A CULTURAL HISTORY OF FAIRY TALES

VOLUME 5

A Cultural History of Fairy Tales
General Editor: Anne E. Duggan

Volume 1
A Cultural History of Fairy Tales in Antiquity
Edited by Debbie Felton

Volume 2
A Cultural History of Fairy Tales in the Middle Ages
Edited by Susan Aronstein

Volume 3
A Cultural History of Fairy Tales in the Age of the Marvelous
Edited by Suzanne Magnanini

Volume 4
A Cultural History of Fairy Tales in the Long Eighteenth Century
Edited by Anne E. Duggan

Volume 5
A Cultural History of Fairy Tales in the Long Nineteenth Century
Edited by Naomi J. Wood

Volume 6
A Cultural History of Fairy Tales in the Modern Age
Edited by Andrew Teverson

A CULTURAL HISTORY
OF FAIRY TALES

IN THE LONG NINETEENTH CENTURY
VOLUME 5

Edited by Naomi J. Wood

BLOOMSBURY ACADEMIC
LONDON • NEW YORK • OXFORD • NEW DELHI • SYDNEY

BLOOMSBURY ACADEMIC
Bloomsbury Publishing Plc, 50 Bedford Square, London, WC1B 3DP, UK
Bloomsbury Publishing Inc, 1359 Broadway, New York, NY 10018, USA
Bloomsbury Publishing Ireland, 29 Earlsfort Terrace, Dublin 2, D02 AY28, Ireland

BLOOMSBURY, BLOOMSBURY ACADEMIC and the Diana logo
are trademarks of Bloomsbury Publishing Plc

First published in Great Britain 2021
Paperback edition published 2025

Copyright © Naomi J. Wood, 2021

Naomi J. Wood and Contributors have asserted their right under the Copyright,
Designs and Patents Act, 1988, to be identified as Author of this work.

Series design by Raven Design
Cover image: Brothers Grimm Fairy Tales 1863 © THEPALMER/ Getty Images

All rights reserved. No part of this publication may be: i) reproduced or transmitted in
any form, electronic or mechanical, including photocopying, recording or by means of
any information storage or retrieval system without prior permission in writing from the
publishers; or ii) used or reproduced in any way for the training, development or operation
of artificial intelligence (AI) technologies, including generative AI technologies. The rights
holders expressly reserve this publication from the text and data mining exception as per
Article 4(3) of the Digital Single Market Directive (EU) 2019/790.

Bloomsbury Publishing Plc does not have any control over, or responsibility for,
any third-party websites referred to or in this book. All internet addresses given
in this book were correct at the time of going to press. The author and publisher
regret any inconvenience caused if addresses have changed or sites have
ceased to exist, but can accept no responsibility for any such changes.

A catalogue record for this book is available from the British Library.

A catalog record for this book is available from the Library of Congress.

ISBN: HB: 978-1-350-09536-6
PB: 978-1-350-59414-2
ePDF: 978-1-350-28756-3
eBook: 978-1-350-28755-6
set: 978-1-3505-9409-8

Series: A Cultural History of Fairy Tales

Typeset by Integra Software Services Pvt. Ltd.
Printed and bound in Great Britain

For product safety related questions contact productsafety@bloomsbury.com.

To find out more about our authors and books visit www.bloomsbury.com
and sign up for our newsletters.

CONTENTS

LIST OF ILLUSTRATIONS	vii
SERIES PREFACE	ix
Introduction: Fairy Tales and the Long Nineteenth Century *Naomi J. Wood*	1
1 Forms of the Marvelous *Laurence Talairach*	25
2 Adaptation *Jan Susina*	43
3 Gender and Sexuality *Amy Billone*	63
4 Humans and Non-Humans: Uncanny Encounters in the Grimms' Tales *Nicole Thesz*	83
5 Monsters and the Monstrous *Sarah Marsh and Zeynep Cakmak*	105
6 Space: Physical, Liminal, and Other *John Pennington*	123
7 Socialization: Civilizing Child's Play *Michelle Beissel Heath*	149

8 Power *Molly Clark Hillard*	167
NOTES	193
REFERENCES	207
NOTES ON CONTRIBUTORS	226
INDEX	228

ILLUSTRATIONS

0.1 Linley Sambourne, "The Great Fairy Science," from Charles Kingsley, *The Water-Babies* (*c.* 1885)   11

0.2 George Cruikshank, title page to *George Cruikshank's Fairy Library* (*c.* 1864)   14

0.3 Richard Doyle, "Feasting and fun among the fuschsias [sic]," from the series *In Fairyland*, 1870   18

2.1 John Tenniel's illustration of Humpty Dumpty from Lewis Carroll's *Through the Looking-Glass* (1872). Many of the characters from Carroll's two Alice books are adapted from nursery rhymes   50

2.2 Andrew Lang created his literary fairy tale, *The Princess Nobody, A Tale of Fairy Land* (1884), by reordering and adapting Richard Doyle's previously published illustrations to Richard Allinghams's *In Fairyland: A Series of Pictures from the Elf-World* (1870)   60

3.1 Pauline Chase as Peter Pan. Unattributed postcard from the early twentieth century   67

3.2 Pauline Chase, actress, notable for playing the part of Barrie's "Peter Pan," postcard, 1905   68

3.3 Anonymous, "The Mermaid," scene from "The Mermaid" by Hans Christian Andersen from a postcard published in Austria, *c.* 1907   72

3.4	*Alice Liddell as beggar-child*. Original photograph taken by Lewis Carroll, 1858	74
3.5	*Older Alice*. Photograph by Lewis Carroll, 1870	76
5.1	Illustration by Willy Pogany from Ignácz Kúnos, *Forty-Four Turkish Fairy Tales* (1913). Courtesy of Lilly Library, Indiana University, Bloomington, Indiana	119
6.1	"Fairy Tale Architecture," from Mary English and Xavier Vendrell, "Fairy Tale Architecture: Little Red Riding Hood," *Places Journal* (2018)	125
6.2	"Little Red Cap," from Shaun Tan, *The Singing Bones* (2015)	127
6.3	Illustration by Edward Burne Jones from William Morris, *The Wood Beyond the World* (Kelmscott edition, 1894)	141
6.4	Illustration by Arthur Hughes from George MacDonald, *At the Back of the North Wind* (1871)	143
6.5	Gustave Doré, "Little Red Riding Hood" (1864)	144
7.1	McLoughlin Brothers' "Little Red Riding Hood," 1887	151
7.2	Milton Bradley's Game of Beauty and the Beast, 1905	164
8.1	"'Choose One'—Little Red Riding Hood or an Assault Weapon?," Moms Demand Action	170
8.2	William (Willie) C. Macready Jr., "Pencil Illustration III," from Robert Browning's "The Pied Piper of Hamelin" (1842)	184
8.3	John Anster Fitzgerald, *The Fairy's Lake*, exhibited 1866. Oil paint on board. Tate	186

SERIES PREFACE

Taking a transnational approach, *A Cultural History of Fairy Tales* seeks to deepen our appreciation for and knowledge about a type of *text* (understood in the broadest sense of the term) that is often taken for granted due to its association with children's literature, old wives' tales, and oral peasant culture. Whether we think of the Brothers Grimm or films by Walt Disney Studios, fairy tales are often viewed as naïve and timeless stories with universal appeal, which suggests they are ahistorical, innocent narratives. This series brings together scholars from a diversity of disciplines to challenge many of these preconceptions about the fairy tale, shedding light on its very complex cultural history.

The chapters included in these six volumes foreground how the fairy tale was deployed in different historical periods and geographical locations for all kinds of cultural, social, and political ends that cross categories of class, age, gender, and ethnicity. "Fairy tale" here serves as a broad umbrella term for what more generally could be referred to as "wonder tale," which encompasses but is not limited to texts that feature fairies, witches, enchanters, djinn, and other beings endowed with magical or supernatural powers; anthropomorphized animals; metamorphosis (humans transformed into animals or other objects and vice versa); magical objects; and otherworlds and liminal spaces. "Fairy tale" also refers to texts that may not include any of these qualities but have been received as—that is, read or categorized as or are generally considered to be—a fairy tale.

By moving from antiquity to the present and transnationally, chapters crossing the six volumes foreground, for instance, how ancient animal fables present both continuities and discontinuities with the representation of animals in later wonder tales; how conceptions of fairies, djinn, and other magical characters change across historical periods and geographical locations; and how the very notion of what is marvelous, natural, or supernatural is understood differently across space and time. Chapters showcase the range of different types of characters and themes one can find in wonder tales as well as the multiple forms and functions tales can take. Together these volumes paint a broad picture of the ways in which different national tale traditions interact with and mutually influence each other, giving us a transnational and transhistorical understanding of the fairy tale. Indeed, readers will discover the rich, complex, and often ideologically charged cultural history of texts that can seem so familiar to us, which helps us understand them in new and exciting ways.

All six volumes cover the same eight themes for the reader to gain a sense of continuities and discontinuities between types of characters, narratives, and traditions over time. Readers will move from *forms* of the fairy tale and the ancillary genres that fed into it to the history of *adaptations*, revealing the ways in which tales are always already a blend of multiple local, regional, and national traditions. A genre often focusing on questions related to development and initiation into adulthood and sometimes (less than we might think) concluding with marriage, tales often feature the norms of *gender and sexuality* grounded in a particular culture. Through the prevalence of non-human characters and problematic human figures, the fairy tale allows for the exploration of the boundaries between *the human and the non-human*, as well as between what is considered normal and *monsters or the monstrous*. As a nonmimetic genre, generally speaking, the fairy tale also plays with the delimitations between real and imaginary *spaces*, opening up both utopic and dystopic possibilities. Tales have often been used in the processes of *socialization*, for both children and adults, men and women, articulating class, gender, and ethnic differences. As such, tales cannot be separated from questions of *power* and ideology.

This cultural history of the fairy tale is divided into the following historical periods:

Volume 1: A Cultural History of Fairy Tales in Antiquity (500 BCE–800 CE)

Volume 2: A Cultural History of Fairy Tales in the Middles Ages (800–1450)

Volume 3: A Cultural History of Fairy Tales in the Age of the Marvelous (1450–1650)

Volume 4: A Cultural History of Fairy Tales in the Long Eighteenth Century (1650–1800)

Volume 5: A Cultural History of Fairy Tales in the Long Nineteenth Century (1800–1920)

Volume 6: A Cultural History of Fairy Tales in the Modern Age (1920–2000+)

Readers will come away with a new and fresh understanding of the fairy tale, which indeed enhances our appreciation for a genre that has touched many of us since childhood. Far from being naïve, innocent, timeless texts, *A Cultural History of Fairy Tales* foregrounds the ways wonder tales are embedded in sophisticated social, cultural, political, and artistic practices across history, anchored in specific cultural contexts that shape their meaning as tales are adapted from one cultural and historical context to another.

Anne E. Duggan, *General Editor*

Introduction

Fairy Tales and the Long Nineteenth Century

NAOMI J. WOOD

Fairy tales were not always for children. At the beginning of the long nineteenth century, German classical and romantic writers from Johann Wolfgang von Goethe to E. T. A. Hoffmann established a place in the canon of German literature for *märchen* (fairy tales). Accounts of fairies and the supernatural appeared in many works with adult concerns and themes—in the poetry of Samuel Taylor Coleridge, John Keats, and William Blake; in the art of Blake and Henry Fuseli; in the tales of Novalis, Friedrich de la Motte Fouqué, and E. T. A. Hoffmann. These works freely explored gothic scenes of madness, terror, and desire. Fairy-tale writing for adults commented on modernity and historical change. Sir Walter Scott's work presented tales of the supernatural and the marvelous as existing only on society's primitive or archaic margins, soon to be crushed by modernity's progress. Some fairy-tale writers used fairy-tale conventions to burlesque them, to draw attention to their own fictionality and to the tension between idea and experience. Foreshadowing modernist techniques such as self-referentiality, intertextuality, narrative fracturing, and metatextuality, William Makepeace Thackeray, Lewis Carroll, and Oscar Wilde incorporated modern attitudes, language, and values into fairy tales not only for humorous effect but also to critique conventions and provoke thought.

By the 1880s, however, fairy tales were seen primarily as a children's genre, providing the foundation for a wide range of diversions. Scottish folklorist Andrew Lang's rainbow of fairy-tale books—Blue, Red, Green, Yellow, Violet—was among the most distinguished of hundreds of collections and adaptations of fairy-tale lore. Fairy tales were staples of theatrical entertainments, especially pantomimes; they were sold as games and toys, referenced in advertisements, depicted in paintings, and featured prominently in Christmas gift lists.[1] Fairies and childhood became so enmeshed that when the Cottlingley photographs were published in 1920, purporting to show the fairy playmates of Frances Griffiths (aged ten) and Elsie Wright (aged thirteen), they seemed to confirm what everyone already knew: that fairies and children were naturally associated (Briggs [1967] 1978: 238–40; Silver 1999: 54).

Fairy tales came to be linked with "childhood" more broadly as theories of development, progress, and change revolutionized the study of language, geology, biology, and culture. Many nineteenth-century thinkers sought in fairy tales the key to human cultural origins. Sanskrit scholar and philologist F. Max Müller argued that myths and folktales were residual expressions of ancient solar myths, a "disease of language"; his view briefly dominated fairy-tale interpretation. Eventually this theory was superseded by E. B. Tylor's notion that fairy tales were "survivals" of prehistoric, proto-scientific humanity (Silver 1999: 43–4). That fairy tales were associated with children neatly aligned with applications of Ernst Haeckel's theory of recapitulation, the idea that embryonic development followed the evolutionary development of the species. Ancient stories and poetry expressed the so-called "childhood of the race," which, by analogy, fitted them for the immature minds of children. In service of these ideas, comparative anthropologists such as Tylor and Lang traced story lines and motifs, speculated on lines of transmission, and theorized the historical conditions that might have produced the fairy tale. Sigmund Freud used fairy tales to build his theories of the mind and unlock dreams and secrets of the unconscious. Seeing in their structure and imagery keys to the history of human evolution, the struggle for existence, and the nature of human striving, nineteenth-century thinkers applied the evolutionary principles of philology, geology, biology, and psychology to narrative, believing the most deeply buried fragments of story or motif gave clues to our beginnings and the genealogy of consciousness.

This chapter traces how nineteenth-century writers found in the fairy tale a flexible form with which to express a wide range of ideas about nation, environment, history, culture, childhood, and faith. The most important influence is Romanticism, a broad movement characterized by idealist metaphysics, gothic imagery, and an obsession with origins, national and personal; Orientalism; natural supernaturalism; and Romantic irony. In addition, an "ante-modernist" aesthetic reacts against Romanticism and anticipates twentieth-century experiments with language and form. Each of these elements extended the epistemological and narratorial possibilities inherent in the fairy-tale form, which combine, mutate, and evolve, perhaps because of fairy tales' association with childhood and the idea of development. Whether they were called *contes des fées*, *märchen*, ballads, or fairy tales; whether they were oral or written or dramatic genres; and whether their implied audience and purpose was child or adult, middle class or working class, radical or conservative, fairy tales of the long nineteenth century both reflect and subvert their cultural moment, seeding the literary and cultural establishment with imaginative responses to the spiritual and intellectual turmoil of the period.

ROMANTICISMS AND THE FAIRY TALE

From the late eighteenth century and into the twentieth, the multinational Romantic movement stimulated interest in fairy tales from both elite and popular perspectives. Elite art fairy tales opposed (neo)classicism by turning from the beautiful, with its values of order, symmetry, and rationality, to the sublime and wildness, irregularity, and the imagination. Art fairy tales were fantastic allegorical narratives for adult readers, a trend persisting throughout the period, despite the dominance of realism and the novel. But Romanticism also inspired new interest in oral folk- and fairy-tale transmission and, with the example set by Jacob and Wilhelm Grimm, mobilized a multinational folklore movement. Chapbooks sold by itinerant booksellers and accessible even to those with limited purchasing power maintained popular familiarity with legends, romances, folk and fairy tales, and ballads (Sumpter 2008: 11). Oral and written forms of the fairy tale intertwined in a "symbiotic relationship," as Jack Zipes argues (2012: 3).

Kunstmärchen, or art fairy tales, flourished in Germany, where they explored ideas about life, the soul, the imagination, and desire. German Romantic writers adopted Emmanuel Kant's notion that the structures of the mind create our experience of reality. According to William Gray, they sought to "overcome the dichotomy between literature and philosophy, and develop a 'progressive universal poetry'" (2010: 12). German fantasist Novalis (Friedrich von Hardenberg) expressed utopian longings in symbolic imagery, such as a blue flower, to evoke divine or spiritual truth in *Heinrich von Ofterdingen* ([1802] 2007) (Gray 2010: 12). Both Ludwig Tieck and E. T. A. Hoffmann probed the shadowy and indeterminate qualities of human consciousness, the thin line between madness and sanity, in "Eckbert the Fair" (*Der blonde Eckbert*, 1797) and in "The Golden Pot" (*Der goldne Topf*, 1814) (Gray 2010: 13, 18), respectively. Like the period's gothic romances with which they share antiquarian and occult imagery, art fairy tales combined folk superstitions and practices and imaginative symbolism that explored the psychological conflicts between social or religious norms and desire.

When nineteenth-century Scottish fantasist George MacDonald asks, "what is a fairy tale?" he offers not a definition, but an example: "Were I asked, what is a fairytale? I should reply, *Read Undine: that is a fairytale; then read this and that as well, and you will see what is a fairy tale*" ([1895] 1976: 162; emphasis in original). For MacDonald, fairy tales are to be experienced, not analyzed, their meaning a matter of individual response rather than authorial intention. German Romantic writer Friedrich de la Motte Fouqué's tale "Undine" (1811) served as the touchstone for many fairy-tale devotees throughout the long nineteenth century. A German *kunstmärchen* (art fairy tale), "Undine" describes the ill-fated romance between the titular character, a water-nymph, and the knight Huldebrand who woos and wins her. After their marriage, Huldebrand's affections stray, and the story ends with Undine's watery punishment of her faithless spouse, whom she weeps to death. The story's gothic trappings of deep forests, crags, and castles, its feudal relationships, and its nature spirits were widely reproduced and adapted as operas, ballets, paintings, and other media. In this and other similar art fairy tales, exotic or archaic imagery offered escape from the sedate, repressed, and banal lives of bourgeois readers.

Oral fairy tales also experienced a period of rediscovery during the long nineteenth century. For many Romantics, oral tales were the true, pure, and authentic form. The work of the Brothers Grimm came to epitomize the oral fairy tale, despite their well-documented editorial work on the seven successive editions of *Kinder- und hausmärchen* between 1812–15 and 1857.[2] In their introduction to the first edition, the Grimms lamented that since "the custom of storytelling is on the wane," their project served a crucial purpose of preserving endangered lore ([1812, 1815] 2014: 4). They praised traditional tales as uniquely pleasurable and offering pure refreshment in contrast with modern "perversities of life" that "obliterate" the imagination (4). Later the art critic and amateur fairy-tale writer John Ruskin echoed these ideas, claiming that the Grimms' collection surpasses modern tales because of roots in "walled cities … surrounded by bright and unblemished country … in which a healthy and bustling town life, not highly refined, is relieved by, and contrasted with, the calm enchantment of pastoral and woodland scenery" ([1869] 2015: 394). Part of the Grimms' mystique has been the notion that their work represents a pure strain of authentic oral lore.

Articulating the philosophical strand of Romanticism, Samuel Taylor Coleridge maintained that written fairy tales offered an antidote to the atomization of modern life. For Coleridge, Enlightenment thought, with its habits of analysis and its denial of spiritual realities, had disenchanted and vivisected the world, leaving nothing but fragments. Fairy tales, by contrast, plant "a love of 'the Great,' & 'the Whole'" that enlarges children's capacity to sense and respond to the sublime:

> For from my early reading of Faery Tales, & Genii &c &c—my mind had been habituated to the Vast—& I never regarded my *senses* in any way as the criteria of my belief. I regulated all my creeds by my conceptions not by my *sight*—even at that age. Should children be permitted to read Romances, & Relations of Giants & Magicians, & Genii?—I know all that has been said against it; but I have formed my faith in the affirmative.—I know no other way of giving the mind a love of "the Great," & "the Whole."—Those who have been led to the same truths step by step thro' the constant testimony of their senses, seem to me to want a sense which I possess—They contemplate nothing but *parts*—and all *parts* are necessarily little—and the Universe to them is but a mass of *little things*.
>
> (quoted in Prickett 2005: 7; emphasis in original)

German idealism reinforced Coleridge's ideas about the creative power of the imagination to make new realities as well as gild old ones. Fairy tales reestablished a link between humans and the cosmos threatened by human intellectual hubris. Fairy tales thus conceived had the potential to raise humanity to a higher spiritual plane. This elevation, however, risked other kinds of alienation. For example, in *The Rime of the Ancient Mariner* (1798, 1817), Coleridge invokes "the Vast" with sublime natural imagery. The narrative enlarges the sympathy and perception of the Mariner as he recognizes the holiness of all living things, along with a sense of humanity's moral failures and responsibilities. However, this realization is also a curse: the Mariner's compulsion to continually find new audiences to whom he must confess aligns him with other mythic wayfarers, such as Cain, the first murderer, or the Wandering Jew.

Indeed, in much of his poetry Coleridge explores the darker aspects of imagination and the supernatural. The imagination produces nightmares as well as visions. *The Rime of the Ancient Mariner* embraces all life, but "Christabel" (1816) imagines malevolent beings who silence and harm. Many Romantic art fairy tales testify to the dangers of enchantment. John Keats's "La Belle Dame Sans Merci" (1820) represents enchantment as both seductive and perilous; those who succumb no longer thrive in the world. Having lost their link to humanity, they are left, like the knight, "alone and palely loitering." Some contemporaries disparaged, as Wordsworth did, this "feverish" and "extravagant" gothic material, superstitious and irrational, that permeated folk-style ballads and stories and defied Enlightenment ascendency (Pask 2013: 105–9). But for those who adopted this mode, it "seem[ed] here to license a radical, even utopian break with modern, novelistic temporality" (115). Thus, the fairy tale variously expresses fears of an unleashed imagination and nostalgia for a simpler, purer, or more archaic state of being.

Hans Christian Andersen's tale "The Snow Queen" (*Sneedronnigen*, 1844) articulates an array of these Romantic themes. Made up of seven linked stories,

"The Snow Queen" first describes a devil's manufacture of a magic mirror whose reflection diminishes everything good, and inflates everything bad or worthless. The devil decides to carry the mirror to heaven to harass the angels; however, on its way the mirror is broken and scatters all over the world instead. The fragments skew vision and turn hearts to ice. The next story shifts abruptly from allegory to sentiment as it describes the idyll of Little Kay and Little Gerda, whose love is symbolized by two entwined rose trees. But Kay's eye becomes infected by a shard of the devil's mirror, and he becomes a cynic, destructive and careless of Gerda's feelings, though adults call him clever. He is taken by the Snow Queen, who kisses him and turns his heart to ice. Kay forgets all about Gerda and drives away with the Snow Queen.

Gerda decides to find Kay. After a long journey, she arrives at the Snow Queen's palace, where Kay is preoccupied with forming patterns out of shards of ice. The allegory is explicit: "He sat arranging and rearranging pieces of ice into patterns. He called this the Game of Reason; and because of the splinters in his eyes, he thought that what he was doing was of great importance. ... He wanted to put the pieces of ice together in such a way that they formed a certain word, but he could not remember what that word was. The word that he could not remember was 'eternity'" (Andersen [1844] 1974: 259). Linking the empty, cold, and sterile icescape with the devil's perverted mirror and with intellectual games, Andersen depicts Kay's affliction as "freezing reason," as Tennyson called it in *In Memoriam* ([1850] 1974: 259). Gerda redeems Kay not through argument but with her tears, which melt the mirror fragment and cleanse his heart. Released from reason's tyranny, his heart opens to Eternity, and he returns home with Gerda. They sit again in their little chairs as adults while the grandmother reads from the Bible: "Whosoever shall not receive the Kingdom of Heaven as a little child shall not enter therein" (Andersen [1844] 1974: 262). Adulthood, seemingly, is incompatible with spiritual enlightenment.

Andersen's hyperborean imagery critiques Enlightenment modes, but many of his readers also found in it a statement of the superiority of European, and particularly Northern European identity. Maria Louisa Molesworth describes Andersen's stories as embodying the "heart and soul of the north":

> Something of this northern spirit is to be felt in the moral atmosphere of all his writings. It is white with the whiteness of child-like purity; cold, though not chilly, reserved and restrained, never overflowing or exaggerated. There is nothing luscious or sensuous even in his rare allusions to southern scenes; he loves the summer and its glories, but the silence and mystery of the winter, like a magnet, are ever drawing him to the sterner regions of the north.
> ([1893] 1976: 142)

Molesworth praises this "moral atmosphere" of restraint along with the privileging of "stern" and ascetic attitudes in contrast with Southern warmth as European countries expand their control over the Global South, as we shall see. Romantic writers who contested neoclassical and Enlightenment dominion discovered in fairy tales material that appealed not only to feelings and desires. For these thinkers, fairy tales also grounded readers in the very things modernity appeared to uproot and destroy. In the wake of revolutionary and national struggle, and in opposition to the atomistic meaninglessness implied by some contemporary science and philosophy, fairy tales seemed to offer a path toward identity, community, and national purpose.

NATIONALISM AND THE FAIRY TALE

The collection of old ballads and other "popular antiquities," as the material was known before the term "folklore" was coined in 1846, was fueled by an idea of national identity rooted in the rural working classes, those seemingly closest to the earth. These projects resisted the hegemonic universalizing tendencies of neoclassicism and Enlightenment rationalism. The Grimms' study of fairy tales, for example, began as a vehicle for German unity opposing French cultural and military imperialism in the Napoleonic era. The brothers responded to Johann Gottfried Herder's patriotic call to recover and record the common people's natural poetry (*Naturepoesie*), recognizing in the lore of household and childhood the formative articulation of a distinctive German identity (Lokke 2006: 140; Neumann 1993: 25–6). German thinkers in their turn had been inspired by popular Scottish ballads and tales, which asserted an identity separate from the English. These projects set in motion a multinational movement to retrieve and preserve regional and national distinctiveness. In the British Isles, for example, Irish and other regional writers likewise resisted absorption into a homogeneous Southern "English" culture by drawing on popular culture and traditions (Killick 2008: 120–1).

Many nineteenth-century nationalist folklore projects followed the lead of the Grimms in collecting and adjusting their finds to suit their theory of national identity. The voice of the peasant storyteller was never unmediated. Even Jacob and Wilhelm Grimm took the position that story variants denoted departures from some original source that could be reconstructed by comparing the variants, just as extinct languages could be inferred by studying their offshoots. Zipes has shown how the Grimms compared variants and combined features that expressed their idea of the most beautiful and authentic tale, essentially fabricating the pure and authentic folktale (2014: xxxii). Whether scholarly, literary, or journalistic, folklorists edited and amended the language and structure of the oral tales they collected. Both Caroline Sumpter and Tim Killick record how journalists and regional writers transcribed and occasionally invented folk literature for publication in contemporary magazines, journals, and newspapers (Killick 2008; Sumpter 2008).[3] Even William Butler Yeats, a late defender of folk belief in fairies, used magazines as sources for his own Irish folklore collection (Sumpter 2008: 24).

On the European continent, the *Kalevala* (1835) was compiled and edited by Finnish philologist Elias Lönrott, who used his recordings of discrete folksongs from Karelia (a region on the border of Finland and Russia) to construct a national epic. According to Zipes, Lönrott adjusted plot and character elements to make them align more readily with fairy-tale, Christian, and pagan motifs (Zipes 2000a). Elsewhere in Scandinavia, the folktale collection *Norske Folkeeventyr* (1841–4), by P. C. Asbjørnsen and Jørgen Moe, strove to distinguish Norwegian identity from Denmark (which ruled over Norway until 1814) and from Sweden (from which Norway separated in 1905) (Ingwersen 2000: 17). In Italy, Giuseppe Pitrè, a Sicilian medical doctor, collected songs, proverbs, and tales during his rounds. He eventually produced a twenty-five volume series of the popular literature of Sicily, *Biblioteca delle tradizioni popolari siciliane* (1871–1913) (Zipes 2012: 109–34). In Russia, Aleksandr Afanasyev, likewise inspired by the Grimms' project, collected, compiled, and organized Russian folktales, culminating in the eight-volume *Russian Fairy Tales* (1855–63) and many other works. Afanasyev's taxonomic work in particular laid the groundwork for the insights of Russian formalists, most importantly Vladimir Propp, whose *Morphology of the Folktale* (1928) continues to be a foundational text in fairy-tale studies. As diverse as these projects and styles were, they established works defining a national identity and linked that identity with membership in a world literary context.

Folk and fairy tales could also be used to challenge centers of political and cultural power by insisting upon local and regional differences. Although Sir Walter Scott's *Minstrelsy of the Scottish Border* (1802–3) did not attempt to reestablish a separate Scottish state, it did glorify Scottish lore and language and defined an audience for other folkloric projects. James Hogg and Allan Cunningham, alongside Scott himself, "created a climate where the role of traditional and popular material in an enlightened world was closely questioned, and where broad-brush, generalist conceptions of Scotland as a cohesive 'nation' were challenged," as Tim Killick writes (2008: 121). In contrast with Scottish writers, Irish Thomas Crofton Croker's compilation *Fairy Legends and Traditions of the South of Ireland* (1826–34) took a more colonial approach. Croker promised to reveal the authentic Irish peasant to his literate audience, though his project was undercut by the ambivalence of his position as a member of the Anglo-Irish ruling class. Croker's framing and voice registers distinguishing the illiterate peasant from his own cultured subject position simultaneously reinforces and subverts English assumptions and prejudices, as Jennifer Schacker has shown (2003: 49, 58). Tensions between collector and informant and between objectification, appropriation, and appreciation continue to haunt folklore research. However, as Tim Killick has noted, widespread publication of regional stories in the early nineteenth century "contested the primacy of progressive, urban, and rationalist thought developed in the post-Enlightenment fiction of the late eighteenth century, and sealed by the arrival of the Scottian historical novel" (2008: 117). And, as we have seen, even Scott played a role in this reclamation and elevation of premodern thought and narrative.

Alongside these nationalistic and colonial fairy-tale collections, another approach emerged. Comparative scholarship began to take interest in the structural and thematic resemblances between tales so that fundamental human similarities could be stressed as well as national differences. The thesis that fairy tales manifested the tastes and traits of a nation's "childhood"—or even the "childhood of the race"—meant that folklorists and educators still positioned themselves as the adults who controlled and updated the material. Folklore was even used to justify cultural overthrow and erasure of the "childlike" tellers of these tales, "a particularly useful concept in an age of imperial expansion," as Carole Silver points out (1999: 45).

For those who linked fairy tales to national identity, the preservation of folktales was a patriotic duty. Many believed that Enlightenment principles of rationality, skepticism, and individualism alienated people from their roots in more than a metaphorical sense. Tales from the peasant classes offered a link to the past that broke through the artificial veneer of civilized society to a more organic, authentic foundation. This foundation, however, was thought to be at risk because of changing technologies, industrialization, and the incursions of modernity. With a sense of urgency that without their intervention key material would be lost, folklorists and antiquarians sought to safeguard the oral tradition and transmit it in writing. With the advent of the most invasive period of the Industrial Revolution in Europe, some fairy-tale writers saw parallels between the despoliation of traditional ways of life and their landscapes.

FAIRY-TALE ECOLOGY

Fairy tales were used to re-enchant natural landscapes and inspire reverence for both the natural world and human ingenuity. Some created tutelary deities expressing nature's agency. In John Ruskin's "King of the Golden River" (written in 1841, but not published until 1851), three brothers are tested by personified natural forces (The South-West Wind, Esquire, and the King of the Golden River). The two older brothers, evil and grasping, believe that the way to get the best of Treasure Valley is to exploit the land and their workers, to kill everything that "did not pay for its eating," to "work their servants without any wages," and to sell their produce at the highest possible price. Though the brothers initially prosper, they run afoul of the South-West Wind because of their greed and selfishness, and the Treasure Valley becomes a "desert": "What had once been the richest soil in the kingdom, became a shifting heap of red sand" ([1851] 1973: 18). Exemplifying utilitarian rapacity, the brothers' dishonorable pursuit of profit exhausts nature itself because it is not moderated by ethical concerns about general welfare.

The youngest brother Gluck, innocent of his brothers' avarice and generous to a fault, learns from the King of the Golden River that he can turn the river to gold if he casts three drops of holy water into it, but that anyone casting unholy water there will be turned into a black stone. His brothers contrive to make the journey first, turning themselves into black stones. Gluck's own trek reveals his selflessness and generosity after he gives the last of his holy water to a dying dog. As the King of the Golden River tells him, what makes water holy is the spirit that animates the user—not whether it has been blessed by a priest. Gluck is rewarded with a river of precious water, not ore, to regenerate Treasure Valley. Ruskin's art fairy tale uses many of the structures and devices of the oral fairy tale, such as the formula of three brothers, three high-stakes magical quests, the triumph of the underdog, and the personification of natural forces. However, Ruskin's hero wins neither kingdom nor princess, but instead restores natural balance. Ruskin's tale promotes ecologically conscious environmentalism more than attainment of political and economic power, unlike most folk fairy tales.[4]

Ruskin's fairy tale rebuked industrial capitalism, but others used fairy-tale allusions and imagery to inspire wonder at scientific inquiry and technological advance. Rather than divorcing the scientific method from the imagination, scientific fairy tales sought to enchant children with wonders of the material world—animals, everyday objects, elementary chemistry. By mid-century, scientific writing for children invoked fairy-tale and romance tropes as a matter of course, as Laurence Talairach shows (2014: 16). Melanie Keene's study of the era's vogue for scientific fairy tales concludes that "The fairy tale remained a favoured analogy for telling the history of life on earth, and for explaining the relationships between past and present, throughout the nineteenth century" (Keene 2015: 127). Of these fairy-tale writing naturalists, the most famous is Charles Kingsley, vicar, geologist, and advocate for evolutionary theory. Kingsley wrote *The Water-Babies* (1863) to persuade his readers to marvel at the wondrous creatures of the river and ocean and to lament "what man has made of man."[5] In Kingsley's view, the "Great Fairy Science" illuminates the natural world for adventurous and upright men ([1863] 1910: 96; see Figure 0.1).

ORIENTALISM AND THE FAIRY TALE

The local and regional focus of some fairy tales may have contributed to nationalism and ecology, but in an era of European expansionism, there was an equally strong push toward the exotic, especially the Global South. Antoine

FIGURE 0.1: Linley Sambourne, "The Great Fairy Science," from Charles Kingsley, *The Water-Babies* (c. 1885).

Galland's *Les mille et une nuits*, translated from the Arabic of *Alf Laila wa Laila* (*The Thousand and One Nights*) and published between 1704 and 1717, fueled a fashion for "oriental" tales persisting through the long nineteenth century. Galland's multivolume work collapsed variations of tales recorded in medieval texts from Persia and India, from Syria, from Baghdad, and from Egypt. By 1800, *The Thousand and One Nights*, or *The Arabian Nights* as it was frequently called, was immensely popular with European readers, and provided a rich source for fantastic images and tropes. The "Orient" was a convenient fiction upon which Europeans could project their desires, fantasies, and fears (Said 1978). The frame story of murderous King Shahryar and the brave Scheherazade became the model of "oriental despotism" filtered through sexual politics. By the end of the eighteenth century, Perrault's "Bluebeard" had been transformed into a Turkish tyrant with a wife named Fatima (Hermansson 2009: 71). Edward William Lane's translation of the *Nights* into English, commissioned by the Society for the Diffusion of Useful Knowledge (SDUK) and appearing between 1838 and 1840, served didactic purposes as well as entertainment, according to Jennifer Schacker (2003: 84). Lane perpetuated the European stereotype that "Oriental" culture was static and homogeneous compared with the dynamism of European powers. Lane posited that his ethnographic observations in contemporary Egypt could explain medieval tales from Iran and Syria, and his work was used didactically as "useful knowledge" disseminated under the purview of the SDUK. Many gothic romances and fairy tales, from William Beckford's *Vathek* (1786) and Coleridge's "Kubla Khan" (1816) to Andersen's "Nightingale" and Wilde's "Happy Prince" (1888) represent the Orient as home to despotic cultures immune from politically liberal yet socially restrained bourgeois mores. Orientalist versions of the Arabian Nights and adjacent stories explored the excessive and the forbidden—luxury, wealth, perversity, power. Sir Richard Burton's unexpurgated translation of *The Book of the Thousand Nights and a Night* (1885-6) recounted sexual mores and practices that defied and titillated bourgeois and European Christian norms in almost every respect.

Orientalism could also be used to comment upon European society. In "The Nightingale" (1842), for example, Andersen deflects his satire onto the distant and othered Chinese, a common Orientalist tactic. The story begins: "In China, as you may know, the Emperor is Chinese, and everyone there is also Chinese"; the ingenuous narrator invites his readers to marvel at this fact, positioning them as geographical naifs. The unsurprising revelation that Chinese people live in China, "as you may know," makes the introduction absurd rather than informative. The narrator's unsophisticated stance invokes Chinese-ness, imagined as the embodiment of art and artificiality, establishing its symbolic rather than mimetic status. China is metonymically conveyed by the Emperor's palace, constructed of "fine porcelain, so costly and delicate that you had to be careful when you touched it" (quoted in Tatar 2017b: 318), a trope carried throughout this story contrasting the natural and artificial. The Emperor's courtiers are likewise ornamental, artful, and contrived. At first Nature's child, the Nightingale, delights the Emperor and his court with its songs, despite its plain appearance. But when the Emperor is presented with a mechanical nightingale "that was supposed to look just like the real one except that it was covered with diamonds, rubies, and sapphires" (quoted in Tatar 2017b: 321), he and his court prefer the artful fake with its single plagiarized song. Only when the Emperor faces Death does he recognize the value of the true folk artist over the elaborate mechanical copy. By the end of the tale, Andersen drops the "Chinese" façade to uphold Romantic values of "art, genius, and the role of the artist," as Zipes puts it (1988: 86).

Tales about the East, as Schacker observes, "must be understood as an ethnographic reality and a marker of cultural difference" (2003: 95) that frequently reinforced a strong sense of European superiority. European Orientalism offered heat and sun, the harem and the walled garden, and physical and sensory delights in place of the supersensual aesthetic of the arctic and of the north evident in Andersen's "Snow Queen."[6] In Wilde's fairy tale "The Happy Prince" (1888), the Swallow's wish to winter in Egypt is developed with luxuriant descriptions drawn from Théophile Gautier's Orientalist poem "Ce que disent les hirondelles" ("What the Swallows Say").[7] The Swallow yearns for the light and heat and color of Egypt, where even the dead are beautifully got up: "The King is there himself in his painted coffin. He is wrapped in yellow linen, and embalmed with spices. Round his neck is a chain of pale green jade, and his hands are like withered leaves" (Wilde [1888] 2017: 336). In the "Orient" the exotic becomes mundane and the fantastic is natural (Schacker 2003: 116). "Oriental" tales provide European fairy-tale readers with windows to their own desires, mirrored back to them in different costumes and with a different accent, opening a world where the "glacial cold of selfish science," as Ruskin put it ([1869] 2015: 392), plays a minor role, and instinctual, sensual pleasure is all.

CHILDHOOD AND THE FAIRY TALE

The Arabian Nights, together with a small store of eighteenth-century romances, saves David Copperfield from despair in Charles Dickens's semi-autobiographical novel. Reading, David writes, "kept alive my fancy, and my hope of something beyond that place and time" ([1850] 1990: 54), despite unjust disgrace and isolation. Dickens promotes fairy tales as necessary for children, a matter of life and death, and holds as sacred the crude chapbooks depicting the triumph of Dick Whittington, Jack the Giant Killer, Cinderella's rescue, and Red Riding Hood's plight. In his famous screed against George Cruikshank's teetotal fairy-tale adaptations, "Frauds on the Fairies" (1853; see Figure 0.2), Dickens writes that altering the stories alters their power: "To preserve [fairy tales] in their usefulness, they must be as much preserved in their simplicity, and purity, and innocent extravagance, as if they were actual fact" ([1853] 1976: 111).

Dickens's advocacy places him solidly alongside Coleridge, Charles Lamb, Ruskin, and many other Romantic and post-Romantic writers. By the end of the century, indeed, fairy tales were understood to be the special

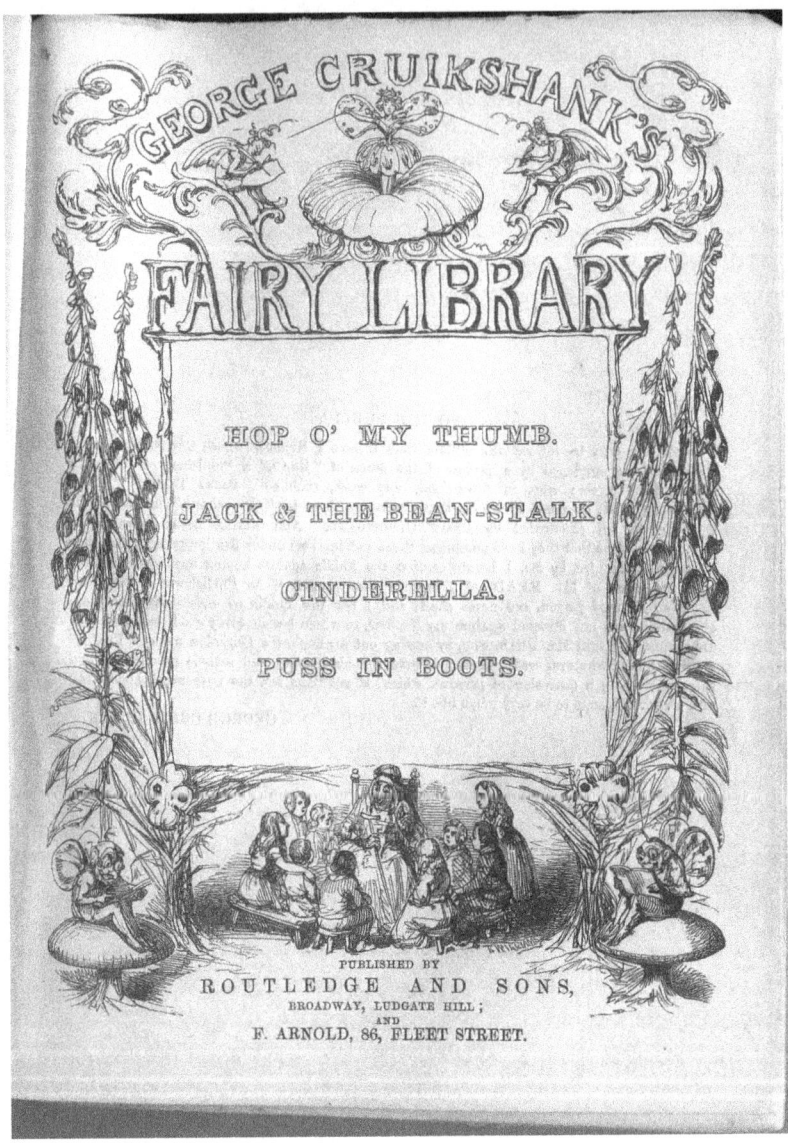

FIGURE 0.2: George Cruikshank, title page to *George Cruikshank's Fairy Library* (c. 1864).

property of childhood. In keeping with Romantic ideas about the unfettered imagination and the taint of modern thought, these writers contended, alongside Wordsworth, that if the modern "world is too much with us," stories and songs from the preindustrial past can rejuvenate adults and nurture children.

Conventional histories of children's literature often posit that late eighteenth-century and early nineteenth-century England completely rejected fairy tales.

However, as M. O. Grenby has shown, fairy tales were never completely eclipsed in England, and in fact distinguished themselves, as they always have done, by their adaptability to the needs of the time and the tellers (2006: 3). Benjamin Tabart's four-volume *Popular Tales* (1804) signals the profitability of the children's fairy-tale market even before the resurgence of fantasy in the 1830s and 1840s with the rise to prominence of Hans Christian Andersen and the Grimms. It is true that many educators viewed fairy tales with suspicion, especially as they were told by lower-class servants. Dickens and Charlotte Brontë both depict the power nurses and governesses wielded over their charges if they were effective storytellers. Jane Eyre's nurse Bessie wheedles Jane into good behavior with promises of a story; Esther Summerson and Sissy Jupe enchant children with their storytelling. But Dickens also recalls the terror his own nurse's tales inspired:

> The young woman who brought me acquainted with Captain Murderer had a fiendish enjoyment of my terrors, and used to begin, I remember—as a sort of introductory overture—by clawing the air with both hands, and uttering a long low hollow groan. So acutely did I suffer from this ceremony in combination with this infernal Captain that I sometimes used to plead I thought I was hardly strong enough and old enough to hear the story again just yet.
>
> ([1868] 1988)[8]

Fearing that nurses and other lower-class servants might bully their charges through such stories, however, some parents opposed them. Moreover, as Sally Shuttleworth has shown, some parents and physicians forbade fairy tales so that their children would not be subject to night fears and mental illness due to a diseased imagination (Shuttleworth 2010; see also Grenby 2006: 8).

Still, it was Edgar Taylor's translation of the Grimms' work in *German Popular Stories* (1823–6), beautifully illustrated by Cruikshank, that stamped the fairy tale as a necessary component of the middle-class nursery in English homes. In keeping with contemporary understandings about middle-class expectations, Taylor adjusted and edited the tales for language, plot, and character. The Grimms themselves followed Taylor's lead and reshaped their work to appeal to the family market by condensing, refining, and illustrating their own collection, publishing an illustrated edition in 1825.[9] Ruth Bottigheimer shows how Wilhelm, especially, edited the tales to conform to German bourgeois norms by removing women's direct speech and foregrounding men's speech and agency (Bottigheimer 1986). As Zipes argues, the many versions of the Grimms' household tales ultimately de-emphasized unmediated folklore in favor of establishing a middle-class canon ([1988] 1991: 47–59). In England, Taylor's *German Popular Stories* became for similar reasons the definitive fairy-tale collection (Sumpter 2008: 28).

Indeed, for many writers, fairy tales were inherently didactic. English children's author Juliana Horatia Ewing defines fairy tales by their moral themes and by their form—"the weak outwitting the strong; the failure of man to choose wisely when he may have his wish; or the desire of sprites to exchange their careless and unfettered existence for the pains and penalties of humanity, if they may thereby share in the hopes of the human soul" ([1888] 2015: 395). In contrast with art fairy tales' sublime landscapes, fraught relationships, and idealist allegory, Ewing's fairy tale favors the down-to-earth: "knowledge of the world," "shrewd lessons of virtue and vice," and "common sense and sense of humour ... in narratives where the plot moves briskly and dramatically from a beginning to an end" ([396). Ewing lauds the fairy tale's simple if not simplistic concerns with growth, survival, and success.

For these writers, fairy tales offered a vehicle for teaching children both humanistic and scientific truths: wonder and morality, science and technology. Ewing updated traditional stories of child-stealing fairies to teach self-reflection and good manners in "Amelia and the Dwarfs" (1870), and her account of the children who decide to take on the role of the Scottish house spirit in "The Brownies" (1865) became an inspiration for the Girl Guides' junior branch. American Nathaniel Hawthorne rewrote classical mythology as fairy tales by adding child characters and removing the gods and unseemly references to sex in *A Wonder-Book for Girls and Boys* (1852) and *Tanglewood Tales for Girls and Boys* (1853). In one of Hawthorne's best-known and most anthologized adaptation, King Midas's daughter is named Marigold and given a more prominent role in the plot. In *The Blue Fairy Book* (1889), Lang followed suit by reframing the story of Perseus as a fairy tale, "The Terrible Head," with all the Greek names removed.

Despite praising fairy tales' robust common sense, adult advocates also made more elevated claims for their contributions to childhood. Ruskin, for example, praised traditional fairy tales for as nurturing belief and idealism against the alienating qualities of modern life. The stories of "any tradition of old time, honestly delivered to them," will provide children with the inestimable gifts of "animating for them the material world with inextinguishable life, fortifying them against the glacial cold of selfish science, and preparing them submissively, and with no bitterness of astonishment, to behold, in later years, the mystery ... of the fates that happen alike to the evil and the good" ([1869] 2015: 392). For Ruskin, as for Coleridge, fairy tales nourished the organ of belief, making children more amenable to spiritual truths and religious faith. George MacDonald, one of the century's greatest practitioners of the art fairy tale for children, combined didactic messages about Christian self-sacrifice and suffering with images of great and beautiful goddess-grandmothers in whose arms the child protagonists receive both love and strength to pursue their quests.[10]

Embedded in the dreamlike fantastic imagery of these didactic and imaginative tales, however, can also be found the very opposite of the "simplicity, purity, and innocence" Dickens found in Taylor's *German Household Stories* (Dickens [1853] 1976: 111). In the work of some artists, fairy-tale waywardness, polymorphous perversity, and other explorations of deviance manifest. The most notorious example may be Christina Rossetti's fairy-tale poem *Goblin Market* (1862), which originally appeared in a volume meant for an adult readership, but was incorporated into school textbooks by the late nineteenth century (Kooistra 1997: 184–5). It continued to be presented as a classic of children's literature for much of the century. Some read it as an innocuous tale about sisterly love, based on the final lines beginning, "For there is no friend like a sister" (Rossetti [1862] 1973: 519). Yet the ferociously sensual imagery both of the goblins' fruit and the sisters' physicality challenges this notion. The goblins' tempting calls lure unwary maidens to anorexic doom through descriptions that make fruit seem prurient: "plump unpecked cherries, … Bloom-down-cheeked peaches, / Swart-headed mulberries, / Wild free-born cranberries" (470). In attempting to sate themselves, the girls instead starve, as Jeanie and Laura can attest. It is only in the shelter of the home where redemptive sexuality may be expressed and appetites satisfied, through sisterly love: "Come and kiss me. Never mind my bruises, / Hug me, kiss me, suck my juices / Squeezed from goblin fruits for you / Goblin pulp and goblin dew. / Eat me, drink me, love me," Lizzie offers herself to her starving sister (512). As with Romantic art fairy tales, enchantment is perilous and largely pernicious.

Perhaps for Rossetti and certainly for fairy-tale illustrators, infantilizing and miniaturizing the fairy tale allowed exploration of polymorphous sexuality that would be scandalous if it were not projected onto tiny humanoids or presumptively innocent children. Richard "Dicky" Doyle, a prominent fairy illustrator, whose masterpiece *In Fairyland* (1870) collected vignettes of sequential art and full-page tableaux depicting fairyland occupying the liminal dreamy space at the point where pleasure and desire overlap. Distancing and diminishing these creatures allows viewers to enjoy but not be overwhelmed (as Rossetti's Laura is) by fairy pleasures. Doyle's illustrations emphasize the minute where a mushroom may serve as an umbrella and a fairy drives a team of butterflies. In another spread, clownish sprites guzzle flower nectar while attenuated females drape themselves across stems and leaves (see Figure 0.3). Even though Victorian publishers felt the images could not stand alone—Richard Allingham was commissioned to write a poem to accompany the pictures, and Andrew Lang later rearranged them to tell the story of "Princess Nobody" (1884)—the critical consensus has been that Doyle's images frustrate attempts to narrate them. As Jan Susina writes, to this day "*In Fairyland* remains the visual archetype of fairies" (2003: 103).

Notwithstanding erotic undertones, children were pervasively associated with fairies and fairy tales.[11] Children's relative size and delicacy readily linked

FIGURE 0.3: Richard Doyle, "Feasting and fun among the fuschsias [sic]," from the series *In Fairyland*, 1870. Reproduced with permission of the Baldwin Library of Historical Children's Literature, George A. Smathers Library, University of Florida, Gainesville, Florida, USA.

them with tropes of the miniature and of evanescence that were already part of fairy lore. Fairies and children, like the dollhouses and other miniature objects discussed by Susan Stewart, paradoxically become artful as they are displayed and alienated from their "natural," unobserved state. Andersen's "Thumbelina" (1835) epitomizes this aesthetic of the miniature: his heroine's walnut-shell bed and rose-petal counterpane can readily furnish a dollhouse, while Thumbelina's trials are likewise miniaturized. This story, and others like it, are "linked to nostalgic versions of childhood and history" that smallness is "manipulatable," "domesticated and protected from contamination" (Stewart 1993: 69), reduced to a picture of idealized life. But many children's fairy stories emphasizing smallness turned toward the cute and the precious, becoming so vacuous that Lang complained in 1892, "We want *story*, and human beings, and human interest, not 'unsubstantial, shade-like, scattered hosts' of fairies, which have nothing to do but float about in glorified Crystal Palaces, gardens, and Brighton Aquariums" ([1892] 1976: 135; emphasis in the original).

The miniaturized, whimsical fairy and the idea of the fairy tale become more fraught in J. M. Barrie's *Peter Pan* (1904), which simultaneously fixes the genre and destabilizes it. Barrie's fairy play presents childhood as the product of children's books and wish-fulfillment, adult desire and child waywardness. Jacqueline Rose has described the instability of Barrie's text, which began as a photograph album, *The Boy Castaways of Black Lake Island* (1901), was incorporated into the novel *The Little White Bird* (1902), then expanded into a play (1904), reframed as a picture book in *Peter Pan in Kensington Gardens* (1906), and novelized in 1911, shifting with each iteration. The narrator of *Peter and Wendy* (1911) describes the similarly unstable components of a child's mind as

> a map ... which is not only confused, but keeps going round all the time. There are zigzag lines on it, just like your temperature on a card, and these are probably roads in the island; for the Neverland is always more or less an island, with astonishing splashes of colour here and there, and coral reefs and rakish-looking craft in the offing, and savages and lonely lairs, and gnomes who are mostly tailors, and caves through which a river runs, and princes with six elder brothers, and a hut fast going to decay, and one very small old lady with a hooked nose. It would be an easy map if that were all; but there is also first day at school, religion, fathers, the round pond, needlework, murders, hangings, verbs that take the dative, chocolate pudding day, getting into braces, say ninety-nine, three-pence for pulling out your tooth yourself, and so on; and either these are part of the island or they are another map showing through, and it is all rather confusing, especially as nothing will stand still.
>
> (Barrie [1911] 1999: 73–4)

Playfully interleaving references to classic adventure novels such as *Robinson Crusoe* (1719) or *The Coral Island* (1858) with fairy-tale motifs such as gnomes, caves, undervalued heroes, and the archetypal storytelling dame, and with ephemera from an upper-middle-class English schoolboy's life, Barrie presents the child's mind as "confused" and "going round all the time." Barrie's invocation of fairy-tale archetypes treats them as interlocking and endlessly interchangeable elements. Their role in the child's mind lacks the synthetic power of Coleridge's vast sublime. It instead emphasizes the spontaneous, experimental, ludic space of a mind that has not yet frozen into conformity. *Peter Pan*'s celebration of play and whimsy made it popular with both adults and children, offering a holiday from real life. Barrie's variations on Peter Pan simultaneously idealize and mock their subject, presenting childhood as a fairyland desired by adults who participate vicariously by performing belief rather than believing. Fairy tales were by this time strongly associated with childlike faith, so fairy tales are "linked to a kind of self-exile from the demands of adulthood" (Pask 2013: 43). Yet, as Barrie's example shows, that whimsy and idealization often provoked reaction and self-ironizing commentary, giving rise to another fairy-tale mode: the anti-Romantic, ante-modernist one.

ROMANTIC IRONY, NONSENSE, AND THE FAIRY TALE

Romantic sentimentality and nostalgia so often dominate discussions of nineteenth-century fairy tales that it is easy to overlook an equally strong orientation toward parody, irony, and meta-narrative. Even Victorians' famous "earnestness" was subject to mockery as fairy-tale creators lampooned forms, subverted characters and plots, questioned old-fashioned norms, and inserted modern skepticism. Not everyone endorsed innocence and credulity. French fairy tales such as Perrault's anticipate one strand of nineteenth-century social satire. In *Histoires ou contes du temps passé* (Stories or Tales from Past Times, 1697), Perrault's ironic asides and morals compare past and present, to the advantage of the present. Sleeping Beauty's Prince notices, but courteously does not mention, that his beloved's dress is a century out of date; a moral to "Cinderella" affirms the difficulty of social advancement without a godparent to pave the way; and "Bluebeard" assures its readers, "You surely know that this tale / Took place many years ago. / No longer are husbands so terrible, / Demanding the impossible" (quoted in Tatar 2002: 157). Alexander Pope's *The Rape of the Lock* (1714) and Jonathan Swift's *Gulliver's Travels* (1735) also influenced a significant vein of fairy-tale parody and burlesque that flourished during our period, using miniature humanoids to satirize contemporary foibles.

When Ruskin objects to modern children's stories' "taint" of the "schoolroom and drawing room," of their "premature imitations of the vanities of elder people," and of his objections to fairies who seem too concerned with "millinery and satin slippers, and appalling more by their airs than their enchantments" ([1869] 2015: 391), he tacitly acknowledges their popularity. On stage, pantomimes burlesqued well-known fairy-tale plots and characters, combining mayhem with sentiment. Rejoicing in intertextual and paratextual references, drawing attention to their own fictionality, questioning plot and character conventions, and scrutinizing the implications of magical transformation, these tales encouraged critical engagement even as they invited laughter and playful appropriations of the fairy-tale form.

Parallel to the burlesque tradition of fairy-tale appropriations and adaptations is another mode, romantic irony. It began as an aesthetic program articulated by Friedrich Schlegel in the late eighteenth century and extended by many of the Romantic writers we have already touched on. The romantic ironist simultaneously creates and de-creates work that is both emotionally charged and aware of its own fictionality (Mellor 1980: 14). In the Romantic ironic fairy tale, closed forms and traditional expectations are cracked and twisted to exhibit instead flux and fertile chaos, experimentation, "throwing up new forms, new creations" (4). Techniques of Romantic irony include breaking the narrative frame through "permanent parabasis," simultaneously controlling and mocking the plot by means of the narrator's "transcendental buffoonery," and incorporating multiple genres and perspectives to emphasize paradox (17, 21). Although Schlegel identified the novel as the premier expression of Romantic irony, a noteworthy strain of nineteenth-century fairy tales exhibit similar qualities, with similar goals.

In children's literature, Romantic irony aligns with literary Nonsense, best embodied in Lewis Carroll's *Alice* books. Kimberley Reynolds outlines the main traits of literary nonsense (as opposed to random "silliness" that characterizes children's play and some works made for them): using rules to challenge meaning (such as grammatically correct nonce sentences), combining incongruous, unrelated, or uncontradictory items, hyperbolic behaviors and actions, and inversion through parody (2006: 161). Nonsense modes gave birth to the most famous literary fairy tale of all time, *Alice's Adventures in Wonderland* (1865), inspired countless others, and led indirectly, as Juliet Dusinberre (1987) has argued, to the experimental techniques of modernism and postmodernism. Thus, we might call this aspect of nineteenth-century fairy tales "ante-modernist."

William Makepeace Thackeray's Christmas book *The Rose and the Ring; or, The History of Prince Giglio and Prince Bulbo: A Fire-Side Pantomime for Great and Small Children* (1854) exemplifies the ante-modernist fairy tale. Based on *Twelfth Night* figures Thackeray had drawn for his children, the story follows two princes, Giglio and Bulbo, and two princesses, Rosalba and Angelica. Giglio and Rosalba are gifted at their christenings by their fairy godmother Blackstick with "a little misfortune." Angelica and Bulbo are blessed by inheriting the Rose and Ring of the title, making them effortlessly appealing and beloved. As toddlers, Giglio and Rosalba are both robbed of their rightful positions, but this misfortune stimulates them (rather belatedly, in Giglio's case) to develop superior characters. The apparently fortunate Angelica and Bulbo, overly indulged by servile courtiers and stunted by their privilege, become ignorant, fatuous, and vain. Thackeray combines and lampoons genres—Shakespearean histories and romances, fairy-tale convention, domestic realism, and the moral tale, among others. The stylistic register ranges from blank verse to journalese to slang. Characters are named after vegetables (Spinachi, Cavolfiore), or as comic allegories (Gruffanuff, Cutasoff Hedzoff). The genial narrator breaks the fourth wall, theatrically speaking, by inviting readers to participate in the text by naming their favorite foods or casting judgment on the absurd situations. After the tide of a battle turns against Giglio's opponent, he complains: "'If,' says he to Giglio, 'you ride a fairy horse, and wear fairy armour, what on earth is the use of my hitting you? I may as well give myself up at once'" ([1854] 2015: 106), undercutting the chivalric code. Indeed, "The Rose and the Ring" repeatedly "burlesques … all male aspirations of heroism" (Knoepflmacher 1998: 81). Skepticism about feudal codes of honor is taken even further by Kenneth Grahame in "The Reluctant Dragon" ([1898] 2015), where Saint George and the Dragon conspire to fake a fight to satisfy the locals, without hurting anyone. Their friend and main mediator, the Boy, impatiently urges, "for goodness' sake do let us have a little straight common-sense, and come to some practical business-like arrangement" ([1898] 2015: 355), inserting into fairy-tale discourse a prosaic desire for "business-like arrangements" that free everyone from the constraints of narrative determinism.

Alice's Adventures in Wonderland (1865) and its sequel, *Alice Through the Looking-Glass* (1871) took nonsense and Romantic irony even further. Carroll's revolutionary text set new expectations for the fairy tale in its own and the next period. Introducing the portal fantasy, *Alice* begins with realistic settings and characters, then pivots to a chaotic yet rule-bound world where language undercuts rather than clarifies meaning, and morals are divorced from wisdom. Alice navigates this confusing world with common sense, logic, and strength of character. Despite meeting no mentors, commissioned with no quest, failing to make friends, and violating most other fairy-tale conventions about survival, maturation, and hope, Alice nonetheless prevails. She marks a shift in what counts as a fairy tale, encouraging other writers to modernize their characters, settings, and themes.[12] American L. Frank Baum's *Wonderful Wizard of Oz* (1900), though less committed to literary nonsense, nonetheless presents Dorothy as a similarly pragmatic child who recognizes a fraud when she sees one in the "wonderful" humbug of the title, despite his plea not to look behind the curtain. And E. Nesbit, in her short stories as well as her novels, highlights the humorous possibilities when the archaic exemplars of fairy-tale determinism collide with independent-minded young people. To choose only one example, at the end of *The Phoenix and the Carpet* (1904), after helping children travel by magic carpet to France, India, the South Seas, and back again and contributing to mayhem at the fire insurance office and the theater, the Phoenix longs for repose: "Time is measured by heartbeats. I'm sure the palpitations I've had since I've known you are enough to blanch the feathers of any bird .... I have lived in these two months at a pace which generously counterbalances 500 years of life in the desert. I am old, I am weary. I feel as if I ought to lay my egg, and lay me down to my fiery sleep" ([1904] 2012: 251). Despite their feelings of loss, the four children are relieved not to continue the responsibility of safeguarding either the Phoenix or the magical carpet they've worn to tatters. Everyone wins.

With less humor but even more subversion, Wilde's fairy tales ironize Andersen's wistful pieties with erotically and politically charged fairy tales, deliberately offering parallel characters and plots to make radically different points about morality. As Silver summarizes, Wilde's "'Nightingale and the Rose' is a tough-minded comment on Andersen's 'The Nightingale'; 'The Devoted Friend' an inversion of 'Great Claus and Little Claus'; and 'The Fisherman and his Soul,' a reversal and complex comment on 'The Little Mermaid'" (2000: 550).[13] Wilde's provocative moral orientation chastens his lushly ornamental description so that readers are arrested and challenged rather than lulled into complacency.

CONCLUSION

Despite widespread dismissal of superstition and embrace of modern skepticism, artists of all media continued to be drawn to the fairy tale as a form and a concept during the long nineteenth century. Antiquarians and folklorists found in the fairy tale and in language a key to identity. Fairy tales provide a link to the vernacular past that seems always already to be lost (like fairies themselves), and whose loss threatens to accelerate the alienation and rootlessness of modern life. Fairy tales expressed faith in the supernatural; they critiqued materialism; they promoted national unity and identity; they reconnected humans with the natural world; they luxuriated in Oriental splendor and justified imperial expansionism; they propped up and developed the cult of childhood; they innovated and invented new modes for play and subversion. Fairy tales expressed utopian longings and desires for a better world, a world more attuned to justice and joy and beauty. At the same time, they offered escape from conformity, morality, and the repressive aspects of bourgeois life.

In all these aspects, authors and collectors of nineteenth-century fairy tales planted seeds for new popular forms that continue to proliferate in the twentieth and twenty-first centuries. By capturing, preserving, freely editing, and reinventing their material, they set in motion imaginative engines fueled by desire. Refusing to be bound by the possible, they gestured toward utopian mindscapes where wishes can come true. Fairy tales continue to enchant, and they continue to reanimate and recombine in comic books and graphic novels, live action and animated film, picture books, novels, music, and dance. As Hans Christian Andersen wrote, "The fairy tale never dies" (Andersen [1865] 1949).

CHAPTER ONE

Forms of the Marvelous

LAURENCE TALAIRACH

It is to story-tellers who lived hundreds of years ago that we owe a great number of our legends, and they help us trace out the connexion between Englishmen of the present day and the children of Japhet, who separated themselves at the Tower of Babel.

Aesop, Phaedrus, La Fontaine, and Bewick would have deserved well of mankind if they had simply written stories which have entertained countless generations of children, and served for proverbs and illustrations of argument to the cleverest men. But, thanks to the labour of an indefatigable German, Jacob Grimm, who lived some seventy years ago, these legends, which were usually looked upon as merely affording amusement for children, have been made to help in throwing light upon various problems of the world's history. He is better known as the means of tracing the connexion of all nations descended from Japhet by their language. He has, however, made fables and fairy tales contribute to the same result by his method of comparison, and he brings them in as witnesses in support of truths which he proves by his comparative grammar. He has shown that the same stories, altered to suit the climate and customs of each country where they are found, exist in every land, from Britain to India; in every language, from Norse to Sanscrit.

—Goldney (1885: 20–32)

As the Reverend S. Goldney put it in 1885, fables and fairy tales relate the story of the "world's history" (Goldney 1885). Rewritten over and over again, appearing in different countries and different languages, fables and fairy tales, from Aesop to Bewick, took many shapes. Goldney's presentation of fables and fairy tales as linguistic materials that bridge the gap between the past and the present, as much as between children's literature and anthropological folklore studies, is characteristic of the last decades of the nineteenth century. Although ballads, tales, legends, and myths had been collected and examined for over a century, leading to the development of taxonomies and indexes as in cabinets of natural history, late Victorian anthropologists' and ethnographers' approach to the fairy tale illuminated the period's search for origins—the origins of fairies and those of human nature. It is therefore not coincidental that the second half of the nineteenth century saw a dramatic rise in the publication of literary fairy tales and fantasies. Frequently revisiting classical literary fairy tales, these publications were increasingly designed for juvenile audiences in the course of the nineteenth century and appeared in various forms, climaxing with the folklorists Joseph Jacobs's *More English Fairy Tales* (1894) and Andrew Lang's fairy books, published from 1889 to 1910, which gathered fairy tales from all over the world.

As this chapter will argue, throughout the long nineteenth century fairies and fairy tales incessantly reflected the period's questionings. As fairies and fairy tales were collected and classified, rewritten and revisited, forms of the marvelous evolved. From the Industrial Revolution to the publication of Charles Darwin's *On the Origin of Species by Means of Natural Selection, or the Preservation of Favoured Races in the Struggle for Life* in 1859, views and definitions of the natural environment changed, and the protean nature of the marvelous served to bridge the gap between old and new visions of the world. As fairies and fairy tales changed faces in the nineteenth century, their transformation served a variety of purposes, from praising science and technology and mapping out new scientific methods, to proposing new definitions of humans—and particularly of women.

TAMING THE FAIRY TALE? FAIRY TALES, FANTASIES, AND CHILDREN'S LITERATURE

With the advent of Romanticism, fairy tales were increasingly accepted as suitable reading material for children,[1] and writers' experiments with the genre opened the gateway to more and more fantasies throughout the nineteenth century. The use of fairies by Romantic poets Samuel Taylor Coleridge, John Keats, and Percy Bysshe Shelley, and the darker and more supernatural tales by Sir Walter Scott or James Hogg,[2] reflected early nineteenth-century folklore collecting. Romantic poetry illuminated the fascination with fairy lore, and sometimes the belief in Queen Mabs and pixies as well, since William Blake claimed he had witnessed a fairy's funeral; it frequently celebrated the close links between fairies and nature, playing therefore with "traditional associations of fairies, sexuality, and the fertile earth" (Silver 1999: 26).[3] The period also saw the resurrection of Shakespearian fairies in painting, from Henry Fuseli's *Titania and Bottom* (c. 1788–90) and William Blake's *Oberon, Titania and Puck with Fairies Dancing* (c. 1786), to later Victorian artists, such as Daniel Maclise's *Priscilla Horton as Ariel* (1838–9) and John Anster Fitzgerald's *Titania and Bottom* in the 1860s.[4]

Furthermore, the Romantic period redefined the child: as children were no longer seen as corrupt creatures, more and more stories designed for a young readership aimed to develop children's imaginative faculties (see Zipes 1987: xviii). Around the same period, however, pedagogues also started exploiting the didactic potential of literary fairy tales. In the preceding century, authors like Gabrielle-Suzanne de Villeneuve had underlined the educational role of the fairy tale, strengthening the part fairy tales could play in the socialization process. Jeanne-Marie Leprince de Beaumont's rewriting of Villeneuve's 1740 *Beauty and the Beast* a few years later intended to educate little girls and to teach them the value of self-sacrifice.[5] Thus, while the French literary fairy tale was diffused throughout Europe—especially after the publication of Charles-Joseph de Mayer's forty-one-volume *Le cabinet des fées* (*The Fairy Cabinet*, 1785–9)—its audience was gradually refined and defined as a younger readership.

As a result, in nineteenth-century Britain, the marvelous took the form of ever new collections of fairy tales designed for children, such as *Popular Fairy Tales; or, a Lilliputian Library*, published in 1804 by the bookseller Benjamin Tabart; and John Harris's *The Court of Oberon; or the Temple of the Fairies: A Collection of Tales of Past Times. Originally Related by Mother Goose, Mother Bunch, and Others* (1823).[6] In Germany, Jacob and Wilhelm Grimm published their first collection of tales in two volumes in 1812 and 1815 (*Children's and Household Tales*). The collection of 156 tales was revised and extended to 170 tales for their second edition in 1819. Little by little, the Grimms' multiple additions, omissions, revisions, and refinements of the tales testified to the changing audience of the literary fairy tale: the first collection of tales in two volumes contained notes that were not intended for children, and which were published separately in the second edition (see Zipes 2006: 82). In the seventh edition of 1857, there were 211 tales, most manifestly aimed at a young bourgeois audience: the sexual elements had been suppressed from the narratives, violence and cruelty played down, domestic chores partook of the heroines' tasks, and Christian references informed a moralistic and patriarchal discourse.

In 1823 and 1826, selections from the Brothers Grimm's fairy tales were translated into English by Edgar Taylor and illustrated by George Cruikshank; new translations also appeared in 1839, 1846, 1849, and 1855 (Zipes 1987: xvii–xviii). The way in which fairy tales were informed by increasingly bourgeois codes of conduct became even more patent when the Danish writer Hans Christian Andersen published his fairy tales between 1835 and 1875. The tales' emphasis on self-abnegation and self-denial and overt Christian principles were much in line with the ideals of the Protestant ethic, thereby suiting the values advocated by the rising bourgeoisie. Published in England in 1846 and translated by Mary Howitt, Andersen's *Wonderful Stories for Children*, therefore, paved the way for a wider acceptance of fairy tales as suitable literature for children in Victorian Britain.

Ironically, it is at the very same time, and, more particularly, from the mid-nineteenth century, that the literary fairy tale most targeted social, political, and cultural issues, showing in so doing its polymorphous capacity for taking ever new forms. As Jack Zipes (1987) has argued, the Victorians construed literary fairy tales as illustrations of their own dreams of better worlds. Consequently, Victorian fairy tales became a means of purveying a social discourse. Seen through the looking glass of the marvelous, British domestic ideology could be investigated, especially as fairy tales traced the rise of the middle classes, underlined the consequences of Britain's Industrial Revolution and the quest for economic possession, and illuminated ideal domesticity and the Victorian double standard. Thus, fairy tales were simultaneously used to educate children and to teach them to distance themselves from the picture of the prescribed social order that such tales offered. Indeed, detaching themselves from the much more moralizing tales of the 1840s and 1850s, juvenile literature became wilder from the 1860s, overtly expressing anger and breaking social taboos. Because in this period the child was seen as a pure and innocent creature and thus non-threatening, children's fiction was subject to less censorship, thereby offering more latitude to the writers of fairy tales.[7] The marvelous hence became a significant means to reflect the flaws of modern society, criticize materialism and utilitarianism, and raise social consciousness, whilst providing a lens for women to look at and represent their social oppression.

Lewis Carroll's *Alice's Adventures in Wonderland* (1865) is a case in point. Following in the footsteps of Edward Lear's "nonsense" literature, Carrol's "fairy tale"[8] questioned (arbitrary) rules and figures of authority, dethroning kings and queens, and giving more liberty to the child's imagination. His little girl's adventure in Wonderland, which mocked earlier didactic children's literature, paved the way for many Victorian experimental fairy tales of the 1860s and 1870s. In fact, Jean Ingelow's *Mopsa the Fairy* (1869) and Christina Rossetti's *Speaking Likenesses* (1874) both revisit Alice's journey in Wonderland, although the heroines' metamorphoses map out much bleaker journeys into discipline and coercion. The trajectory of Carroll's "fairy tale" and its gradual transformation into darker fantasies by women writers provides a significant instance of Victorian fairy tales' preoccupation with women's education and limited conditions in patriarchy. Another example of the recycling of fairy tales can be seen in the tales of Juliana Horatia Ewing, much influenced by the Brothers Grimm, Hans Christian Andersen, and Ludwig Bechstein, as hinted at in the title of her *Old-Fashioned Fairy Tales* (1882).

Ewing's tales also conflated rewritings of literary fairy tales with oral folklore, as in "Amelia and the Dwarfs" (1870), inspired by "Wee Meg Barnileg and the Fairies," an Irish folktale.[9] For authors such as George MacDonald, Mary de Morgan, Anne Isabella Thackeray Ritchie, and later Mary Louisa Molesworth, the fairy tale offered manifold ways of playing with the conventions of the genre. More often than not, the stereotypes of the fairy tale were comically or satirically debunked, as suggested by MacDonald's or de Morgan's princesses (who may be selfish or cruel), or rewritten as realistic short stories or novellas as in the case of Ritchie's "Cinderella," "Beauty and the Beast," "Little Red Riding Hood," and "The Sleeping Beauty in the Wood." Other examples of adaptations of fairy tales were also found in Dickens's fiction, Dickens using fairy-tale motifs and plot-patterns as a way of toning down the materialistic and utilitarian environment of Victorian Britain (see Stone 1979). If at times heavily moralistic, Dickens's fairy tales nonetheless shaped his utopian vision of society and typify the pervasive presence and use of the marvelous in the Victorian period.

Zipes's dualistic classification of the fairy tales of the second half of the nineteenth century is interesting in this context. He contends that, despite the many forms Victorian fairy tales could take, some remained conventional and (sometimes heavily) moralistic, featuring protagonists who finally integrate into the prescribed social order. This is the case of Dinah Mulock Craik's *The Little Lame Prince and his Travelling Cloak* (1875) and Harriet Louisa Childe-Pemberton's *The Fairy Tales of Every Day* (1882); and tales by Jean Ingelow, Anne Thackeray Ritchie, and Christina Rossetti. By contrast, other writers favored utopianism, as illustrated by the fairy tales and fantasies of de Morgan, Ewing, MacDonald (notably in *Dealing with the Fairies*, 1867), Oscar Wilde (exemplified in *The Happy Prince and Other Tales* from 1888 and *The House of Pomegranates* from 1891), and Molesworth, with *The Cuckoo Clock* (1877), *The Tapestry Room: A Child's Romance* (1879), *The Magic Nuts* (1898), and *Fairies Afield* (1911). These latter works pictured strong heroes and heroines eventually reaching autonomy and independence (Zipes 1999: 125–7). The fantasies of MacDonald—including *Phantastes* (1858), *At the Back of the North Wind* (1871), *The Princess and the Goblin* (1872), *The Princess and Curdie* (1883), and *Lilith* (1895)—and those of Molesworth undoubtedly paved the way for twentieth-century fantasists such as J. R. R. Tolkien and C. S. Lewis, showing once again the potential of the marvelous to endlessly metamorphose into new forms and patterns. However, through their rewritings, these fairy tales and fantasies nevertheless showed that although fairies offered journeys away from the Victorians' disenchanted world, they were intricately linked to many aspects of modernity, be it technological advances, scientific ideas, or even political issues. Fairies also stood for the marvels of the world of industry, for technological advances and scientific progress, and the (dis)enchanted kingdoms presented in these literary fairy tales and fantasies were more often than not the wonderlands of Victorian society.

THE MARVELS OF SCIENCE AND TECHNOLOGY: THE FAIRY TALE AND POPULAR SCIENCE

When Queen Victoria, privately dubbed "the Faery" by her favorite prime minister Benjamin Disraeli (Lambourne 1997: 53), entered the Crystal Palace for the first time in 1851, she claimed the place "had quite the effect of fairyland" (quoted in Gere 1997: 64). At the entrance, a tableau of fairies representing "Art, Science, Concord, Progress, Peace, Wealth, Health, Success, Happiness, Industry and Plenty" welcomed visitors, but the jarring contrast between the world of fairies and the industrial world became a regular source of satire in the popular press, as in W. H. Wills and George A. Sala's 1853 article:

> The magician is right; but as Beauty's chamber was guarded by griffins, and all enchanted castles are defended by dragons, so is Fairyland guarded by gnomes; blue, and uncompromising. One occupies the little crypt on either side of the door by which visitors are admitted to Fairyland in crystal. To judge from the costumes of these gnomes you would take them to be plain constables of the Metropolitan Police; but, my word for it, they have all the gnomical etceteras beneath their uniform and oilskin. The entrance to Fairyland is not effected by rubbing a lamp, or clapping the hands three times, or by exclaiming "Open Sesame"; but, as a concession to the non-magical tendencies of some of the visitors, a commutation is accepted in the shape of five shillings current money of the realm.
>
> (Wills and Sala 1853: 313)

The disenchanting experience of modernity and progress that the 1851 Great Exhibition proposed, miles away from enchanted Fairyland, show how fairies and Fairyland were both a retreat for Victorians striving to cope with humans' increasing power over nature *and* images of themselves—their tiny size and fragile-looking appearance illustrating humans' bodies, dwarfed by the height and power of factories and machines, as Nicola Bown has shown (2001: 96). However, different forms of the marvelous—as illustrated by the many paintings and illustrations, advertisements (used to promote ordinary commodities for ordinary people) and stories informed by fairy-tale stereotypes, motifs, or plot-patterns—helped to capture the wonders of the world of industry. For instance, in Ritchie's realistic short stories, which updated classical fairy tales, the Crystal Palace, and glasshouses more generally (which enable the maturation of pumpkins), become magical places where heroines are turned into princesses. In her 1868 "Cinderella," Ritchie turns her heroine into one of the wonderful commodities displayed at the Crystal Palace, the glasshouse functioning as the magic place where the prince and princess meet and fall in love, and where the princess exhibits her series of brand new dresses and accessories ([1868] 1987: 101–26).[10] Similarly, Andersen's "The Dryad" (1868, English translation 1869) relates a dryad's wish to visit the 1867 Paris Great Exhibition, "the great and wonderful time of Fairy-Tale" (Andersen 1869: 296). Not only does Andersen's fairy tale link progress with the world of magic but it also ironically associates the world of art and industry with natural metaphors: the exhibition is short-lived; the palace that hosts the exhibition grows up with the spring and vanishes at fall. Thus, the world, miniaturized in the palace, literally becomes a fairy world, as every country is downsized to a single room. Visitors can travel the world in a day: in this way, the place encapsulates the modern changes of rhythm and the hectic pace of modern society, miles away from the slow cycles of nature.[11]

Though many celebrated the marvelous achievements of modernity, however, numerous rewritings of classical fairy tales published in the second half of the nineteenth century used the form of the marvelous to denounce industrialization, utilitarianism, and materialism, from John Ruskin's *The King of the Golden River, or the Black Brothers* (1841) to Wilde's "The Happy Prince" (1888) and Kendall and Lang's *That Very Mab* (1885). Industrial England, discreetly found in the background of a few fairy paintings,[12] was often prominent in Victorian fairy tales, conveying these tales' social and political discourse. Moreover, many of the fairy tales aimed at children made explicit that scientific materialism had divorced humans from nature. This idea permeated as well Victorian art, peopled with fairies and the little people. By playing upon the nostalgia for a lost natural world threatened by pollution and massive urbanization, paintings hinted at the dangers of technological and scientific developments.

Such contemporary anxieties resonated, for example, in the microscopic quality of Victorian fairy painting, as illustrated by Richard Dadd's *The Fairy Feller's Master Stroke* (1855–64). Dadd's work presents an unknown territory that hinges on variations on the fairies' size, constructing in this way the little people as new species to be cataloged. The fairies merge here with the natural world, whilst the grass in the foreground gives the viewers the impression that the painter's brush has provided them access to an invisible universe, as if seen through a microscope. Among fairies, elves, and gnomes of different sizes, a dragonfly plays the trumpet, a gnat acts as coachman. Aligned with insects, the little people's diversity is evaluated as if by a naturalist. Though many argue that Victorian fairy paintings entail a dreamlike atmosphere, their play with proportion, resulting in a disorientating effect, is nevertheless in keeping with the politics of observation of the time. For Lynn Merrill, indeed, the use of the microscope produced "a disoriented sense of fragmentation ... a loss of unity ... Too many details signal a failure of meaning, a collapse of unity, the death of hope" (1989: 123).

Victorian fairy painting, in particular, illustrates how this form of the marvelous alongside Victorian art more generally could mediate between science and popular culture. In the second half of the nineteenth century, natural history illustrations in popular science books and paintings uncannily echoed one another, and undoubtedly showed the interchange between science and art throughout the period. Painters linked to fairy painting looked at nature not so much with an artistic eye, but with a scientific one, offering a microscopic realism and scientific accuracy in their depiction of fairy lands. Moreover, natural historians' highly visual prose appealed to Victorian artists eager to experiment with perspective and to take their viewers into invisible realms beyond the reach of human perception.[13] Victorian fairy painting offered journeys to some unknown worlds that look like expeditions to worlds invisible to the naked eye, and which only the artist's paintbrush was able to reveal. They too recall the period's attempt at giving shape (and reality) to the invisible world that science and technology were daily revealing to the public.

Despite its affinity with contemporary science illustration, Victorian art often used fairies and fairy lands to offer viewers an escape into romantic natural worlds. On those canvases, fairies mingle with the natural environment, hide in trees or behind mushrooms. As exemplified by the works by John Anster Fitzgerald (1819–1906), Joseph Noel Paton (1821–1901), John George Naish (1824–1905), Richard Dadd (1817–86), and Richard Doyle (1824–83), Victorian fairy painting was, in addition, characterized by an attempt at combining fairy art with "truth to nature,"[14] reconciling reality and fantasy in detailed descriptions of fairies in a natural environment. In so doing, Victorian fairy art testified to the period's association of fairy lands with natural wonders, since fairies, sharing their land with other animals and insects, from birds and squirrels to snails, beetles, and butterflies, proposed imaginative views of other ecosystems.

The precise and minute realism of Victorian fairy painters (or "microscopic optics"; see Axton 1977: 281–308, 288), directly spurred by the Pre-Raphaelite movement, committed to the faithful depiction of the natural world, capitalized on the vision of nature as a source of wonder and astonishment. Their fairies' resemblance to insects and animals allegorized the Victorians' vision of nature, its secrets, mysteries, and wonders. Furthermore, Victorian fairy painters' insights into more folkloric and rural settings, especially John Anster Fitzgerald's fairy banquets—as in *The Fairies's Banquet* (1859)—and funerals (*The Fairy's Funeral*) echoed the scientific and anthropological studies of the time. The sometimes random cruelty evident in many Victorian fairy paintings, though enabling the artists to evade censorship and add sadomasochistic and erotic elements on the canvases, could be read as revelatory of anxieties related to life's competitiveness and the struggle for life, or even the way in which savage elements of folktales seen after 1859 were deemed examples of primitivism and less evolved cultures, primitive races of humankind.[15]

In the same way as Victorian fairy painting's hyperrealism testified to the close links between the artistic and scientific worlds, literary fairy tales likewise used, referred to, or alluded to natural historical knowledge throughout the Victorian period. In both cases, the connection with natural history suggested that fairy tales were a relevant literary material to negotiate tensions at a time when the meaning of nature changed and "nature" became a much debated word. Indeed, shifts in the understanding of natural history, especially after the publication of Darwin's *On the Origin of Species* in 1859, had a significant impact on fairy stories and Victorian experiments with the literary fairy tale.[16] Carroll's *Alice's Adventures in Wonderland* is a case in point: Alice's obsession with size throughout her journey mirrors the text's interest in questions of scale in ways very similar to Victorian fairy painters' microscopic realism and scientific accuracy. Furthermore, in *Alice's Adventures in Wonderland* Alice first believes she is falling through the earth, reaching lands situated on the other side of the globe, and the tale calls to mind the period's urge to travel farther and to see farther, peering into unknown worlds—or even planets, as the motif of the telescope, mentioned by the little girl who wishes she could shrink to go through the door, intimates. In fact, *Alice's Adventures in Wonderland* easily reads as a humorous rewriting of a travel narrative, with the young naturalist entering a wild territory where codes of conduct and signs of civilization have become useless or turned upside down. The case is similar in its sequel, *Through the Looking-Glass and What Alice Found There* (1871): both narratives take us into a realm inhabited by talking animals and flowers, extinct species, mythical creatures, and imaginary beings.

Carroll's reappropriation of the marvelous in his *Alice* books, both aimed at children, is also highly representative of the issues that concerned the Victorians. The marvelous, here represented by Wonderland, encapsulates debates revolving around representations of nature at a time when such definitions were changing; it also serves to allude to the development of scientific knowledge linked to a new mapping of the world and the discovery of exotic, unknown or unseen species and peoples; it is used as well to tackle the diffusion of such knowledge, either through references to specimens exhibited at the time in museums (like the Dodo in the Oxford University Museum) or to popular science works. Furthermore, the little girl's experience of natural selection and struggles for life in Wonderland is reminiscent of the journeys that writers of natural history books proposed at the time, inviting their readers to travel into unknown territories to discover new species and constantly triggering wonder and curiosity.

Literary critics William Empson and Rose Lovell-Smith have shown how Carroll's fairy tale, like many other mid- and late Victorian experimental fairy tales, was much influenced by the publication of Darwin's *On the Origin of Species* (see Empson [1935] 1995; Lovell-Smith 2007). As suggested above, the naturalist and collector's book gave to the wonders of the natural world new meanings that the Victorians tried to grasp and appropriate. Like the worlds of fairies, evolutionary theory could not be visualized, casting empirical science away to favor a radically different scientific method. Though epitomizing science's materialism, Darwin's vision of nature, as Gillian Beer and George Levine have underlined, "radical[ly] *re*-enchant[ed]" the natural world through a scientific method that gave some room to the invisible or the impossible (Levine 2006: 22; Beer [1983] 2000; Levine [1988] 1991). In so doing, evolutionary theory opened up the world of nature to the world of a new type of marvelous, possibly inhabited by fairies, as popularizers of natural history suggested. Hence, though "nature had to be objectified," even if the Victorians were progressively moving away from a Romantic perception of nature, science nonetheless pointed out the natural world's marvels (Knoepflmacher and Tennyson 1977: xix).

As a consequence, fairies and fairy tales were frequently used throughout the Victorian period to depict the wonders of nature or of science or to express doubt and anxieties related to the implications of scientific knowledge. Forms of the marvelous could, in some cases, serve to explain natural history without undermining revealed religion; in others, it was used to deal with a theory that could not be seen and was not empirically verifiable, demanding therefore to be conceived through the use of the imagination. In Bown's terms, fairies connoted both "the marvels and difficulties of science" (2001: 102) in the second half of the nineteenth century, and were often to be found whenever popularizers aimed to introduce their readers to the latest scientific developments and conceptions of the natural world. Because the latest scientific discoveries—and especially, of course, evolutionary theory—touched on the foundations of religious belief, their implications were to permeate Victorian culture, and were refracted in such popular science works. If science appeared to disenchant the world, scientists increasingly explaining away the mysteries of natural phenomena,[17] Victorian popularizers played a key part in re-enchanting the natural world. Although the wonders of science could account for some mysteries of nature, nature nonetheless remained a fairyland, and the explanatory power of (evolutionary) science, suggesting, for instance, that transformations of all kinds were always possible, could appear magical. Thus, beneath this contradictory construction of fairies and Fairyland one may discern not just the Victorians' ambivalence toward science but also the way science seemed to desecrate the world, robbing religion of its authority.

Surprisingly enough, perhaps, this view of nature as charged with religiosity was increasingly emphasized in the popular science books that followed the publication of Darwin's *On the Origin of Species*. This shows, in fact, how fairies and the fairy-like played a role in reconciling the findings of material science with the tenets of Christianity. Popular science works, such as Arabella Buckley's *The Fairy-Land of Science* (1879), or Charles Kingsley's *Madam How and Lady Why* (1870), as well as Kingsley's fairy tale *The Water-Babies: A Fairy Tale for a Land-Baby* (1863), were significant examples of the ways in which fairy-tale discourses strongly contributed to the mediation of knowledge about nature. These new forms of the marvelous typify the difficulties that popularizers encountered in the years that preceded and followed the advent of evolutionary theory. In both Kingsley's and Buckley's writings, the world of nature is filled with wonderful creatures still unknown to humans, and the images and tropes they use show how wonder and religion are not only compatible with science but also essential to the scientific method. Indeed, although before 1859 fairies and the rhetoric of wonder generally served to illustrate the wonders of creation and help convey a Christian message in popular science works, mid-Victorian fairies also helped disseminate new representations of nature.

This is well illustrated in Kingsley's "fairy tale" *The Water-Babies*, which aimed at popularizing evolutionary theory whilst reconciling science and religion. The story does not merely foreground species transformation; it also makes clear that species that fail to evolve will inevitably become extinct, as the example of the last Gairfowl, who refuses to share the attributes of lower—more recent—creatures, demonstrates. The "Lady Gairfowl," whose wings have become "two little feathery arms" with which she fans herself, is doomed to extinction because of her aristocratic arrogance, wings serving, in her opinion, the "vulgar creatures" who seek to "rais[e] themselves above their proper station" (Kingsley [1863] 1995: 249).

As these scientifically inflected fairy tales mediated knowledge about nature, moreover, they increasingly helped raise the Victorians' awareness of environmental issues. The story of Lady Gairfowl relates, in fact, the extinction of the great auk, deemed to have vanished due to climate change and because sailors took their eggs and ate them.[18] This idea became most prominent at the close of the Victorian period, in fantasies such as Edith Nesbit's *Five Children and It* (1902), where an endangered "sand fairy" educates children about the reality of extinction. As the last Psammead suggests, all prehistoric creatures, including sand fairies, have become extinct due to overhunting—or "wishing" too much for delicacies to grill and eat. Nesbit's critique of consumerism is ironically rendered by her depiction of the children's wishes systematically going wrong throughout the fantasy. Another example is found in Rudyard Kipling's *Puck of Pook's Hill* (1906), in which the nature spirit Puck explains that the fairies have now all left England. As Kipling's text suggests, at the turn of the century, writers increasingly characterized fairies as extinct so as to evoke the nostalgia that fairies conjured up and represent the disenchantment of modernity: the little people were the victims of massive industrialism and of the destruction of natural ecosystems. Fairies therefore illustrated and encapsulated the growing awareness of the world as an ecosystem—Darwin's vision of a cruel environment where the weakest could not survive.

These changes in the meaning of fairies and Fairyland were not unrelated to the understanding of fairy tales as primitive stories of humankind, at a time when anthropologists increasingly studied folklore through an evolutionary lens, as suggested. Indeed, fairies could also take the form of primitive models of humans, as Charles Kingsley explains in *Madam How and Lady Why; or, First Lessons in Earth Lore for Children* (1870), his words echoing the Reverend S. Goldney, quoted in the introduction to this chapter:

> But what has all this to do with my fairy tale? This:—
>
> Suppose that these people, after all, had been fairies?
>
> I am in earnest. Of course, I do not mean that these folk could make themselves invisible, or that they had any supernatural powers—any more, at least, than you and I have—or that they were anything but savages; but this I do think, that out of old stories of these savages grew up the stories of fairies, elves, and trolls, and scratlings, and cluricaunes, and ogres, of which you have read so many.
>
> (Kingsley [1870] 1888: 125)

As Silver has argued, the rise of Darwinism made the study of fairies possible because the debate on origins launched the development of theories of social, cultural, and spiritual evolution (1999: 32). In Darwin's theory as applied to culture, fairies were therefore reimagined as "savage" societies. The popular Thomas Crofton Croker's *Fairy Legends and Traditions of the South of Ireland* (1825–8), the Brothers Grimm's essay "On the Nature of the Elves" (1825–8),[19] or Thomas Keightley's *The Fairy Mythology* (1828, revised in 1850, newly prefaced in 1860) were signs of the era's interest in fairy scholarship on the part of artists and folklorists alike (Silver 1999: 29). For Silver, the "linguistic analysis, categorization and systematization" initiated by such research into fairy lore were the first steps toward turning "the quest for fairies into science" (31), all the more so with the development of anthropology and ethnology.

The debate on origins, moreover, which fascinated naturalists as much as anthropologists, included that of the origins of matrimony, as Silver contends, and became reflected in the many tales of swan maidens of the period, which dealt with female sexuality. Indeed, the multiple shapes that fairies and fairy tales could take in Victorian literature and art show how forms of the marvelous also aimed at addressing fears and anxieties related to women, femininity—and "female bestiality" (Silver 1999: 8).

FORMS AND TRANSFORMATIONS: THE "BEASTLY" NATURE OF WOMAN

The sensational advances in technology that marked the nineteenth century, proudly symbolized by the commodities on display in the Crystal Palace in 1851, benefited book production and book illustration, enabling artists, writers, and publishers alike to imagine ever new forms of the marvelous. Indeed, the books published in the Victorian period became increasingly beautifully crafted and illustrated. Images likely to spur the reading public's interest appeared in a variety of publications, from newspapers and journals to magazines and books, climaxing with picture books in which images dominated the text. Edmund Evans (1826–1905) was one of the influential printers who participated in the boom of illustrated children's books and whose collaboration with Walter Crane (1845–1915) led to the production of a series of toy books. Among the stories Crane illustrated, Perrault's versions predominate. They also include a version of "Beauty and the Beast."[20] As both illustrator and designer, Crane carefully ornamented his illustrations, using them as a surface on which to project his aesthetic theories. Decoration, for Crane, as a reflection of taste, had a moral significance: beauty was linked to design and craftsmanship. Merging the tales for children with his reflections on decorating ideas, his illustrations were firmly rooted in Victorian England. However, as technological improvements gave the fairy tale new forms, as in picture books, these forms sometimes mirrored the many shapes women could take, as the era more and more questioned the definition of woman, as we will see.

Walter Crane's 1874 plates for "Beauty and the Beast" are significant in this context, for one of the plates describes Beauty and the Beast quietly having tea in a typically bourgeois environment. Crane's colorful illustration of the classical fairy tale—originally aimed at teaching little girls the value of self-sacrifice—has frequently been read by feminist criticism as paradoxically highlighting the link between woman and creature. The symmetry of the picture, as Beauty and the Beast face each other on the sofa, is broken by the hem of Beauty's dress, which seems attracted to the Beast and slightly reveals feet shaped in stark contrast to the Beast's cloven hooves. In her study of Victorian representations of women, Nina Auerbach develops this idea further by highlighting the role played by complementary colors in the illustration: the red slashes in Beauty's dress, hair, and fan mirror the Beast's red waistcoat and hooves (Auerbach 1982: 65). The picture is also striking in the way that the Beast vanishes under fashionable clothes in the garish bourgeois surroundings, with hints at Japanese decoration, Greek and Renaissance art. These choices testify to Crane's involvement with the Arts and Crafts movement, like many other illustrators of his time such as Randolph Caldecott, Kate Greenaway, and Arthur Rackham, and recall the heavy decoration of mid-Victorian middle-class homes. As Betsy Hearne suggests, "there is no wildness in either the setting or the Beast" (1989: 43): the Beast's monocle and eighteenth-century French court costume, or Beauty's profiled face, hinting at Greek pottery, turn Beauty and the Beast into fashionable and colorful curios that cancel the tale's potential fierceness. Playing as it does with conventional postures and decorative clichés, Crane's illustration becomes a gaudy surface with little depth. As the characters become flat surfaces, the illustration erases the tale's concerns with sex and marriage to stress decoration instead. In doing so, it foregrounds much more modern concerns, such as the importance of appearance and class, emphasizing therefore the visual signs that make the lady and the gentleman. Consequently, the form of the picture book shows how the marvelous turns into a lesson about fashion and decoration rather than morality. The construction of Beauty as housekeeper and elegant lady is shaped by the play on lines and colors, thereby radically revisiting a classical fairy tale aimed at advising young readers to read through appearances.

The new form that Crane's illustration proposes for Leprince de Beaumont's classical fairy tale is telling. Crane's picture book epitomized the era's vogue for illustrated fairy tales for children. The numerous toy books Crane illustrated for Routledge in the last decades of the nineteenth century, foregrounding the significance of the image, are good examples of the close relationship between fairy tales and the development of children's literature at the turn of the twentieth century.[21] This is one of the reasons why, in his last collection of tales, the folklorist Andrew Lang (1844–1912) complained about the increasing number of published fairy tales targeting children, which as a result were gradually severing their connections with the morally ambiguous fairies of folklore (Introduction to *The Lilac Fairy Book* [1910], quoted in Silver 1999: 186). However, Crane's toy book also revealed his decorating ideas, showing how Victorian reality and bourgeois culture suffused the literary fairy tales of the period, adapting the classical fairy tales to the social and cultural environment of Victorian England. By simultaneously suggesting Beauty's wild nature and her relationship with the Beast and proposing an image of the ideal Victorian lady, fated to be objectified and sold in marriage, Crane's illustration points out the tensions that informed Victorian fairy tales dealing with the nature of woman.

The many versions of "Beauty and the Beast" that appeared in Britain in the second half of the nineteenth century illuminated, in fact, an increasing interest in form. Transformations and metamorphoses of all sorts fascinated the Victorians in the decades that followed the publication of Darwin's *Origin of Species*, hence the fairy tale's popularity. But "Beauty and the Beast" also attracted many women writers eager to tackle the violence of male sexuality, which the heroine must learn to tame—and accept—and which marks the main stage of her education into womanhood. In her revisions of classical fairy tales, Ritchie frequently featured frightening or ugly suitors, such as in

"Bluebeard's Keys" or in "Riquet à la Houppe," interestingly often erasing the male characters' wildness in ways very similar to Walter Crane.[22] Opening her *Five Old Friends and a Young Prince* (published as *Fairy Tales for Grown Folks* in America), Ritchie's "Beauty and the Beast" hinges on middle-class interests and bourgeois mores and manners.[23] Ritchie cancels all magic from the narrative, her Beast symbolizing a man who has no taste for society life and social obligations, appearing thereby "uncouth and uncivilized" (1867a; 1868: 104). Ritchie's transposition of the classical fairy tale into the modern world indeed makes clear that the beast is the man who is not fashionable enough to figure in society gossip columns and whose marriageability is directly related to his use of "tailors and hair-oil" (125). Ritchie's Beast is therefore neither monstrous nor threatening, and his power is exclusively economic; Griffiths is a member of the wealthy commercial middle classes, and his money is the magic aid that transforms him into the ideal suitor despite his manners and appearance. Beauty, standing for ideal femininity, is also constructed in materialistic terms: the heroine becomes an object that can be purchased. Hence, Ritchie replaces marital consummation with male consumption, effacing thereby sexuality from the narrative. Like the tiger's pelt in the foreground of Crane's illustration, men's and women's beastly natures have been domesticated and turned into decorative items.

Ritchie's revision of the classic fairy tale and her erasure of sexuality from the narrative bring to light how, by the mid-Victorian period, fairy-tale motifs and characters purveyed bourgeois patriarchal ideology. Throughout the period, toy-like and angel-like fairies could be found in advertising or used for home decoration. Fairies and fairy tales were part and parcel of the Victorians' material culture, and the domesticated fairies found on soap (Oval fairy soap), mustard (Coleman's), ointments (Sanford Camphor ice), shoe polish, clothes, wallpapers, pottery, and so on, often symbolized the Victorian feminine ideal, inviting women to literally consume bourgeois ideology. These angelic fairies were ironically used to spur women's urge for consumption at a time when fairy ballets such as *La Sylphide* or *Giselle*, which featured supernatural women, and operas like E. T. A. Hoffmann's *Undine* (based on Friedrich de la Motte Fouqué's 1811 fairy tale), as well as fairy plays or "extravaganzas," many of them showcasing more and more technologically complex and sensational magical transformations,[24] explored female desire.[25]

In realist fiction, the fairy metaphor was an integral part of representations of femininity. The doll-like Paulina Home in Charlotte Brontë's *Villette* (1853) appears as an emblem of the diminutive feminine ideal whose clipped wings condemn her to an indoor life. Rooted in early nineteenth-century folklore of the kind that inspired Coleridge, Keats, and Shelley, references to changelings continued to be made in Victorian novels and tales, such as Catherine Earnshaw in Emily Brontë's *Wuthering Heights* (1847),[26] Dinah Maria Craik's deformed heroine in *Olive* (1850), or Juliana Horatia Ewing's "Amelia and the Dwarfs" (1870) and George MacDonald's "Cross-Purposes" (1867). But despite these references, Victorian fairies increasingly seemed to sever their links with folklore the better to represent (or frame) the modern Victorian woman.

In different ways, all these forms of the marvelous nonetheless continually suggested that fairies and fairy tales could map out more transgressive models of womanhood. In Charlotte Brontë's *Jane Eyre* (1847), for instance, the heroine refuses to conform to the stereotype of the fairy Edward Rochester sees in his ward's governess, flirting rather with that of the ugly duckling or Little Red Riding Hood. In the sensation novels of the 1860s, many of the fairy-like heroines are scheming criminals. Mary Elizabeth Braddon's *Lady Audley's Secret* (1862) cites the eponymous protagonist's "fairy" accessories (such as her bonnet, scissors, and embroidery) as telltale devices intimating the artificiality of the character and her transgressive role-play.[27] In realist fiction, likewise, much informed with forms of the marvelous through stereotypes, motifs, and plot-patterns directly borrowed from classical fairy tales, fairy-like women conceal darker natures, as in the case of Olive's selfish mother in Craik's novel,[28] or the manipulative Rosamond Vincy in George Eliot's *Middlemarch* (1871), who lures Lydgate into marriage. Embedded fairy tales—used in many of the fantasies of the period, such as MacDonald's *Adela Cathcart* (1864), Molesworth's *The Tapestry Room* (1879) and *Christmas-Tree Land* (1884)—also functioned as mirroring devices in gothic texts. Bram Stoker's *Dracula* (1897) at the end of the century refers to "Little Red Riding Hood" and "The Ugly Duckling" to explore the nature of female sexuality at the transition between the Victorian and Edwardian periods, a time when more and more educated and independent women, embodied by the feminist ideal of the New Woman, current in the late nineteenth century, increasingly threatened the patriarchal status quo.

Such play with forms of the marvelous is in keeping with contemporary scientists' and medical professionals' attempts at understanding and controlling the nature of woman. Like rewritings of "Beauty and the Beast" in the second half of the nineteenth century, revisions of "Little Red Riding Hood" particularly addressed the issue of woman's nature.[29] Perrault's literary fairy tale not only dealt with the relationship between woman and nature—the wild nature of woman—but also highlighted the artificiality of woman through the red riding hood, which frames and defines the female character in the tale. Both Ritchie's and Childe-Pemberton's rewritings of Perrault's "Little Red Riding Hood" use the classical fairy tale to foreground the social condition of Victorian women and the few choices offered to women outside marriage. Though Perrault's fairy tale does not feature a marriage, Ritchie's "Little Red Riding Hood" (1867) emphasizes the significance of marriage for women and the equation between women and commodities.[30] In her tale, women are literally sold in marriage, since the wolf, Rémy de la Louvière, has lost his money at gambling and wants to marry his cousin, Patty, who is to inherit their grandmother's fortune. However, the fairy tale ironically brings to light her heroine's sexual nature more than it effaces it, proposing a less conventional reading of the classical cautionary tale.

Indeed, as Rémy falls in love with his cousin, forgetting "all about his speculation" and "his part of wolf altogether," the fairy tale becomes a means of mapping out the young girl's passion: Patty is "heedless," "impulsive," an "Undine-like" creature yielding to her instincts for pleasure (often rendered through allusions to food) (Ritchie 1867b; 1868: 186, 198, 195). Thus, whilst the heroine becomes more and more commodified in preparation for her wedding,[31] donning "a scarlet 'capeline'—such as ladies wear by the seaside—a pretty frilled, quilted, laced, and braided scarlet hood, close round the cheeks and tied up to the chin," Patty's physical transformation and the stress on her appetite mark her sexual maturation, foreshadowing her meeting—and mating—with the wolf (Ritchie 1868: 197). Moreover, Ritchie's rewriting of Little Red Riding Hood eventually disrupts the moral lesson the reader might have expected, since trusting nature pays here more than decking oneself in fashionable red clothes, and Patty's innocence, if it costs her her inheritance, enables her to marry the wolf.

Like Ritchie, Childe-Pemberton revised Perrault's classical fairy tale in the 1880s, transposing the narrative into Victorian reality. Little Red Riding Hood's journey through the forest has been replaced by a train journey—the train epitomizing, perhaps more than any other machine, the Victorians' changing environment. The heroine's growth is mapped out by the train's speed: as the female character "steam[s] out" of the station, her evolution marches hand in hand with the pace of fashion (Childe-Pemberton [1882] 1987: 219). She explains: "I wore red stockings, and a violet dress, and a scarlet cloak, and nobody ever thought, as they would now, of calling my taste vulgar. What I must have looked like you can very well imagine" (213). Made to signify through the accumulation of accessories, Childe-Pemberton's Little Red Riding Hood matches the visual stereotypes of the period. Her cloak, "made in a particular shape, a sort of double cloak, the upper one being shorter than the under, and drawn in at the waist with a rosette," shows how the riding hood becomes an emblem of mechanical reproduction and artificiality, turning the female character into a commodity whose value is essentially economic and effacing, as a result, her (natural) body (214).[32]

In both cases, either tamed or freed, woman's nature, as captured by Ritchie's and Childe-Pemberton's rewritings, shows how the image of the beast and definitions of bestiality followed the scientific and technological developments of the period. By the turn of the twentieth century, however, as science seemed to have explained away many of the mysteries of the natural world, fairies were often left to explain psychic phenomena and "reconnect the actual and the occult" (Silver 1999: 3). The marvelous thus defied extinction, enduring through multiple forms: fairies continued to sprinkle fairy dust on a modern world, as exemplified by the mischievous and quick-tempered Tinker Bell in J. M. Barrie's *Peter Pan; or, the Boy Who Wouldn't Grow Up* (1904) and in *Peter and Wendy* (1911), whilst others haunted photographs, as shown by Elsie Wright and Frances Griffiths's 1917 fraudulent Cottingley fairies.

Hence, throughout the long nineteenth century, forms of the marvelous both served to tone down or raise tensions; to challenge ideologies or reinforce them; to reassure or threaten. All in all, fairies and fairy tales helped artists, writers, viewers, and readers alike come to terms with modernity and their changing world, and their polymorphous capacity for taking ever new forms was crucial to lead the Victorians into the twentieth century. Some refused to let them go, however, and as they linger on for ever and ever, they continue to enchant us with their haunting presence.

CHAPTER TWO

Adaptation

JAN SUSINA

As Linda Hutcheon has noted in *A Theory of Adaptation,* adaptation is both a process and a product (Hutcheon 2012: xvi). At its most basic, adaptation is about intextuality and the ways texts can be reimagined or transformed into something new, be it within the same genre or in a different medium. Children's books are frequently based on, or draw inspiration from, previous books; many children's books are adaptations or simplifications of preexisting adult texts. The borders between what constitutes adult literature and children's literature have always been surprisingly fluid and over time texts often change their readership. Nineteenth-century children's literature is filled with crossover texts, those stories that were initially intended for adults but over time have been given to children, usually following revision to make them more child appropriate, according to the cultural and social codes of the period.

Along with fairy tales, three other well-known crossover texts from the long nineteenth century intended for children were John Bunyan's *Pilgrim's Progress* (1678), Jonathan Swift's *Gulliver's Travels* (1726), and Daniel Defoe's *Robinson Crusoe* (1726). While none of these three texts are specifically fairy tales, Bunyan's religious allegory, Swift's fantasy, and Defoe's desert island story each contain fantastical or fairy-tale elements and would be adapted by subsequent writers of literary fairy tales. Each of these adult texts appeared in multiple editions intended for children during the period. Andrew Lang's *The Blue Fairy Book* (1889), the first of his many collections of fairy tales for children, included "A Voyage to Lilliput," an extract from *Gulliver's Tales* along with Marie-Catherine d'Aulnoy's "The Yellow Dwarf," Charles Perrault's "Cinderella," and Jacob and Wilhelm Grimm's "Hansel and Gretel."

While fairy tales were not originally intended for children, by the midpoint of the nineteenth century due to changing attitudes toward fairy tales and fantasy literature, traditional and literary fairy tales had entered the canon of children's literature. The very term "fairy tale" is an adaptation from the French term "contes des fées" or "stories of the fairies." D'Aulnoy's *Les contes des fées* (Tales of the Fairies, 1697–8), her three-volume collection of tales, was translated into English as early as 1699. While d'Aulnoy's fairy tales were popular with adults in Parisian high society, by 1776, Francis Newbery, the nephew of John Newbery, had published *Mother Bunch's Fairy Tales,* one of the first editions of her tales intended for younger readers. D'Aulnoy's fairy tales—such as "The Yellow Dwarf," "The White Cat," and "The Blue Bird"—circulated in chapbook form as attributed to Mother Bunch, just as Perrault's fairy tales would subsequently be associated with the figure of Mother Goose. By the beginning of the nineteenth century, chapbooks specifically intended for children were produced containing fairy tales, nursery rhymes, Aesop's fables, or abridged versions of *Robinson Crusoe* or *Pilgrim's Progress*. D'Aulnoy's elaborate and lengthy fairy tales had much in common with heroic romances and would eventually find their most popular form as entertainment for children as the basis for pantomimes and extravaganzas produced by J. R. Planché and other dramatists during the 1840s and 1850s.

In England at the beginning of the nineteenth century, many people continued to have a strong distrust of fairy tales, with the fear that such tales were a waste of time or that they lacked sufficient morals for young readers. The fiery Evangelical writer Mary Martha Sherwood was an outspoken opponent of fairy tales and removed the fairy tales from her 1820 edition of Sarah Fielding's *The Governess, or The Little Female Academy* (1749), considered the first children's novel. Instead of fairy tales, Sherwood composed two adaptations of Bunyan for children: *The Indian Pilgrim* (1818), based on her experiences of living in India, and *The Infant's Progress* (1821). The continued popularity of *Pilgrim's Progress* as a book for young readers is confirmed in Louisa May Alcott's *Little Women* (1868) where the March girls enjoy "playing pilgrims" and many of the chapter titles in the first volume refer to places or characters taken from Bunyan's religious allegory. While Alcott is best known for her domestic fiction, prior to the success of *Little Women*, Alcott published two collections of moralizing fairy tales, *Flower Fables* (1854) and *The Rose Family* (1864), and continued to write fairy tales long after the success of *Little Women* and its sequels.

Adaptations of *Robinson Crusoe* were so popular as children's texts that they spawned an entire subcategory of children's books known as Robinsonades, those deserted island stories inspired by Defoe's novel. Johann David Wyss's *Swiss Family Robinson* (1813) was translated from the German by William Godwin and was first published in English in 1814. Wyss's adventure story of a shipwrecked family of four boys became the inspiration for Captain Frederick Marryat's *Masterman Ready, or the Wreck of the Pacific* (1841–2), which was written to serve as a sort of continuation in the manner of *Swiss Family Robinson*. Marryat's story featured the Seagrave family wrecked on an island during passage to Australia, who survive due to the assistance of the pious but resourceful old sailor. Another notable Robinsonade was M. Ballantyne's *The Coral Island* (1858), which became one the most widely read boys' adventures stories of the nineteenth century, featuring the exciting exploits of three boys: Ralph Rover, Jack Martin, and Peterkin Gay. This variation of Robinson Crusoe would in turn become one of key the inspirations for Robert Louis Stevenson's *Treasure Island* (1883), as well as J. M. Barrie's *Peter and Wendy* (1911). Both authors read and admired *Coral Island* in their youth. Most adaptations of *Robinson Crusoe* were written by men, directed toward boy readers and featured overt imperialistic overtones. But Catharine Parr Traill's *The Canadian Crusoes* (1852) shifts the setting from a tropical island to the Canadian woods where two boys and a girl manage to survive a challenging environment with the help of a Mohawk girl. Jules Verne's fantasy, *L'Ile mysterieuse* (*The Mysterious Island*, 1874–5) is based on *Robinson Crusoe* and began with a working version titled *Wrecked Family: Marooned with Uncle Robinson*.

In a similar fashion, William Shakespeare's plays, given appropriate editing, were considered appropriate for children. Twenty plays were adapted into prose by Charles and Mary Lamb in *Tales from Shakespeare, Designed for the Use of Young Persons* (1807), with Mary abridging the comedies and Charles simplifying the tragedies. In an attempt to make the plays suitable for children, the Lambs toned down and removed some of the more violent and sexual scenes. Shakespeare's plays were much more rigorously expurgated by Thomas Bowdler for younger readers in his *Family Shakespeare* (1818). Bowdler omitted what he considered to be vulgar language and sexual references so that the plays could be read aloud as a family and in doing so popularized the term "bowdlerize." With its uses of fairies, Shakespeare's *Midsummer Night's Dream* was considered the most child-friendly of the plays and appears in Lambs's, Bowdler's, and later E. Nesbit's children's editions of Shakespeare. The popularity of fairy painting extended from 1840 to 1870, and many of these paintings by artists such as John Aster Fitzgerald, Richard Dadd, and John Doyle were based on literary sources, with the most common references being to Shakespeare's *A Midsummer Night's Dream*, *The Tempest*, and the "Queen Mab" speech from *Romeo and Juliet*.

This sanitizing of children's texts tended to be the norm for crossover texts during the Victorian period, although not so extreme as Bowdler. Charles Dickens would poke fun of such excessive monitoring of reading material for younger readers, especially for girls, with the character of Mr. Podsnap in *Our Mutual Friend* (1864–5), who was constantly worrying whether a text might "bring a blush into the cheek of the young person" (Dickens [1865] 1997: 131). Following the Lambs' lead, Nesbit's *The Children's Shakespeare* (1897) provided prose adaptations of twelve of the plays in less complex language.

Given the importance placed on the classics in public schools during the Victorian period, there were numerous adaptations of Greek mythology for younger readers, with editors oftentimes referring to them as Greek fairy tales. Andrew Lang is best known as the editor of a twelve-volume collection of fairy tales for children, beginning with *The Blue Fairy Book* (1889), which included an adaptation of the myth of Perseus, which Lang titled "The Terrible Head." He was also a classics scholar at Oxford University and his prose translation of Homer's *Odyssey* (1879), done in partnership with Samuel Henry Butcher, and a companion translation of the *Iliad* (1883), would become standard school editions for the period. Lang also wrote *Tales of Troy and Greece* (1907), a child's retelling of the *Odyssey* and *Iliad*, with additional stories of Theseus and Perseus. Lang's adaptations of Greek mythology joined Nathaniel Hawthorne's *Wonder-Book for Boys and Girls* (1852), which was followed by his *Tanglewood Tales for Boys and Girls* (1853). The frame tale for Hawthorne's retellings involves a young college student, Eustace Bright or Tanglewood, who narrates a series of tales from Greek mythology to a group of children as they wander through the New England countryside. Charles Kingsley considered Hawthorne's adaptation of Greek myths for children vulgar and produced his own version of Greek myths for children, *The Heroes, or Greek Fairy Tales for my Children* (1856).

It was during the nineteenth century that fairy and folktales became adapted and accepted as children's literature. Gradually, fairy tales, along with Greek myths, nursery rhymes, and short selections or adaptations of Shakespeare were revised and recognized appropriate reading material for children rather than exclusively adult texts. Previously, the Puritans objected to folktales, which they associated with witchcraft and superstition. Both John Locke, in *Some Thoughts Concerning Education* (1693), and Jean-Jacques Rosseau, in *Emile* (1762), dismissed fairy tales and warned against their foolish and frightening aspects for younger readers. As a result, most children's texts in English during the eighteenth century tended to be stories of daily life. As early as 1818, Benjamin Tabart published *Popular Fairy Tale; or a Lilliputian Library*, which reprinted in one volume a collection of twenty-six tales intended for children that had previously circulated in chapbook form. While English translations of fairy tales by d'Aulnoy and Perrault had been previously published in the eighteenth century, wider acceptance of fairy tales as children's literature occurred with the English translation of the Grimms' folktales by Edgar Taylor as *German Popular Stories* (1823–6). When Jacob and Wilhelm Grimm initially published their two-volume collection *Kinder- und Hausmärchen* (1812–15), their purpose was to preserve German oral culture; their two-volume collection of folktales was aimed at other scholars. In contrast, Taylor redirected his English translation to children, and edited out some of the more violent and sexual elements in the tales; he had them illustrated by the popular cartoonist George Cruikshank. The Grimms were surprised that a scholarly edition of folktales that encouraged other folklorists to collect similar national collections of folktales would also become popular with children. Eventually they followed Taylor's lead in 1825 and produced a small edition of fifty folktales intended for children and illustrated by their brother Ludwig Grimm.

The Grimms were part of the German Romantic movement that promoted folktales and literary fairy tales for adults which included Ludwig Bechstein, Friedrich de la Motte Fouqué, and E. T. A. Hoffmann. These German writers would, in turn, influence English authors of literary fairy tales for children, such as John Ruskin and George MacDonald. The noted art critic, Ruskin, who praised Cruikshank's illustrations to *German Popular Stories* in a lengthy introduction in the 1868 reissue of the volume, composed his own literary fairy tale as an imitation of Grimms' folktales, *The King of the Golden River* (1851), illustrated by Richard Doyle. MacDonald praised Fouqué's *Undine* (1811) as "the most beautiful" of all fairy tales in his influential defense of fairy tales, "The Fantastic Imagination" (MacDonald 1895: 313), which was first published in *A Dish of Orts: Chiefly Papers on the Imagination and on Shakespeare* (1895). MacDonald published his own fairy tales in *Dealings with the Fairies* (1868) as well as book-length fantasies, *The Princess and the Goblin* (1872) and *The Princess and Curdie* (1875), which both owe a great deal to his knowledge of German Romantic literary fairy tales. Hoffman's *Nussknacker und der Mausekönig* (1816) would be translated into English as *The Nutcracker* but would become best known through Piotr Ilyich Tchaikovsky's ballet *The Nutcracker and the Mouse King* (1892). With the success of the Grimms' folktales as children's texts, children's editions of Perrault's fairy tales in English were quick to follow, including Tom Hood's *Fairy Realm* (1865), which featured the striking black-and-white illustrations by Gustave Doré. D'Aulnoy's fairy tales were often featured as the basis of the pantomimes and extravaganzas by J. R. Planché and other Victorian dramatists that combined special effects, music, and dance loosely framed around the plot of a fairy tale. Lewis Carroll regularly attended the theater and enjoyed pantomimes; the *Alice* books show the performances' influence with their transformation scenes, sudden changes in locations, and frequent use of puns and songs. The theatrical aspects of the *Alice* books made them easily adapted to both the stage and film.

The popularity of the Grimms' fairy tales in English as children's literature paved the way for other traditional folktales and fairy tales to be considered appropriate reading material for children. While the Grimms' scholarship encouraged other folklorists to collect and publish collections of traditional tales, folklorists discovered that England, in comparison to other European countries, had a limited body of traditional folktales. Lang's *Blue Fairy Book* and its subsequent volumes in his Color Fairy Book series adopted an international approach to folk and fairy tales. While Joseph Jacobs published *English Fairy Tales* (1890) and *More English Fairy Tales* (1894) to prove that the English were not lacking in traditional fairy tales, he, like Lang, used the British Empire for his sources and padded his two volumes with legends, ballads, beast fables, and nonsense verse.

As the result of the subtitle of Perrault's fairy tales, *Contes de ma mère l'Oye* (Tales of My Mother Goose), in France, Mother Goose was associated with the telling of fairy tales. But in England, Mother Goose was associated with the sharing of nursery rhymes, short anonymous poems that were spoken or sung to young children. Mother Goose rhymes, like folktales, were a collection of crossover texts and included bits and pieces of material created originally for adults, such as ballads, riddles, and amusing verse that had moved into children's literature. Some nursery rhymes—like lullabies, counting rhymes, or rhyming alphabets—were always intended for young children. Since nursery rhymes tend to be short verses and often their original context has been lost over time, their pleasure is found chiefly in the rhyme and rhythm of the language, emphasizing the sound of the words over their sense. Since many of these folk verses include odd or comical characters—an old woman who lives in a shoe, a wise man who scratches his eyes out and scratches them back again—nursery rhymes have often been considered nonsense verse with their grotesque and sometimes violent humor. Due to their brevity, children's editions of nursery rhymes are generally illustrated.

All three leading children's book illustrators of the late Victorian period adapted collections of nursery rhymes into the picture book form, highlighting their particular artistic skills. Randolph Caldecott generally adapted a single nursery rhyme, such as *Hey Diddle Diddle* (1882) or *Bye Baby Bunting* (1883), into a single picture book full of lively characters who seemed to be dancing to the music of the nursery rhyme. Caldecott would often add a visual detail that would give an unexpected meaning to the nursery rhyme. Working with the master wood-block printer Edmund Evans, Caldecott is considered the most accomplished picture book artist working in color during the Victorian period. The Caldecott Medal, which is given annually to the illustrator of the most distinguished illustrated book for children by the American Library Association, is named in his honor. Walter Crane's *The Baby's Opera* (1877) is an elegant picture book version of a collection of nursery rhymes, which also provided the musical notations for the tunes associated with specific nursery rhymes. Kate Greenaway's *Mother Goose* (1881) featured beautifully dressed, but rather stiff, children who seem at odds with the zany actions of the nursery rhymes she illustrated. Greenaway had established herself as a successful children's book illustrator with *Under the Window* (1878), an earlier collection of children's verses. The eighteenth-century clothing that children in Greenaway's illustrations wore inspired a popular style of clothing for girls during the 1880s and 1890s. Liberty of London designed a line of clothing based on Greenaway illustrations. The Kate Greenaway Medal is given annually to the most distinguished illustrated children's book published in the United Kingdom; it is the British counterpart to the Caldecott Medal. Christina Rossetti's *Sing-Song: A Nursery Rhyme Book* (1872) illustrated by Arthur Hughes, includes a number of nonsense poems, but her updating of Mother Goose rhymes into a Victorian context is dominated by a number of moralizing poems of appropriate behavior in children. L. Frank Baum began his career as children's writer with *Mother Goose in Prose* (1897), illustrated by Maxfield Parrish, which provided the back stories to well-known nursery rhyme characters. Baum's second children's book, *Father Goose, His Book* (1899), was a picture book of nursery rhymes illustrated by W. W. Denslow. The author and illustrator would subsequently collaborate on *The Wonderful Wizard of Oz* (1900), the first volume of Baum's fourteen *Oz* books.

Nursery rhymes provided a refreshing antidote to the overt moralizing poems for children by authors such as Issac Watts or Anna Laetitia Barbauld. William Roscoe's *The Butterfly's Ball and the Grasshopper's Feast* (1807) and Catherine Ann Doreset's *The Peacock "At Home"* (1807) were early examples of humorous children's poetry that prompted entertainment rather than education. It is not surprising that author/illustrators such as Heinrich Hoffmann and Edward Lear would draw inspiration from nursery rhymes with their own nonsense verse. Hoffmann's *Struwwelpeter* (1844) was written and self-illustrated after the German physician became frustrated with the limited options of children's books available for his young son. Rather than purchasing one of the many moralizing tales intended to improve and make obedient children, Hoffmann created a series of poems that satirize such stories with their overt messages and harsh punishments for disobedient children. Like Mother Goose rhymes, *Struwwelpeter* became popular with children who enjoyed Hoffmann's exaggeration, and was translated into English in 1848. Hoffmann's ironic poems feature misbehaving children: Harriet, who plays with matches and burns to death; Conrad, who sucks his thumbs and has them cut off by the scissor-man; and Augustus, who refuses to eat his soup, withers away, and dies. Hoffmann illustrated his grotesque poems with amateur but compelling colorful illustrations.

Along with Edward Lear's nonsense poetry, which also featured mischief and mayhem, these poems provided a refreshing change from didactic children's verse. While Lear was an accomplished landscape painter and a noted illustrator of birds, his crude, sketch-like illustrations in his *A Book of Nonsense* (1846) and his subsequent volumes of limericks resemble those of Hoffmann. The eccentric characters of Lear's limericks exhibit quirky behavior, such as birds

fell off the wall in doing so) and offered Alice his hand. She watched him a little anxiously as she took it. "If he smiled much more, the ends of his mouth might meet behind," she thought: "and then I don't know what would happen to his head! I'm afraid it would come off!"

"Yes, all his horses and all his men," Humpty

FIGURE 2.1: John Tenniel's illustration of Humpty Dumpty from Lewis Carroll's *Through the Looking-Glass* (1872). Many of the characters from Carroll's two Alice books are adapted from nursery rhymes.

nesting in their beards, or dancing a quadrille with a raven; they have much in common with the odd figures of nursery rhymes. Given his many limericks and longer poems like, "The Owl and the Pussy-Cat" and "The Dong with the Luminous Nose," Lear is considered, along with Lewis Carroll, as one of the two great children's writers of nonsense literature of the nineteenth century.

Carroll also drew inspiration from nursery rhymes. Many of his memorable characters that appear in his two *Alice* books are based on figures from nursery rhymes, such as Humpty Dumpty and Tweedledum and Tweedledee (Figure 2.1). Like Hoffmann, Carroll's *Alice* books poke fun at the overly moralizing children stories. Before Alice drinks from the bottle marked "Drink Me," she remembers the many stories she has read about children who get burnt or eaten by wild animals because they didn't remember the rules their friends have told them. Both *Alice* books include a number of nonsense poetry—"Jabberwocky" and "The Walrus and the Carpenter"—as well as other comic poems that parody the moralizing children's verse of Isaac Watts and Robert Southey.

It was the remarkable international success of the literary fairy tales written by Hans Christian Andersen that would serve as the model used by many English authors of literary fairy tales written for children during the second half of the nineteenth century. With the publication and success of *Eventyr, fortalte for Børn* (Fairy Tales, Told for Children, 1835), his first collection of literary fairy tales, Andersen rapidly became the first internationally recognized children's author. His tales were translated from Danish into English in 1848, with three separate translations: Charles Boner's *Danish Story-Book*, Mary Howitt's *Wonderful Stories for Children,* and Caroline Peachey's *Fairy Legends and Tales*. Over time, Andersen would complain that he was being pigeon-holed as only a writer for children. His international success helped to establish the fairy tale as the dominate genre of children's literature during the nineteenth century. The status of Andersen's popularity is confirmed in that his birthday, April 2, is celebrated as International Children's Book Day, and the most prestigious international award given in children's literature remains the Hans Christian Andersen Award. Subsequent English writers of literary fairy tales, including Oscar Wilde in his two collections, *The Happy Prince* (1888) and *A House of Pomegranates* (1891), reveal a marked influence of Andersen with their own sentimentality, moralizing, and emphasis on suffering.

Using the pseudonym Felix Summerly, Henry Coles edited the *The Home Treasury* series (1841–9) which promised to cultivate the affections, fancy, and imagination in children's taste. He published a number of fairy tales in the series, which helped to promote the acceptance of fairy tales as appropriate children's reading material. Catherine Sinclair's *Holiday House* (1839) is a story about the daily life of two mischievous children, Laura and Harry Graham; unlike children in moral tales, they escape their misadventures without punishment. Sinclair's novel includes the interpolated fairy tale, "Uncle David's Nonsensical Story about Giants and Fairies." Lewis Carroll enjoyed the book enough to give an inscribed copy to Alice Liddell and her sisters.

F. E. Paget's *Hope of the Katzekopfs: A Fairy Tale* (1844) is considered to be the first full-length children's fantasy in English, although it uses fairies to offer a lesson about self-control and the need for discipline. Frances Browne's collection of literary fairy tales, *Granny's Wonderful Chair* (1856), helped to reintroduce the fairy tale for children and was a great favorite of Frances Hodgson Burnett, whose *The Little Princess* (1905) is an adaptation of "Cinderella" set in London. In a similar fashion, Charles Kingsley's *The Water-Babies: A Fairy Tale for a Land-Baby* (1863) is a book-length fairy tale about Tom, the mistreated chimney sweep who is transformed into a water-baby. Under the guidance of the two fairies, the stern Mrs. Bedonebyasyoudid and the loving Mrs. Doasyouwouldbedoneby, Tom learns forgiveness and basic tenets of Christianity. *The Water-Babies* had a strong influence on Carroll's composition and book design of *Alice's Adventures in Wonderland*. William Thackeray both wrote and illustrated *The Rose and the Ring* (1855), a comic fairy tale in the manner of a Christmas pantomime. It is much less moralizing than those written by Kingsley or Paget, although the story suggests that a little misfortune is helpful for building character.

While fairy tales were becoming more accepted as children's texts, to do so they often featured a moral as in the case of Norman Macleod's *The Golden Thread* (1861) or George Cruikshank's ill-fated *George Cruikshank's Fairy Library*, which was begun as a series of booklets issued in parts beginning in 1853 and subsequently published as a single volume in 1870. Earlier, Cruikshank significantly helped popularize the fairy tale as appropriate reading for children with his humorous illustrations in Edgar Taylor's *German Popular Stories*. Formerly a heavy drinker, Cruikshank had become a teetotaler, and with his fairy-tale collection he not only illustrated the fairy tales but also rewrote them to include messages against the dangers of alcohol. Cruikshank's versions of traditional French and German fairy tales so irritated Charles Dickens that the latter penned the biting "Frauds on the Fairies" published in *Household Words* in 1853, ridiculing these fairy-tale revisions, insisting that fairy tales ought not be tampered with, and maintained that they already provided younger readers with lessons of kindness and good behavior. Dickens's literary influence damaged the success of the *Fairy Library* and ended his friendship with Cruikshank, who had illustrated Dickens's *Sketches by Boz* (1836–7) and *Oliver Twist* (1837–9). As a boy, Dickens had found solace in fairy tales, and numerous critics have observed that many of his novels, especially the Christmas Books, use fairy-tale elements. While Dickens was against the revising traditional fairy tales, he was not opposed to creation of new literary fairy tales. His own modern fairy tale, "The Magic Fishbone," appeared as a section of *A Holiday Romance* (1868). Here Dickens suggests magic should only be used as the last necessity after trying all other options.

It is with Lewis Carroll's *Alice's Adventures in Wonderland* (1865) that literary fairy tales for children began to shed their lessons and emphasize entertainment over education. Carroll's illustrated children's novel became a landmark in children's literature and is often credited, perhaps even given too much credit, for single-handedly causing the shift from education to entertainment in children's literature during the nineteenth century. While Carroll consistently referred to *Alice's Adventures in Wonderland* as a fairy tale, he borrowed widely from the traditions of beast fables, nonsense verse, pantomime, nursery rhymes, dream visions, and upside-down books in his attempt to "strike out some new line of fairy-lore." He even had Alice identify her adventures as a fairy tale when she is trapped in the White Rabbit's house as she expressed her surprise in finding herself in the middle of one. There had been previous English literary fairy tales, but Carroll decidedly broke with those earlier moral fairy tales, which were meant to merely amuse younger readers. *Alice's Adventures in Wonderland* also helped establish a distinctly English tone to literary fairy tales. Alice wanders in the lovely gardens, plays croquet, and travels by railway rather than entering the Fairy court of French fairy tales or the dark and dangerous woods of German fairy tales. Carroll's Wonderland is not so much the world of "once upon a time," set in the past, as it is an inverted mirror or looking-glass version of the Victorian society that Alice inhabits before falling down the rabbit hole. This Victorian setting enabled Carroll to introduce into his fairy-tale world many contemporary references and parodies of events and poems in the tradition of the theatrical pantomimes that he enjoyed. The narrative frame of Alice falling asleep and dreaming her way into an imaginative world has been widely imitated by later writers of literary fairy tales. Carroll's technique of the protagonist entering this fairy world by way of a portal located in the real world has been widely adapted by children's writers including as L. Frank Baum, C. S. Lewis, Neil Gaiman, and J. K. Rowling.

While Carroll was the most prominent children's author to challenge and change the tone of children's literature during the nineteenth century, earlier children's writers such Sinclair, Hoffmann, and Lear were also responsible for this cultural shift. Still many subsequent popular children's texts published after *Alice's Adventures in Wonderland* contained religious and moral lessons. These include children's books published by some of Carroll's close acquaintances, including George MacDonald's *At the Back of the North Wind* (1874) and Christina Rossetti's fairy-tale collection *Speaking Likenesses* (1874), as well as Juliana Horatia Ewing's *The Brownies and other Tales* (1870), Lucy Lane Clifford's *Anyhow Stories* (1882), and Alice Corkran's *Down the Snow Stairs* (1886). While Carroll maintained there were no lessons for young readers in either *Alice* books, that is certainly not the case in his final, two-volume fairy tale *Sylvie and Bruno* (1889) and *Sylvie and Bruno Concluded* (1893).

With the popular success of *Alice's Adventures in Wonderland*, Carroll confirmed the fairy tale and its companion, the literary fairy tale, as wholesome reading material for children. By the second half of the nineteenth century, the so-called battle of the fairy tales had been won in favor of the genre. Fairy tales were gradually replacing moral tales, those short or book-length realistic stories that promote social or religious lessons for children. Well-known moral tales included the stories found in Maria Edgeworth's *Early Lessons* (1801) and Mary Martha Sherwood's *The History of Fairchild Family* (1818).

Carroll's own process of creating *Alice's Adventures in Wonderland* as well as the manner in which he consciously adapted it into different versions and media, as well as the many imitations of the *Alice* books published by other authors, are useful examples of how adaptation in children's literature functioned during the nineteenth century. Carroll first told an oral version of what would eventually become *Alice's Adventures in Wonderland* to Alice Liddell and her two sisters during a boating expedition on May 2, 1862. Alice was so charmed by the story, undoubtedly in part because she was the protagonist, she requested the Oxford mathematical lecturer to write it down for her. Carroll did and he eventually provided her with *Alice's Adventures Under Ground* as an early Christmas gift in November 1864. This first written version of *Alice's Adventures in Wonderland* was a handwritten and self-illustrated manuscript by Carroll. While Carroll would become an accomplished amateur photographer, especially of children, despite his lifelong interest in visual arts and drawing, he never became more than an amateur visual artist. Nevertheless, Carroll's crude illustrations share some of the simple energetic style found in Hoffmann and Lear's published illustrations. Carroll subsequently borrowed the manuscript from the Liddell family and had his friend and published children's author MacDonald and his family read *Alice's Adventures Under Ground*. They encouraged him to revise it for publication and also encouraged him to consider using a professional artist to illustrate the book. Carroll, who had seen Arthur Hughes's illustrations for MacDonald's forthcoming *Adela Cathcart* (1864), which included a series of interpolated fairy tales including "The Light Princess," took their recommendations to heart.

After the commercial success of *Alice's Adventures in Wonderland*, MacDonald would extract the fairy tales from *Adela Cathcart* and publish them for children as *Dealings with the Fairies* (1867), along with Hughes's illustrations. In revising *Alice's Adventures Under Ground* to *Alice's Adventures in Wonderland*, Carroll almost doubled the length of text, adding some of the most memorable characters such as the Cheshire Cat and episodes like the Mad Tea-Party. He was able to secure the well-known *Punch* cartoonist John Tenniel to illustrate *Alice's Adventures in Wonderland*, realizing the importance of illustrations to a children's book with Alice observing, "what is the use of a book ... without pictures or conversations?" Many of the earliest reviews of *Alice's Adventures in Wonderland* focused on and praised Tenniel's striking black-and-white illustrations as much, if not more, than Carroll's humorous prose. Carroll had been impressed by Tenniel's illustrations of animals in Reverend Thomas James's edition of *Aesop's Fables* (1848), realizing that he needed an illustrator skilled at drawing animals and other creatures that Alice would meet in his book.

While John Locke argued against giving fairy tales to children, he encouraged the reading of Aesop's fables as they embodied his belief in combining instruction and delight; he also felt illustrated editions of the fables would make them more attractive to younger readers. The nineteenth century was a golden age of children's books and children's book illustration. In addition to Tenniel's illustrations, there were a series of well-illustrated editions of Aesop fables for children including Crane's *The Baby's Own Aesop's* (1857) and Caldecott's *Some Aesop's Fables with Modern Instances* (1883). Perhaps the most innovative is Charles H. Bennett's *Bennett's Fables from Aesop and Others Translated into Human Form* (1857), which represented the animal figures in Victorian dress and settings.

Just as Aesop's fables used animals to express human behavior, animal stories for children involving humanized animals were extremely popular. Anna Sewell's *Black Beauty* (1877) is the most famous of the animal autobiographies and did much to improve the treatment of horses in the nineteenth century. Rudyard Kipling's two volumes of *The Jungle Books* (1894, 1895) featured adventures of a young boy, Mowgli, adopted by a wolf pack. Beginning with *The Tale of Peter Rabbit* (1902), Beatrix Potter wrote and illustrated twenty-three compact picture books, which could fit comfortably into a child's hands. Potter's tales featured animals behaving, and misbehaving, like children. Although now recognized as racist, Joel Chandler Harris's *Uncle Remus, His Songs and Sayings* (1880) and *Night with Uncle Remus* (1883) were popular animal fables collected and adapted by the white author but taken from the African American oral tradition. Kenneth Grahame's *The Wind in the Willows* (1908) successfully moved the animal fable into the twentieth century, with Mr. Toad's obsession with motor cars.

Since its publication, *Alice's Adventures in Wonderland* has been illustrated by hundreds of illustrators in addition to Tenniel, with the first rush to provide new visual interpretations to *Alice's Adventures in Wonderland* when the copyright for Tenniel's illustrations expired in 1907. None of the subsequent illustrators have seriously challenged Tenniel's status as the defining set of illustrations of the text. Despite the difficulties of working around Tenniel's demanding schedule, when Carroll published the sequel, *Alice Through the Looking-Glass*, he once again chose Tenniel as his illustrator. With the success of the *Alice* books, Carroll also published various adaptations of his work, including *The Nursery "Alice"* (1889), in which Carroll greatly simplified the text for children five years old or younger. This picture book adaptation was the first authorized edition to feature Tenniel's illustrations in color, which were also enlarged and reduced in number from the original edition.

Carroll was actively involved in the translations of *Alice's Adventures in Wonderland* from English into German, French, and Italian, oftentimes locating the appropriate translator himself. The adaptation of Carroll's nonsense words often proved to be a challenge for some translators. These translations sold modestly during Carroll's lifetime and at his death in 1898 *Alice's Adventures in Wonderland* had only been published into seven languages. But by the beginning of the twentieth century, when Carroll's book was recognized as a classic of children's literature, the flood of translations began. As of 2015, the 150th anniversary of the publication of *Alice's Adventures in Wonderland*, Carroll's book has been published in 174 languages.

Carroll also published a facsimile edition of *Alice's Adventures Under Ground* (1886) as a collector's edition and as a way of affirming himself as the originator of the *Alice* stories, which had come under question given the spate of imitations of that had been published by other authors. The facsimile edition of *Alice's Adventures Under Ground* was released the same week as the first production of Henry Savile Clarke's operetta *Alice in Wonderland: A Musical Dream Play* (1886), with music by Walter Slaughter. Carroll authorized and contributed lines to the operetta, which combined episodes from both of the *Alice* books. In addition to the play, Carroll wrote the essay "'Alice' on Stage," which appeared in *The Theatre* in April 1887, where he provided an appreciative evaluation of the child actors in the production. The essay also included his most detailed recollection of his process of composing *Alice's Adventures in Wonderland* and how he imagined some of the key characters.

By 1886, an anonymous critic in *The Nation* jokingly remarked in a review of recent children's books that if the author of *Alice's Adventures in Wonderland* had foreseen the long procession of imitations of his book and been forced to read them, he never would have written it in the first place. The popularity of the *Alice* books resulted in an increased publication of children's books that resembled *Alice's Adventures in Wonderland*. Carroll himself began collecting what he referred to as "books of the 'Alice' type" and listed in his diary Tom Hood's *From Nowhere to the North Pole* (1874), Edward Holland's *Mabel in Rhymeland* (1885), F. E. Weatherley's *Elsie's Expedition* (1874), Jean Jambon's (J. K. MacDonald's) *Our Trip to Blunderland* (1877), Maggie Browne's *Wanted—A King* (1890), and anonymous's *The Story of a Nursery Rhyme* (1883). The sales catalog of Carroll's library after his death mentions he also owned a copy of Mark Lemon's *Tinykin's Transformations* (1869), Mary De Morgan's *On a Pincushion and Other Fairy Tales* (1877), Juliana Horatia Ewing's *The Brownies and Other Tales* (1870), and A. M. Richards's *A New Alice in the Old Wonderland* (1895), as well as a number of other unnamed books based on *Alice's Adventures in Wonderland*.

Given the popularity of the *Alice* books, several less talented children's authors produced imitations or variations on the *Alice* books for readers who desired more adventures of Alice, or at least adventures like those of Alice. "Ernest" by Edward Knatchbull-Hugessen (Lord Brabourne) is one of the earlier examples of an *Alice* imitation that appeared in *Puss-Cat Mew and Other Stories for my Children* (1869), one of his many collections of grotesque fairy tales. In this literary fairy tale, a young boy follows his ball down a well and finds himself in Toadland where he meets the Royal Toad who is smoking a cigar on a toadstool and entertains the young boy with parodies of nursery rhymes. In his introduction to his collection of fairy tales, Knatchbull-Hugessen dismissed the issue of adaptation from Carroll, acknowledging that while his story might seem to have a family resemblance to *Alice's Adventures in Wonderland*, his idea of parodying familiar rhymes was written before the publication of Carroll's book. Given the popularity of the *Alice's Adventures in Wonderland*, which was ranked the top children's book in the "What Children Like" poll sponsored by the *Mall Pall Gazette* in 1898, there was an ever-expanding family of stories inspired by the *Alice* books. Some of the titles make the link between Carroll's books explicit, such as George Hartley's *A Few Chapters More of "Alice Through the Looking-Glass"* (1875), Charles Carryl's *Davy and the Goblins; or What Followed Reading "Alice's Adventures in Wonderland"* (1885), and John Rae's *New Adventures of "Alice"* (1917). There are also a number of parodies of *Alice* books for adults that use the characters and episodes from the books to poke fun at current events such as Saki's (H. H. Munro's) *The Westminster Alice* (1902), John Kendrick Bangs's *Alice in Blunderland* (1907), Laurence Housman's *Alice in Ganderland* (1911), and R. C. Evarts's *Alice in Cambridge* (1913). The majority of adaptations of the *Alice* books loosely borrow the plot of a young protagonist who falls asleep after reading, enters an alternative world, has a series of comical adventures with various supernatural characters in this strange world, and eventually returns home. Just as Carroll synthesized bits and pieces from preexisting folk and fairy tales, nursery rhymes, dream journeys, and pantomimes to create the *Alice* books, many nineteenth-century children's authors produced book-length literary fairy tales or fantasies following Carroll's lead. While in the tradition that Carroll helped to popularize, many of these books are much more than pale imitations of the *Alice* books, and can be enjoyed on their own merits as compelling children's books.

Jean Ingelow's *Mopsa the Fairy* (1869), while having a few similarities with *Alice's Adventures in Wonderland*, is a strikingly different literary fairy tale, in which the protagonist, Jack, is befriended by Mopsa, a female fairy who outgrows, matures, and eventually abandons the boy, who then returns from fairyland. A number of critics read Ingelow's book-length fairy tale as an attempt to revise *Alice's Adventures in Wonderland* and provide female characters with power, which Alice seems to lack. Two writers who began as imitators of Alice but developed as outstanding writers of fantasy and nonsense are Maggie Browne (Margaret Hamer Andrewes) and G. E. Farrow. Their many children's books can be appreciated beyond their similarities to Carroll and can be judged on their own merits. Maggie Brown's *Wanted—A King, or How Merle Set the Nursery Rhymes to Right* (1890) and *The Book of Betty Barber* (1900) are both clever fantasies that draw on a number of literary sources in addition to Carroll. Farrow's popular *The Wallypug of Why* series began in 1895 as an imitation of *Alice* but took on a life and readership its own as Farrow produced ten volumes of humorous fantasy stories.

Baum's *The Wonderful Wizard of Oz* (1900) has long been recognized an an Americanized version of *Alice's Adventures in Wonderland*, with Dorothy being swept by a cyclone and dropped into Oz rather than Alice falling down a rabbit hole into Wonderland. Unlike the class-conscious Alice, Dorothy is a much more independent girl who leads her companions to the Emerald City. In his 1909 essay "Modern Fairy Tales," Baum praises *Alice's Adventures in Wonderland* but felt that Carroll's story lacks plot or motive and is bewildering for children. Baum published *A New Wonderland* (1900), which featured humorous fairy tales set in Phunnyland, in the same year as *The Wonderful Wizard of Oz*. With the success of *The Wonderful Wizard of Oz*, Baum renamed and reissued the book as *The Surprising Adventures of the Magical Monarch of Mo* (1903), with Mo being located in a magical valley beyond Oz. In his "Introduction" to the *Wonderful Wizard of Oz*, Baum showed himself to be familiar with the fairy tales of the Grimms and Andersen, but argued that children needed a new modernized fairy tale. *The Wonderful Wizard of Oz* and well as Baum's subsequent *Oz* books celebrate technology as the modern equivalent of magic. With the success of *The Wonderful Wizard of Oz*, Baum adapted the novel into a musical, but had to make adjustments to the plot and characters, including the change of Dorothy's dog, Toto, into Imogene, a calf. With the success of the *Oz* series and his own interest in technology, Baum moved to California in 1914 and started his unsuccessful Oz Manufacturing Company that produced a number of silent films, including some based on books from the *Oz* series such as *The Patchwork Girl of Oz* (1914).

While literary imitations and adaptations of *Alice* flourished, Carroll also authorized a number of non-book items as well. Carroll created "The Wonderland Postage-Stamp Case" (1890), whose outer sleeve featured Tenniel's Alice holding a baby; when the inner sleeve was revealed, it transformed into Alice holding the pig. Another spin-off was the *Alice's Wonderland Birthday Book* (1884), with short passages from the *Alice* books selected by E. Stanley Leathes. Carroll also authorized a "Mad Tea-Party" tablecloth and parasol handles in shapes of Wonderland characters. "The Looking-Glass Biscuit Tin" (1892) was intended as a storage container. Carroll explored the possibility of authorizing a set of magic lantern slides for public presentations of *Alice's Adventures in*

Wonderland, but never could come to terms with the manufacturer; however, an unauthorized set of twenty-four slides based on the book's illustrations and a lantern lecture was produced in 1893. The first of many film adaptations of the Alice books was Cecil Hepworth's *Alice in Wonderland* (1903), a ten-minute silent film produced only three years after Carroll's death.

Adapting fairy tales to nineteenth-century settings was a typical feature in the realistic novels of Frances Hodgson Burnett. There are elements of "Cinderella" in the mistreated protagonists of *The Secret Garden* (1911) and *Little Lord Fauntleroy* (1886). Her best-known "Cinderella" story is *The Little Princess*, which evolved through three distinct revisions. It was first published serially as "Sara Crewe: Or, What Happened at Miss Minchin's" in *St. Nicholas Magazine* in 1887 and 1888. It was later revised and expanded into a three-act play, *A Little Unfairy Princess*, which was retitled *A Little Princess*. The final and best-known version of the story is the novel *A Little Princess*, published in 1905.

J. M. Barrie's story of Peter Pan, which combines elements borrowed from fairy tales, pantomime, *Robinson Crusoe*, and *Treasure Island*, went through a more complex series of revisions and adaptations. It began with a series of oral stories Barrie told to the sons of Arthur and Sylvia Llewelyn Davies and became a series of captioned photographs of the boys on holiday, called *The Boy Castaways of Black Lake Island* (1901). This story was reimagined as the interpolated tale told to a young boy, David, in Barrie's adult novel *The Little White Bird* (1902). This story was revised and expanded into the play, *Peter Pan, or The Boy Who Wouldn't Grow Up*, first performed in 1904. Barrie then extracted the chapters featuring Peter Pan from *The Little White Bird* and had them illustrated by Arthur Rackham to become *Peter Pan in Kensington Gardens* (1906). Later, he novelized the play as a children's novel, *Peter and Wendy* (1911). However, the novel, unlike the play, included a final chapter, "When Wendy Grew Up," a pivotal scene where Peter returns to find Wendy an adult and then takes her daughter, Jane, to Neverland. The scene was only performed once during Barrie's lifetime at the conclusion of the play as "When Wendy Grew Up: An Afterthought" in 1908. Barrie only published the script for *Peter Pan, or The Boy Who Wouldn't Grow Up* in 1928, by which time the play had expanded from three to five acts and included extensive director's notes. Like Carroll's multiple adaptations of *Alice's Adventures in Wonderland*, Barrie's *Peter Pan* is a children's text that the author remade in a dizzying series of adaptations.

Andrew Lang, who edited and helped popularize fairy tales for children with his twelve-volume *Color Fairy Books*, eventually took his familiarity of fairy tales to create his series of literary fairy tales, *The Gold of Fairnilee* (1888), which borrows from the Scots ballad tradition. His *Chronicles of Pantouflia* series is composed of three comic literary fairy tales, *Prince Prigio* (1889), *Prince Ricardo* (1893), and *The Tales of a Fairy Court* (1906), that all poke gentle

FIGURE 2.2: Andrew Lang created his literary fairy tale, *The Princess Nobody, A Tale of Fairy Land* (1884), by reordering and adapting Richard Doyle's previously published illustrations to Richard Allinghams's *In Fairyland: A Series of Pictures from the Elf-World* (1870).

fun at the fairy court tradition. Lang's most ambitious literary fairy tale is *The Princess Nobody, A Tale of Fairy Land* (1884), a fairy tale based on Richard Doyle's previously published illustrations for Richard Allingham's *In Fairyland: A Series of Pictures from the Elf-World* (1870). Lang reordered and in some cases divided Doyle's colorful illustrations of elves and fairies into separate parts to produce a new fairy tale (Figure 2.2).

Perhaps the most nimble and imaginative adaptor and writer of children's literary fairy tales and fantasies of the second half of the nineteenth century was E. Nesbit, famous for her Psammead trilogy: *Five Children and It* (1902), *The Phoenix and the Carpet* (1904), and *The Story of the Amulet* (1906). Nesbit is noted for her fantastical worlds, and for extensively and openly borrowing from her own vast reading. The child characters in the Psammead books are an extremely bookish lot. In "Town in the Library in the Town in the Library," one of the literary fairy tales in *Nine Unlikely Stories* (1901), two children construct a city made of books they find in the library. Nesbit would later adapt and expand this plot for her novel *The Magic City* (1910). It was an activity that Nesbit would play with her own children and she was subsequently commissioned to create an extensive imaginary city for the 1912 Children's Welfare Exhibition. A year later Nesbit published *Wings and the Child, or Building of Magic Cities* (1913), a how-to-do book for children to build their own magic cities. A literary magpie herself, Nesbit's children's books are very much like these magic cities in that they borrow and adapt from a range of authors including Lewis Carroll, Charles Dickens, Charlotte Yonge, and Rudyard Kipling. Using and reimagining these authors' characters and plots in innovative and imaginative ways these became the building blocks for Nesbit's own literary magic.

The nineteenth century has long been considered one of the golden ages of children's literature. The children's writers of his period, like Rumpelstiltskin, were able to transform the previous moralist children's literature of the earlier era into to more golden, imaginative books for children. It is also seen as the period that saw a significant shift from education to entertainment as the primary purpose of children's literature, although neither entertainment nor education are completely rarely absence in books written for children. The acceptance and publication of folktales and literary fairy tales for children was pivotal to that change. This was a gradual shift and children's books remained limited and marketed for the most part, to middle- and upper-class children. It wasn't until 1887, twenty-two years after its initial publication, that Carroll authorized a *People's Edition of Alice* that sold for a more affordable 2 shillings 6 pence in contrast to the original price of 6 shillings. Carroll himself thought it wasn't a book in which poor children would have much interest. Despite the changes to children's literature often attributed to Carroll's *Alice's Adventures in Wonderland*, it is worth noting that by the end of the nineteenth century Hesba Stretton's (Sarah Smith's) *Jessica's First Prayer* (1867), a deeply moralistic "street Arab" story, had sold ten times as many copies as *Alice's Adventures in Wonderland*.

Children's literature in the nineteenth century tended to be conservative, not necessarily in the political sense. Children's books have been primarily written by white authors for white children. The images of nonwhite children in most nineteenth-century children's books often engage in racist stereotypes as in "The Story of the Inky Boys" from Heinrich Hoffmann's *Struwwelpeter* or Helen Bannerman's *The Story of Little Black Sambo* (1898). These negative stereotypes were not challenged until the publication of W. E. B. Du Bois's short-lived, but highly influential, *The Brownies' Book* magazine, begun in 1920, which featured children's stories and poems by Jessie Fauset, Nella Larsen, Langston Hughes, and other African American writers. While children's publishers were more open to woman authors, children's literature remained male-dominated. It was primarily conservative in that it was slow to change. Many of the children's books of the period were crossover texts and adaptations or revisions of books that originally had an adult audience. Miles Orvell has noted the importance of that imitation in the nineteenth century and observed that Victorians were fascinated by reproductions of all kinds ranging from furniture and architecture to the visual arts. Children's books of the nineteenth century were not immune from the impulse to borrow, imitate, and adapt from preexisting texts. That is not to suggest that the nineteenth-century children's literature was lacking original and innovative authors and illustrators. In "Notes on Deconstructing 'The Popular,'" Stuart Hall observes that transformations are at the heart of the study of popular culture and that popular texts, which would include fairy tales for children, are constantly being reworked from existing traditions to create something new (Hall [1981] 2005: 65). Like Lang in his process of creating *Princess Nobody* or Nesbit in creating her many magical literary cities, nineteenth-century children's authors oftentimes reimagined preexisting texts or literary forms and creatively rearranged them to create something new for child readers.

CHAPTER THREE

Gender and Sexuality

AMY BILLONE

Over the course of the long nineteenth century, fairy tales began to question, modify, pull against, and refashion models of gender and sexuality that the history of the fairy tale had established. In spite of the way that fairy tales had always engaged in revisions to and reactions against earlier versions of themselves, new meditations about gender and sexuality began to develop. These innovations were exciting and revelatory during the period, culminating in the golden age of children's literature. Nevertheless, revolts against conventional patterns could not entirely remove social and logistical restraints between 1800 and 1920. Compulsory heteronormativity haunts the fairy tales from this period.

Because of the tensions that they magnify, nineteenth-century fairy tales might be read as edging more toward tragedy than comedy or as finely balancing comic and tragic tones, often hinging on questions of gender or sexual identity. As this chapter will show, revolutions were made evident not only in the fairy tales themselves (both in their shorter and in their longer formats) as they developed but also via the illustrations, postcards, and performances or pantomimes related to these works that evolved throughout the long nineteenth century. However, just as they kept breaking open, gender constraints also remained firmly in place. Women spoke but their voices were often silenced or erased.[1] The children who collaborated with adults were often sexualized by these same adults and by the public in general.[2] Acting upon same-sex attraction was legally forbidden.[3] Building from previous models that they reenvisioned and also building from each other as the long nineteenth century progressed, authors made imaginable what was before unimaginable. But they also found themselves revealing problems that even their own brilliance could not solve. In fact, the genius of these fairy tales overall lies in their ability to illuminate euphoric new dreamscapes at the same time that they realize the potentially tragic consequences of their own ventures into the unknown. J. M. Barrie's *Peter Pan*, with which this chapter will conclude, serves as a leitmotif of the discoveries and the disturbances that came to both motivate and to unsettle fairy tales from the period as a whole.

THE GRIMM BROTHERS' INTERVENTIONS

With respect to gender and sexuality, current scholars study the homoerotic suggestions and counternormative affiliations in the Grimm brothers' fairy tales, exemplified by Kay Turner and Pauline Greenhill's *Transgressive Tales: Queering the Grimms* (2012). More than any other collection of fairy tales in the world, Jacob and Wilhelm Grimm's *Kinder-und Hausmärchen* (Children's and Household Tales, 1857) has influenced the way fairy tales are perceived today. The Grimms' work began to be translated in 1816, four years after their first volume appeared in 1812 in a Danish edition, spreading to Dutch, English, French, then moving rapidly around the globe.[4] Their fairy tales have been translated into 150 languages. In the 1980s and 1990s, scholars such as Ruth Bottigheimer and Maria Tatar took a feminist approach to the Grimms' corpus. Now a more recent subfield of fairy-tale studies is emerging since the 2010s, queer fairy-tale studies, which is shedding new light on the works of the Brothers Grimm and others.[5] Since the word "queer" is multivalent, these recent approaches offer a range of different methods for how to frame the spectrum of gender roles and sexuality that both include and extend beyond the homoerotic.

Scholars in queer fairy-tale studies propose that while the Grimm brothers were careful to omit overtly sexual details as they revised their tales to make their stories more child friendly, they did not think (or simply chose not) to eliminate homoerotic or counterhegemonic relationships.[6] One of the Grimms' fairy tales that draws particular interest in queer fairy-tale studies is "The Frog King, or Iron Heinrich."[7] This story is especially interesting to consider because the Grimms began every edition of their fairy tales with this same piece. The story not only includes transbiology but it also concludes with an unforgettable allusion to same-sex love between men. It is with Iron Heinrich's heart that the story ends. The hoops Heinrich needed to have placed around his chest so that his heart would not break from grief when he saw his beloved prince transformed into a frog finally snap open. This ending could be read as celebratory since the prince is on his way to be married. However, the prince mistakes the "cracking noise" he hears when the hoops around Heinrich's chest snap open for the sound of his coach "breaking," which hints at heartbreak (Zipes 1987: 5).

The same-sex love finale to "The Frog King, or Iron Heinrich" is absent from the Grimms' initial companion story "The Frog Prince," which appeared in their second volume of tales in 1815, as Heinrich is not a character in the story. However, the Grimms never included "The Frog Prince" in any edition of their stories that they published after its first appearance in 1815.[8] Certainly, an enormous amount of emotion between female characters also explodes within the Grimms' fairy tales, which might be understood as sexually charged (Greenhill and Turner 2012: 15). Still, in spite of recent arguments about the sexually transgressive nature of the Grimms' fairy tales, it is impossible not to note that girls and women are shown to be most beautiful when they are dead ("Snow White"), asleep ("Briar Rose"), imprisoned in towers ("Rapunzel"), chased by wolves ("Little Red Cap"), abandoned and starving to death ("Gretel" from "Hansel and Gretel"), or magically dressed in gorgeous gowns ("Cinderella"). Violence done to women either by other women or by themselves in the Grimm fairy tales is much more extreme than in earlier counterparts by Charles Perrault.[9] The stepsisters' hacking off of their heels and toes to fit into Cinderella's slipper in the Grimm version, the prince's inability to realize that neither one of them is his true bride, and by the Grimms' 1857 version of the story, the plucking out of the stepsisters' eyes by vengeful pigeons communicate the terrible price nineteenth-century women were compelled to pay for marriage to wealthy powerful men.

Sadomasochistic relationships between characters of both genders notwithstanding, the Grimms also grant potency to traditionally disempowered figures. Even in the case of "Cinderella," the Grimms give her a conversation with her dying mother, a contract between them and a means of communication to enlist her services after the mother has died. This alliance between mother and daughter strengthens relational ties between women in a way that Perrault's fanciful fairy godmother cannot. Unlike in earlier versions of "Rapunzel" by Friedrich Shulz (1790) and by Charlotte-Rose de la Force ("Persinette," 1698), after the prince's vision has been restored with Rapunzel's tears of love alone, he and she save themselves without the miraculous aid of the witch/fairy/sorceress who has imprisoned her since birth.[10] By 1857, the Grimms also make the prince fall in love with Rapunzel at the start of the story and find his way back to her (blind) at the end through the power of her *voice* and not by her stunning appearance. Instead of imitating the end of the Perrault version of "Little Red Riding Hood" where the girl and her grandmother are devoured and die, the Grimms used the more optimistic ending by Ludwig Tieck in *Life and Death of Little Red Cap* (1800) as Tieck was the first to introduce the huntsman saving Little Red Cap's life.[11]

Ultimately, the Grimms' complication of preconceptions regarding gender and sexuality together with their remarkable alertness to the plasticity of the fairy tale inspired countless adaptations—which themselves influenced the

Grimms' rewriting of their own tales—not only in print but also in other forms of art: the illustration, the postcard, and theatrical performance.[12]

FROM ILLUSTRATIONS TO POSTCARDS

In addition to novel interpretations of gender and sexuality that nineteenth-century fairy tales themselves propose, illustrations and postcards began to communicate and even reinterpret gendered and sexual subtexts from these same tales. Fairy-tale illustrations in the Western world began approximately in 1800 (Zipes [1983] 1993: 352). Suddenly, fairy tales appeared in thousands of illustrated books. Later in the nineteenth century, fairy-tale postcards began to be produced on a global scale. As do the illustrations, these postcards illuminate and make personal publicly written or performed fairy tales, often revealing unexpected visions of gender and sexuality in the stories, and at times presumably functioning as private jokes between the sender and the recipient. A major shift took place in Austria in 1869 when the government authorized the postcard as an officially approved method of correspondence. In the next four months, more than three million postcards were sold in the Austro-Hungarian Empire. After that, other countries such as England, the United States, Canada, Switzerland, and most other European countries authorized postcards. Of these postcards, millions were sent on a global scale so that examples can be found from Finland to Japan.[13] In this way, in the 1880s, the postcard began to link fairy tales (historically transmitted, adapted, written, read, and publicly performed) to intimate forms of communication with counterhegemonic implications for gender expression.

Moreover, benefiting from the Victorian invention of photography, photographic postcards exhibited the dizzying permutations of gender and sexuality enabled by both public and private performances of nineteenth-century fairy tales. For example, photographic postcards were sent as souvenirs from theatrical productions. Numerous pictures of "Miss Pauline Chase," who played the part of Peter Pan, circulated as postcards when she starred in the role at the start of the twentieth century (Figure 3.1). She appears in many of Peter's poses, one showing her holding his phallic dagger. Yet Chase's curling flowing hair, developed figure, and erotically charged feminine figure and face stress the off-kilter nature of *Peter Pan*, in which gender roles do not remain fixed.

In stark contrast to the postcards showing Pauline Chase reveling in the many parts she played on stage in the role of eternal boy child Peter Pan, another postcard from 1905 shows Chase looking seductive with one nipple exposed (Figure 3.2). These drastically different images of the same woman call attention to both the sexualization of the child and to the mutability of gender that nineteenth-century fairy tales exposed.

FIGURE 3.1: Pauline Chase as Peter Pan. Unattributed postcard from the early twentieth century. Courtesy of Mary Evans Picture Library.

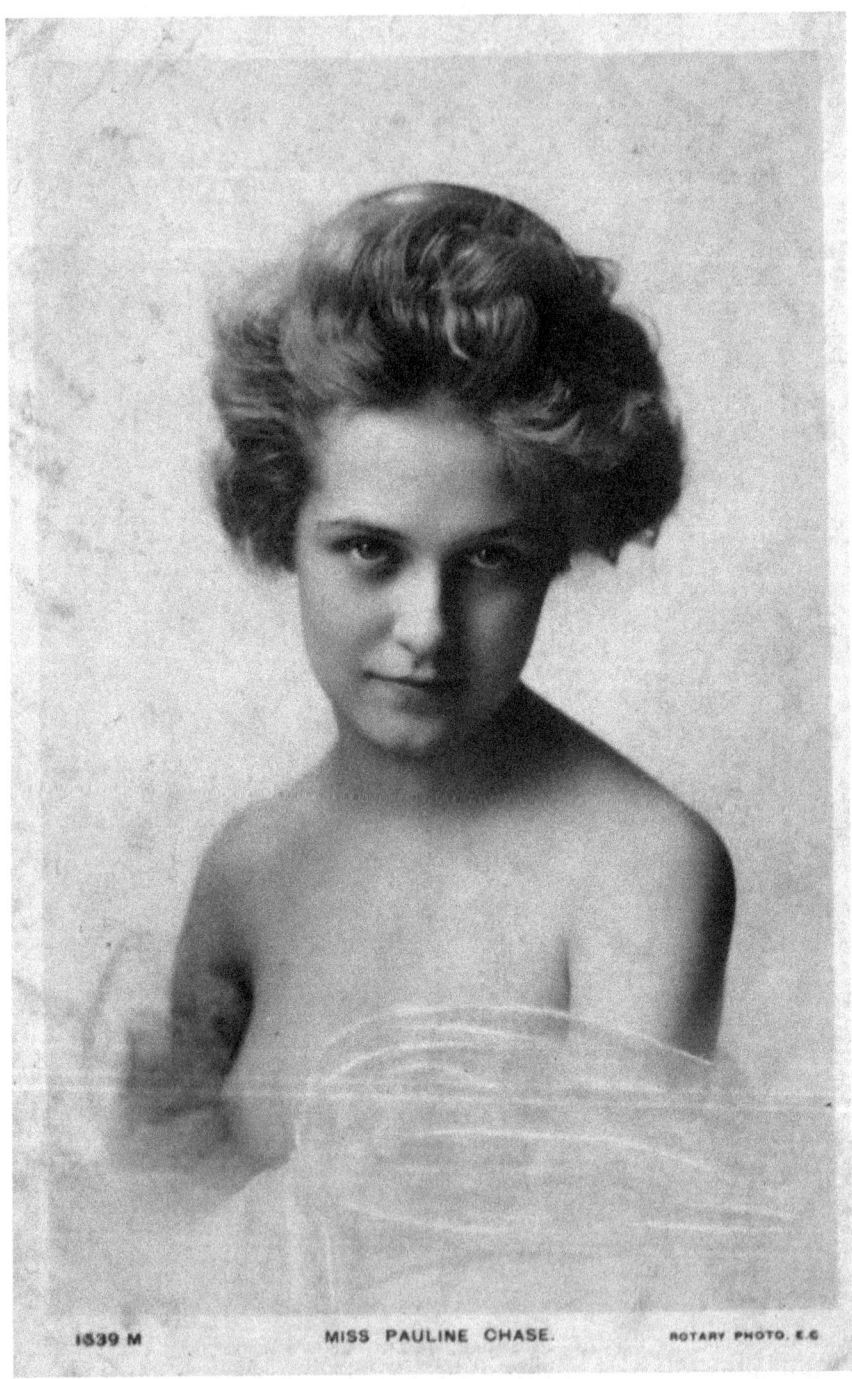

FIGURE 3.2: Pauline Chase, actress, notable for playing the part of Barrie's "Peter Pan," postcard, 1905. Courtesy of Mary Evans Picture Library.

PERFORMING FAIRY TALES, CROSS-DRESSING, AND THE CULT OF THE CHILD

Just as gender and sexuality were reconceptualized during the long nineteenth century in the form of illustrations and postcards, so too were they reconfigured theatrically in popular performances.[14] With the frequent use of cross-dressing, nineteenth-century pantomimes, which were both comedic and musical, upended the way that gender and sexuality appeared in written plots of stories. Pantomimes combined cross-dressing with plot twists that gave the stories happy endings. It is perhaps because of the comic slant of the pantomime that tales by the Grimms, considered more scholarly during the period, did not extend to the stage in England. Neither did the popular translation of Peter Christen Asbjørnsen and Jørgen Moe's Norwegian tales by George Webbe Dasent (Schacker 2018: 180). However, the pantomime versions of "Little Red Riding Hood," which was first adapted in 1803, and which involved an abundance of cross-dressing and hilarity, were more in keeping with the optimistic ending the Grimms would choose for their story as opposed to the tragic ending of Perrault's version (188–9).

One helpful way to understand how cross-dressing revolutionized written fairy tales through pantomimes during the long nineteenth century would be to comprehend their format. Pantomimes featured burlesque performances of gender as a key component, which ultimately let off subversive steam. In general, pantomimes starred a cross-dressed "Principal Boy," who would fall in love with a "Principal Girl," and they also starred a cross-dressed "Dame." Nineteenth-century audiences enjoyed watching two comely actresses flirting with each other, kissing each other and marrying each other at the end of the narratives just as much as they loved watching a grandiose male "Dame" marry a man in the happy conclusions to pantomimes. The role of the "Principal Boy" was beloved by Victorian and Edwardian audiences because it allowed a lovely sexually developed girl to display parts of her body such as her waistline and legs. Both the man who played the "Dame" and the actress who played the "Principal Boy" would headline performances (Schacker 2018: 192–3). When considering how gender and sexuality were approached during the long nineteenth century, it is important to be aware that Victorian and Edwardian audiences flooded to cross-dressed performances that played with gendered and sexual roles on stage.

Theatrical performances not only affected notions of how gender and sexuality operated in fairy tales through the use of cross-dressing in pantomimes but they also altered the role of the child. On stage, the child began to be sexualized. Child actors and actresses became a phenomenon on stage in the nineteenth century. The parts children played involved both cross-dressing and cross-generational talents as they were often asked to play adult roles. Many acolytes of the cult of the child such as Lewis Carroll (1832–98), John Ruskin (1819–1900), Frances Hodgson Burnett (1849–1924), and Barrie (1860–1937) adored the theater and were fixated on professional child actors, often taking their child friends to shows with them (Gubar 2009: 149–79). Carroll took at least three of his child friends each time to six showings of an all-child production of *Robin Hood*, where the child actors pretended to be adult lovers and rolled on the stage together (157).

In spite of questions of pedophilia that the sexualization of the child during the long nineteenth century has raised, specifically with respect to biographies of famous male writers such as Barrie, Carroll, and John Ruskin, the gender and generational fluidity that theatrical performances made apparent helped to give unusual authority to girls and to women. As shown earlier in this chapter in the discussion of Pauline Chase, women were able to play the parts of boy heroes. The "Principal Boy" character gave a developed girl the opportunity to star in a role that took her outside of her own gender while also permitting her to flaunt her feminine figure.

This gender fluidity can be seen in stage versions of *Little Lord Fauntleroy*, which plays on many fairy-tale motifs. Frances Hodgson Burnett (1849–1924) made use of the longer fairy-tale form and achieved great fame as a writer and playwright for both children and for adults.[15] Burnett's most successful fictional work of the period, *Little Lord Fauntleroy* (1885–6), which premiered as a play at Terry's Theatre in London in 1888, starred female child actresses such as Elsie Leslie and Vera Beringer in the leading role of Cedric, a fictional boy Burnett based on her own son Vivian.[16] Cedric, like Burnett's son Vivian, wore a lush suit with a fancy blouse, a large collar and a cut-away jacket. This outfit set massive fashion trends. Burnett was inspired in her choice of clothes for her own sons and for her character Cedric by another celebrity of the period, Oscar Wilde. A good friend of Burnett's, Wilde also dressed in velvet and lace.

Burnett's play *Little Lord Fauntleroy* emphasized the androgynous/genderqueer roles that women and girls were able to play on stage in the nineteenth century. Furthermore, Burnett's success as both a writer and a playwright in England and America highlights the fact that women from the long nineteenth century lacked none of the skills that their male counterparts possessed. Neither did women always lack the recognition for their accomplishments that male fairy-tale writers received. Burnett's fame notwithstanding, many other women writers of fairy tales during the period were silenced or—as in the case of female informants to the Grimms such as Dorothea Viehmann or Marie and Jeannette Hassenpflug—relegated to the role of domestic storytellers or folk informants to professional male authors.[17] It is more as characters (often based on real-life children and adults) that disenfranchised groups such as women, children, and queer people were foregrounded in the long nineteenth century. Ironically, illustrations, postcards, and theatrical productions made queering and cross-dressing highly visible to a ravenous audience during the same period that would sentence Oscar Wilde to two years of hard labor due to his sexual involvement with other men.

FROM HANS CHRISTIAN ANDERSEN TO OSCAR WILDE

When read next to each other with respect to gender and sexuality, Hans Christian Andersen (1805–75), born in Denmark, and Oscar Wilde (1854–1900), born in Ireland, wrote fairy tales that open themselves up to queer readings. Andersen may have had romantic interest in both genders but was rejected by women, who were not attracted to him, and by men, who only wanted to be with women. He never married. Wilde married the wealthy Constance Lloyd in 1884 and had two sons with her: Cyril in 1885 and Vyvyan in 1886. But in 1895, at the height of his fame, Wilde was arrested for gross indecency due to his promiscuous sexual involvement with men. Wilde was sentenced to two years of hard labor, followed by impoverishment, exile, sickness, and death only three years after he was released, in 1900, at the premature age of forty-six years old.

A good example of a fairy tale that queers gender and sexuality, Andersen's "The Little Mermaid" (1837) aches with complex, painful desire for unattainable love. The tale was begun just after the marriage of Edvard Collin, a man with whom Andersen was in love but who had rejected him to be with women instead.[18] Andersen would never be able to compete with women to win Collin's love. Neither can the Little Mermaid, whose body is in the wrong shape, compete with a woman to win the heart of the man she loves.[19] Because of its theme of body dysphoria, "The Little Mermaid" has frequently been read as a performance of transgender identity. With "The Little Mermaid," Andersen tells a poignant story about longing for impossible love, desperate efforts to transform one's body to realize it, and the beloved's rejection despite everything. The story presents a view of utopian happiness only in this case to brutally take it all away.[20] A captivating postcard printed in Austria in 1907 shows the Mermaid gazing at and pining for the prince who will neither look at her nor return her love (Figure 3.3).

As is the case in Andersen's "The Little Mermaid," Wilde frequently treats love as crossing gender, species, and other boundaries, rarely happily. He published his first book of fairy tales, *The Happy Prince and Other Tales*, in 1888, and his second volume, *The House of Pomegranates*, in 1891, the same year that he published the novel *The Picture of Dorian Gray*. In one story a hideous dwarf falls in love with a girl but after the dwarf recognizes his own monstrosity in a mirror and after the girl laughs at him, he dies of a broken heart.[21] In Wilde's "The Fisherman and his Soul," which was influenced by Andersen's "The Little

FIGURE 3.3: Anonymous, "The Mermaid," scene from "The Mermaid" by Hans Christian Andersen from a postcard published in Austria, *c.* 1907. Courtesy of the Mary Evans / Peter and Dawn Cope Collection.

Mermaid," a fisherman falls in love with a soulless mermaid and must give up his own soul to be with her (see Tatar 2007: 120). The story takes turn after turn and at the end the fisherman drowns himself out of love for the mermaid when she dies. Religious orthodoxy inverts at the end of the story and the true love between the fisherman and the mermaid is shown to transcend all.

Both Andersen's "The Little Mermaid" and Wilde's "The Fisherman and his Soul" are about the difficulty of forbidden love. Both stories are preoccupied by the impasses to love that was deemed inappropriate due to constraints that might be associated with nineteenth-century sexual/gender taboos. In Wilde's "The Happy Prince," the statue of a beautiful male prince and a male swallow fall in love after the swallow has left his lady-love, a reed. The story results in the death of both out of love for each other. In "The Star-Child," a boy child is so beautiful that he falls in love with himself. After a series of punishments (including transbiology) resulting from his rejection of his own mother, his beauty is restored. He is made king but he dies three years later at the age of sixteen and never shows any interest in the opposite sex.[22] The Selfish Giant ceases to be selfish in the story of that name by falling in love with a tiny little boy. The boy proves at the end to be a Christ figure and the Giant dies of love for the boy.[23]

The extent to which Andersen and Wilde queered the fairy tale during the nineteenth century is remarkable. Both were also hugely successful writers (Wilde in all genres). In spite of writing fairy tales that were immensely popular during their lifetimes and that have now become canonical, Wilde's spectacular persecution for "gross indecency," which ended his career, changed the vocabulary and conceptions of what homosexuality was thought to be. No intellectual vitality was enough to protect Wilde from the life-threatening consequences of what both his work and that of Andersen so fervently divulged. Paradoxically, the long nineteenth century was able to appreciate and even to idolize fairy tales that could not at that time play out harmlessly in daily life.

PLUNGING INTO WONDERLAND

As explained earlier in this chapter, the child began to be sexualized during the long nineteenth century.[24] The results of this sexualization at once gave children agency and compromised it. Children were able to act as collaborators with adult authors who may have felt sexual longing for them. They were also able to perform major roles in plays involving cross-dressing and cross-generational activities—parts that enraptured an overwhelming number of fans. Innocence itself became queered in the nineteenth century. However, the confusion between the child's body and the adult's body threatened children who may have been victimized by the same adults who fetishized them. Audiences and readers today are still implicated in a perplexing process of sorting out what is real from what is imaginary in texts that ask us to sympathize and even fall in love with children who may or may not be fictional in origin.

Carroll's Alice books—*Alice's Adventures Under-Ground* (1864), *Alice's Adventures in Wonderland* (1865), *Alice Through the Looking-Glass* (1871), and *The Nursery Alice* (1890)—blend the real and the illusory with respect

FIGURE 3.4: *Alice Liddell as beggar-child*. Original photograph taken by Lewis Carroll, 1858. Courtesy of Mary Evans Picture Library.

to gender and sexuality in baffling ways. Controversy remains about whether Charles Lutwidge Dodgson (pseud. Lewis Carroll) (1832–98) was in love with the real-life little girl Alice Pleasance Liddell (1852–1934), for whom he wrote his stories, or whether his dream-child, who, as he laments in the acrostic closing frame poem to *Looking-Glass* (1871), perpetually haunts him "phantomwise" for more elusive reasons (Gardner [1960] 2000: 273).[25] Clearly, on some level

Alice is both illusory and real as she was the one of the three Liddell girls who asked him to write down the story that he made up for them.²⁶ Not only was she a real person but she was a ravishingly beautiful child. Carroll shows us Alice Liddell's beauty with the mesmerizing photographs he took of her (Figure 3.4). When Carroll's breathtaking photograph of the six-year-old Alice Liddell dressed as a beggar maid (1858) is compared to the revealing postcard of Pauline Chase (Figure 3.2), it is evident that Alice Liddell, too, has one nipple exposed in Carroll's erotic photograph.

Alice's primary problem in Carroll's books is that, because of her gender, she seems unable to enter the childhood fantasyland she wants to be in.²⁷ All older female characters in the Alice books—Alice's older sister, the Queen of Hearts, the Duchess, the Cook, the Red Queen, and the White Queen—are shown to be uninteresting, furious, repulsive, or incompetent. Alice's own anger increases throughout *Alice's Adventures in Wonderland* (1865) until she at last grows inexplicably out of her dream. The Queen of Hearts shouts, "Off with her head!" and does so "at the top of her voice," but only after Alice grows to her full size and cries, "Who cares for *you*? ... You're nothing but a pack of cards!" (Gardner [1960] 2000: 124; emphasis in the original). At this point, "the whole pack" rises into the air and flies down upon Alice so that she has to try to "beat them off," screaming partly in "fright" and partly in "anger" before waking up to realize that what she thought were cards are "dead leaves" her older sister is brushing gently off of her face (124). Here, the dead leaves represent the innocence that Alice has lost by this point in the story if she has not already lost it with her initial fall down the rabbit hole. Perhaps due to the eroticization of her innocence, she was never able to luxuriate in child-land at all.

Alice's real-life identity as a beautiful child who can neither stay a child nor return Carroll's love and from whose family Carroll was inexplicably barred seems to be mourned in the frame poems. Carroll's final poem in *Looking-Glass* (1871) is an acrostic in which every line begins with the first letter of Alice's full name, ALICE PLEASANCE LIDDELL. The last line of the second tercet starts with the initial of Alice's middle name, Pleasance: "Pleased a simple tale to hear—" (Gardner [1960] 2000: 273). But everything harshly shifts in the next stanza: "Long has paled that sunny sky: / Echoes fade and memories die: / Autumn frosts have slain July" (273). By May 1865, soon before the publication of *Alice's Adventures in Wonderland* (a book starring the seven-year-old Alice), the real-life Alice Liddell was thirteen years old. When Carroll took his last picture of Alice, in 1870, after having minimal contact with the Liddells for the past five years, due to having been banned from continuing to see the children for reasons that still remain mysterious, she was eighteen years old and so different in appearance from her child self in Carroll's photograph; indeed, the grown Alice looks so plagued by melancholy she is almost unrecognizable

FIGURE 3.5: *Older Alice*. Photograph by Lewis Carroll, 1870. Courtesy of Mary Evans Picture Library.

(Winchester 2011: 74–5) (Figure 3.5). In Carroll's view, time is no friend to young girls, any more than it is to the Mad Hatter.[28]

In the combination of her impossibility and her reality, Alice both resembles and differs along gender lines from another canonical nineteenth-century fairy-tale character from Italy: Pinocchio.[29] Pinocchio's creator, Collodi, a pen-name for Carlo Lorenzini (1826–90), initially published *Pinocchio* as a series of installments in a children's newspaper, *Il giornale per i bambini*, in 1881. Pinocchio was first published in English in 1892; Alice appeared in translation in Italy in 1872. The two characters are now globally beloved. Alice and Pinocchio are both "transtextual"; both do not give any indication of knowing they are fictional characters and not real people, even when Alice learns she has been dreaming (or the Red King has been dreaming her) and Pinocchio from the beginning knows he is a puppet.[30]

Just as the character Alice seems always on the verge of death even in the famous early scene in *Wonderland* where she almost drowns in a pool of her own tears, Collodi kills Pinocchio at the end of his story. Collodi was forced to resurrect Pinocchio, but some critics believe that the first book, *Pinocchio I*, originally called *Storia di un Burattino* (*Story of a Puppet*), and which ends with Pinocchio's death in chapter 15, is a different book from *Pinocchio II*, which includes the first and second parts and ends with chapter 36. According to this reading, Pinocchio the puppet/boy dies at the end, and the first book is the story of his postponed death, while the second book replaces him with a different character. Like Alice, Pinocchio seems to be at once constantly on the verge of death and perpetually returning to life. Yet he never comfortably is a "real boy" in the same way that the dream-child Alice never reassuringly is a "real girl." In spite of their liminality, both characters believe themselves to be real to such an extent that audiences cannot stop resurrecting them in new adaptations.

As a wooden puppet who wants to be a real boy, Pinocchio recalls E. T. A. Hoffmann's wooden doll Olympia who successfully poses as animate and female in his German story "The Sandman" ([1818] 2004). The difference here is that Olympia has no humanity in her at all: she is simply an automaton that has been programmed to play the harpsichord, sing, dance, and respond "Ah, ah!" However, the deranged Nathaniel not only perceives her to be real but also falls in love with her, later mistaking his real fiancée for a wooden doll, whom he tries to kill. Hoffman's story suggests that women in general can be successfully duplicated by wooden puppets, but with Pinocchio, Collodi takes a wooden puppet and, by gendering him male, makes it conceivable that the wooden doll might actually come to life as a little boy.[31]

Unlike Pinocchio, Alice is forced to grow up in Carroll's books at the same time that she purportedly remains only seven years old in *Wonderland* and seven and a half years old in *Looking-Glass*. This requirement that a girl grow up while still remaining a child can be seen in another interesting counterpart to Alice, George MacDonald's (1824–1905) "The Light Princess" ([1864] 1999).[32] Carroll would already have been familiar with "The Light Princess" in 1862. According to U. C. Knoepflmacher, "On July 9, 1862, Lewis Carroll recorded in his diary that he had run into Mr. MacDonald 'on his way to a publisher with the MS. of his fairy tale "The Light Princess" in which he showed me some exquisite drawings by Hughes'" (1999: 125). Even though MacDonald failed to secure publication of "The Light Princess" in 1862, in Knoepflmacher's words, "Carroll apparently was already familiar with the text" (125). MacDonald strongly encouraged Carroll to expand and convert his 1864 private gift to Alice Liddell, *Alice's Adventures Under-Ground*, into what became the 1865 *Alice's Adventures in Wonderland*. MacDonald, too, was a serious writer both of fairy tales and of longer fairy-tale narratives.[33] Carroll admired MacDonald's *Phantastes* or *A Faerie Romance for Men and Women*, published in 1858. Even though *Phantastes* is also a dream-narrative and even though Carroll certainly drew inspiration from it when he composed his Alice books, MacDonald's book is a quest narrative in which a boy strives to become a man. Carroll's work, on the other hand, is about a little girl who is not permitted to be a child or on some level to be anything at all.

Indeed, Alice bears closer resemblance to MacDonald's nameless Light Princess from 1864. Revising and satirizing both Hoffmann's *Princess Brambilla* and "Sleeping Beauty," MacDonald tells the story of a baby girl who is cursed to lack gravity—both physical and emotional. While at first her floating and flying resembles that of Peter Pan, unlike Peter she ages. The Light Princess's levity is both innocent and problematic as she laughs hysterically when she learns that a General has been cut to pieces with all of his troops and that the city might be abandoned to the mercy of the enemy. In fact, her laughter not only begins to sound more like screaming than laughing but moreover her name, the Princess, doubles as the name for the wicked witch in the story who first cursed her. It is only when the Light Princess meets a prince and falls into the water with him that she is able to experience a sexual awakening: significant enough to begin to pull her from innocence to experience, from levity to gravity.

Worried about Victorian readers' reactions to MacDonald's valorization of sexual experience over innocence, John Ruskin (1819–1900), the author of the fairy tale "The King of the Golden River" (1841), which features another innocent idealized child in the boy Gluck, expressed his misgivings about the story's content and style in a letter to MacDonald one year before the 1864 publication of "The Light Princess." Ruskin feared that audiences offended by MacDonald's extreme approach to gender and sexuality would misinterpret MacDonald's comic tone. Like the Light Princess, and unlike the boy Gluck, Alice ages even while apparently retaining the levity of childhood. Another similarity to Alice in "The Light Princess" is that even after the Princess gains her gravity, falls in love, and watches her lover nearly die for her, the happy ending she wins at the end is ridiculed by the narrator. Once again infantilized, the Princess finds it difficult to learn how to walk. If the Light Princess cannot fly happily forever as a little girl, her progression to an absurd marriage at the end of the story does not compensate for her maturation.[34] Carroll's Alice, too, while she cannot remain a child (or ever be a child at all) has nothing to look forward to once she reaches adult womanhood.

FROM WONDERLAND TO OZ

In his effort to replicate Lewis Carroll's tremendous success with the Alice books, the American L. Frank Baum (1856–1919) created *The Wonderful Wizard of Oz* (1900), the first in a series of books whose characters have become popular lesbian, gay, bisexual, transgender, and queer/questioning (LGBTQ) icons.[35] The novelty of Baum's renovation in speculations about gender and sexuality was only magnified and reinforced by the 1939 musical fantasy film *The Wizard of Oz*, starring Judy Garland. Baum's fourteen Oz novels were published between 1900 and 1919, with two published posthumously the year that he died.[36] It is thought that fairy tales came of age in America with Baum's *The Wonderful Wizard of Oz* (1900).[37] What was it about Baum's novel(s) that yielded such an effect with respect to gender and sexuality?

Unlike the fairy tales by the Brothers Grimm with which this chapter began (1812–57), there is no "happily ever after" in Baum's *The Wonderful Wizard of Oz* series (1900–19). In other words, as is the case for Carroll's Alice and for Barrie's Peter Pan, Dorothy will not conclude her adventures with a happy heterosexual marriage (see Pugh 2008: 225). In fact, it remains unclear if any sexual reproduction takes place in the Oz books at all. Later in the series, an orphan boy named Tip learns he is actually a girl and a queen, Ozma. After Tip transforms his gender, he takes the throne in Oz.[38] In the world of Oz, as Tison Pugh (2008) has convincingly argued, Baum created an erotically antisocial queer utopia: an alternative world where erotic attachment and reproduction take place in previously unthinkable ways.

GENDER AND SEXUALITY IN NEVER-NEVERLAND

Like Carroll's Alice books and Baum's Oz series, Barrie's Peter Pan destabilizes happy matrimonial endings. While Wendy Darling might eagerly grow up, marry, and have children, Barrie's dream-child Peter Pan can never reach sexual maturity. Consequently, he vehemently resists anything that growing up might entail. Due to the sexualization of the child that troubles the long nineteenth century, however, Peter Pan's incomprehension of sexual maturity is contradicted by every other element of the story he is in, including by the emphasis Barrie places on his own infatuation with the actual little boys who inspired his narrative about the boy who can never grow up.

As appears to have been the case for Carroll with the real-life little girl Alice Liddell, Barrie's mythological wonder-boy came into being through his interactions with and love for real-life little boys: the Llewelyn Davies brothers.[39] Before writing the first version of Peter Pan, Barrie met the four- and three-year-old George and Jack Llewelyn Davies in 1897, in Kensington Gardens, and began telling them stories about their baby brother Peter who had been born that year. Barrie grew obsessively devoted to what became the five Llewelyn Davies brothers, George (b.1893), Jack (b.1894), Peter (b.1897), Michael (b.1900), and Nico (b.1903). After the deaths of both Llewelyn Davies parents in 1910, Barrie adopted all five of the boys (aged from seven to seventeen years old).

In 1909, the year before Barrie's adoption of the five Llewelyn Davies boys, Barrie's wife since 1894, Mary Ansell, with whom he had no children due to Barrie's likely impotence, divorced him to be with her lover. The earliest version of Peter Pan, *The Boy Castaways of Black Lake Island*, consisted mainly of photographs Barrie took of the Llewelyn Davies brothers as they played fantasy games with Barrie about being shipwrecked on an island while they summered in Surrey in 1901. The book contained a preface and thirty-six captioned photographs of the Llewelyn Davies boys, scantily clad or at times naked. The next version of Peter Pan appears in Barrie's adult novel *The Little White Bird* (1902), a story about a bachelor resembling Barrie, who falls in love with, or who at least becomes irrationally devoted to, a little boy, only tricking the boy's mother that he is really interested in her.

Most famously, Peter Pan appeared in 1904 in the phenomenally popular play that Barrie managed on every level, ceaselessly rewriting it.[40] Barrie's play premiered in London and in America, starring 37-year-old Nina Boucicault in London and 33-year-old Maude Adams first in Washington, DC, and then on Broadway in the role of the eternal boy child Peter Pan. In 1911, Barrie converted his play to a novel, *Peter and Wendy*. Barrie's choice to cast grown-up women in the role of a beloved boy child reminds us that Peter can play the part of anyone he wishes, from a mermaid to Wendy to a crocodile to Captain Hook, all the while being played by a grown-up woman. Still, as a character, Peter remains nothing other than a wonderful boy who refuses to age. Yet Wendy, like Alice, grows up, it is implied, before she is ever a child at all.

No girls are normally allowed entrance into the dreamscape of Never-Neverland. As an exception, Wendy is invited to Neverland to tell the boys stories the way her own mother has been telling her children the story of "Cinderella," a fairy tale that Peter has listened to at the Darlings' window but has not yet heard to the end. "Cinderella" is a story that Wendy wishes to live out herself, identifying with a girl in need of a prince, whom she links to Peter Pan, and hoping that he will recognize her as his true partner and happily marry her at the end of their story. This outcome can never take place, however, for Peter is doomed to remain trapped in eternal childhood: at once an ecstatic state and a tragic condition.

Wendy's role in Neverland, which she cheerfully plays, at least initially, is of the pretend wife to Peter and the pretend mother to both Peter and to the Lost Boys. It is Wendy's choice to leave Neverland, which was never a real home to her, just as Wonderland is never a home to Alice. Wendy must grow up, has already grown up, while Peter never can. Peter's relegation to Neverland, a dreamland that he controls and from which he can never fully escape, makes him a tragic boy because he is also never able to live in the real world. As a result, he acts like a dead child that children dream about, but who exists only on the other side of the grave.[41]

In a sense mirroring Peter Pan himself, who flies away with three children but is unable to hold onto them, Barrie endured a similar fate. His frantic devotion to his five muses, the Llewelyn Davies boys, resulted in heartbreak when George was killed on the battlefield at the age of twenty-one in 1915, just after Barrie mailed him a love letter that was never opened. Michael Llewelyn Davies, about whom Barrie added much to the character of Peter Pan, even giving a picture of Michael to the sculptor who created the statue of Peter Pan in Kensington Gardens, most likely committed suicide by drowning himself with his male lover Rupert Buxton in 1921: a fate both of these young men may have planned in the wake of what had recently happened to Oscar Wilde. For unknown reasons, Peter Llewelyn Davies, too, would eventually take his own life, throwing himself beneath an underground train in London in 1960. These traumatic biographies aside, Barrie's ghost-child Peter Pan still refuses to age and will never die.

CONCLUSION

Even with his lack of tangible physical form, the dream-child Peter Pan embodies the conflicts about gender and sexuality that dominate fairy tales from 1800 to 1920. As was the case in Carroll's creation of the dream-child Alice from the hauntingly seductive real-life little girl Alice Liddell, Barrie's Peter Pan shows how the fetish of innocence that developed during the long nineteenth century at once glorifies cross-generational attraction and reveals the impossibility of its actualization.

The instability of the dream-child, the surprising gender reversals, the tearing apart of distinctions between past and future, between dream and reality, the humor generated as every rule of ordinary existence is broken at will, the sexual attraction between men and boys, girls and women, children and grown-ups, all of whom keep performing each other's parts: everything that makes Peter Pan extraordinary today comes from its fascinating contradictions, which result in both exhilaration and in heartbreak. All points of view explode before us, all become imaginable and real and then the pressures of gender, sexuality, and temporality itself strike with a greater force than they have done before. Throughout the long nineteenth century similar effects were taking place, all echoing one another and all striking different tones. Because these works are masterpieces, they not only changed history but they also contain within themselves glimpses of startling revisions and adaptations that even today we still have yet to bring alive.

CHAPTER FOUR

Humans and Non-Humans

Uncanny Encounters in the Grimms' Tales

NICOLE THESZ
In memoriam James M. McGlathery (1936–2020)

INTRODUCTION

This chapter explores the varied encounters with the non-human in German fairy tales, arguing that these entities uncover a narrative attempt to test and validate humankind. My ecocritical rereading of Jacob and Wilhelm Grimm's *Kinder- und Hausmärchen* (hereafter, KHM; Children's and Household Tales) is only at first glance anachronistic. The climate crisis may elicit new perspectives on humanity's trajectory, but the fear of extinction and obsolescence—of self, species, or environment—is already manifest in the folkloric tradition. Such anxieties arise in fairy-tale conflicts that are perhaps less symbolic than existential and are derived from real-world threats such as predators, illness, crime, and warfare. Indeed, tales address biological and sociopolitical fears in stark terms, utilizing the non-human world to express humans' struggle for survival. Reference to the non-human extends beyond myth and fiction, probing human relations to others at several levels. Yet the anthropocentric reference-point remains a constant in the equation. Therefore, the present analysis of the non-human examines the fairy-tale world as a model for human self-exploration in service of survival, attempting an ecocritical rethinking of the human condition as presented in folk and fairy tales.

The Grimms' collection is closely associated with German Romanticism, a period marked by nostalgia, yearning for transcendence, and proto-ecological thought, as seen in the portrayal of nature in both idyllic and uncanny terms by Ludwig Tieck in "Der blonde Eckbert" ("Eckbert the Fair," 1797) and "Der Runenberg" ("The Runenberg," 1804) or by Wilhelm Hauff in "Das kalte Herz" ("The Cold Heart," 1827). E. T. A. Hoffmann's literary tales "Der Sandmann" ("The Sandman," 1816) and "Nußknacker und Mausekönig" ("The Nutcracker and Mouse-King," 1816) offered spooky visions of blurred lines between fiction and reality, human and animal, as well as human and automaton, as seen in the lovely but robotic Olimpia of "The Sandman." In a more naturalistic vein, Johann Wolfgang von Goethe's "Novelle" ("Novella," 1828) problematically contrasted urban artifice with the supposed simplicity of childhood and nature, as exemplified by a group of Roma and their powerful but tamed lion. Indeed, gaining a sense of authenticity through "Naturpoesie" (natural poetry) was a preoccupation of German Romantics, evident in the Grimms' work as well as in Achim von Arnim and Clemens Brentano's folksong and poetry collection *Des Knaben Wunderhorn: Alte Deutsche Lieder* (The Boy's Magic Horn: Old German Songs, 1805–8).[1]

In the *Kinder- und Hausmärchen*, edited and published between 1812 and 1857, the Grimms established a complex landscape of idyll, mystery, and danger, but the brothers also explicitly commented on the natural realm and the depletion of habitats through human activities: "die großen viel Tage langen Wälder sind ausgehauen worden, und das ganze Land ist mehr und mehr in Wege, Canäle und Ackerfurchen getheilt" ("the woods that went on for days have been cut down, and the entire country is more and more divided into rows, canals, and furrows").[2] The brothers' fairy tale collection remains relevant for its exploration of family structures, psychology, and socio-economic portraits as well as for its attention to the human experience of biological environments. The following sections explore five categories of the non-human in fairy tales, examining characters in temporary beastly form as well as encounters with animal helpers, plants, inanimate objects, and magical humanlike creatures. The shared role of flora, fauna, objects, humanoids, and animal-human hybrids is to evaluate humanity, albeit with varying scenarios regarding judgment and consequences. All told, fairy-tale humans' liminal encounters with their "non-human others" offer lessons about human aspirations and limitations. These entities serve as reminders of humankind's egocentric shaping of the world, its selfishness and wickedness, and its ultimate mortality.

THE STRUGGLE FOR HUMANITY IN "BEAUTY AND BEAST" TALES

As Maria Tatar suggests in the context of "Beauty and Beast" reinventions, ecocritical readings involving the non-human make sense in a world that is increasingly "biocentered" (2017a: xi). Stories about beauties and beasts conjure up the "Missing Wildness" for audiences living "in a hyper-civilized society" (Griswold 2004: 23). The "Beauty and Beast" narrative enters twenty-first-century European culture most prominently through the literary tale by Jeanne-Marie Leprince de Beaumont (1756), but was preceded by versions in Greek mythology (Apuleius, "Cupid and Psyche") and Indian folklore (the Panchatantra), folktales about frog suitors, Marie-Catherine d'Aulnoy's "Le Mouton" ("The Ram," 1697) as well as Gabrielle-Suzanne de Villeneuve's novel-length *La Belle et la Bête* (Beauty and the Beast, 1740). The myth of Psyche indicates a fascination with transcending human boundaries, albeit with a prominent warning against female curiosity, since Psyche's glance at Cupid causes their long separation. Narrative tropes associated with the tale type are the obstacles to love, a quest, courtship, and the recognition of unique worth in the chosen partner. Beauty and Beast tales often foreground a test of female loyalty, although stories of animal brides place some of the burden on the male partner. A tale from nineteenth-century collector Alexander Afanasev, "Tsarevna liagushka" ("The Frog Princess"), has the prince prove his perseverance before he can regain his bride. At the same time, the "Animal Bridegroom" tales (ATU 425,[3] including the "Beauty and Beast" subtype) relate to stories about human beasts (e.g., Perrault's "La Barbe bleue," "Bluebeard"; ATU 312) given that "Bluebeard" tales are often more focused on the brides' disobedience than their husbands' murderous impulses, as critics point out (Tatar 2003: 171–2).[4]

Versions of the "Beauty and Beast" tale type present variations in terms of the heroine's agency, the groom's plight, and the couple's parents, but the most popular tales develop the bride's ability to look beyond social appearances. The beast's form is not simply an unfortunate curse but an opportunity for the human partner to prove integrity. Thus, d'Aulnoy's "The Ram" centers on the heroine's failure to keep her promise: the ram dies when Merveilleuse does not return at the agreed-upon time. In contrast, Leprince de Beaumont's story validates the bride's social power in marital relationships that were in reality skewed toward male socio-economic dominance, but the author also added an implicit lesson about female love representing the unconditional acceptance of flaws in one's partner. This acceptance extends to Beauty's father, who allows her to be sacrificed in his place, one example among many of tales that conceal the role of daughterly sacrifice in connection with the choice of a marriage partner. In Anne Thackeray Ritchie's Victorian-era version, however, this weakness is clearly spelled out by a critical discussion of the father's dishonest business dealings (Ritchie 1867a: 8, 11–13). Unlike other versions, both those predating and those following hers, Leprince de Beaumont modernizes and complicates the plot by making the courtship more than a litmus test of obedience, as in the case of "Cupid and Psyche" or in the folktale collected by the Grimms, "Der Froschkönig" ("The Frog King," KHM 1), which surely circulated prior to the nineteenth century. Instead, Leprince de Beaumont transforms it into an opportunity for the partners to become acquainted—the opposite, thus, of the arranged marriages that may have prompted this tale type (Tatar 1992: 141). This recasting of the heroine's imprisonment as a period of slow courtship that includes the development of friendship is taken up in Ritchie's tale as well as in twentieth- and twenty-first-century retellings.[5] Leprince de Beaumont's fiction about the castle's inclusion of "Beauty's room" (Tatar 2017b: 45)—a first indicator that Beauty is not destined to be devoured—also plays into modern notions of "a room of one's own," as Virginia Woolf put it. Setting the stage for the future, French female authors such as Leprince de Beaumont reinvented the animal-human constellation as an opportunity for friendship and female "self-realization" (Zipes 2003: 788), albeit one that misfires in "The Ram" and that would be put on hold in the nineteenth century by returns to patriarchal views on female submissiveness in the Grimms' collection, though upheld in Ritchie's Victorian romance.

Yet the dramatic element of the "Beauty and Beast" plot is not limited to the girl's fear of marriage and sexuality. Hidden drama is found in the beast's struggle for his humanity as he resides involuntarily in the form of an often-unexplained monster, a frog, a boar, a ram, or some other shape. Leprince de Beaumont's Beast abhors flattery, feeling perhaps that his state is so humiliating that any flattery reveals the speaker's lack of honesty (Tatar 2017b: 42).[6] At the same time, his insistence on being recognized as a "monster" and "stupid" (46) indicates psychological concerns that transcend those of a simple tale of love, loyalty, and redemption. After all, in certain versions, the Beast is in fact a human; Ritchie's hero Guy Griffiths is uncouth, but his fear of displeasing is due to a lack of self-esteem and smooth manners, a fact the author relates to his upbringing by a cold, selfish mother (Ritchie 1867a: 4, 16–17). His sole transformation is the proverbial look of love (24), a sentimental resolution similarly adopted by Charles Perrault in "Riquet à la houppe" ("Riquet with the Tuft," [1697] 2001b).[7] Rather than just an unfortunate suitor, the Beast in most tales represents a human who doubts his fundamental right to exist as a social being. Leprince de Beaumont's Beast, too, craves his lost humanity, which is not simply his shape or "intelligence" (Tatar 2017b: 45), but his identity as part of a species that rather proudly makes being humane an expression of ultimate kindness and integrity. Leprince de Beaumont and Ritchie suggest that psychological factors play a role in the beast's self-perception.

If the Beast's struggle is the fear of rejection, which often causes death or near-death (indicating that social membership is vital, and that romantic love is a test of the ability to be accepted by one's species or society),[8] then the human partner's experience in tales about animal bridegrooms (ATU 400, 402, and 425) is to endure a test. Such scrutiny encompasses keeping promises, demonstrating self-sacrifice and perseverance, and balancing the needs of parents and spouse. Speaking to the role of "Beauty and Beast" stories in examining humankind, the tales often emphasize that the animal partner is the more steadfast of the two, whether because they understand better the existential necessity to play it safe or because humans—in the storytellers' imagination—are more distracted by externals. Flailing humans and steadfast animal partners abound. D'Aulnoy suggests that Merveilleuse is drawn back to her father's kingdom not only to reunite with her family but also to regain her status as her father's favorite. Leprince de Beaumont's Beast patiently courts her, whereas Beauty seeks to return to her family and temporarily succumbs to her sisters' flattery. A German folktale collected by Johann Gustav Büsching, "Das Märchen von der Padde" ("Puddocky," 1812), features an enchanted bride in the form of a frog that patiently helps her human suitor satisfy his father's demands.[9] The Grimms' bride in "Das singende, springende Löweneckerchen" ("The Singing, Springing Lark," KHM 88) seeks to attend balls for her sisters' wedding, and the petulant heroine in "The Frog King" tries to evade her repugnant suitor at every turn. Exhibiting a more drastic test, in "Hans mein Igel" ("Hans My Hedgehog," KHM 108), the half-human suitor's unworthy first bride scorns Hans and is terribly punished by his quills, whereas the more accepting second bride is kindly treated and rewarded by his final transformation (Zipes 2003: 363–4).

Yet these tales not only evaluate humans in comparison to "down-to-earth" animal brides and grooms. In addition, the plots display remarkable gendered differences since females are tested even when they are the animal partner. Afanasev's frog princess, akin to "Puddocky," must perform tasks after she is married to Prince Ivan, completing household chores to be evaluated by the king and mesmerizing an audience through her dancing at a ball. On the other hand, Hans Christian Andersen's "Den lille Havfrue" ("The Little Mermaid," 1837)—a special case given that hybridity, and not human form, is her original state—gives up her voice to become human, and when she fails to secure the prince's love, she continues to be tested as an air spirit (Tatar 2017b: 300). In contrast, animal grooms usually woo their human brides with the help of confinement, luxuries, and polite company; they are not, like Andersen's mermaid or the heroine of the Grimms' "Marienkind" ("The Virgin Mary's Child," KHM 3), deprived of their voices, the logic perhaps being that women would need only physical beauty to entice the male. In fact, Ruth Bottigheimer suggests that this ideal of the "silent woman" became more and more prevalent in German mid-nineteenth-century culture than, say, in France, and is thus reflected in the Grimms' editing and selection process (1986: 115–18). In a variation upon the theme of confining brides as a form of "courtship," a Persian tale describes a man who tricks his wife, a Peri or winged mythological creature, by hiding her garments, but loses her in the end (Tatar 2017a: 76–8). Here, the human is seen as "below" the non-human—a pattern reminiscent of the relationship between Psyche and Cupid—but the examples of the Peri, the Scottish Selkies, the French Melusine, and other animal brides also reveal a striking difference in the portrayal of female and male animal-human hybrids. As Carole Silver writes, women's "mysterious ties to nature … made them threatening and dangerous," whereas animal bridegrooms are simply transformed, handsome humans (2016: 41), whose ties to nature are erased after regaining their human form.

According to fairy-tale logic, the animal brides and grooms need a woman's (or man's) love to be transformed, while the human counterpart is tested in the process regarding patience, acceptance, and loyalty. To some extent, the animal's vulnerability, as seen in d'Aulnoy's, Leprince de Beaumont's, and the Grimms' tales, seems to communicate a greater need for humanity's compassion and self-examination. In these tales, we can see glimpses of proto-ecological thought regarding transspecies relationships and equality. However, "Beauty and Beast" stories habitually display the human form as the ultimate goal. Indeed, on a psychological level they suggest fantasies of control over a partner otherwise perceived as monstrous and overpowering: the prospective husband in marriages between young girls and older men. Animal bridegrooms, such as the lion in the Grimms' "The Singing, Springing Lark," express social vulnerability but also hint at a mixture of fear and titillation at animalistic masculine sexuality.[10] While critics have read stories about animal bridegrooms as rooted in anxiety about arranged marriages (Tatar) or as proof of the inseparability of human and animal nature (Seifert 2011: 245), I also argue that the beasts' predicament communicates deep-seated anxiety regarding the loss of humanity, selfhood, and concomitant social isolation (a fate that similarly befalls female animal brides such as Afanasev's frog princess or Büsching's Puddocky). In "The Singing, Springing Lark," the groom's challenge to be humanized is made easier by his daily shift between human and lion form; yet his subsequent beastly form, a dove, suggests that his animality stands for humankind's unacknowledged vulnerability. Indeed, failure to return to human form is sometimes associated with death, as seen in d'Aulnoy's "The Ram." Moreover, the Grimms' "Frog King" endures abuse, tacitly accepting violence as his ticket back to a human form. The loyal servant, Henry, whose heart was held by iron bands, even calls into question the notion of humanness. His modified heart suggests a model of hybridity, as if humanity's outer form might pose a mechanical means to hold back an emotional essence for the sake of social propriety or survival.

Emotionally speaking, "Beauty and the Beast" tales may be driven by the desire to overcome social and physical constraints. The king in "The Singing,

Springing Lark" is turned into a dove because his wife insists that he accompany her to her sister's wedding. This suggests two areas of problematic social bonds: on the one hand, the heroine is unable to accept a short separation from her husband; and on the other hand, she has not yet fully overcome her ties to her birth family. The heroine's lack of maturity is conveyed by her fear of separation, and the threat to their relationship is emphasized by the groom's various animal shapes as well as by the appearance of the false bride, or dragon princess. "The Singing, Springing Lark"—which in several respects emulates the Grimms' Cinderella variant "Aschenputtel" (KHM 21) given the request for a gift from the father's journey; the gift that relates to nature; the temporary separation; and the token of recognition—suggests that the disparity between bride and groom follows two patterns: either a separation based on species difference and need for maturation ("Beauty and Beast" tales) or a separation due to social class distinctions ("Cinderella" tales). What the tale types have in common, however, is the message that an individual's essence, and not their appearance, should determine their worth.

Ultimately, tales about animal brides and grooms reveal a fascination with transcending species barriers, perhaps as a means to access a broader, more authentic human experience, much as the Cinderella tales evoke the need to appeal to nature for help in a world distorted by greed and social barriers. Whereas French tales (e.g., d'Aulnoy, Villeneuve, and Leprince de Beaumont) test the heroines' ability to see beyond social appearances, the German variants (Grimms' "The Frog King" and "The Singing, Springing Lark" or Büsching's "Puddocky") more explicitly frame the encounter with animal brides and grooms as part of a larger encounter with natural spaces and symbols, such as the cool well in the woods or the gift of a lark and quest for the dove. Certainly, stylistic choices in "Beauty and Beast" tales reflect social, aesthetic, and scientific preferences of a particular era; individual storytellers introduce "psycho-social"[11] concerns; sexual drives and emotional layers intermingle with legal, economic, and sentimental aspects of marriage; and natural surroundings and the visual arts inspire the fictional visions of animal spouses. However, given that "Beauty and Beast" tales retain over the course of many centuries and throughout oral traditions the basic pattern of difficult courtship, I would argue that they are indicative of an archetypal preoccupation with alterity and physical boundaries as well as a projection of sexual fantasies and fears onto animalistic or monstrous bodies.

ANIMAL JUDGES: TESTS OF CHARACTER AND THE HUMAN QUEST

Although fairy tales can mirror more rural times, animals in these stories are less often wolves in the woods than helpers encountered on human quests. However, assistance is generally contingent on passing tests of loyalty and kindness. Whereas "Rotkäppchen" ("Little Red Cap," KHM 26) features a real-life predator, the most common animal character in fairy tales—classic fables excluded—is the anthropocentric helper-judge. Strikingly, the species involved are often non-mammals, with many occurrences of birds, fish, or insects. Ants appear in a number of tales, fish frequently intervene in human affairs, and birds help the Grimms' Cinderella to attend the ball and warn her that the false brides—her stepsisters—are riding off with the prince. In fact, the doves—a species often aligned with the divine—render punishment, starting in the Grimms' second edition (1819), by pecking out the sisters' eyes at the wedding.[12]

The fish in "Von dem Fischer un syner Fru" ("The Fisherman and His Wife," KHM 19), who metes out rewards and punishment, is primarily a judge of humankind despite the gifts he bestows on the couple.[13] His proximity to nature is indicated by the increasingly stormy and discolored waters after each successive greedy wish. Yet the fisherman's claim that he would not have kept *"eenen Butt, de spreken kann"* ("a talking fish"; Grimm and Grimm 1997: 119; Zipes 2003: 65) anyway suggests that he senses the uncanny in this breach of nature. There is an implied line between human and nature, and whereas both the fish and the wife are willing to cross it, the fisherman would prefer to avoid any transgression of such boundaries. At the same time, the fish's claim that he is an enchanted prince does make him a part-human or quasi-divine entity, given his ability to speak, grant wishes, and to direct the elements. His voice appears ecocritical, though his revolt at the wife's wish for divinity reveals mainly sociopolitical concerns, as if he were seeking to keep the poor in their place by warning against greed.[14] The tale's alignment of fish and the divine recalls the New Testament account of Jesus's power over water, which follows the broader biblical theme of subjugating nature for human benefit—a theme found in other folktales and also reflected in the frequent use of a power differential between heroes, heroines, and their non-mammalian helpers.

In "Die Goldkinder" ("The Golden Children," KHM 85), also collected by the Grimms, a golden fish caught by a poor fisherman confers a castle that is lost due to the wife's curiosity and the husband's inability to keep a secret. The fish's unnatural ability to speak is not addressed in this tale, and moreover, the fisherman only relinquishes his catch after being promised rewards (Zipes 2003: 284). This lesser-known tale emphasizes mercy over moralism. Less punitive than the stern flounder of "The Fisherman and His Wife," the fish of "The Golden Children" sacrifices himself first to be partly eaten by the wife and their horse, and then to be buried, yielding magical lilies, while he also grants the couple two golden children (285). Thus, the folktale blurs the origins of life, deriving the children's (humanity's) existence from his own body, as a biological (food), spiritual (divine), or quasi-sexual procreation.

Already in the ninth-century Chinese Cinderella version "Yeh-Hsien," a fish's bones grant wishes and are associated with a divinity in human form that descends from the sky (Tatar 2017b: 146–8). The crucial difference between these various renderings lies in the fact that the Grimms' judgmental fish in "The Fisherman and His Wife" objects to even the simplest wish. Whereas the husband initially returns the flounder *"in dat blanke Water"* ("into the clear water"; Grimm and Grimm 1997: 119; Zipes 2003: 65), the sea is already *"gröön un geel"* ("green and yellow"; 120; 67) as he returns to make the very first request, even though it is a rather modest one for a cottage that would replace their *"Pißputt"* ("dirty hovel"; 119; 65). However, the fact that the released fish leaves behind *"enen langen Strypen Bloot"* ("a long streak of blood"; 119; 67) would indicate that even the fisherman's mere subsistence-fishing causes irreparable harm to the divine order of nature, or alternatively, that the fish already predicts further exploitation on the part of humans. In contrast, Yeh-Hsien receives limitless wishes; only at the very end do the fish bones lose their power after her husband overuses them. Similarly, the prince of d'Aulnoy's "Le Dauphin" ("The Dolphin," 1697) enjoys unlimited wishes without any judgment regarding his requests (Zipes 2001: 116–31).

Like "The Fisherman and his Wife," the Grimms' tale "Die Gänsemagd" ("The Goose Girl," KHM 89) aims to protect the authorities and aristocracy from social upheaval. Here, the horse Falada is the voice of truth, much like the handkerchief with the mother's blood that protects the girl from her servant earlier in the tale, until the handkerchief's loss. The animal in this tale is not only a loyal companion (who also conferred status as a steed), but, like the fish of "The Golden Children" and "Yeh-Hsien," ultimately serves the human in a sacrificial capacity. Falada continues to remind the girl of her status even after his death, speaking as a dismembered head nailed to a barn door. Like the fish characters, the sacrificed horse bears connections with Christian symbolism, though here referring to crucifixion. Yet aside from the anti-revolutionary allegory of "The Fisherman and His Wife" or the horse's role in "The Goose Girl," animals in German fairy tale are in fact frequently allies of the working class.

Numerous tales condone upward mobility. In "Die weiße Schlange" ("The White Snake," KHM 17), a servant secretly eats part of the ruler's magical snake dish and thereby gains the ability to understand the language of animals. Rather than punishing this transgression, the tale marries him to a princess, who only accepts her lowly suitor after a number of grateful animals he had previously saved—fish, ants, and ravens—help the young man to complete a series of challenges, the last one being to retrieve an apple from the Tree of Life.[15] A snake holds power over life and death in "Die drei Schlangenblätter" ("The Three Snake Leaves," KHM 16), in which a servant marries a princess with the promise to be buried alongside her if she were to die first; he is able to resurrect her with magical leaves after watching a snake heal another snake. Both stories allude to Eve's transgression but recast the serpent in the service of humankind, and to be sure, men. In "Der getreue Johannes" ("Faithful Johannes," KHM 6), the eponymous servant understands the words of ravens, who predict the ruler's fate in wooing a princess but also warn Johannes that he will turn to stone if he reveals this knowledge. Johannes prevents his master's death three times, only to be sentenced to death for his seemingly inexplicable behavior; telling the truth spares him from execution but not petrification. Interestingly, the happy ending in all three tales is not simply due to the protagonist's proven kindness but also his willingness to risk his life (in "The White Snake," failure to perform tasks will cause suitors to be executed). Moreover, these similar stories not only cast animals in the role of testers and helpers but also associate them with the pursuit of knowledge and resurrection: after being petrified, as the ravens predicted, for saving his master's life, Johannes is revived by the blood of the ruler's children, and they are resurrected by their own blood, which may carry special strength due to their youth, innocence, or their royal birth ("Faithful Johannes"); ravens locate the Tree of Life ("The White Snake"), and snakes hold the key to resurrection in the hands of men ("The Three Snake Leaves").

In a more modern narrative, the ants in "Furnica" ("Furnica, or The Queen of the Ants," 1883), a semi-modern literary tale by Carmen Sylva (Elisabeth of Neuwied and later Queen of Romania [1843–1916]), are not grateful helpers but rather hive-minded totalitarians who end up imprisoning their human queen for daring to make contact with human society. In this tragic tale, the author imagines a benevolent but lonely queen whose life at the ants' "court" seems to mirror the writer's own. This literary addition to Romanian folklore (or, possibly, the establishment of "fakelore")—which alludes to the real mountain Furnica in the Bucegi National Park, near the Peleș Castle—would have served the native German to demonstrate her assimilation into her new culture. Instead of portraying the loyal helper ants of Grimms' tales, however, Carmen Sylva conveys modern sentiments of isolation and alienation, which are not, moreover, resolved in the end. The finale shows Viorica trapped in a stifling Kafkaesque chamber secured by the ants' continuous rebuilding. Kafka would transform humanity into an insect to communicate inescapable victimization, self-hate, and revulsion by others, whereas Sylva paints a protagonist whose beauty makes her desirable but does not protect her. Akin to Rapunzel, Viorica's long hair is an indication of her long stay away from civilization, but it provides no means of escape. Her initial retreat from humanity shortly after losing her mother and her turn to animalkind yields only a short reprieve. Her experience indicates that other species are no more kind than humanity, as suggested already in the fables of Aesop and Jean de La Fontaine, in which the industrious ant refuses to help the grasshopper in need (Aesop sixth century BCE; La Fontaine

1668). In "Furnica" as well, the ants' controlling and inhumanly efficient nature embodies human failings such as avarice, ruthlessness, and lack of forgiveness. Sylva probes both the supposed authenticity of nature and the difficulties of human society, ultimately finding a measure of solace and cruelty in both spheres.

MEETING FLORA: THE PLANT WORLD IN GERMAN FAIRY TALES

Plants often reside in the background of literature, like the proverbial wallflower, but they do move into the spotlight and are anthropomorphized based on aesthetic qualities, religious beliefs, medical customs, and everyday plant awareness. A legendary, unattainable "blue flower" serves as the symbol of yearning and beauty in Novalis's unfinished novel *Heinrich von Ofterdingen* (Henry of Ofterdingen: A Romance), an image adopted by such authors as Joseph von Eichendorff and Goethe. In addition to a given society's knowledge of biology, various forms of spiritual and supernatural beliefs are expressed in literary encounters with plants.[16] The biblical visions of paradise seem to indicate that flora contains beauty and innocence, but also temptation, as seen in the Tree of Knowledge that is instrumental in humanity's alleged Fall. Much as the judgment and banishment of humankind takes place in a gendered framework, fairy-tale nature appears to shift its hues according to a gendered logic. Bottigheimer argues persuasively that Wilhelm Grimm emphasized the "social isolation" of heroines in the tales (1987: 102), as seen in the poignant images of the abject heroine of "The Virgin Mary's Child" abandoned in the forest. On the other hand, fairy-tale trees also relate to women's supposed close ties with nature. In the Grimms' "Von dem Machandelboom" ("The Juniper Tree," KHM 47), the eponymous tree is the site of the mother's wish for a child, and she experiences her pregnancy as part of nature's seasonal cycle. Yet when she eats juniper berries in the seventh month, she falls ill, as if the tree had reminded her that her fertility had been unnaturally begotten (Zipes 2003: 159). The connection between human vitality and the tree's powers over life and death is further emphasized by the burial of the mother, and later her son's bones, under the juniper tree, and the son's resurrection as a phoenix from flames erupting between its branches, enabling his revenge (161).

Whereas encounters with other non-human entities—animals, fairies, or objects—are often directly focused on judgment, the plant realm appears to express a more subtle aspect of human experience, namely, that of fundamental vitality and material existence. Much as the juniper tree gives life and contributes to the cycle of death and rebirth in the eponymous tale, the hazel tree in the Grimms' "Cinderella" version mediates the deceased mother's presence in the heroine's life, as does a date tree in Giambattista Basile's "La gatta Cenerentola"

("The Cat Cinderella"; Zipes 2001: 447). As I have noted elsewhere, the 1812 version of the Grimms' tale still has the mother suggest to her daughter that she plant a tree, from which the mother promises to issue help, whereas later versions refrain from pagan imagery and instead imply that the daughter is drawing on her mother's remembrance as she plants the twig, waters it with her tears, and receives assistance from birds by the tree (Thesz 2019: 428). Plants confer or correspond to life in several German tales. In "Jorinde und Joringel" ("Jorinda and Joringel," KHM 69), *"eine blutrote Blume"* ("a flower as red as blood") takes the witch's power and returns birds to their human shape (Grimm and Grimm 1997: 365; Zipes 2003: 250). Golden lilies mirror the vitality of the "Golden Children" once they have left their home (Zipes 2003: 287–8). In the Grimms' "Die Nelke" ("The Pink Flower," KHM 76), the protagonist turns his wife temporarily into a flower, which then implicitly holds her spirit or soul (Zipes 2003: 261–4). Parsley or lettuce restore health to the pregnant mother in the Rapunzel tales, and cabbages are able to turn humans into a donkey and back again in "Der Krautesel" ("The Lettuce Donkey," KHM 122). In "Der Gevatter Tod" ("Godfather Death," KHM 44), an herb (*"ein Kraut"*) supposedly saves lives—although ironically, the "herb" is a prop since in reality it is Death's position at the patient's bed that determines the outcome (Grimm and Grimm 1997: 228; Zipes 2003: 150).

Against the background of Bottigheimer's argument regarding the isolation of women in the Grimms' tales, I suggest that the plant world altogether frequently presents a more indirect and less judgmental relationship to humans than seen in encounters with other non-human entities. While heroines such as the Virgin Mary's adopted daughter or Rapunzel are certainly isolated in their natural realms, these surroundings are more often nurturing and stable presences than threatening entities, perhaps rooted in the mute and unmoving impression that plants leave on humans. In "Das Mädchen ohne Hände" ("The Maiden Without Hands," KHM 31), the devil threatens first the father, and then the daughter; the father betrays his daughter; and the devil returns to threaten the heroine after her marriage to the king. Among these dramatic encounters, the pear tree that feeds the maimed maiden is a silent, benevolent, and nurturing presence (Zipes 2003: 110). Instead of judging either in favor of the heroine or intervening in the devil's plans, the tree offers a haven much like the forest at the end of the tale, where king and queen are reunited (112–13). Likewise, a pear tree harbors Cinderella in the Grimms' version, offering passive protection to the heroine, but unable to resist violence when the father, eager to please the prince pursuing his daughter, willingly chops down the tree, never considering that his daughter may be harmed in the process (Zipes 2003: 82; see also Thesz 2019: 434).

Plant nature can appear a witness to both good and evil, though more often seeming to perform for the greater good. In "Dornröschen" ("Briar Rose,"

KHM 50), a briar hedge grows around the enchanted castle, impenetrable much like the forest in Perrault's version, but more threatening since the Grimms' tale specifically references the unsuccessful suitors who die in the thorns (Zipes 2003: 173–4). Interestingly, the successful prince is not simply permitted entrance because the hedge judges him to be the right one. The tale instead offers a combined effect: the prince has been warned and proceeds nevertheless, with courage that in narrative terms makes him worthy, but perhaps more importantly, the 100-year spell is just up as he reaches the hedge. Thus, biology, magic, and psychology intersect in implying that humans are bound to the cycles presented by seasons and temporal limits more than they are masters of their destiny. The ambiguity or neutrality of thorns is reinforced in "The Virgin Mary's Child," when the recalcitrant heroine is imprisoned by *"dichten Dornhecken"* ("thick hedges of thorns"; Grimm and Grimm 1997: 38; Zipes 2003: 8). The phallic thorns that keep the heroines of "The Virgin Mary's Child" and "Briar Rose" in their places, and which also blind Rapunzel's prince, are distinct from the womb-like hollow trees that offer safety in "The Virgin Mary's Child" or "Allerleirauh" ("All Fur," KHM 65; Zipes 2003: 240). Plants can be protective, life-giving, or stern guardians and at times exploited by evil, but overall seem to represent balance—giving and taking life in "The Juniper Tree," providing food and shelter but also isolation and danger in "The Maiden Without Hands" and "Rapunzel." In the Grimms' "Cinderella," the birds determine the false brides and the true one each time the couple passes the hazel tree (Zipes 2003: 83–4), while a nettle bush in the similar tale "Jungfrau Maleen" ("Maid Maleen," KHM 198) acts as Maleen's witness and interlocutor as she hints at her identity as the rightful bride (Zipes 2003: 575–7). Flora in fairy tales cannot enact justice but does provide protection, nurture, and even at times a site conducive to the rendering of narrative justice.

DANGEROUS OBJECTS: THE REVOLT OF THE NON-HUMAN SPHERE

In folk and fairy tales, objects and witchcraft regularly represent existential threats, expressing human anxieties at being constrained by the material and the supernatural world. The scrutiny of things has been seen in the recent "material turn" of literary criticism, but even Karl Marx's theories on commodification is predated by the close attention paid to objects in the oral and literary fairy-tale tradition. As Elaine Freedgood comments, literary texts modify the nature of things for the purpose of representation, seen both in verbal sketches of mundane backgrounds and in the portrayal of symbolic items: "The object as reality effect loses its potential as a material thing outside the conventions of representation; the object as metaphor loses most of its qualities in its symbolic servitude" (2006: 11). At the same time, even Marx's theory about the alienation produced by capitalist systems objectifies matter. Perhaps any scrutiny of objects denaturalizes them, since the human view of matter is necessarily a probing one that limits the focus on economic dynamics, scientific properties, or aesthetic effects. Yet fairy tales, while often framing the non-human in terms of utilitarian gain, also invest considerable power into objects, thus narrowing the agency gap between human and non-human.

In Grimms' tales, supposedly inanimate objects, such as millstones, become murderous in "Herr Korbes" (KHM 41) and "The Juniper Tree." The eponymous bone in "Der singende Knochen" ("The Singing Bone," KHM 28) is all that is left of the protagonist, but the object and spirit voice remain devoid of vitality. Such objects appear both uncanny and ominous because their inanimate status is reminiscent of death, given that their comparative permanence, their "objectness," does without the animating but ephemeral quality of life. Yet from another perspective, fairy tales are dealing with what critics such as Serenella Iovino and Serpil Oppermann would call the recognition of "agency" on the part of matter.[17] The fact that the uncanny lifelike behavior of supposedly inanimate household objects is successively rewritten in the "Beauty and Beast" tradition—from spooky hands in Jean Cocteau's film *La Belle et la Bête* (1946) to the cutesy cup and teapot in Disney's 1991 animated rendition—points toward the idea that the potential threats of the non-human world have become increasingly painful to acknowledge in the age of escalating technological invention. Historically, however, humans have invested their surroundings with agency, less from scientific perspectives than from quasi-totemic beliefs in the ways objects might absorb the human lives around them.

In the Grimms' "Herr Korbes," a hen and rooster seemingly off-handedly assemble a group of animals and inanimate objects (a team of mice, a cat, a millstone, an egg, a duck, a pin, and a needle) to visit the eponymous character, who is later assaulted by them and ultimately killed by the millstone perched on his door: "Wie er aber an die Haustür kam, sprang der Mühlstein herunter und schlug ihn tot" ("just as he got through the front door, the millstone jumped down and killed him"; Grimm and Grimm 1997: 224; Zipes 2003: 146). The verb *"sprang"* ("jumped") leaves no doubt as to the storyteller's perspective: jumping is not a passive, gravity-induced occurrence but rather purposeful action.[18] Other events are murkier: the hen and rooster assemble the carriage and invite the animals but themselves do not take part in the attack on Herr Korbes, raising the question as to whether they are innocent bystanders, accomplices, or ringleaders. The red wheels of their carriage suggest the latter role. In fact, their color and circular motion allude to revolution[19] and, given the class difference between the animals, objects, and the presumed feudal lord *"Herr"* Korbes, offer the option of classifying the events as premeditated revolt and murder.[20] Although the Grimms attempted to ease the sense of wanton cruelty toward the main character by adding the line, "der Herr Korbes muß ein recht böser Mann gewesen sein" ("Herr Korbes must have been a very wicked man"; Grimm and Grimm 1997: 224; Zipes 2003: 146) in the third edition (1837), the ominous atmosphere outweighs any slapstick humor in the tale.[21] In fact, the fear of matter extends to the broader international tradition: in the *Popol Vuh*, household objects attack early humans in an act of revenge for having been exploited (Christenson [2003] 2007: 75).[22] References to such scenes—"the revolt of the objects"—are found in Peruvian Moche artwork as well, signifying "social upheaval," an interpretation that is also applicable to "Herr Korbes."[23]

At the same time, the Grimms' story capitalizes on the humor arising from the absurd setup (the duck splashing water, the egg breaking into Korbes's eyes) and the grotesque, even *unheimlich*, nature of inanimate objects reanimating and putting their mundane qualities—that usually serve humans—to murderous use in their home (i.e., the *Heim* turning *unheimlich*). The "revolt" of the oppressed objects, who might be interpreted as serfs, can be construed as goal-directed political action against the feudal lord "Herr Korbes." However, in a similar story published by the Grimms, "Das Lumpengesindel" ("Riffraff," KHM 10), political revolution cedes to thuggery. There, similar animal and inanimate "characters" take advantage of an innkeeper's hospitality, only to assault (but not kill) him the next morning. Part of the story's humor derives from the animals' jousting for power, as the hen and rooster put on airs, not wanting to pull their carriage home, leading them to force a duck (who had overestimated his fighting power) to do so instead. The human realm, in turn, proves susceptible to *"süße Reden"* (sweet talk) and the promises of the hen's and duck's eggs (Grimm and Grimm 1997: 78; Zipes 2003: 37). Relating back to "Herr Korbes," part of the birds' resentment in these tales may be grounded in the human use of their offspring, which the tales underscore by having the egg (or egg shells) blind Korbes (the innkeeper). In both tales, therefore, the "revolting" household objects lend themselves to political allegory and social farce, suggesting that this story communicates the general sense of an unpredictable, even resentful material world rather than offering specific allegorical messages inherent in the household objects themselves.

In the Grimms' "Die sieben Raben" ("The Seven Ravens," KHM 25), multiple layers of the non-human world surround the heroine, who indirectly gives rise to her brothers' loss, and then assists in the retrieval of their human shape. The girl's journey is marked by the items she packs (bread, a cup, a chair, and a family ring) and the star's gifts (the bone), which serve as literal means of survival but also indicate human limitation by demonstrating the need for material protection. The heroine's access to material things possibly suggests the storyteller's critique of entitlement since these objects signal property rights or affluence, and thus exhibit a proto-capitalist pattern of setting material bulwarks against life's vicissitudes. Privilege is also evident in the ring, which connotes family tradition and bonds. Fairy-tale objects are derived from real life but also employed judiciously as symbolic objects, as seen in the star's gift: the little bone ("*Hinkelbeinchen*"; Grimm and Grimm 1997: 155) is both an object with certain qualities (its key-like shape) and a symbolic item as a gift. It represents a reminder of mortality and a link between humans and the inanimate realm.

However, "The Seven Ravens" suggests that the attitude toward objects also involves an ethical dimension. On the one hand, the story shows the girl drawing on a celestial realm for help, and on the other, she subjugates the world of objects for her purposes. The girl's existence has caused only suffering in the tale, though inadvertently, since her frailty at birth puts her brothers' existence in danger. Indeed, by the time she has reached the glass mountain, she has received life, parenting, objects, and help, but she has not yet given anything of herself, as the tale seems to imply. Her loss of a finger represents a permanent sacrifice that appears to be required of the female, but not of males, in the tale. This sacrifice is, moreover, necessary even in the 1812 version of the tale, "Die drei Raben" ("The Three Ravens"), where the boys' initial transformation is the consequence of their mother's anger that they had played cards under the church, a deed unrelated to the sister's birth (see Grimm and Grimm 1812).

Although regaining humanity represents the impetus for the tale's plot, the non-human dominates the narrative's emotional economy. The brothers' transformation into ravens turns them from alleged truants into objects of melancholy. Their abuse at the hands of a parent both objectifies them and lends them dignity, while their sister is set up for a sacrifice simply because her existence "caused" the brothers' departure, a pattern that ironically aligns males with nature and females with alienation. The narrative also underscores the limits of humankind by offering a cosmological encounter with powerful figures—the sun, moon, and morning star—whose actions suggest a stern, but anthropomorphic, universe. As in numerous of the Grimms' tales, the non-human tests the heroine, who must prove compassion (to seek her brothers), perseverance, and sacrifice (her finger) to enter the glass mountain, the latter of which signifies an imprisonment of humans in their vulnerable creaturely form as well as humanity's fundamental alienation from others.

At the moment of the terrible sacrifice of a limb, we come to understand that the inanimate and animate worlds in fairy-tale perspective are deeply connected: if humans underestimate an object (the material world "matters"), they must pay with their own, animate bodies, because nothing—not even a bone—is easily retrievable once lost. The non-human universe (seen in celestial bodies, ravens, a dwarf, and the glass mountain) tests the heroine's loyalty before relinquishing the brothers from the non-human sphere—a realm, incidentally, in which they have not seemed entirely discontent. Another way of reading the sister's quest for her brothers' humanity would be to note that the various entities she encounters suggest a counter-quest for a multivalent understanding of the universe, which is never fully human, nor ever fully inanimate. Yet although the heroine has to some extent learned the value of the non-human (the bone), the transformation of the brothers is ultimately seen as a liberation. The siblings return home, turning their backs on the instructive non-human guiding forces they have encountered. A happy end for humanity? Another, more Marxist interpretation of these tales might be that the overly utilitarian approach to the world—be it a bone refashioned as a key, ravens, household objects, or oppressed serfs—represents an immoral state of affairs, one that the material world, in its seemingly inanimate agency and timeless persistence, would force humans to ultimately relinquish.

SUPERNATURAL WOMEN: ELECTIVE AFFINITIES AND DISAFFECTION

Humanlike figures in folktale are frightening precisely because of their uncertain status as a "species," their resemblance to humans, and their ability to anticipate and interfere with human behavior. Witches' power derives in part from masking their inhumanity, as seen in "Hänsel und Gretel" ("Hansel and Gretel," KHM 15), when the witch pretends at first to feed the children. In "Brüderchen und Schwesterchen" ("Little Brother and Little Sister," KHM 11), the stepmother-sorceress seeks to destroy the siblings' bond and to usurp the sister's position as queen and wife for her own daughter. The fascination of supernatural beings for the world of humans, as in Rumpelstiltskin's wish for a child or Mother Gothel's imprisonment of Rapunzel, suggests an anthropocentric foil to humankind's privileging of humanity over planet. Witches and their kin both entrap and test humans, doing so out of their affinity for human society but also out of their desire to gain control, echoing the hierarchies of the human world.

It may seem a rather broad stroke to discuss fairies, angels, ogres, ogresses, sorcerers, and witches side by side, but despite the nuances, these characters do share some key properties. Above all, they are focused on the fates of humans (rather than their own kind), seeking them out for trickery, profit, and for relationships. Facing an often hostile world, the human storyteller is drawn to imagine beings that resemble humans but transcend their powers, entities that would focus their lives on humans—indeed, make them the center of all their plans and attention. This is apparent when angels appear in "The Pink Flower" to grant the wish for a child and to rescue the unfortunate queens of this tale and of "The Maiden Without Hands." However, many of the stories offer another, darker option: namely, that the world is intent on undermining the semblance of free will offered to humanity in a Christian worldview, evident in scenes of temptation, as in biblical accounts or in "The Virgin Mary's Child."

Images of supernatural interference in human lives is found in both religious and secular contexts, each time spanning the spectrum of selfless help and relentless destruction.

The argument that supernatural characters are fundamentally similar can be further justified by the fact that they appear fairly interchangeably within similar tales (e.g., the "Rapunzel" variants of Basile, Charlotte-Rose de la Force, Friedrich Schulz, and the Brothers Grimm; Zipes 2001: 475–91). In the "Rapunzel" tale type, the older female's affinity for the human child derives from a maternal attitude and a desire to control. The maternal nature is most pronounced in the fairies (de la Force and Schulz), whose inherently kind and noble qualities lead them to provide food for the heroine even after her banishment. Ultimately, the supernatural women, such as the Grimms' sorceress, seek to protect the baby they have removed from the parents' care. This act is somewhat legitimized given the ease with which the parents in these tales relinquish their children. The non-human, thus, functions as a means to chastise humans for their lack of protectiveness of their young, though perhaps overshooting the mark since the guardians imprison these young girls in towers that are more reminiscent of phallic power than of maternal nurture, which suggests that part of the supernatural women's uncanny framing is rooted in overstepping traditionally accepted female roles.

Whereas fairies commonly appear in French and Italian tales, the Grimms' stories often feature witches, suggesting differences in mentality between Catholic and Protestant contexts regarding magic, ritual, and the inclusion of female figures in religious narratives.[24] Even though the Grimm brothers based "Rapunzel" on Friedrich Schulz's 1790 version,[25] which essentially is a copy of de la Force's tale of 1698, they changed the fairy to a stern sorceress who banishes the heroine after her "marriage" to the prince. Unlike the fairies in earlier versions, the Grimms' sorceress neither provides food at the site of banishment nor returns to reconcile with her ward. Clearly, the brothers' editing builds on the tradition of the evil stepmother that they added to tales such as "Hansel and Gretel" or "Schneewittchen" ("Snow White," KHM 53).[26] At the same time, the fact that the guardians in the Rapunzel tales beautify the young girl suggests, as James M. McGlathery writes, that the older females identify to some extent with their younger charges; they combine maternal pride with a "vicarious participation" in the young girl's romantic future (1991: 113). This act backfires, however, when the captress finds herself sidelined by the girl's love affair, despite her isolation in the tower. Altogether, the Grimms downplay the maternal element of Rapunzel's guardian by evoking a more malicious warden, whose domineering treatment of the unsuspecting prince heightens the impression that her actions are driven by envy and jealousy of the prince's attention, and by the desire to punish the girl rather than protect her from the attentions of a man.

Supernatural women are not inevitably malign, however. Victimization and jealousy are completely lacking in the popular story of "Frau Holle" ("Mother Holle," KHM 24), where a witch-like character tests two sisters and rewards them with gold and pitch for their diligence and laziness, respectively. This tale rests entirely on the motif of testing women's sense of duty, primarily connected to the activity of spinning, although related versions extend the virtuous girls' qualities to physical attractiveness, as seen in Marie-Jeanne L'Héritier's "Les enchantements de l'éloquence" ("The Enchantments of Eloquence," [1696] 2001: 550–64), which similarly connects work ethic to physical beauty or disfigurement. At the same time, many of these tales emphasize the physical deterioration, through age and malice, of the witch-like antagonist. The older female humanoids can be ambiguous figures, however, encompassing identification with and resentment of youth and fertility (cf. McGlathery 1991: 113). Frau Holle in the Grimms' tale is scary-looking due to protruding teeth, and has been compared both to Hulda in Nordic myths and to the Russian Baba Yaga. Like Frau Holle, Baba Yaga controls clouds, tests spinning skills, and is alternately fiend and friend, although this ambiguity is, as Andreas Johns notes, less common in Western Europe (2004: 6). Seen from a broader perspective, Frau Holle, Baba Yaga, and older females test younger women's adherence to duty and assist in their romantic affairs, and at the same time are linked to a society's productivity by influencing both overall climatic and human reproduction. References to supernatural older females such as Frau Holle thus point toward a more practical, biological understanding of women's lives than in the romanticized heterosexual encounters found in French courtly tales.

Much as Rapunzel tales align beauty, fertility, food, and love, the Grimms' tale "The Lettuce Donkey" combines different elements of the non-human, containing humanoid figures, plants, potions, as well as a "Beauty and Beast" trope. The humanlike characters whom the protagonist, a young hunter, encounters, embody stark contrasts: a helpful hag initially tests his kindness and an evil witch, in turn, procures his gifts (a bird's heart conferring riches and a magic traveling cloak) by exploiting her beautiful daughter's attractions. Interestingly, the third presumed humanoid creature is never named, yet the young hunter enters a garden reminiscent of Rapunzel tales, in which magical cabbages turn humans into donkeys, and back again. This tale offers a spectrum of humanness: the human in animal shape, which renders "it" helpless (the evil witch will die in her donkey form), the hag in various forms, and the human, who is seemingly the most desirable creature, being the moral and romantic subject that prevails. The fact that the evil witch's daughter and servant almost die as donkeys because "sie sind so traurig" ("they are so sad") further suggests that in comparison, animality is abject (Grimm and Grimm 1997: 591; Zipes 2003: 404). In contrast, humanoid shape allows figures such as the helpful hag, evil witch, and witch's daughter a worthwhile, albeit human-focused existence.

The frequent portrayal of similar characters suggests that the activities of supernatural women are prominent but ambiguous in fairy tales given their affinity for and power over humans. Tieck's novella "The Runenberg" features a naked temptress who ruins the hero's life as she hands him a jewel-studded tablet: "der Jüngling vergaß sich und die Welt im Anschauen der überirdischen Schönen" ("the youth forgot himself and the world around him as he gazed at her supernatural beauty"; 1992: 33; my translation). Although the protagonist, Christian, succeeds for a time in rejoining human company and leading a seemingly normal life, the temptress ultimately reappears in the guise of an old woman to complete her deed.[27] Unlike the beneficent ageless fairies in French and Italian folklore, witches and sorceresses in German tales tend to outnumber helpful hags, although the latter do counter evil in such tales as "Der Teufel mit den drei goldenen Haaren" ("The Devil With the Three Golden Hairs," KHM 29) and "Der Teufel und seine Großmutter" ("The Devil and His Grandmother," KHM 125), thus undermining the stereotypical alignment of witches with the Devil (Thurston 2007: 7). Altogether, these supernatural females in folktale are denied an independent existence, remaining focused on either helping or hindering younger characters. Whether exhibiting caretaking (helpful hag), exploiting biology (parsley, lettuce, or cabbages), or creating intrigue (jealous elders in "Rapunzel," "Briar Rose," and "Snow White"), supernatural women in German tales remain closely linked to the maternal and seductive tropes of the feminine. These stories about witches who imprison maidens and turn boys into deer express the societal fear of women's power over nature, and yet the storytellers ultimately, begrudgingly, suggest that humans might find answers about the secrets and evils of the world with precisely these uncanny, shunned older women.

CONCLUSION

While human stories have long converged on anthropocentric concerns and biases, fairy tales in particular incorporate the non-human, which permeates the narrative landscape as a means to test, assist, validate, and humble humanity. Based on the international and cross-temporal survey presented in this chapter, different aspects of the non-human contribute to distinct reflections on the human condition. The "Beauty and Beast" framework offers scenarios that scrutinize human behavior, while also serving to satisfy romantic yearnings of unity with nature, whether by approaching animalkind, re-naturing the self in an abandonment of societal constraints, or restoring humanity through fulfillment of the terms of a "curse." The real animals of fairy tales are placed in the roles of judges and helpers, matching the desire to subjugate nature and to imagine linear consequences for human conduct. Encounters with plants, on the other hand, lack some of the dramatic reactivity of other non-human entities;

instead of judging humans, plant nature seems to offer presence and protection despite the fact that it can prove dangerous to those who find themselves in the wrong place at the wrong time. For the most part, the silent, immovable green of plantkind makes it a rather peaceful and steadfast companion of fairy tale humans. In contrast, the seemingly inanimate objects of everyday life do not play a passive role, which indicates a deep skepticism even in premodern cultures regarding human inventions of any kind. Why else would the silent tree be benevolent but the household tool return to harm its owner? Indeed, such fantasies of revenge on the part of matter reappear in twentieth- and twenty-first-century dystopian visions of artificial intelligence and technology attacking civilization. Fairy tales similarly suggest that humanity's utilitarian approach to the material world and fellow humans (and even the self, if we remember Cinderella's stepsisters' efforts to fit the shoe) is in need of correction. Certainly, the manifold interventions by humanoid creatures in the fairy-tale world indicate humanity's assumptions regarding its own importance. Yet the tests presented by the non-human world offer a "timeless" model that measures worth as a qualitative, rather than quantitative, entity. Essence, and not productivity, is the magic of the fairy-tale realm.

CHAPTER FIVE

Monsters and the Monstrous

SARAH MARSH AND ZEYNEP CAKMAK

Inter the corpse where the road forks, so that when it springs from the grave, it will not know which path to follow. Drive a stake through its heart: it will be struck to the ground at the fork, it will haunt that place that leads to many other places, that point of indecision. Behead the corpse, so that, acephalic, it will not know itself as subject, only as pure body.
—Jeffrey Jerome Cohen, "Monster Culture (Seven Theses)" (1997)

INTRODUCTION

In his "Seven Theses," Jeffrey Jerome Cohen elaborates a framework for understanding cultures through the monsters they produce. The monster, for Cohen, is a sign of what the culture expels; monsters occupy "the gap between the time of upheaval that created [them] and the moment into which [they are] received, to be born again" (1997: 40). In this sense, Cohen's theses describe several dimensions of monstrosity in the nineteenth-century fairy tale. Most immediately, Cohen helps us see nineteenth-century fairy-tale monsters—hungry beasts, murderous stepmothers, brutal enslavers, animal-humans, devil-mothers, racially marked giants, and lurking daemons—as narrative signs of social disaggregation within the tales themselves: the *deus ex machina* by which difference (of body, of culture, or of ideology) is encircled and purged from the family, the state, or the imagination. Cohen's theory also describes the fairy tale's global cultural movements during this period. Throughout the nineteenth century, fairy tales were mass produced, and they extended their "civilizing" role to both the nursery as well as the work of nation-building, imperial expansion, and political resistance.[1] In the case of the Turkish fairy tales included in this chapter, they had only circulated in oral tradition and first made their way into print when Hungarian professor Dr. Ignácz Kúnos collected and anthologized them under *Turkish Fairy Tales and Folk Tales* in 1889.[2]

As Benedict Anderson has theorized, the emergence of mass-print culture during this period was "key to the generation of wholly new ideas of simultaneity" that make it possible for a country full of readers to imagine a nation held in common (1991: 37). Fairy tales were no exception to this trend; and, because of their unique importance to notions of cultural purity or authenticity, the tales took a formative role in nation-building movements, as well as political resistance to them. As knowledge was scientized and labor increasingly industrialized during this period, the genre's writers often repurposed its older, agrarian, and pastoral motifs in response to new sociopolitical realities of capital. The tales, like the monsters who inhabit them, were thus born again into a new moment. And the question that the nineteenth-century fairy tales have sometimes raised—who are these stories *really* for? —bespeaks the category crisis that monsters always signify (Tatar 2003: 3–38).[3]

This chapter elaborates these insights about monstrosity in and of nineteenth-century fairy tales from selected Western and Eastern traditions, as well as from the globally displaced tale traditions of nineteenth-century African Americans. Our purpose here is not exhaustive but, rather, comparative and suggestive of how these tales use the narrative forms of monstrosity to grapple with the nineteenth century's incarnations of politicized otherness, family and national formation, trauma, and empire. At the same time, we examine how monstrosity functions in these tales to operationalize the "civilizing" processes traditionally ascribed to fairy tales: the formation of children's reading practices; the orientation of their moral understanding; and their indoctrination into dominant cultural values.

The function of monsters in the nineteenth-century tales is, as in earlier eras, not strictly subversive or oppressive; rather, the nineteenth-century tales demonstrate monsters' protean power to take a variety of forms that disrupt categorization, particularly the work of binaries.[4] As we will see, the monster in the nineteenth-century fairy tale was a malleable vessel for complex anxieties about global modernity itself as well as those modern subjects who "refused to participate in the classificatory 'order of things'" in an era defined by its commitments to global taxonomy and the hierarchies it afforded (Cohen 1997: 45).

GENDER, SEXUALITY, AND THE NINETEENTH-CENTURY GENETIC IMAGINATION

"The monster's very existence," Cohen writes, "is a rebuke to boundary and enclosure," and these boundaries are fundamentally aligned across cultures with normative notions of gender, sexual reproduction, race-making, and the role of these processes in constructing the category "human." Thus, cultural meanings of race, gender, and sex(uality), procreative or otherwise, are intimately bound up in the creation of monsters (Cohen 1997: 46). Nineteenth-century fairy tales often stage monstrosity as the transgression of gender, sex, and race binaries; these transgressions take the form of both violence and play. The Grimms' tale "The Wolf and the Seven Little Kids," for example, is the story of how a mother goat leaves her "children"[5] alone at home, returning to find that a wolf, in disguise, has gained entry into the house and eaten all of the kids but one. The mother goat and her remaining child, horrified by what has happened to their family, go looking for the wolf, whom they find in a field, digesting—but with a belly that is still moving. In a bid to save her eaten offspring, the mother goat gruesomely cuts the wolf open with a pair of scissors, and her "children" emerge from the male "monster's stomach" in an intersexed Caesarian section that delivers questions about gender, violence, and the story's real sources of monstrosity (Grimm and Grimm 1988). In the Turkish tale, "The Brother and Sister," a Padishah similarly cuts open the belly of a fish to rescue his wife and little son after the princess had been pushed into a fountain by an "evil Moor Slave and g[iven] birth inside the fish's belly" (Kúnos 1913: 10). Each story transgresses bodily and generational boundaries, underscoring the necessity of corporeal and kinship integrity to the production of monsters.

Monstrous births and bodies such as these are a recurring plotline in nineteenth-century tales, as is their corollary: sexual coupling of humans with non-humans. Trans-species narrative forms were also common in earlier tale traditions, but they took on new meanings in the 1800s as Darwinian theory, Mendelian genetics, and scientific racism altered conceptions of human heredity and its socio-economic implications. Earlier, in seventeenth-century England, human-animal hybrids often signaled a family's ancient (and thus, politically powerful) identity: according to family legend, Siward, Earl of Northumberland under Edward the Confessor, had descended from a grandmother raped by a bear; and the Sucpitches of Devonshire claimed a forebear who had been nursed in Prussia by a wild dog, no doubt an anglophone retelling of Rome's founding myth. During the eighteenth century, the burgeoning field of natural history engaged the possibility of human-animal hybrids in its own ways: Swedish taxonomist Linnaeus, in his *Systema Naturae* (1735), created a category for wild men, *homo ferus*, and included examples dating back at least two hundred years (Thomas 1983: 134). These elements of the Western tradition raised the monstrous possibility that human beings were not a species distinct from animals—contrary to the Great Chain of Being's postlapsarian promise that, though fallen from grace into a profane world, humans still held dominion over terrestrial flora and fauna. Rather, these hybrids held open the imaginative possibility that this hierarchy was mutable, open to transgression, and perhaps a generally incorrect way to envisage the relationships among living things—thus troubling the Adamic (and, later Lockean) model of male, human dominion over non-human, female nature.

The Adamic model of human domination persisted into the nineteenth century in Eastern Islamic tradition, and the human-animal hybrids in Turkish fairy tales represent a different type of anxiety from their Western counterparts. As Cohen stresses, "monsters must be examined within the intricate matrix of relations (social, cultural, and literary-historical) that generate them" (1997: 4). In Eastern Islamic tradition, humankind is believed to be and is held as a "higher" form of being than animals. This is not to suggest that animals are without value in Eastern culture. However, human will and consciousness places them above animals; in other words, while animals exist in the material world, humans carry both a material and a spiritual life, allowing them to use their will in a more complex way.[6] The human-animal hybrids we see in Turkish fairy tales usually signify the anxiety of humankind to fall to—in a rough translation of a Turkish saying—"the level of animals." In other words, this animal-human hybridity does not signify a positive relationship between the two but the tension of the hierarchy between animals and humans the culture upholds. The hierarchy manifests in the Turkish tale "The Brother and Sister" when a failed-prince turns into a stag after drinking enchanted dirty water. The prince's downfall comes both from having to run away after spending all the palace money after his father's death and not listening to his sister's cautions against the poisonous water. As these tales were told by the peasantry, the prince's dismal metamorphosis can be read as the cultural desire for the economic and political downfall of authorities who misuse their power in the palace.

In the nineteenth-century Western tradition, anxiety and excitement about blurred human-animal categories were, as in earlier periods, centered around nubile and maternal female bodies as primary sites of taxonomic breakdown and the (pro)creation of hybridity. In the anglophone tradition, this breakdown troubled imperial ideals of "progress" and "improvement" with the possibilities of degeneration, fractured family lineage, and racial contamination. The fairy tales of this era are no exception. Writing in 1905, the English anthropologist J. A. MacCulloch recorded across cultures a variety of nineteenth-century tales centered around what he viewed as socially repugnant "beast-marriages," or the marital (and ostensibly sexual) union of humans with animals in gender-normative formations, typically a female human paired at her parents' behest to a male animal (1905: 51, 253). Sometimes the animal is a prince enchanted into brute form and reconstituted as human by the love of a sexually pure young woman, but permanently animal husbands are also recorded in these stories.[7]

The marriage of girls to animals exists in Turkish fairy-tale tradition as well. In "The Horse Dew and the Witch,"[8] when the palace horse allows only the youngest daughter of the Padishah to feed him, her father marries the princess to the horse. However, unbeknownst to anyone but the princess, the horse turns into a "handsome youth" every night (Kúnos 1913: 71). At initial glance, the tale seems like an allegorical story of an authoritarian father's extreme control over his daughter's life. One day, despite the husband's request to keep his hybridity a secret, the princess brags about him to her sisters. Because of this "betrayal" the prince disappears as a retribution: "'Woe is me!' she groaned, 'I have betrayed my husband, I have broken my promise, thus am I punished!'" (72). The princess's punishment highlights the importance of the family values of fidelity and loyalty that persisted in nineteenth-century Turkish culture. Similarly, in "Shah Jussuf" a poor father sells his youngest daughter (with her will) to an Arab (307). The harsher punishment comes when the girl tries to trick her husband, who vanishes after telling his wife that "as a punishment, [she] shal[l] be shod with iron shoes and with an iron staff in [her] hand and shal[l] seek [him] for seven years" (311). In the tale "The Rose Beauty," the youngest daughter of the Padishah insists that she wishes to marry despite her young age, and her father punishes her by marrying her to a poor woodcutter. Here, the similar trope of marriage-as-punishment equates the undesired husbands: the horse-devil, the Arab, and an impoverished man.

The connubial trope of a male-animal and female-human may seem to invert male supremacy, with the woman as the "higher" human animal in the pairing—but the plotlines of these stories reveal deeper, gender-based subordination transacted by marital and kinship violence as well as financial coercion. The most famous of these in the Western tradition, "Beauty and the Beast," was first published in French as *La Belle et la Bête* in 1740 by Gabrielle-Suzanne Barbot de Villeneuve; in 1756 Jeanne-Marie Leprince de Beaumont adapted the tale by significantly streamlining the narrative and inserting it within an explicitly didactic context aimed at young girls. Both versions would be translated, reprinted, and popularized in English in anthologies throughout the century through 1889, when Andrew Lang published his *Blue Fairy Book*. In Lang's version of the story, the heroine, Belle, is offered to a monster husband in exchange for her merchant father's life. By giving Belle to the Beast, the plot rectifies the father's financial failures, and his imprisonment, an iteration of the transcultural narrative form that the feminist anthropologist Gayle Rubin famously called the traffic in women. Animal predation and female sexual subordination are naturalized as analogues for marriage and kinship by Beauty's regular reference to herself as the Beast's "prey," even though his intention is to marry her, not devour her. Beauty's will to stay with the Beast is asserted as a condition of the exchange between her father and her betrothed, but this ostensibly feminist gesture is foreclosed by the absence of meaningful alternatives for Belle within the structure of the story. Thus, the tale offers a relatively tight allegory for marriage under the old Roman law of coverture. Common in both Europe and the Near East during the nineteenth century, coverture is a practice in which a woman's legal personhood is "covered," or subsumed under, the legal personhood of her husband (OED Online 2020a: s.v. "coverture"). Similar to predator-prey relations, one body is subsumed by another to consolidate the natural order of things. Indeed, in Leprince de Beaumont's version, the Beast's monstrosity transmutes into normalized human form only after Belle aligns her so-called will to wed with the patriarchal mandates for exogamous marriage between the merchant and aristocratic classes—one of the only methods of class mobility during the period—and the attendant retrenchment of family wealth.

Women's will or "curiosity"—code for female intellection and sexual autonomy—often is figured in the nineteenth-century tales as a site of monstrous boundary-crossing. According to Cohen, cultural definitions of gendered monstrosity typically dictate that female curiosity is punished, implying that "one is better off safely contained within one's own domestic sphere" (1997: 12). The borders that monsters create or signify are "in place to control the traffic in women, or more generally to establish strictly homosocial bonds, the ties between men that keep a patriarchal society functional" (13). The "Bluebeard" tale is a suggestive case in point, particularly because it was adapted in the nineteenth century from Charles Perrault's 1697 story, the major source of the tale type, to include imperialist intertexts. In Perrault's late seventeenth-century "Blue Beard," a newlywed young woman is forbidden by her husband to enter a particular room in his luxurious home. When the young woman transgresses her husband's order and goes into the forbidden room, she finds it full of corpses: the previous wives of Bluebeard, all with their throats slashed and lying in pools of their own blood. In a variant of the tale by the Brothers Grimm, "The Fitcher's Bird," the young woman avenges these deaths by arranging the death of her murderer-husband; in others, the heroine is spared the fate of her predecessors by the last-minute interventions of her brothers, or by revealing the true nature of her betrothed, as in the Grimm brothers' "Robber Bridegroom," which leads to his arrest and punishment.

As Maria Tatar has documented, however, Bluebeard's serial killing of his spouses (a transgression of both his marriage vows and cultural prohibitions against murder) is almost always elided by the fairy-tale narrator's focus on his "wife's curiosity and infidelity" (2003: 161). Yet, this is not the case in the Jamaican iteration of the tale, which highlights instead the still-living people freed from the killing room by Mrs. Bluebeard (Gates and Tatar 2018: 471–2). Even when an animal is cast in the role of the murderer-husband, as in the Russian and Scandinavian iterations of this tale type, the "moral" of the story still focuses on female (sexual) curiosity as the true sociopolitical taboo. Certain versions of this tale, then, posit that women's transgression of gender and sex hierarchies is more monstrous than male-committed homicide or trans-species marriage, with its implications of bestiality and racial corruption. When Bluebeard was adapted in nineteenth-century pantomimes—with Bluebeard as a "Turk" and his wife as "Fatima"—the European gender politics of the earlier tale were transvalued by the new orientalist frame of Western cultural imperialism, relocating the monstrosities of domestic violence onto the contact zones of the empire (Simmons 2011). As Jack Zipes has argued, fairy tales thus possess a fundamental "art of subversion," a discourse with many levels, shifting meanings, "implicit adult and young readers, and with unimplied audiences," which generates room for multiple and politically complex readings (1983a: 9).

The "beast marriages" of nineteenth-century tales thus invite several methods of critical interpretation. They articulate a cultural form that Coventry Patmore called "the angel in the house" in his 1854–6 poetic sequence by that title, in which women are posited as being/represented as the moral regulators of the home. Sometimes, the conceit was extended to frame women as responsible for uncontrollable male sexual desire that is sanctioned (in both senses of that word) as fundamentally animalistic. Typical of early twentieth-century anthropologists, MacCulloch thought that tales about beastly marriages represented the persistence of primitive narrative forms in the present; they showed the durability, in MacCulloch's view, of that "stage of primitive thought in which the possibility of [a human-animal] union was far from being incredible" (1905: 253). Charles Darwin, in *On the Origin of Species*, defines the term "monster" in temporal terms, as a large, terrible, but extinct creature, or a class of living animal made monstrous by the presence of atavistic features:

> We have plenty of cases of rudimentary organs in our domestic productions,—as the stump of a tail in tailless breeds,—the vestige of an ear in earless breeds,—the reappearance of minute dangling horns in hornless breeds of cattle, more especially, according to Youatt, in young animals,—and the state of the whole flower in the cauliflower. We often see rudiments of various parts in monsters.
>
> (1859: 454)

In this sense, nineteenth-century fairy tales, which were being translated from older oral and written traditions into newer print forms, embody the period's fascination with the persistence of the past in the present—a kind of temporal hybridity—as a type of monstrosity. Individuals born with phenotypic differences often were classified during this period as evolutionary throwbacks or monsters. As Melinda Cooper has shown, for example, the Shelleys' doctor,

William Lawrence, treated a boy in his home who had been born with his brain partly outside of his skull. This patient later inspired Lawrence's definition for "monster" in *Rees's Cyclopædia* (Cooper 2008: 87–98). Paradoxically, as Schacker notes, the rise of folklore as an area of academic study during this period was linked "to the quest for national identity and cultural purity ... as nationalist movements, particularly in Europe, were fueled by the 'discovery' of popular culture" by aristocrats whose political and economic interests were advanced by the elevation of folk culture to hegemonic national identity, not its denigration into the categories of the monstrous (2003: 2). In this vein, Jacqueline Rose has noted fairy tales' frequent nineteenth-century association with "cultural infancy and national heritage" in politically problematic ways that fetishize either the purity, or the atavism, of particular tale traditions and the people groups who tell them ([1984] 1993: 56). Thus, as Cohen notes, "history itself becomes a monster: defeaturing, self-deconstructive, always in danger of exposing the sutures that bind its disparate elements into a single, unnatural body" (1997: 47).

If history is an unnatural body, its vessel across generations is a monstrous woman. During the early modern period, the primary source of monsters in many tale traditions was the maternal imagination, as Marie-Hélène Huet (1993), Dennis Todd (1995), Holly Tucker (2003), Lisa Forman Cody (2005), and others have shown: a mothers' imaginings during conception or pregnancy were thought to have a direct impact on her growing child's plastic physical form. The idea can be traced back to at least the first century when Pliny the Elder, the Roman naturalist, suggested that mother bears licked their cubs to form them into bear-shape. Perhaps the strangest example in the anglophone history of this idea is the story of Mary Toft, who in 1726 was said to have given birth to seventeen rabbits after craving hare meat during her pregnancy. The Grimms' wolf, who eats six goat children only to give monstrous birth to them later, or Kúnos's fish, which gobbles up the pregnant princess who later gives birth inside the fish's belly, are folkloric parallels. While Toft's story was later exposed as a hoax (an otherwise unidentified knife-sharpener's wife apparently had convinced Toft to insert the animals into her vagina in a bizarre act of sexual victimization), its popularity was extraordinary. The Royal Society and even King George I himself became interested in the case (Cody 2005: 120–33). In addition to Toft's real-life story, maternal imprinting also enjoyed a long life in the anglophone print culture of the early modern period, from the poetry of Abbot Claude Quillet to Aphra Behn's *The Dumb Virgin; or, The Force of Imagination*, published posthumously in 1700 (Wilson 2002: 2–3). The idea of maternal imprinting has been well-documented globally in the folklore traditions of Africa, India, Europe, Asia, and the Americas, and—as recently as the 1980s—it persists in the sociology of childhood morphological conditions, such as cleft palate (Shaw 1981: 237–46).

During the nineteenth century, this theory of the maternal imagination as a source of monstrosity did not disappear entirely, though it was transvalued by Victorian bourgeois social conventions, the rise of teratology during the 1820s, the new "sciences" of physiognomy and phrenology, and the persistence of "imaginationists" in British and American schools of gynecology, including the United States Surgeon General William Hammond (Wilson 2002: 11). Fascination with the idea of mothers creating monstrous children was articulated variously in nineteenth-century literature in stories such as Nathaniel Hawthorne's "The Birthmark" (1843) and Oliver Wendell Holmes's "medicated novel," *Elsie Venner: A Romance of Destiny* (1861), in which Holmes imagines a serpentine child whose mother had been bitten by a snake during pregnancy. Capitalist popular culture articulated this trope with its monetization of Chang and Eng Bunker (the "original Siamese Twins"), "Elephant Man" Joseph Merrick, and the many human subjects exploited by carnival men such as P. T. Barnum as "freaks" for public consumption. As Wilson has shown, pregnant women sometimes were documented as taking fright at these exhibitions and thus imprinting their children with further deformity as a lasting biological mark of the freak-show cultural experience (2002: 12–15). Although Darwin's theory of evolution was known during this period, it did not necessarily limit the persistence of older Linnaean notions of the biological heritability of acquired traits.

Nineteenth-century fairy tales in the anglophone tradition often rearticulate the culture of maternal imprinting by figuring the maternal body itself as a source of childhood trauma. Using the characterological duality articulated by *The Madwoman in the Attic* (Gilbert and Gubar 1979), Anita Moss (1988) analyzes two versions of motherhood in Lucy Lane Clifford's 1882 tale, "The New Mother." The first is Patmore's angel in the house, who keeps her home immaculately clean and cares selflessly for her two children, the Turkey and Blue Eyes; her husband, a sea captain, is away from home and absent from the story except for his letters. The second is a monster mother, a New Mother, with glittery glass eyes and a wooden tail, who emerges from the fatigue and tedium of solo-parenting two small and sometimes unruly children. As Moss notes, this New Mother "taps deeply into any child's worst terrors—the fear of losing one's mother and the anxiety that terrible transformations will occur, that what is beloved and familiar will somehow, inexplicably become strange and terrifying" (1988: 57). The body of the mother, turned monstrous by empire's absentee husbands and fathers, is thus refigured in Clifford's tale as a source of childhood trauma. Later, this vein of discourse on maternal imprinting would give birth to the mechanical "refrigerator" mothers of mid-twentieth-century psychiatry, who, by withholding maternal warmth and selfless care, were imagined responsible for their (usually male) children's homosexuality.

Also salient in the nineteenth-century tale tradition is the recurring trope of the dead or missing mother, which exposes children to various kinds of monstrosity in the form of social and sexual predation. In "The Storm Fiend," the three sons of the Padishah promise their dying father to give his daughters to the first one who asks for them: the eldest marries a lion; the middle, a tiger; and the youngest, a bird (Kúnos 1913: 105–6). The mother is missing from the story, not mentioned even in passing, and the girls' fates are controlled by men. The missing mother trope brings with it the recurring event of a Padishah or a father marrying his daughter(s) off to suitors in human or non-human form.[9] The only tale among Kúnos's collection where the mother is present and active in marriage arrangements is "The Wizard Dervish," where the mother is, in fact, a witch.

In the Grimms' "Aschenputtel" ("Cinderella") and its many variations, the death of Cinderella's mother exposes her to the cruelty of her stepmother and stepsisters, who first express their monstrosity in their treatment of their sister, but who themselves become mutilated by the end of the tale, when they amputate parts of their feet to fit the slipper used to identify the prince's bride (Grimm and Grimm 1857: 119–26). This body horror recalls the Greek myth of Procrustes, an urtext of societies' creation of monsters by fitting bodies into a preconceived mold. While Cinderella ultimately is rehabilitated in the Grimm tale by the interventions of a supernatural mother, the story emphasizes the domestic grief and childhood trauma born of absent and morally compromised maternal figures, who tend to wreak havoc on the entire kinship system.

The powerful mothers present in the Turkish tales are either devil-mothers or witches. In "The Horse-Devil and the Witch" two lovers have to fight off the evil-witch/mother-in-law to have their happy ending. In many of the tales, one of the obstacles the voyager faces in his or her journey is the Dew-Mother/Mother of Devils:[10]

> On a boundless plain [the Prince] found himself suddenly confronted with the gigantic Dew-Mother. Standing astride upon two hills, one foot on each, she crunched resin in her jaws and the sound could be heard two miles away. Her breathing raised storms, and her arms were nine yards long.
>
> "How do you do mother?" the young said to her, putting his arm round her waist.
>
> "Hadst thou not called me 'mother' I would have swallowed thee" returned the woman.
>
> (Kúnos 1913: 21)

Then, the mother takes the traveler to her house and orders her Dew-sons to accept him as their brother and help his quest. As Barbara K. Walker highlights in *The Art of the Turkish Tale*, "the tales serve as preservers of Turkish social practices and material culture. The customs attached to hospitality provide a sound example" (1993: xxix). The monstrous mothers perform the pedagogic function of teaching young readers politeness and hospitality, the cornerstones of Turkish culture, which conserves these traditions. As Roy Porter has noted, to think in this way about maternity's generational effects is to imagine the entire "future of the race": maternal imprinting suggested that this future depended upon "what chanced to be racing through the mind of the weaker vessel, whose rationality was doubted at the best of times" (quoted in Wilson 2002: 9).

MONSTROSITY AND THE INVENTIONS OF RACE

In this sense, maternal and racial purity share a locus in the reproductive and hereditary ideologies of the West. In nineteenth-century tales, this is particularly evident in Charles Kingsley's 1862 *Water-Babies*, which follows the travails of a young, motherless chimney sweep named Tom as he is transformed from a boy into a water-baby "complete with external gills, just like an eft, or salamander" (Hale 2013: 561). The occasion for Tom's interspecies transformation is a scene of implied category mixing of complexions and classes. When Tom is cleaning the chimneys of a local squire, Sir John Harthover, he becomes lost in the branching wings of the sprawling home—a winding taxonomic tree of corridors and staircases added by each generation of the Harthover family. Ultimately, Tom lands in the bedroom of Sir John's lily-white daughter Ellie (the most recent of the family line), who screams after seeing the "little black ape" in her room. This "black ape" is Tom, covered in soot from his labors in the Harthover mansion, which, having been added to the home by each generation, is a spatial representation of the family's hereditary history. Ellie's characterization of Tom, coupled with his blackface appearance in some illustrations of the text,[11] stages a variety of racist ideas, most obviously the myth of black men's sexual depredation of white women. Just slightly more subtle in this scene is Tom's horror in realizing his own race and class inferiority, just as Ellie screams at his monstrous appearance. These are the discursive effects of a robust and popularized scientific racism that consolidated the institution of slavery in the anglophone Atlantic world and understood racial mixing as a form of sociological monstrosity. The scientific racist narrative is ultimately consolidated in Tom's degeneration into an amphibian in a pool of water, suggestive of that primordial soup out of which a transitional species crawled so many generations ago. Tom's ontogeny recapitulates a phylogeny dramatizing anglophone societal hierarchies that posited both white supremacy over people of African descent and the social pathologies of other classes of white people, including the working poor and the Irish, who also are assigned to lower orders in Kingsley's text.

Because tale collections in the anglophone tradition also were politically invested in recovering a kind of national purity during the nineteenth-century rise of nationalist and proto-fascist states, the textual authenticity—indeed, the purity—of the tales themselves was persistently interrogated. "Beauty and the Beast," for example, ultimately was removed from the Grimms' *Kinder- und Hausmärchen* (Children's and Household Tales) for being contaminated by French influence from Leprince de Beaumont's earlier version. As Tatar has documented, even modern efforts to categorize the tales in the West have sometimes deployed a vocabulary redolent of racial science. "Monogenesis" is the folkloric theory that thematic similarities among tales are the result of an original set of stories that were disseminated by travel routes from a central location (posited as India by German folklorists during the nineteenth century). "Polygenesis," by contrast, described discrete folk- and fairy-tale traditions arisen from independent sites of invention whose topical or structural similarities result from the commonalities of human experience (Tatar 2003: 64–5). In racialist theories of human descent, which enjoyed broad academic interest from the eighteenth century to the twentieth, "monogenesis" analogously posited a single human ancestor for all people while "polygenesis" imagined that human races had sprung from different racial ancestors not shared in common. Both theories of natural history were leveraged toward racist ends, albeit in different ways.

The written African American folk tradition, and the oral tradition out of which it grew, necessarily grappled with racist cultural attitudes that figured people of African descent as monstrous. However, while at stake for European-descended writers was the "purity" of their tale traditions, "originality" became a primary rubric for assessing the value and political necessity of an African American folk tradition in the struggle for civil rights and an end to racial discrimination in the United States. When Hampton Normal School (later Hampton University), a historically black institution, inaugurated the project of collecting African American folklore in 1888, they wrestled with the problem of what historian Evelyn Brooks Higginbotham famously called "the politics of respectability": were the folk practices of enslaved, African-descended people cultural embarrassments to their descendants? Something to be bracketed by African Americans under the rubric of slavery's tragic history to assimilate more fully into white American culture? Or should African Americans insist on deep cultural continuities through which they could trace a folk lineage back through slavery, the Middle Passage, and ultimately to the pre-chattel-slavery societies of West Africa? As Henry Louis Gates Jr. (2018) notes, the latter became the consensus position in the African American academic tradition after important debates in the late nineteenth and early twentieth centuries. This position foreclosed the notion that the oral cultures of the enslaved were a source of monstrosity. Bound up in these debates is the persistent American problem of race in cultural politics; as Walter Benn Michaels has argued, notions of "heritage" or "tradition" in the United States historically have *required* biologized ideas of "race" to do their most important cultural work (1992: 655–85). The anti-racist cultural project of saving the oral traditions of enslaved people is thus inherently caught up in what Audre Lorde famously called "the master's tools"—in this case of establishing national identity through the construction of an archive or canon, in which some stories are elevated to the level of "tradition" while others inevitably are forgotten or misunderstood (Gates 2018: xxv–xxx).

While academic conservators of the African American tale tradition have defied its categorization as "monstrous" by saving it from oblivion under complex political circumstances, the tales themselves are a testament to how the category of monstrosity was deployed by enslaved people to assert their humanity, in all its complexity, in the face of unfreedom and flattening racist stereotypes. Perhaps the best example of this complexity is the story of the "Tar Baby." As Gates and Tatar have emphasized, the transcultural variations of this tale type popularized by Joel Chandler Harris are notoriously difficult to interpret, and in this sense the type enacts upon readers the central category-foiling work of monsters in the inscrutable stickiness of the tale's central figure (Gates and Tatar 2018: 133–40).

The "Tar Baby" tale type typically begins with a person or animal who has stored up food to eat at a later time; a "thief" next arrives in the story, wishing to take some of this food—and often actually taking it, prompting the food's owner to create a figure out of tar: a tar baby, a tar woman, a tar monkey, or a tar man. The tar figure is designed to draw the thief in and prevent further pilfering. The thief then returns to the scene and, before stealing any food, engages the tar figure first verbally and then physically, ultimately becoming stuck at various points of contact. Typically a threatening monologue ensues: the thief berates the tar baby for its failure to respond but is further ensnared by interactions with the tar figure, both verbal and physical. Following this encounter with the tar baby, the owner of the food returns to catch and punish the thief, gluey and immobilized with tar, but who typically escapes the situation alive (Espinosa 1943: 129–209). But who is owed our sympathy: the forward-looking food saver or the hungry, searching thief? And what host of things must the tar baby symbolize? Thus deflecting readers' abilities to identify with particular characters, or tether themselves ethically with reference points in the plot, the Tar Baby tale-type[12] deploys protean messages about social hierarchies, their maintenance through narrative customs and manners, and the various social meanings of silence.

While this tale type has been traced by folklorists to India, Lithuania, Mexico, Venezuela, Chile, Santo Domingo, the Cherokee Nation of North America, Portugal, and Jamaica, the first version of the famous African American iteration of the tale was published in the United States in 1875 in *Leslie's Comic Almanac*, which situated it alongside children's tales such as "Little Red Riding Hood" and "Cinderella," though Gates and Tatar note that it never has belonged solely to the cultures of childhood, itself a racial category under chattel slavery. In 1877, the story of the tar baby was reprinted by William Owens in *Lippincott's Magazine*, who offered it as evidence of a variety of racist stereotypes about so-called "negro character," including passion for pastimes "requiring little exertion of either mind or body" and "a very low standard of morals" (quoted in Gates and Tatar 2018: 139). The persistent inscrutability of the tar baby across tale traditions—its mutable gender; its speechlessness; its gooey featurelessness; its "whatever it was" qualities, as in the tradition of the Ewe-speaking people of Ghana and Togo—suggest the deep degree to which the construction of fairy-tale monsters depend not only upon the teller of the tale, as James Baldwin reminds us, but upon its readers (Gates and Tatar 2018: 143–5).

Similarly, the monstrous depictions of Arab slaves in the Turkish fairy tales are rooted in the Western audience that the book was produced for and the writer and illustrator who produced it. In the Ottoman Empire, the majority of the slaves were brought to the Anatolian lands from Africa—specifically Sudan and Ethiopia—and Eastern Europe.[13] However, the lack of historical evidence for the existence of Arab slaves in the Ottoman Empire raises the question of why Dr. Kúnos chose to mark these characters as Arabs in his translation. In Robert Nisbet Bain's translation of the tales, he does not use the word Arab; instead, the same characters are described as "ifrit" (devil). In his own translation, Kúnos replaces many of the devil characters with Arabs. Since the original texts of the fairy tales were produced in Hungarian and English by Kúnos, and not Turkish, how the Turkish peasantry described the slave-characters to Kúnos remains a mystery.[14]

Resembling the way people of African descent are portrayed in Western fairy tales, in the Turkish tales Arabs are depicted as monstrous: the words "dew," "Arab," "devil," and "slave" are used interchangeably. Arab characters are described as having thick "monstrous lips" or "such immense lips that one swept the sky and the other the earth" and giant bodies. However, though there is obvious racism in these textual elements of the tales, Willy Pogany's illustrations of the Arabs in Kúnos's collection are unlike anything one might come across in a Turkish text (Figure 5.1), but resonate with Western illustrations of characters of African descent, as in Kingsley's *Water-Babies*.[15] Though the depictions of monstrous Arab are predominantly male, the antagonist of "The Brother and Sister" is a jealous Arabian "black slave-woman," who pushes the

FIGURE 5.1: Illustration by Willy Pogany from Ignácz Kúnos, *Forty-Four Turkish Fairy Tales* (1913). Courtesy of Lilly Library, Indiana University, Bloomington, Indiana.

sister into the fountain out of jealousy, causing her to be swallowed by the fish. In "The Three Orange Peris" a black slave thrusts her hairpin into the skull of the damsel and takes her place in the palace. She tricks the prince, saying that he left her out in the sun too much, causing the sun to spoil her complexion; this is the explanation she uses for everyone in the castle who directs racist remarks at her or calls her a "negress" (Kúnos 1913: 27). At the end of both tales, lies are exposed and both slaves are executed.

ADULT READERS, CHILD READERS, AND THE MAKING OF MONSTERS

The same year that African American folklorists at the Hampton Normal School began archiving their ancestors' oral tradition not only to save it from oblivion but also to seize upon a unique cultural history as an argument for civil rights, authors such as Oscar Wilde were deploying the fairy tale in Britain to critique Victorian bourgeois culture, including the same global capitalism that had stolen the history of people of African descent in the Americas. While Wilde noted in his usual aphoristic mood that his fairy-tale collection, *The Happy Prince and Other Tales* (1888) was "intended neither for the British child nor the British public," *A House of Pomegranates* (1891) was pointedly anti-capitalist, articulating Wilde's socialist vision, and involving his parent and child readers in this critique. Wilde's "The Devoted Friend," for example, suggests that it is not bodily difference but rather unfettered greed—and the social predation of the working poor by the moneyed classes—that is a society's real source of monstrosity. Throughout Wilde's tale, a wealthy miller named Hugh systematically deprives his poorer friend, Hans, of all of his worldly possessions by exploiting Hans's altruism. In the story's frame narrative, animals comment on the "dangerousness" of this altruism, suggesting that the maintenance of class hierarchies through the emiseration of the laboring poor is this society's real monstrosity. In his other fairy tales, like "The Happy Prince," "The Selfish Giant," "The Star Child," "The Birthday of the Infanta," and "The Fisherman and His Soul," Wilde would further elaborate the problem of Christian kindness and its tendency to become an exercise in self-effacement in an era of unbridled capitalist exploitation. Manipulations of the monster category, in which moral monstrosity is hidden beneath aesthetic beauty, are characteristic ways that Wilde developed his literary program of aestheticized socialism.

"Like all real folklore," Kúnos notes in a similar vein, Turkish fairy tales "are not for children, though it is the children who are most strongly attracted by them" (1913: x). Barbara Walker elaborates that these tales were more of and for the adult world:

> In any given culture the personal and sociological needs of the members were and still are served by the tales told within the community. Among these are the need to laugh, to see those in power reduced through some failing or another, to enjoy wish fulfillment, to share heroic values, and to be entertained and refreshed by a break in the ordinariness of their own days.
> (Walker 1993: xxii)

The monsters of the Turkish tale tradition, whether they are natural or supernatural, are the products of the Turkish peasantry's fancy, allowing them to envision a palace life in which they, as storytellers, are in control of the authorities. Walker continues, "this feature is tonic to the one presently in a post of authority who might abuse that position: there is the possibility, born out of [the] tradition, that a seemingly unlikely contender will topple him" (1993: xxiv). Though princes, kings, and padishahs face some challenges—whether the monster they face is a seven-headed dragon or an evil Moorish slave—the tales all end with the royal family's success, reflecting or perhaps reinforcing the peasantry's inherent trust in Ottoman rule. In addition to the warnings these tales cast for the people in power, they also disseminate cultural ideals throughout the land. As Cohen argues, "every monster is in this way a double narrative, two living stories: one that describes how the monster came to be and another, its testimony, detailing what cultural use the monster serves by calling horrid attention to the borders that cannot—and must not—be crossed" (1997: 15). In other words, monsters express the strength and significance of cultural borders between husband and wife, parents and children, master and slave, rich and poor, human and animal—while also blurring those borders to suggest their arbitrary qualities.

The monstrous birth of fairy-tale elements within nineteenth-century discourse is perhaps best epitomized by Mary Shelley's *Frankenstein; Or, the Modern Prometheus*, in which a fragmented body made of human and animal parts is brought to life through a combination of old magic and new science. Marketed as children's fiction since its publication in 1818, Shelley's novel is not a fairy tale, but, through this combination of magic and science, carries major themes of fairy-tale monstrosity into the novel: monstrous birth, human-animal mixing, missing parents, marriage gone wrong, and racial formation (Showalter 2018). Certainly, since that time, *Frankenstein* has continued to illuminate these important fairy-tale themes in stories for adults and children alike. As Karen Coats and Farran Norris Sands observe, Shelley's story has become a touchstone for childhood questions about embodiment, growing up, and familial relations (2016: 241–55). If we envision a scene of adult-child reading, which authors such as Shelley and Wilde invite us to imagine through the use of frame narratives, and which families the world over elevate as a primary scene of childrearing and cultural transmission, the tales export monster-making to the dialectic between generations. As Cohen notes, "monsters ask us how we perceive the world, and how we have misrepresented what we have attempted to place. They ask us to reevaluate our cultural assumptions about race, gender, sexuality, our perception of difference, our tolerance towards its expression. They ask us why we have created them" (1997: 20). In the nineteenth-century tales, monsters raise these questions to the old and young alike, enacting the perennial necessity of building and breaking the categories that organize human life. Across the tale traditions we have examined here, monsters emerge as important signatories of enduring ruptures in hegemonic sexual politics, empire-building, and racial formations—and these systems' salient interconnections in families and the bodies of individuals. As such, monsters' appearances in and across these tales, and in the imaginations of their readers, represent opportunities for disruption and reimagination of the very systems whose inconsistencies monsters always illuminate.

CHAPTER SIX

Space

Physical, Liminal, and Other

JOHN PENNINGTON

In George MacDonald's 1895 fantasy romance *Lilith*, Mr. Vane, after entering the "region of the seven dimensions" ([1895] 2001: 21), is told by Mr. Raven (who is actually a raven) that "if you understood any world besides your own, you would understand your own much better" (25). A bit later, Vane admits: "I was lost in a space larger than imagination" (40). For the rest of his journey in this fantastical realm of the seven dimensions, Mr. Vane must lose his self by accepting the reality of this alternative world, a similar journey that Anodos encounters in Fairy Land in MacDonald's 1858 *Phantastes*, which has as its subtitle *A Faerie Romance for Men and Women*.

Vane's space that is larger than the imagination is an apt metaphor for the variety of spaces and places that are found in fairy tales. Fairy-tale writers of the long nineteenth century were equally consumed by timeless spaces and places in fairy tales. Three examples below will highlight the importance of such spaces in fairy tales:

> Once upon a time there was an ancient castle in the middle of a deep forest, where an old woman lived all by herself. She was a powerful witch.
> (Brothers Grimm, "Jorinda and Joringel" [2012])

> Once there lived a King, whose wife was dead, but who had a most beautiful daughter—so beautiful that every one thought she must be good as well, instead of which the Princess was really very wicked, and practiced witchcraft

and black magic, which she had learned from an old witch who lived in a hut on the side of a lonely mountain.

(Mary De Morgan, "The Necklace of Princess Fiorimonde" [(1880) 1988])

Once upon a time, the Queen of Fairyland, finding her own subjects far too well-behaved to be amusing, took a sudden longing to have a mortal or two at her Court. So, after looking about her for some time, she fixed upon two to bring to Fairyland.

(George MacDonald, "Cross Purposes" [(1874) 1999])

Each tale reflects what Max Lüthi describes in *Once Upon a Time* ([1962] 1976) as "a timeless world" that relies on "formulaic" functions to create a sense of time and space—"'Once upon a time' and 'They live thus today' are the most widely distributed," argues Lüthi in *The Fairytale as Art Form and Portrait of Man* ([1975] 1985: 49). In fairy tales, there is the past time evoked by the "once" that suggests a sense of the universal. That past time, in turn, is made concrete by particular spaces—castles, forests, a hut in the mountains, and fairyland, the places that are identified by the Brothers Grimm, De Morgan, and MacDonald. When "once" gives way to a variation of "ever after," the tales are projected into the future, creating a double universality of time and space, "once" and "after."

Time and space, it appears, are central to the fairy-tale enterprise. H. G. Wells, who was intrigued by MacDonald's conception of the seven dimensions in *Lilith*, explored the space-time connection in *The Time Machine* (1895, the same year as *Lilith*), having the Time Traveler remark that "Time is only a kind of Space," further suggesting—in italics no less—that "*there is no difference between Time and any of the three dimensions of Space except that our consciousness moves along it*" ([1895] 2005: 4). A bit earlier in the century, Edwin A. Abbott published *Flatland: A Romance of Many Dimensions* (1884), where the main character A. Square, from a strictly two-dimension world of Flatland, travels about to Pointland (no dimension), Lineland (one dimension), and Spaceland (three dimensions), in an attempt to learn from Sphere that there is, contrary to our perceptions, a fourth dimension:

> What therefore more easy than now to take his servant on a second journey into the blessed region of the Fourth Dimension, where I shall look down with him once more upon this land of Three Dimensions, and see the inside of every three-dimensional house, the secrets of the solid earth, the treasures of the mines in Spaceland, and the intestines of every solid living creature, even of the noble and adorable Spheres.
>
> (Abbott [1884] 2002: 168–9)

A. Square lands in prison for his perceived heretical attempts to convince others of other space dimensions that go beyond the second.

POETICS OF SPACE: THEORETICAL SPECULATIONS

In an exhibit in *Places Journal*, fairy-tale writer and editor of *Fairy Tale Studies* Kate Bernheimer and architect Andrew Bernheimer curate a collection of architectural "retellings" of classic fairy tales, which include "Little Red Riding Hood," "Rapunzel," "The Juniper Tree," "The Little Match Girl," "The Snow Queen," and "Jack and the Beanstalk." Abbott's *Flatland* is also depicted. Figure 6.1 illustrates one of the physical spaces architects imagined for "Little Red Riding Hood": the grandmother's house, where the wolf has

FIGURE 6.1: "Fairy Tale Architecture," from Mary English and Xavier Vendrell, "Fairy Tale Architecture: Little Red Riding Hood," *Places Journal* (2018). Reproduced with the permission of Kate Bernheimer.

consumed Little Red (her red cape glowing in the black-and-white belly of the beast), which on another level becomes a womb space where, the Architects visually remind us, Little Red may be reborn (depending on which version you choose). The house space was influenced by Robert Venturi's Mother's House near Philadelphia, designed in 1959 and completed in 1964, thus connecting a classic fairy tale to modern architecture and demonstrating the continual pull of the fairy tale in contemporary life. Mary English and Xavier Vendrell imagine "Little Red Riding Hood" as comprising multiple spaces, both inner and outer (English and Vendrell 2018). Kate Bernheimer suggests that the architectural spaces concretely capture the essence of the fairy tale: "girl, wolf, woods."

Kate Bernheimer and Andrew Bernheimer write about the Fairy Tale Architecture project, which contextualizes their project with the history of the fairy tale:

> Fairy tales have transfixed readers for thousands of years, and for many reasons; one of the most compelling is the promise of a magical home. How many architects, young and old, have been inspired by a hero or heroine who must imagine new realms and new spaces—new ways of being in this strange world? Houses in fairy tales are never just houses; they always contain secrets and dreams. This project presents a new path of inquiry, a new line of flight into architecture as a fantastic, literary realm of becoming.
>
> (Bernheimer and Bernheimer 2018)

One final example that connects the fairy tale to unique spaces can be seen in Shaun Tan's *The Singing Bones* (2016) where Tan creates three-dimensional sculptures to evoke the essence of particular fairy tales. In "Little Red Cap" he has a seemingly gentle wolf looking at Red as she stands on his back near his tail, looking at his eyes and snout (Tan 2016; Figure 6.2). Yet the brief narrative—which reduces the tale to "girl" and "wolf"—ends with the classic lines from the Charles Perrault version: "The better to eat you with!" Neil Gaiman writes in the foreword to the book that Tan's sculptures evoke "a tactile quality ... [that] feel primal, as if they were made in a long-ago age of the world, when the stories were first being shaped, and that perhaps the sculptures came first" (Gaiman 2016: 2). Tan's sculpture would fit comfortably in the imagined Grandmother's house conceived by English and Vendrell.

That *Flatland* appears as one of the fairy-tale appropriations for the Fairy Tale Architecture project suggests—as Abbott, MacDonald, and Wells intimate—that fairy tales and romances are concerned with imaginative spaces that go beyond our known world. These modes evoke a version of the space-time continuum that physicists argue allows for a better understanding of the macro- and microscopic workings of the universe. For that last statement to make sense, though, we need to explore how space and time are intertwined in the fairy tale.

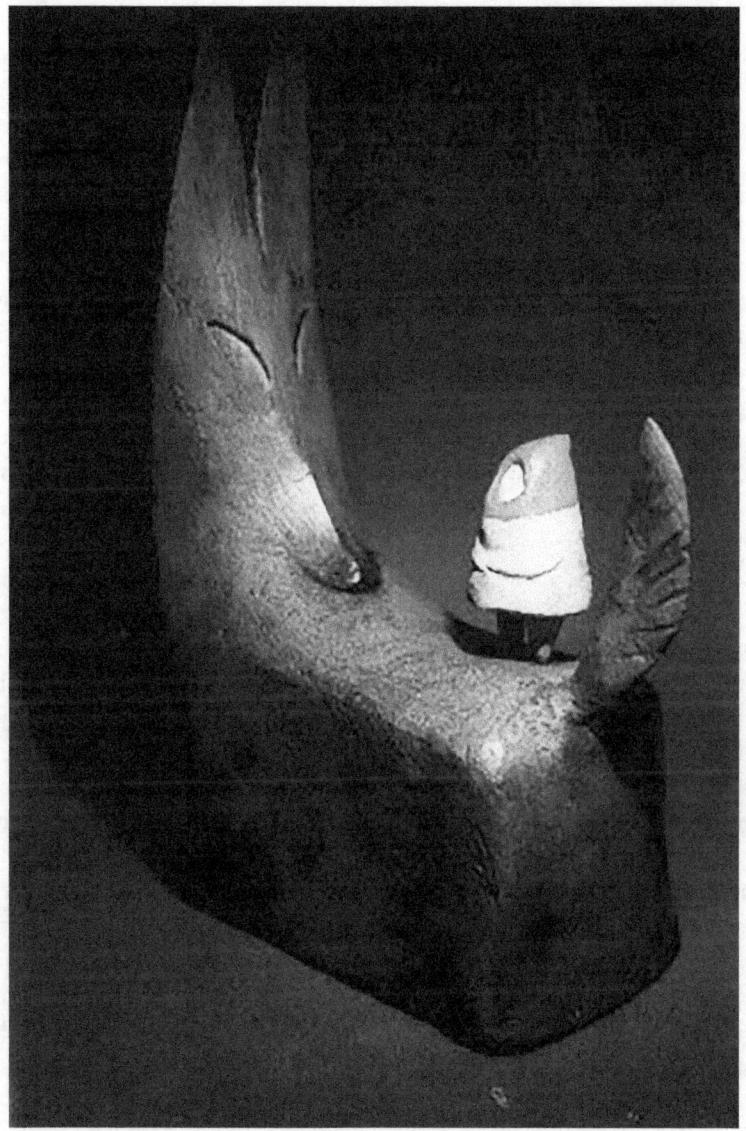

FIGURE 6.2: "Little Red Cap," from Shaun Tan, *The Singing Bones* (2015). Reproduced with the permission of Scholastic, Inc.

Gaston Bachelard in *The Poetics of Space* (1964) examines how poetic images become "quite simple images of *felicitous space* …. They [these spaces] seek to determine the human value of the sorts of space that may be grasped, that may be defended against adverse forces, the space we love" ([1958] 1964: xxxv; emphasis in the original). Bachelard's spaces—which include houses, cellars, garrets, huts, drawers, chests, wardrobes, nests, shells, corners, forests, and doors (any enclosure, it seems)—all appear in fairy tales and comprise what he argues about space generally as "the dialectics of outside and inside" (211), where "everything is circuitous, roundabout, recurrent, so much talk; a chaplet of sojournings, a refrain with endless verses" (214). "Once upon a time" and "they lived happily ever after," those proverbial phrases often used to structure fairy tales, create these internal and external felicitous spaces, like Little Red in the wolf's belly or atop the wolf's back as seen in Figures 6.1 and 6.2. Space in fairy tales can be comforting and menacing simultaneously—in the Grimms' version the wolf's belly becomes a womb space that regenerates Little Red and her grandmother. Christopher Clausen describes this tension as *home* and *away*, where the home space is primarily a child's space of safety and comfort, the away space an escape from home (Clausen 1982). In this way, the fairy tales appeals to both the child (*home*) and the adult and younger reader (*away*). Bachelard ends his study with a short chapter "The Phenomenology of Roundness" ([1958] 1964: 232), which describes the "hypnotic power" of such images—or poetry—of spaces: "Suddenly we find ourselves entirely in the roundness of this being [of space], [as] we live in the roundness of life …. A philosopher, a painter, a poet and an inventor of fables have given us documents of pure phenomenology" (234). Bachelard's roundness complements the suggestion that a fairy tale's time and space connection creates a fullness of narrative. Consequently, the variety of spaces and places evoked in fairy tales provide concrete ways for readers to structure their reading experiences that might reflect, in such seemingly simple tales, the complexities of the physical struggle to survive and the internal fear and fascination made external by the variety of these struggles presented.

Space and time, we are continually reminded as we read fairy tales, are intertwined, for space is often situated in a past time that defines a particular place, described by Bachelard as "roundness" reflected in the very form of the fairy tale itself: "once" and "happily ever after." In "Forms of Time and of the Chronotope in the Novel," from *The Dialogic Imagination* (1981), Mikhail Bakhtin posits that the *chronotope* ("'time space'") reflects "the intrinsic connectedness of temporal and spatial relationships that are artistically expressed in literature" (1981a: 84). For Bakhtin, time in literature "thickens, takes on flesh, becomes artistically visible" (84). Such a claim is important to the fairy tale: the sparseness of the fairy-tale setting, plot, characters—those very elements of these tales—become "thickened" or fleshed out because time is a central component to the fundamental operation of the fairy tale.

Readers are familiar with the physical spaces that fairy tales use to structure action. Readers are also familiar with the element of time that is the foundation to these spaces. A few examples illustrate the connection of the space-time continuum in fairy tales. Domestic spaces are central to many tales: the house and hearth, which can be spaces of comfort or unease, as seen, for example, in "Sleeping Beauty" and "Hansel and Gretel." These tales are foundational to the fairy-tale canon, having become timeless tales that continue to resonate. Castles and towers also play significant roles, for many of the so-called classic tales that define the foundation of fairy tales are aristocratic in setting and concern kings and queens, princes and princesses. "Beauty and the Beast" and "Sleeping Beauty" make castles central, this last tale suspending time in its castle. Relatedly, forbidden rooms and imprisoning towers suggest taboo or dangerous places: "Bluebeard" and "Rapunzel" are classic examples. And going into the woods is also a device, making forests a central narrative space that can be foreboding or liberating. "Little Red Riding Hood" encounters the dangers of the forest by meeting the wolf—in Perrault's version she is punished for going off the path, the moral of the tale warning young women to be fearful of the woods (an *away* space) where men lurk in wolves' skins. In the Brothers Grimm's "Little Red Cap," the womb space of the wolf returns Red and her grandmother to the *home* space, but only after they are saved by a male woodcutter. (Gender is an important space in fairy tales, discussed in Chapter 3, this volume.) In "Snow White" the Queen orders a servant to take Snow White into the forest to be killed, but he spares her and she wanders to find the dwarfs' compact house. "Beauty and the Beast" ties all these spaces together: the father must leave the home to attend to business, he wanders through a forest on his journey home, he encounters the castle of the Beast, and he picks a rose for Beauty, creating the central conflict in the tale. Fairy tales of the nineteenth century will engage in these fairy-tale trope spaces in a myriad of ways.

Foundational Spaces

The long nineteenth century is often seen as the golden age of the fairy tale. Humphrey Carpenter contends that the garden is a central metaphorical space to capture the spirit of a "golden-age" of children's literature that defines this period. He writes:

> While it [the fantastic strain, which includes fairy tales] was not overtly "realistic" and purported to have nothing to say about the "real" world, in this fantastic strain of writing may be found some profound observations about human character and contemporary society, and (strikingly often) about religions. It dealt largely with utopias, and posited the existence of Arcadian societies remote from the nature and concerns of the everyday world; yet in doing this it was commenting, often satirically and critically, on real life.
>
> (Carpenter 1985: 16)

Carpenter's "yet" in the last sentence is central to the thesis of this entry: that fairy tales occupy spaces that are simultaneously timeless and timely.

The blossoming of the fairy tale in the nineteenth century did not happen in isolation, for these writers were influenced by the variety of fairy tales that were being released from diverse cultures and editorial enterprises. These writers can be called key foundational writers, who defined foundational fairy-tale spaces that inspired Victorian writers and beyond to explore the potential of the fairy tale for children and adults. When George MacDonald begins "The Light Princess" with a christening that goes wrong, as a powerful sorcerer is forgotten to be invited, he is evoking Charles Perrault's "Sleeping Beauty" and the Brothers Grimm's "Briar Rose." In *Once Upon a Time: A Short History of Fairy Tale* (2014), Marina Warner asks readers to "imagine the history of fairy tale as map." She then asks,

> Unfurl this imaginary terrain in your mind's eye, and you will see two prominent landmarks, Charles Perrault's *Histoires ou contes du temps passé* (Tales of Olden Times, 1697) and a little nearer in the foreground, the Grimm Brothers' *Kinder- und Hausmärchen* (Children's and Household Tales, 1812–57). These collections dominate their surroundings so imposingly that they make it hard to pick out other features near or far.
>
> (Warner 2014: xiii)

But Warner's sight is fine, and she is able to read her map in more detail, as she includes a variety of geographical spaces that include *The Tales of the Thousand and One Nights*, Hans Christian Andersen, Russian spaces that include Baba Yaga and Vasilissa the Beautiful, and the ocean that includes Salman Rushdie and *Haroun and the Sea of Stories* (1990). The fairy tale, while an elusive entity, is past, present, and future. The classic fairy tales provide a foundational cartography for writers to redraw their fantastic creations during the nineteenth century. As with the MacDonald example above, the classic fairy tales also become an intertextual space, where the fairy-tale writer expects the reader to understand the intertextual play that a fairy tale may be making.

Warner's map extends to places ordinarily seen as hostile spaces to fairy tales—the realm of realism, particularly as related to the nineteenth century's penchant for social realism. Harry Stone maps a bit of a different route. In *Dickens and the Invisible World* (1979) Stone argues that Charles Dickens appropriated fairy-tale motifs in most of his novels, having read from youth a variety of tales from Perrault and Madame d'Aulnoy to *The Arabian Nights*. For Stone, Dickens's brand of social realism is contingent on the fantastic to bring fullness to his narrative world. To Dickens, it seems, a fairy tale is as real as any story. In fact, Dickens once quipped that he wished he could have married Little Red Riding Hood! Dickens also admired Hans Christian Andersen, even inviting the Dane to stay with him, where Andersen proceeded to wear out his welcome. Dickens had a spat with his former illustrator George Cruikshank (who had illustrated an edition of Grimm) for writing didactic tales. In "Frauds on the Fairies" (1853) Dickens argues for letting the tales speak for themselves. Even John Ruskin, the preeminent art and social critic, dabbled with one fairy tale and wrote about them positively. The fairy tales of the past permeated the long nineteenth century.

The fairy-tale influence on novels ostensibly seen as primarily realistic in the nineteenth century also led to some of the most memorable full-length fantasies often labeled as fairy tales because they defy easy categorization: George MacDonald's *Phantastes* (1858), *At the Back of the North Wind* (1871), *The Princess and the Goblin* (1872), *The Princess and Curdie* (1883), and *Lilith* (1895); Charles Kingsley's *The Water-Babies* (1863); Lewis Carroll's *Alice's Adventures in Wonderland* (1865) and *Through the Looking-Glass* (1872); Jean Ingelow's *Mopsa the Fairy* (1869); William Morris's *The Wood Beyond the World* (1894) and *The Well at the World's End* (1896); L. Frank Baum's *Wonderful Wizard of Oz* (1900); E. Nesbit's *The Story of the Amulet* (1906); Kenneth Grahame's *The Wind in the Willows* (1908); and J. M. Barrie's *Peter and Wendy* (1911). These longer works of secondary-world fantasy became the basis of modern fantasy, a genre made popular by J. R. R. Tolkien and C. S. Lewis, both writers influenced by the Victorian George MacDonald.

The rise of the fairy tale in the long nineteenth century did not happen in isolation: writers were guided by some foundational maps as they created unique fairy-tale spaces that comprise this golden age.

INFLUENTIAL MAPS FOR FAIRY-TALE SPACES

Italian and French fairy-tale writers provided an early map for Victorian writers to use to navigate various fairy-tale spaces. In Italy Giovan Francesco Straparola (1480–1558) and Giambattista Basile (1575–1632) were important influences. In France, one of the most influential writers to define the fairy-tale tradition was Charles Perrault (1628–1703), who wanted to revise fairy tales to advance a more modern sensibility, which reflected the debate in France over the ancients and the moderns. That Perrault retold folk and fairy tales suggests the importance that he put onto these tales, for he believed that myths could promote the modern sensibility of enlightenment. His *History of Past Times* (1697) included updated versions of "Sleeping Beauty," "Little Red Riding Hood," "Bluebeard," "Little Tom Thumb," and "Puss in Boots." Other key writers from France include Marie-Catherine d'Aulnoy (1650/1–1705), Gabrielle-Suzanne Barbot de Villeneuve (1685–1755), who published an extensive version of "Beauty and the Beast" (1740), which was adapted by Mme Leprince de Beaumont (1711–80) and has become the most famous version in the world, the inspiration for Disney's two versions of *Beauty and the Beast*.

The Brothers Grimm and the German Romantics: Physical and Liminal Spaces

One could argue that the most influential fairy-tale spaces can be centered around the following: the Brothers Grimm and the German Romantic writers, Hans Christian Andersen, and *The Arabian Nights*, which brought an exoticism to the fairy-tale genre.

The Brothers Grimm have become synonymous with fairy tales, so much that they have become cultural icons—Grimm fairy-tale tours in Germany take visitors to the castles that may have inspired the tales, journeys through the Black Forest, even tracing the routes that the Grimms used to collect the fairy tales. History tells us, however, that the Grimms did not necessarily travel the countryside recording folk tales—instead, as good collectors, they invited people to their offices to recite these tales. Whatever is the reality, the fact is that the Brothers Grimm created popular renditions of fairy tales and a mythology of this tradition.

Jacob (1785–1863) and Wilhelm (1786–1859) were interested in linguistics and the German language and dedicated their lives to documenting the importance of the German literary and linguistic tradition. One of their major undertakings was the *German Dictionary*, which first appeared in 1854. But their most famous work by far is the collection of fairy tales that they collected and edited throughout their lives. *Children's and Household Tales* went through multiple editions from 1812 to 1864 and included many fairy tales that have become cultural touchstones: "Rapunzel," "Hansel and Gretel," "Cinderella," "The Twelve Brothers," "Little Red Riding Hood," "The Elves," "The Robber Bridegroom," "Briar Rose," "Rumpelstiltskin," "The Goose Girl," "The Singing Bone," to name only a select few. The importance of the Grimm fairy tales became more manifest with Edgar Taylor's translation *German Popular Stories* (1823), with illustrations by George Cruikshank. John Ruskin, the preeminent art and social critic of the Victorian period, provides a defense of fairy tales in "Fairy Stories" (1868), which uses Cruikshank's illustrations to Taylor's translation to highlight "the power of genuine imaginative work" that is both the fairy tale and the illustrations (Ruskin [1868] 1905: 239).

Though the Grimms are the most influential German writers in the fairy-tale tradition, other German Romantic writers also were significant to the tradition, particularly creating fairy tales that were more expansive in scope and more centered on the mingling of the quotidian with the mystical and magical. The German Romantics lauded individual liberty, the longing for the unattainable—what C. S. Lewis would examine as *Sehnsucht*—journeys into the unconsciousness, and the desire to evoke a sense of the uncanny. As important, though, was the German Romantics' penchant for blurring the real with the fantastic, paving the way for the fascination with liminal spaces by the Victorian writers. Friedrich von Hardenberg (Novalis) (1772–1801), Ludwig Tieck (1773–1853), E. T. A. Hoffmann (1776–1822), and Friedrich de la Motte Fouqué (1777–1843) merit mention. Novalis's most famous work may be *Heinrich von Ofterdingen* (1802), a fantastical romance that concerns a young poet in search of love, who has a series of dream visions. Novalis believed in the power of the imagination and believed that fairy tales had the power to transform—the fairy tale could be a well-wrought literary form designed for sophisticated audiences. Novalis also promoted a radical aesthetic of the fairy tale that George MacDonald included at the beginning of his fairy romance *Phantastes* (1858). Novalis argues that a fairy tale should align itself with chaos, like a dream or a musical sonata, and defy rationality. As he writes: "In fairy-story the time of anarchy, lawlessness, freedom, the natural state of Nature makes itself felt in the world" (Novalis 2017: 198), pinpointing how *time* is intricately connected to *space*, which was often liminal. Ludwig Tieck also saw the potential in fairy tales and was influenced by folktales. As a playwright he retold the classics "Puss in Boots" (1797), "Bluebeard" (1797), and "Little Red Riding Hood" (1800), by bringing a self-consciousness to these adaptations and often a satirical tone. Hoffmann may be the most famous of these German Romantic writers, partly because Sigmund Freud focused on one of Hoffmann's tales to discuss his psychoanalytic theory—"The Sandman" (1816), a tale that blended the fantastic with the realistic to evoke a hesitant sense of the uncanny. But more important, Hoffmann wrote "Nutcracker and the Mouse-King" (1816), which became a Tchaikovsky ballet and perennial Christmas-time favorite. Finally, Fouqué's *Undine* (1811), a mermaid/water-spirit tale, influenced both Hans Christian Andersen and George MacDonald, and was adapted into an opera by E. T. A. Hoffmann in 1816. These German Romantic writers instilled in the fairy tale a space where other writers could explore the liminal, the space that blurred the real with the fantastic. In *The Fantastic: A Structural Approach to a Literary Genre*, Tzvetan Todorov argues that "the fantastic occupies the duration of this uncertainty. Once we choose one answer or the other, we leave the fantastic for a neighboring genre, the uncanny or the marvelous. The fantastic is that hesitation experienced by a person who knows only the laws of nature, confronting an apparently supernatural event" (Todorov 1975: 25). These liminal spaces of the German Romantic writers create, to a degree, the hesitation that occupies the fantastic. Todorov, however, implies that most fairy tales accept or explain the fantastic mechanism, moving such tales into the uncanny or marvelous categories.

Hans Christian Andersen and the Space of Original Invention

Hans Christian Andersen (1805–75), a Danish writer, is often seen as the most important writer of original fairy tales of the nineteenth century. While Perrault and the Grimm Brothers were retelling stories that were part of the oral folktale tradition, Andersen, while often influenced by the oral tales of his culture, created stories from the detritus of common life, imbuing inanimate objects with magical properties to capture his unique view of life that was ironic, melancholic, pessimistic, and primarily tragic. Andersen's fairy tales pushed the proverbial "happily ever after" ending of fairy tales into a new direction. That his autobiography is titled *The Fairy Tale of My Life* (1847) suggests that Andersen was conscious of his importance to the fairy-tale tradition. Andersen called his tales *eventyr*, which is translated into English as *fairy tale*. He published four volumes: *Fairy Tales, Told for Children* (1835–42), *New Fairy Tales* (1844–8), *Stories* (1852–5), and *New Fairy Tales and Stories* (1858–72). His tales have become as iconic as those by Perrault and the Brothers Grimm. A short list of his tales include "The Little Mermaid," "The Little Match Girl," "The Ugly Duckling," "The Emperor's New Clothes," "The Princess and the Pea," "The Tinderbox," "The Steadfast Tin Soldier," "The Red Shoes," and "The Snow Queen," based on the Norse legend of the Ice Maiden. Andersen's tales first appeared in English translation in 1846, so they were readily available for the Victorians. Andersen's focus on a variety of fairy-tale spaces make his tales highly original—he could blend a fantastic liminal space in "The Snow Queen" with the domestic space of common life, as he does in "The Little Match Girl," where the bleak social space of the city transforms into a desirous world of death, where the little girl can escape her sordid living conditions.

The Arabian Nights *and Exotic Spaces*

The Arabian Nights, or *The Thousand and One Nights*, has a complicated history, as the collection contains tales from Indian, Persian, and Arabian cultures. Antoine Galland's French translation, *The Thousand and One Nights* (12 volumes, 1704–17), made the tales readily available, with a focus on genies, demons, and jinni. As Ulrich Marzolph writes: "With the tremendous success of Galland's translation, hardly a major European writer of the eighteenth and nineteenth centuries could avoid being in some way or other influenced by *Arabian Nights*" (2011: 59), which evoked a foreign and exotic space that was certainly not European. The frame device of Scheherazade spinning tales to save her life has become a central narrative technique that nineteenth-century writers used to interject fairy stories into longer narratives: Catherine Sinclair's *Holiday House* (1839), for example, used interpolated fairy tales to teach moral lessons to two rambunctious children; George MacDonald's *Adela Cathcart* (1864) incorporated fairy tales as ways to heal a young woman of ennui.

Liminal and Crossing Spaces

Whereas the forest, the castle, and the forbidden chamber are concrete spaces used in fairy tales, other spaces are more difficult to pin down, what we may call liminal spaces. Liminal spaces, according to Mihai Spariousu, are "indeterminate ontological landscapes located in between alternative worlds" (1997: 9). Victor Turner identifies a liminal space as a threshold to something other, a condition of ambiguity, where the self resides nowhere (Turner 1982). Bachelard finds doors such a space, "for the door is an entire cosmos of the Half-open ... the very origins of a daydream that accumulates desires and temptations" ([1958] 1964: 222). The German Romantic fairy-tale writers often focused on such liminality, for many of these tales were caught between the real and the fantastic or dream. In fact, George MacDonald quotes from Novalis—"Our life is no dream; but it ought to become one, and perhaps will"—in *Phantastes* (1858: 318) and his final fantasy *Lilith* ([1895] 2001). To use a phrase from Turner that echoes *Peter Pan*, each of these fantasy romances follow young men who are "betwixt and between" the real and the other: *Phantastes* finds the bedroom of the protagonist Anodos transformed into Fairy Land before his own eyes, where he must enter a world that he is not certain actually exists. In one scene an old woman warns Anodos not to open a door; but he does and acquires his shadow, which makes everything in Fairy Land that is magical mundane. His overall goal becomes to lose his shadow, a nebulous thing that in Fairy Land is a menacing entity, but in the real world a simple reflection from the sun. Something similar happens in *Lilith*, as Mr. Vane discovers that his library is connected to an alternative world of the seven dimensions, where an object can reside in two spaces simultaneously. *Phantastes* and *Lilith* are indebted to the German Romantic tradition and are geared for an adult audience, yet they use fairy-tale spaces to convey profound ideas on the nature of reality and the afterlife. Both works are quite radical, for they depict the appeal of death by depicting it as a tempting liminal space. MacDonald will do something similar in his full-length children's fantasy, *At the Back of the North Wind*.

Another fairy narrative that plays with liminal spaces is Charles Kingsley's *The Water-Babies* (1863). A young chimney sweeper, Tom, runs scared from a house that he has just swept, falls into a river, and presumably drowns. Instead, he wakes from a profound sleep to discover that he has transformed into a water-baby: "[He] found himself swimming about in the stream, being about four inches, or—that I may be accurate—3.87902 inches long" (Kingsley [1863] 2008: 76). As a water-baby Tom explores the natural realm of the stream and is guided by a variety of people and sea creatures, the most important are three motherly figures: Mrs. Bedonebyasyoudid, Mother Carey, and Mrs. Doasyouwouldbedoneby. Kingsley mingles scientific discussions with nonsense to question how science—in a world after Darwin—can also be spiritual, the liminal space of the water a way to philosophize about the new world order. Tom evolves as a water-baby and is ready to return to his world, a changed person. Kingsley adds a moral to the end, only to undercut it: "But remember always, as I told you first, that this is all a fairy tale, and only fun and pretense;

and, therefore, you are not to believe a word of it, even if it is true" (232). Tom's return to the real world demonstrates the interconnectedness of the real with the liminal. By creating this dual space of the real and the liminal, Kingsley can have readers contemplate larger spiritual and philosophical ideas. The liminal world of water raises comparisons with the cruel domestic space of child labor abuse and the clear distinction between the "haves" and the "have-nots" in Victorian England.

MacDonald's *At the Back of the North Wind* ([1871] 2011), a work geared for a younger audience, combines, like *The Water-Babies*, the social realism of a Dickens novel with fantasy as North Wind takes the main character Diamond on various journeys, including the very liminal space at the back of the north wind. MacDonald also includes an original fairy tale—"Little Daylight"—and various retellings of nursery rhymes and original nonsense verses to blur the boundaries between the real and fantastical worlds. MacDonald's intent in *North Wind* is to create a space for the most liminal world of all—that of death, which is a timeless space that is made a concrete space at the back of the north wind. He does something similar in a shorter fairy tale, "The Golden Key" (1867), which finds a young girl Tangle and boy Mossy travel to fairyland and meet a variety of sage seers on different journeys: the Old Man of the Sea, the Old Man of the Earth, the Old Man of the Fire, who is a child. In fact, when Tangle and Mossy are reunited in fairyland, they have grown old and are led into a rainbow to climb some mysterious stairs: "They knew that they were going up to the country whence the shadows fall. And by this time I think they must have got there" (Knoepflmacher 1999: 144). This shadow land, a liminal space, seems to be death, that liminal realm that in MacDonald's theology is the beginning of life. Thus we see in MacDonald how liminal spaces in fairy tales allow for abstract discussions of life and death.

Another important work that plays with the space/time elements of liminality is Jean Ingelow's *Mopsa the Fairy* (1869), which Nina Auerbach and U. C. Knoepflmacher describe as "a conscious reversal of the story of 'Sleeping Beauty'" (1992: 208). Echoing MacDonald's *Phantastes* (1858), *Mopsa* begins with a young boy Jack meeting a fairy, who tells him of a liminal world of Fairyland. An albatross agrees to take Jack to Fairyland, and the bird alludes to that great liminal poem by Coleridge, *The Rime of the Ancient Mariner*, a poem that finds the ancient mariner wandering the countryside with the goal of relating his tale of sin. The opening poem to the fantasy captures the variety of liminal spaces that Jack will encounter:

> "And can this be my own world?
> 'Tis all gold and snow
> Save where scarlet waves are hurled
> Down yon gulf below."

> "'Tis thy world, 'tis my world,
> City, mead, and shore,
> For he that hath his own world
> Hath many worlds more."
>
> (Ingelow [1869] 1992: 215)

The notion that one can "hath many worlds more" suggests that the realistic realms of "city, mead, and shore" exist in parallel to otherworldly space. When Jack reunites with Mopsa in Fairyland, he discovers that the fantastical realm operates much differently from the real word he has come from: "'That's because you've got something in your world that you call Time,' said Mopsa, 'so you talk about NOW, and you talk about THEN'" (Ingelow [1869] 1992: 270). Fairyland's timeless world confounds Jack as he returns home and Mopsa gains power as the ruler of Fairyland. Jack soon forgets about Fairyland since "it was a long time ago." Yet Mopsa remembers: "You know that your people say there was a time when there were none of them in the world—a time before they were made. Well, THIS is that time. This is long ago" (270). Auerbach and Knoepflmacher argue that Ingelow revises the liminal space of such writers as Lewis Carroll by gendering that very space: instead of perpetuating the innocence of Alice, which Carroll is fixated on, Ingelow focuses on the importance of Mopsa's growth: "As Ingelow implies, Victorian boys who grew into men found it easier to forget what could not be ignored by girls, who, by growing into women, became more acutely conscious of an impairment of their former freedom" (Auerbach and Knoepflmacher 1992: 210). At the end of *Mopsa the Fairy*, Mopsa rules the liminal world of Fairyland, the world of the timeless, a world much older than even Adam and Eve—the liminal space of Fairyland remains alive as a gendered space.

MacDonald's friend Lewis Carroll does something different, as Auerbach and Knoepflmacher attest. In *Alice's Adventures in Wonderland* ([1865] 2013) and *Through the Looking-Glass* (1872) Carroll creates liminal spaces for Alice to explore her identity. In her first adventure, Alice tumbles down a rabbit hole and enters Wonderland, a topsy-turvy world that Alice must navigate. The rules of Alice's "real" world no longer hold true in Wonderland—she encounters fantastical creatures, including those from various nursery rhymes. While in Wonderland Alice recognizes the absurdity of her own world as she journeys through a world of nonsense. In Looking-Glass Land, Alice recognizes that a mirror, or looking glass, reflects an alternative world, equally as nonsensical as Wonderland. At the end of this adventure, Alice becomes Queen Alice and returns to her Victorian world by waking from a dream. While Carroll uses the dream mechanism as a device that gets Alice delivered to the fantastical realms, the dreams are spaces of the liminal, recalling Novalis's desire that the dreamworld replace the real.

Christina Rossetti in *Speaking Likenesses* ([1874] 1992) directly responds to Carroll's fantastical worlds, with the intention, it appears, to create a liminal space that teases out the implication of childhood and adulthood while simultaneously centering the liminal space in the domestic. Whereas Carroll allows Alice agency in Wonderland and Looking-Glass Land, he keeps her a perpetual child, much like Peter Pan, Rossetti is more interested in interrogating the liminal space between child and adult. In *Space and Place in Children's Literature, 1789 to the Present*, Maria Sachiko Cecire, Hannah Field, Kavita Mudan Finn, and Maline Roy argue that children's literature creates "a conceptual space of childhood" (2015: 1). Peter Hunt in "Unstable Metaphors: Symbolic Spaces and Specific Places" suggests children's literature becomes a "negotiation" (Hunt 2015: 21) between the adult writer and the child reader to create a space where children can enjoy autonomy while being directed by an adult (24). While many fairy tales—particularly those of Perrault and the Brothers Grimm—were not originally conceived as being solely for children, many of the Victorian fairy tales were, with Carroll's Alice books and Rossetti's *Speaking Likenesses* as prime examples. Rossetti's liminal world is created by the domestic spaces where knitting accompanied by storytelling transports the reader to fantastical worlds that allow characters to play out their desires. Like Carroll's dream mechanism in the Alice books, Rossetti had her first character Flora, celebrating her eighth birthday, enter a violent fantastical realm that seems a mirror inversion of Wonderland. The difference between the two works is that Rossetti uses a frame story to transport her characters to the liminal space: the aunt tells three stories to her nieces. Each tale in *Speaking Likenesses* uses violence and aggression to demonstrate to readers that the transition from childhood to adulthood is cruel, probably responding to Carroll's more benign world of Wonderland and Looking-Glass Land, where danger is mostly hinted at. The final story about Maggie has her finding a wounded woodpigeon nearly frozen to death; she nurses the bird back to life, rescues a kitten and puppy, both of which seem destined for death without her help. With her companions she journeys forward, sees the glowing of the northern lights (a literal liminal space), and spots a door that returns her to her "familiar step and bell of home" (Rossetti [1874] 1992: 359). With echoes of MacDonald's *At the Back of the North Wind*, Rossetti's tale creates a liminal fantasy world that depicts the struggles between that child and adult—and the reality that any transition from child to adult will lead to the ultimately liminal space of death, a timeless space.

A final example of a liminal space is J. M. Barrie's *Peter Pan*. For the purposes of this study, *Peter Pan* will refer to the 1911 novelization of the play *Peter and Wendy* and "Peter Pan in Kensington Gardens" (1906), a version of this tale also appearing in *The Little White Bird* (1902). In "Peter Pan in Kensington Gardens" the reader finds Peter Pan caught in the liminal realm that the bird Solomon

Caw calls "Betwixt-and-Between" (Barrie [1911] 2004: 172)—after Lock-Out Time, Peter cannot return to his family and can never grow up. He is stuck in a state of limbo. In *Peter and Wendy* Barrie fills out the narrative of Neverland, the liminal space that Peter and the Lost Boys reside, a place "second to the right, and straight on till morning" (35). The opening chapter is called "Peter Breaks Through," which suggests that Peter resides in an alternative reality. Mrs. Darling tidies up the minds of her children each evening, suggesting that their dreams access that alternative space and provide a way for Peter to break through. Neverland is a world of desire, or potential, but a space that does not allow for maturation—once one leaves Neverland, once one grows up, one can never return, being in a different Lock-Out Time. The novel paints Peter as a tragic figure, one that remains youthful as the world ages and dies, including Wendy, Jane, and the Lost Boys, who leave Neverland for Victorian England. At one point in the novel Peter exclaims: "To die will be an awfully big adventure" (84). Yet Peter, stuck in Neverland, can never go on that adventure.

UTOPIAN AND ARCADIAN SPACES

Thomas More's *Utopia* (1516) asked readers to envision a perfect world, one that operated on communal agreement of societal principles that ranged from politics, family governance, to education. Utopia, this "nowhere" island, has been appropriated by fairy-tale writers of the nineteenth century to push the fairy tale into social and political spaces. An important early tale is by John Ruskin (1819–1900), who took the fairy tale seriously, as attested to by his essay "Fairy Stories" (1868), which lauded the significance of the Grimms' fairy tales and the illustrations by George Cruikshank. Ruskin's "The King of the Golden River" was written in 1841 for twelve-year-old Effie Gray, and was eventually published in 1851. Ruskin's tale demonstrates the evils of greed and self-interest that he felt permeated Victorian society; he envisioned in the tale a utopian world of the Treasure Valley and the Golden River where "the Treasure Valley became a garden again, and the inheritance, which had been lost by cruelty, was regained by love" (Ruskin [1851] 1987: 36). Jules Zanger contends that Ruskin's tales are somewhat "burdened by a great deal of fairly transparent allegorizing and overt moralizing" (1977: 154) about the need for a return to a nostalgic ideal agrarian past.

Ruskin's friend and confidant George MacDonald was also influenced by utopian zeal in some of his tales. "The Golden Key" finds the two characters Mossy and Tangle climbing the stairs to some utopian world where men and women will be on equal footing. "The Light Princess" (1864), a comic tale that inverts many fairy-tale conventions, concerns a young princess who has lost her gravity, thus is unable to confront the world with any seriousness (gravity) and unable to be tethered to the ground since she has no gravity. The tale shows how compassion can create a more perfect world, as the prince sacrifices himself to save the princess who, in turn, gains her gravity and saves the prince, leading to a happy ending. "The Light Princess" posits a utopian goal of gender equality, while framing the tale within the fairy-tale world of kings and queens, princesses and princes. For MacDonald, this utopian impulse can also be found in *At the Back of the North Wind*, which uses the liminal space to imagine a utopian world beyond the real world of our senses. Yet MacDonald did not always evoke a utopian and Arcadian space through a happily-ever-after ending. In *The Princess and Curdie* (1881), a veiled response to Ruskin's utopian world in "The King of the Golden River," MacDonald finds that greed will win out. Though the protagonists Irene and Curdie from *The Princess and the Goblin* (1872) return and marry and become King and Queen, they have no children, reflective of the sterile greed of the kingdom Gwntystorm. At the end of *Curdie*, the King and Queen die, leave no heir, and an earthquake destroys the kingdom, with a flicker of hope that "all round spreads a wilderness of wild deer, and the very name of Gwyntystorm has ceased from the lips of men" (MacDonald [1871, 1881] 1990: 256). Here MacDonald proposes a utopian space without humans, which raises the question: is *Curdie* a pessimistic tale about humanity or an uplifting eco-tale about nature's healing powers?

William Morris (1834–96) is normally not seen as a writer of fairy tales, but his utopian romances *News From Nowhere* (1891) and *The Well at the World's End* (1896) follow in the movement of the fairy tale to morph into longer fantasy narratives. These works envision utopian spaces that mirror the Christian Socialist movement that gained traction during the nineteenth century. His collection of poems *The Earthly Paradise* (1868–70) focuses on the myths of Greece and Scandinavia, suggesting ideal worlds from past myths. An interesting connection is that Morris's house in Hammersmith was named Kelmscott Manor, a site that helped define the utopian spirit of the Arts and Crafts movement; Morris moved into the house, which was owned previously by George MacDonald, then called The Retreat. Both men imagined their domestic spaces as a kind of utopian retreat. Morris, who founded the Kelmscott Press at his home, creates a utopian space for the book: *The Wood Beyond the World* returns to an archaic past of bookmaking, rejecting the mass-market production of books during the nineteenth century. In a sense, *The Wood Beyond the World* is a material object that reflects Morris's utopian zeal—the utopian fantasy reflects a long-ago past that is no longer reflected in the market conditions of the Victorian age (Figure 6.3).

Oscar Wilde (1854–1900) was also influenced by John Ruskin's focus on social issues of the day; he was also influenced by Walter Horatio Pater's argument for art for art's sake philosophy. Wilde published two collections of fairy tales—*The Happy Prince and Other Tales* (1888) and *The House of Pomegranates* (1891)—which suggested that the world could be improved by

FIGURE 6.3: Illustration by Edward Burne Jones from William Morris, *The Wood Beyond the World* (Kelmscott edition, 1894). Public Domain.

embracing the spirit of Christian Socialism that Wilde defined in *The Soul of Man Under Socialism* (1891). In that work, Wilde argues that to make socialism human is simply to follow the ways of Christ, an anti-authoritarian figure who shows the way to a new kind of utopia. "The Selfish Giant" and "The Happy Prince," from his first collection, capture his approach. In the first tale, a selfish giant prohibits young children from playing in his garden; only when he sees the error of his ways does the garden blossom again, as he sacrifices himself for the children—the tale follows a fairly obvious connection to Christ's story. "The Selfish Giant" reimagines a new Eden where death leads to resurrection of the innocence of childhood. In "The Happy Prince" we see a society that never achieves a semblance of a more perfect world, except for the love a little swallow has for the Happy Prince, a statue, who asks the bird to distribute his jewels that adorn him to those in need—a struggling playwright and a young match-girl (a direct reference to the influence Andersen had on the tale) as two examples. The love the swallow has for the Happy Prince leads to the bird's death, as he freezes to death, and the melting down of the statue since the city fids it no longer beautiful. The unhappy ending reminds readers of the importance of Christian love—and of earthly love between the bird and the statue, a veiled attempt of Wilde to imagine a world where humans can love one another, regardless of sexual preference. The city in "The Happy Prince" reflects the jaded world of human greed and pride that is balanced by the hope that in the future a world of love and compassion will prevail.

Any discussion of fairy tales and utopian space would be incomplete without mention of L. Frank Baum, the creator of the Oz series. Michael Patrick Hearn writes that Baum's *The Wonderful Wizard of Oz* (1900) "has entered American folklore" (Hearn 2000: xiii), with help, of course, from the iconic 1939 MGM musical starring Judy Garland. In *The Wonderful Wizard of Oz* the young protagonist Dorothy is trapped in the gray, dusty world of Kansas, only to escape by having a tornado uplift her house and drop it into Oz. There she meets various creatures, the most famous being the Scarecrow, the Tin Man, and the Cowardly Lion, as well as the Good Witch of the North and the Wicked Witch of the West. Dorothy's quest is to help her companions get a brain, a heart, and courage from the great wizard Oz, and for Dorothy to find her way home, for the domestic space is like no place else. However, Baum eventually reminds the readers of the limits of America, and in *The Emerald City of Oz* (1910), the sixth of the fourteen volumes, Dorothy embraces the socialist utopia of Oz, overseen by Princess Ozma. Baum has Dorothy emigrate to Oz, leaving America—she has no desire to return to her home space because the utopian impulse that drives Oz is much more appealing.

ILLUSTRATIVE SPACES

Illustrations provide a visual commentary or supplement of a written work. Illustrators of fairy tales become collaborators since their illustrations add depth to a narrative by fusing the verbal with the visual. George Cruikshank's illustrations to the 1823 translation of the Grimm's fairy tales by Edgar Taylor depicted the importance of illustrations and paintings to capture the fairy-tale spirit. Cruikshank went on to illustrate his own didactic fairy tales, though the popularity of his illustrations and his tales waned after Dickens's attack in "Frauds on the Fairies." Richard Doyle (1824–83) illustrated John Ruskin's "The King of the Golden River." That Ruskin viewed fairy-tale illustrations as a legitimate form of art help lead to the acceptance of fairy-tale art.

The most famous collaboration is between John Tenniel (1820–1914) and Lewis Carroll. Tenniel was a satirist for *Punch* magazine, and he found in Carroll's nonsensical, absurdist world in *Alice's Adventures in Wonderland* and *Through the Looking-Glass* a space for his satiric spirit. Tenniel's illustrations are simultaneously humorous and grotesquely exaggerated, capturing the absurdity and danger of Alice's adventure. In one of the most famous illustrations for the Mad Tea Party, Tenniel creates a Victorian space that should reflect civilized society—a tea party. In the illustration, however, chaos reigns as Alice tries

FIGURE 6.4: Illustration by Arthur Hughes from George MacDonald, *At the Back of the North Wind* (1871). Public Domain.

to take the animal partygoers seriously, thus undercutting any clear message a reader may be expecting.

Another productive collaboration was between George MacDonald and Arthur Hughes (1831–1915). Hughes, who was associated briefly with the Pre-Raphaelite Brotherhood, illustrated *Dealings with the Fairies* (1867), *At the Back of the North Wind* (1871), and *The Princess and the Goblin* (1872). Hughes also did illustrations for the 1905 edition of *Phantastes*, commissioned by George's son Greville. *At the Back of the North Wind* intertwines a realistic narrative of the young protagonist Diamond who navigates a harsh London with the fantastic journeys he takes with the supernatural North Wind. The illustration in Figure 6.4 defines clearly the space between the real and the fantastic—North Wind could easily be in a Pre-Raphaelite portrait, and Diamond from an illustration in a Dickens novel. But North Wind's extraordinary hair that embraces Diamond creates a space that is both real and fantastic, precisely matching the narrative technique of the novel.

One of the most infamous artists of faery is Richard Dadd (1817–86). The infamy resides in the fact that Dadd stabbed his father to death in 1843, convinced that his father was the Devil incarnate. Dadd was institutionalized in mental hospitals, where he concentrated on his paintings. His most famous is *The Fairy Feller's Master-Stroke*, which he worked on from 1855 to 1864. Other significant paintings include *The Haunt of the Fairies* (1841), *Titania Sleeping* (1841), and *Contradictions: Oberon and Titania* (1854–8).

As much of Dadd's work suggests, Shakespeare was a popular topic for fairy-tale painting, the two most illustrated plays being *A Midsummer's Night Dream* and *The Tempest*. Gustave Doré (1832–83), from France, illustrated

FIGURE 6.5: Gustave Doré, "Little Red Riding Hood" (1864). Public Domain.

The Tempest in 1860, as well as the tales of Perrault in 1862. His illustration for "Little Red Riding Hood" is iconic: Doré foregrounds the sexuality of Perrault's version by making it visual and a bit disconcerting (Figure 6.5). One of the most famous Freudian studies of fairy tales is Bruno Bettelheim's *The Uses of Enchantment* (1976). Bettelheim believed that the Grimms' version of "Little Red Cap" provided children with a needed happy ending of rebirth and resurrection of Little Red and the grandmother—Perrault's version ends with the grandmother and Little Red devoured by the wolf, a much more sexualized version. Doré's illustration makes the domestic space dangerous.

Other artists of note who concentrated on illustrating and painting fairy tales include Joseph Noel Paton (1821–1901), who was asked to illustrate *Through the Looking-Glass* but suggested Tenniel continue from *Alice*; John Anster Fitzgerald (1832–1906); John Atkinson Grimshaw (1836–93); Walter Crane (1845–1915); Kate Greenaway (1846–1901), who John Ruskin admired; Arthur Rackham (1867–1939); and Edmund Dulac (1882–1953).

MODERN AND AESTHETIC SPACES

The fairy tale occupied a significant place in the literature that was created during the nineteenth century. Yet the fantastic itself seems to exist in a liminal space in the canon of Victorian literature. *The Norton Anthology of English Literature: The Victorian Age* (10th edition, 2018), for example, has no space for the fairy tale or fantastic, beyond Christina Rossetti's *Goblin Market* and an excerpt from Lewis Carroll's *Alice's Adventures in Wonderland*—as an example of grappling with educational policies of the period. Oscar Wilde, of course, is represented by various poems and the play *The Importance of Being Earnest*, but not by one of his fairy tales. While the editors are willing to shun this rich fairy-tale tradition of the nineteenth century, they did find space to include "The Speckled Band," a detective story by Arthur Conan Doyle. As a fringe genre, the detective story is cemented in the real, with reasoned observation driving the Sherlock Holmes narrative. The follow-up volume, *The Twentieth and Twenty-First Centuries* (2018), has no writer of the fantastic represented, though two writers continue to dominate reading tastes, C. S. Lewis and J. R. R. Tolkien, who followed in the tradition of the great fairy-tale writers. One can forecast that Philip Pullman and J. K. Rowling, the two most influential contemporary practitioners of the fantastic, will find a similar fate in updated Norton anthologies. Lewis claimed that his reading of MacDonald's *Phantastes* "baptized" his imagination, while Tolkien wrote in his influential "On Fairy-Stories" that MacDonald's great feat was his ability to describe the realm of death, the ultimate liminal space. T. S. Eliot owned a copy of MacDonald's edited anthology *England's Antiphon* (1868) and appears to have read some of the fairy tales; W. H. Auden wrote an afterword to Maurice Sendak's illustrated edition of *The Golden Key* (1967). Eliot and Auden are two of the major poets of the twentieth century and found uses for the enchantment in fairy tales. The golden age of the fairy tale during the nineteenth century did not disappear during the long nineteenth century, so it might be productive to examine briefly the transitional spaces that fairy-tale writers used to usher in the twentieth century.

L. Frank Baum is credited with creating a space for the American fairy tale, though some believe that Washington Irving showed the potential for an American myth in "Rip Van Winkle" (1819) and "The Legend of Sleepy Hollow" (1820). In the Introduction to *The Wonderful Wizard of Oz* (1900) Baum sets the parameters for a new kind of fairy tale. Extolling the virtues of the classic tales by Grimm and Andersen, Baum argues for "newer 'wonder tales' in which the stereotyped genie, dwarf and fairy are eliminated together with all the horrible and blood-curdling incident devised by their authors to paint a fearsome moral to each tale" ([1900] 2000: 4). To Baum the new wonder tale should teach morality, but primarily through entertainment—*Oz* "aspires to be a modernized fairy tale, in which the wonderment and joy are retained and the heart-aches and nightmares are left out" (4). W. W. Denslow's (1856–1915) illustrations to *Oz* capture the spirit of Baum's new wonder tale aimed at younger readers. The illustrated space is clearly geared for a younger audience: Denslow hints at a more menacing forest in the background, but Lion, Scarecrow, and Tin Man are clearly nonthreatening.

Taking a different approach to the fairy tale than Baum and Denslow is Laurence Houseman (1865–1959; brother of E. A.), who was both an illustrator and writer of fairy tales. Housman's illustrations to Christina Rossetti's *Goblin Market* (1893), for example, draw out the erotic and exotic qualities of the poem. Unlike Denslow's more "childish" illustrations from *Oz*, Houseman's goblin fairy space is lush and exotic, the images distorted to create discomfort as the goblin men tempt the innocent young woman. Houseman, who was a friend of Oscar Wilde (even after Wilde's conviction for gross indecency), believed that fairy tales should be aimed at adults, not children, and he created fairy spaces where he could comment on social issues, including rigid gender stereotypes. He published four collections of fairy tales: *A Farm in Fairyland* (1894), *The House of Joy* (1895), *The Field of Clover* (1898), and *The Blue Moon* (1904). Embracing Pater's art for art's sake manifesto, Houseman created fairy tales that privileged the exotic and erotic over the moral. In 1907 he published *Stories from the Arabian Nights*, illustrated by Edmund Dulac.

Edith Nesbit (1858–1924) was a collaborator with Laurence Houseman and shared similar political views promoted by George Bernard Shaw and the Fabian Socialists. Nesbit's collection of more modern fairy tales *The Book of Dragons* appeared in 1900, often using humor and satire to poke fun at fairy-tale conventions while respecting the genre itself. "The Last of the Dragons" is an example. "Of course you know that dragons were once as common as motor-omnibuses are now, and almost as dangerous" (Nesbit [1900] 1987: 353), opens the tale, as Nesbit tells a tongue-in-cheek story about the King of Cornwall's daughter. At the end of the tale the reader witnesses the transformation of the fairy tale and its conversion into a modern realm: "The dragon, indeed, became the first aeroplane" (358). Nesbit also ushered in the long form of the fairy-tale fantasy that had its roots in the works of Charles Kingsley, Lewis Carroll, and George MacDonald. *Five Children and It* (1902) concerns a sand fairy—a Psammead—who grants the children one wish a day. Of course, the children's wishes lead to comically unintended consequences that give the work a lighthearted tone that respects the fairy-tale tradition while satirizing it simultaneously. Other fantasy novels by Nesbit include *The Phoenix and the Carpet* (1904), *The Story of the Amulet* (1906), and *The Enchanted Castle* (1907), which starts out as high comedy but moves toward more serious implications. Nesbit's tales often involve time travel that H. G. Wells made popular in *The Time Machine* (1895), thus connecting time and space to round out her fantasy creations.

Other important writers in the transition of the fairy tale into new modern and aesthetic space would need to include Kenneth Grahame (1859–1932), J. M. Barrie (1860–1937), and Rudyard Kipling (1865–1936). Grahame's *The Wind in the Willows* (1908) is not ostensibly a fairy tale but a full-length fantasy that mingles animals and humans. *Willows* captures the desire to return to a golden age before industrialization. In fact, Grahame published a collection of fairy tales in *The Golden Age* (1895), where fairy tales are seen as real to the more modern characters. "The Reluctant Dragon," which appears in *Dream Days* (1898), encapsulates how Grahame transformed the fairy tale to a new age: in this fairy tale the Boy meets a reluctant dragon and urges him to fight St. George because that is what the story requires the dragon to do. The Boy negotiates a fight between St. George and the reluctant dragon that fakes the outcome and allows knight and dragon to maintain face and the spirit of the fantastic story.

Barrie's character Peter Pan is iconic and challenges the notions of the innocence of childhood. Whether one has seen the play or read the novel, one knows the story of the boy who would not grow up. The novelization of the Peter Pan play *Peter and Wendy* (1911) creates a fantasy of empowerment and loss: Peter remains a perpetual boy but refuses to grow up, able to recreate dangerous adventures in Neverland. Wendy, and eventually the Lost Boys, will return to civilization and become adults, but only by abandoning any hope to return to Neverland. Barrie's work updates William Blake's tension created in *Songs of Innocence* (1789) and *Songs of Experience* (1794), "shewing the two contrary states of the human soul" ([1794] 2018: 127)—the child and the adult, the of tension that fairy tales face.

Rudyard Kipling (1865–1936) is another transitional figure. His *Rewards and Fairies* (1910) and *Puck of Pook's Hill* (1906) engage in the fairy-tale tradition. *Puck* has Puck from Shakespeare grant magical power to children so they can go back in the past; *Puck* is both historical fiction and full-length fantasy that honors the myth of the past. The stories, told by the characters, feel like a return to the folktale tradition. *Rewards* follows a similar pattern, though the events take place one year before those in *Puck*. Of course, Kipling's most enduring work is *The Jungle Book* (1894), a series of stories about Mowgli who has been raised by wolves. The proverbial fairy-tale forest is a very real one in India, where Mowgli learns from his various animal encounters the "law of the jungle."

The modern and aesthetic spaces reflected in Oz, Neverland, the Riverbank and the Jungle transform the classic fairy-tale space into secondary-world creations that Tolkien and Lewis made most famous. These spaces reflect the importance of fantasy at the turn of the century, a time more focused on productivity than imaginative escape. Yet these writers returned, to use Humphrey Carpenter's term, to the "golden age" that provided escape from a growing modernized world. Nesbit's dragon that transforms into an airplane is an apt metaphor for that new space for the fantastic, one that was generated by the nineteenth century's love of fairy tales, which became essential space where readers could lose themselves in that "space larger than imagination" (MacDonald [1895] 2001: 40).

CHAPTER SEVEN

Socialization

Civilizing Child's Play

MICHELLE BEISSEL HEATH

In the long nineteenth century, fairy tales were viewed as ideal means of socializing and civilizing children to adapt to and internalize British and US middle-class values.[1] Not only did they dominate children's literature, fairy tales also reigned as a preferred theme for a favorite entertainment at the newly developed playgrounds at the end of the nineteenth century. Performances, reenactments, and play productions acting out fairy tales emulated the pantomimes and tableaux present in nineteenth-century British and US games books and paralleled the use of skits as well as games in Robert Baden-Powell's Boy Scouts movement, which began to flourish around the same time.[2] As Marta Gutman and Ning de Coninck-Smith observe, "organized play on dedicated spaces was intended to socialize immigrant and working-class children, to inculcate gender norms, and to create a foundation for citizenship in democratic societies" (2008: 10). Similarly, in the 1980s and 1990s formative fairy-tale critics repeatedly noted the use of the tales for purposes of socialization and civilization. In his 1983 book, *Fairy Tales and the Art of Subversion*, revealingly subtitled *The Classical Genre for Children and the Process of Civilization*, for example, Jack Zipes emphasizes that "folk tales and fairy tales have always been dependent on customs, rituals, and values in the particular socialization process of a social system. They have always symbolically depicted the nature of power relationships within a given society. Thus, they are strong indicators of the level of civilization, that is, the essential quality of a culture and social order" ([1988] 1991: 67).[3] In the nineteenth century, Zipes argues, fairy tales increasingly targeted the young and were therefore altered to reflect nineteenth-century middle-class values, mores, morals, and educational ideas. In agreement, Maria Tatar discerns that "the literature we read to our children by and large stands in the service of productive socialization" and observes that reliance on "bodily punishment" in earlier centuries, rather than indicating "real concern for the welfare of the child" instead represents a tendency to "deeply resent the child as a representative and reminder of everything that is unruly, untamed, and uncivilized" (1992: xvi, 53). This tendency may help to account for the punitive and even violent aspects of many fairy tales used in service of civilizing and socializing efforts in the nineteenth century. Ultimately, "socialization" and taming/civilizing the child were, have been, and continue to be crucial objectives of fairy tales.

In this chapter I will build on the work of previous scholars to examine the use of fairy tales for socialization in several countries. I will explore the socializing and civilizing elements on display in adapted and original fairy tales, in fairy-tale-based games, and in movements such as scouting. In the process, I will point to ways in which socializing elements of fairy tales may either support or subvert the status quo. Some tales sought to civilize or indoctrinate children, at times with bouts of nationalism, exoticism, and jingoism, but others critiqued governmental, political, societal, and cultural systems, or offered alternate pathways for children and others to break out of the limits of class and gender.

GAMES AND ADAPTATIONS: COMPETING PATHWAYS

Fairy tales' function as socializing agent becomes clear in nineteenth-century games. Children's and family games flourished in this period and frequently connected with children's literature, if only because booksellers often invented and sold the games. Both media experienced notable growth at the end of the nineteenth century, so much so that Roger Tilley suggests that "perhaps the main feature of [the 'last quarter' of the nineteenth century] in England" was "the great output of children's games" (1973: 168). Margaret K. Hofer observes a similar trend in the United States, related to "improvements in printing and paper making [that] enabled the large-scale commercial production of board games" (2003: 14). Game manufacturers frequently started out as book publishers and, in their attempts to win over youthful audiences (and their parents), published not only picture and toy books but also toys and games. As Hofer points out, "the earliest game known to have been produced in America ... was made by a New York City bookseller in 1822," and some games were even designed to look like books when stored (16, 19).

Likely as part of this bookstore legacy, fairy-tale-based games are frequently predicated on retelling or adapting the tale. In an 1887 McLoughlin Brothers (New York) card game of "Little Red Riding Hood" (Figure 7.1), for example,

FIGURE 7.1: McLoughlin Brothers' "Little Red Riding Hood," 1887. Reproduced with the permission of The Strong, Rochester, New York.

the dealer is instructed to begin the game by telling the story of Little Red as printed in the game's instructions booklet: "Once on a time, in a far-off country, there lived a very good little girl, who wore a bright red mantle, with a riding hood to it, and all the people about there called her Little Red Riding Hood" (Little Red Riding Hood 1887). The story instructs Little Red to locate items from four categories, with a caution that reinforces the Grimm Brothers' version of the tale more than Charles Perrault's seventeenth-century French one: "'But remember, my dear,' her mother continued, 'that there is a bad wolf near grandmother's house: take care not to go near him!'" (Little Red Riding Hood 1887). As Wilhelm and Jacob Grimm adapted "Little Red Riding Hood" between their first edition in 1812 and the last one in 1857, they de-emphasized the tale's sexual aspects in a bid to make it more palatable to middle-class audiences (and despite maintaining what is obliquely referred to in popular culture as the "stranger danger" point of the tale). Instead of either warnings about sexual activity or encouragement of female child agency, the Grimms focused on a primary moral of listening to your mother emphasized through instructions such as "don't go peeping in all the corners of the room," "walk properly and don't stray from the path," and ending with Red Riding Hood's resolution "never again [to] stray from the path and go into the woods, when your mother has forbidden it" ([1812, 1857] 1999: 14–16). McLoughlin Brothers' game reinforces the lesson of "listening to your mother" with its allusion to the mother's warning against the wolf. It also pointedly emphasizes good behavior with the assertion that Little Red is "a very good little girl," a reminder to child players of what they should strive to be. The note that this "very good little girl" "lived" "in a far-off country," suggests, perhaps, that there is room for improvement in US children's behavior.

But more than simply repeating the story's lessons, the "Little Red Riding Hood" game cards themselves highlight US values of the period by promoting industry, consumerism, and luxury. The mother instructs Little Red to locate "something to wear" (ironically, few of the items depicted on the cards for articles of clothing appear to be red), then "something to take to grandmother for supper," "something pretty for grandmother," and finally "something to carry it in" (Little Red Riding Hood 1887). Players collect cards from each category to win the game. As items to wear, Little Red can choose from "a string of beads," a "cape trimmed with fur," or a "mantle"; she can bring grandmother such food delicacies as cheesecakes or a cranberry tart; and "pretty" items of (generally feminine) industry and luxury, such as a warm "foot-stove," a "velvet pin-cushion," "a little bird," or an exotic "Morocco work-box," alongside the more useful knitting needles, thimble, thimble-case, bodkin, and spectacles (Little Red Riding Hood 1887).[4] In addition to insisting on the importance of the "goodness" of children and their need to listen to adult authority figures, the game follows previous versions of the Little Red tale by specifically highlighting what good little *girls* should be doing, not only now, but as they grow into responsible, productive women: knitting, sewing, producing articles both necessary and ornamental, privileging middle-class commodity consumption.

The McLoughlin Brothers' "Little Red Riding Hood" game dovetails with UK and US concerns earlier in the century about the "usefulness" of fairy tales and fantasy versus more overtly didactic and/or religious texts for children, such as those by Sarah Trimmer and Maria Edgeworth. The game's focus on women's trinkets and products echoes debates about women's work and usefulness that flourished throughout the long nineteenth century, evident, for example, in the novels of Charlotte Yonge and throughout the pages of her periodical *The Monthly Packet*. The conservative Yonge frequently insisted that women's work and duty was first and foremost to the home and family, particularly male relatives in need. Yet middle-class girls in her novels struggle to find useful life paths, and Yonge entertained debates over what girls and women should do in *The Monthly Packet's* "correspondence" sections, where young women and girls wrote letters agreeing and disagreeing with various positions on the subject.[5]

Fairy tales took up these debates over women's work. Edith Nesbit's fairy tale "Fortunatus Rex & Co." (1901) gently mocks notions of the work available to middle-class women during the long nineteenth century. A corrupt magician kidnaps a school of princesses in revenge for not being offered a position at the school. The school is run by a middle-class woman, Miss Fitzroy Robinson, who powerfully and comically dictates her terms to royalty, primarily highlighting middle-class values of respectability and domesticity.⁶ The tale opens by stressing her insistence on "the highest references" and her choice of "polite letters" for the "brass plate fastened to the door" indicating that she is in charge of a "select boarding establishment for the daughters of respectable monarchs" (Nesbit [1901] 1992: 192). The reader quickly learns that Miss Fitzroy Robinson has the power to determine who is and who is not respectable, for "a great many kings who were not at all respectable would have given their royal ears to be allowed to send their daughters to this school, but Miss Fitzroy Robinson was very firm about references" (192). She has the power to turn down any royal applicant who fails to satisfy her standards, and we are told that "only one monarch refused to send his daughter ... on the grounds that so cheap a school ['ten thousand pounds a year'] could not be a really select one, and it was found out afterwards that his references were not at all satisfactory" (192). Indeed, the final moral of the tale is "I always say that you cannot go far wrong if you insist on the highest references!" (205). Primarily, however, the tale critiques middle-class expectations for women and the ideas of women's work of the period as it highlights notions of feminine power.

At the same time that the story conforms to traditional fairy-tale plot conventions, the narrative ironically highlights the superfluous nature of much of middle-class women's "work" of the period, as well as the period's encouragement of conspicuous consumption. When the king of the realm comes looking for his daughter Daisy and is told of her kidnapping, the text digresses into a description of the fancy work and refined consumerism evident in the school's décor: "So the King was shown into the best parlour where the tasteful wax-flowers were, and the antimacassars and the water-color drawings executed by the pupils, and the wool mats which Miss Fitzroy Robinson's bed-ridden aunt made so beautifully. A delightful parlour full of the traces of the refining touch of a woman's hand." He then "sat down heavily on part of the handsome walnut and rep suite (ladies' and gentlemen's easy-chairs, couch, and six occasional chairs)" (Nesbit [1901] 1992: 195). Described in the style of a catalog or advertising circular, these middle-class commodities and feminine "touches" are recurred to once the rescuing princes come to town in search of the princesses, their brides-to-be. They discover the school is closed, but they are compelled to rent the house, as "the wax fruit under the glass shade still showed attractively," "they were charmed with the furniture, and the refining touch of a woman's hand drew them like a magnet" (199–200). The elevation of middle-class womanly work perhaps reaches its apex in the depiction of the Queen, Daisy's mother, whom we are told "was much more broken-hearted than the King, but of course she had the housekeeping to see to and the making of pickles and preserves and the young Prince's stockings to knit, so she had not much time for weeping" (196). She gets tired of her husband's moping and sets about finding him something to do as a distraction, which ends up being a development project that offers an environmental and aesthetic critique of conspicuous consumption (196–7).

These versions of Little Red and the Nesbit fairy tale offer alternate pathways of expectations for middle-class girl- and womanhood even as they both attempt to socialize children, and particularly girls, into societal views and expectations of what they should be and do as ideal citizens or subjects. Taking the idea of the home as symbolizing womanly influence and power according to sage John Ruskin and poet Coventry Patmore, Nesbit elevates that power into a man-trap. Not only are the princes lured by the touch of a woman's hand, but the corrupt magician is literally confined by Miss Fitzroy Robinson in the school's terrestrial and celestial globes until the princesses are rescued (Nesbit [1901] 1992: 200).[7] The tale's depiction of women's power over the home and over men becomes even more hyperbolic when it literally and symbolically places the earth and universe in the realm of the house and under "a woman's hand."

FAIRY TALES AND FEMININE SOCIALIZATION

Still, in both their adherence to and critiques of the socializing values of previous tales and the cultures in which they arise or are produced, McLoughlin Brothers' "Little Red" game and Nesbit's "Fortunatus Rex & Co." simultaneously offer alternate pathways and follow a path set by fairy-tale writers and adapters throughout the century and in a variety of countries. As Zipes and others (Bottigheimer, Tatar) have shown, the Grimms over time repeatedly altered the fairy tales they published to make them more suitable for nineteenth-century children and more German. As Ruth Bottigheimer explains it, "the process of editing, codifying, and translating [the tales] produced a distinctly nineteenth-century text, incorporating the gender-related assumptions of Grimms' informants and of Wilhelm Grimm himself" (1986: 117).[8] An example illuminating nineteenth-century expectations for good German (and, really, Western) girlhood can be found in early changes to "Snow White." In the Grimms' 1810 Ölenberg Manuscript, Snow White's explanation for her appearance and acceptance by the dwarfs is described rather quickly: "She told them everything … The dwarfs took pity on her and persuaded her to remain with them and do the cooking for them when they went to the mines" (Zipes 1999: 72). By 1812, however, that description becomes much more elaborate and imperative:

> Then she told them how her mother had wanted to have her put to death, but the hunter had spared her life … So the dwarfs took pity on her and said, "If you keep house for us and cook, sew, make the beds, wash and knit, and keep everything tidy and clean, you may stay with us and you will have everything you want. In the evening, when we come home, dinner must be ready."
>
> (Zipes 1999: 72)

In addition to cooking, Snow White now has a detailed list of household chores to accomplish as well as an expectation to have dinner ready as soon as the dwarfs are home. This list of chores is a clear signal to child readers of what types of tasks good, obedient, and grateful girls should do or what feminine duties are.[9]

Although he did not focus as much on chores, the Dane Hans Christian Andersen also offered views of ideal nineteenth-century girl- and womanhood in "The Little Mermaid" (1837). To win the love of a human prince and gain an immortal soul, the mermaid princess gives up her beautiful voice but maintains other attributes of ideal femininity, including, in the words of the sea-witch, "lovely form," "light gait," and "speaking eyes."[10] She must endure—just as her grandmother forced her to endure the painful grandeur of oysters clinging to her tail—the physical pain of feeling "as if she trod on a sharp knife" as she dances. As she attempts to achieve her goal, she also endures the emotional pain of being desexualized by being dressed in boy's clothes; of being treated like a pet, "given leave to sit outside [the prince's] door on a velvet cushion"; and of holding her rival's bridal train as her rival weds her love (Andersen [1837] 2000: 108, 113–14). She even sacrifices her life for her love as she hears him whisper her rival's name in his sleep, even though killing him would save her own life (116–17). In the end she gains the possibility of an immortal soul, but only because of her willingness to die rather than exact revenge, underscoring the virtue of feminine self-sacrifice.

Perhaps not surprisingly, given debates, ideals, and realities of women, work, and duty throughout the century in many Western countries, many literary fairy tales of the long nineteenth century vacillate or are ambiguous with regards to their portrayals of girls and societal expectations of feminine duty, at times undermining societal values even as they attempt to socialize children into them. Christina Rossetti's famed *Goblin Market* (1862), for instance, ends with a bland moral about friendship between two sisters who are now wives and mothers. The bulk of the poem, however, offers erotic, homoerotic, and even potentially incestuous allure as it powerfully invokes temptation and warns against the dangers of men, marketplaces, and consumption (Rossetti [1862] 1988: 208).[11]

Both Lewis Carroll's and J. M. Barrie's book-length fairy tales, *Alice's Adventures in Wonderland* (1865) and *Peter and Wendy* (1911), respectively, offer similarly vacillating, ambiguous approaches, simultaneously conforming to and critiquing social expectations about gender roles, particularly for girls and women, in ways perhaps not dissimilar to Nesbit's mocking deployment of feminine and middle-class cultural respectability in "Fortunatus Rex & Co."[12] The Wonderland Alice encounters is a domestic realm: the tunnel Alice falls through mirrors a pantry and study; concerns over baked goods form the basis for public trials; and thimbles serve as prizes. (Alternately, thimbles become kisses in Neverland.) Adventures consist of domestic social activities: tea, croquet, singing, dancing, and cards. It is here, though, that Carroll offers his simultaneous critique and adherence to nineteenth-century socialization of girls in particular. At the end of the text, Alice awakens merely to return to her house to do it all over again: to get her tea and repeat the cycle of female domestic social obligations on display throughout her Wonderland journey. Carroll critiques this very cycle through such things as the circular, never-ending tea party and the vicious and arbitrary croquet game. Carroll depicts rudeness and violence barely kept in check by social conventions, for as James Kincaid discerns, when "genteel disguises are quietly removed in Wonderland," their removal often emphasizes why they should be maintained in the first place (1992: 291).[13] Even as he illustrates the potential traps of houses, domesticity, and nineteenth-century ideals of girls' socialization, Carroll insists they are necessary and shapes his characters' interactions persistently around considerations of manners, demonstrating that a lack of socialization leads to chaos. The Mad Hatter and March Hare commit many social blunders at their tea party—rudely offering nonexistent wine and insulting Alice's appearance and ideas—but Alice's behavior is not much better (Carroll [1865] 2013: 52–3). Indeed, throughout her time in Wonderland she threatens and insults creatures, as when she praises cats for their hunting to an audience of mice and birds, and insults the "exactly three inches high" Caterpillar by informing it that "three inches is such a wretched height to be" (18, 25, 40).

By contrast, *Peter and Wendy* (1911), the novelized version of Barrie's play, shows Wendy to have been well socialized for all things domestic. She is—and desires nothing more than to be—"a nice motherly person" (Barrie [1911] 2004: 65). The narrator dwells on her aptitude for domesticity, femininity, and motherhood: she "grew up of her own free will a day quicker than other girls," immediately sets up housekeeping in Neverland despite many other options, and delights in domestic drudgery:

> I suppose it was all especially entrancing to Wendy, because those rampageous boys of hers gave her so much to do. Really there were whole weeks when, except perhaps with a stocking in the evening, she was never above ground. The cooking, I can tell you, kept her nose to the pot …
>
> Wendy's favourite time for sewing and darning was after they had all gone to bed. Then, as she expressed it, she had a breathing time for herself ….
>
> When she sat down to a basketful of their stockings, every heel with a hole in it, she would fling up her arms and exclaim, "Oh, dear, I am sure I sometimes think spinsters are to be envied!"
>
> Her face beamed when she exclaimed this.
>
> (Barrie [1911] 2004: 146, 60, 69)

Even as the text seems to offer a fully domestic, socialized Wendy, however, the narrator's tone here (hinting at playful, if not mocking or sarcastic) reminds us that perhaps not all is as it seems, that what much of what Wendy enjoys is the child's play of emulating adult activities, an idea that may well undermine the text's apparent promotion of Wendy's feminine socialization by instead offering a critique of it: who really enjoys spending weeks underground doing housework—and creating pretend meals rather than actually eating— or staying up late to mend clothes? As Jacqueline Rose reminds us, Barrie's narrator in the novel is hard to place at best, unreliable at worst.[14] Perhaps the passage ironically points out that societal expectations for girls and women are actually unreasonable and dreary? Such portrayals of "playing at" femininity, housekeeping, motherhood, marriage, and even middle-class life are on display at other points in the text as well. Mrs. Darling's need for a nurse—even if it is a dog—and her account-keeping are as fanciful—and "game"-playing— as her daughter's housekeeping in Neverland: "Mrs. Darling was married in white, and at first she kept the books perfectly, almost gleefully, as if it were a game, not so much as a Brussels sprout was missing; but by and by whole cauliflowers dropped out, and instead of them there were pictures of babies without faces" (Barrie [1911] 2004: 6–7). Ambivalence toward women's roles also surfaces repeatedly in other texts and figures of the period. For example, the feminine or matriarchal or gender-fluid power in L. Frank Baum's *Oz* series (1900–20) falls under scrutiny at times, while the Russian Baba Yaga figure is utterly ambivalent, powerful, helpful, hindering, and as hard consistently to place as Barrie's narrator.

FAIRY TALES AND BOYS' DOMESTICATION

Ambivalence and yet practical recognition of the importance of domesticity is evident—for boys—in Robert Baden-Powell's use of Juliana Horatia Ewing's fairy tale "The Brownies" (1865) as a model for the Scouting movement in *The Wolf Cub's Handbook* (1916). Although the term "Brownies" eventually was adopted by the Girl Guides and Girl Scouts side of the movement, Baden-Powell viewed the tale as suitable for boys as he tried to instill in his young Cub Scouts adherence to duty and obedience. Time and again throughout his handbook, he offers moralizing and socializing statements such as "it may sometimes be a trouble to them if they are feeling tired or want to be playing, but they must remember that it is their Duty, and Duty comes before everything else" ([1916] 1918: 48). To help illustrate this importance of duty, Baden-Powell retells Ewing's tale. Ewing's original tale is based on a medley of fairy tales (such as the "Elves and the Shoemaker") with a goal of convincing a couple of lazy, unhelpful children to turn into good little "fairies" who get up early to do chores and clean up around the house to help out their poor, overworked parents (see Ewing 1871). In retelling the story, Baden-Powell emphasizes that, just like Cub (and Boy) Scouts, "Brownies do their work quietly and without wanting to be thanked or rewarded for it. They do it because it is their duty to their father and mother and family" ([1916] 1918: 48).

Baden-Powell masculinizes the tale's domestic messages for his Cub Scouts by setting it in "the jungle" so it is relevant to the "wolves" the Cubs are to become, based on Rudyard Kipling's *The Jungle Books* (1894). By aligning Ewing's tale with Kipling's, he also strove to ensure his use of the fairy tale did not threaten his audience's presumed masculine identity (Baden-Powell [1916] 1918: 46). Like Kipling's protagonists on whom Baden-Powell based his movement—Mowgli from *The Jungle Books* and Kim from his eponymous novel (1901)—the Cub and Boy Scouts comprised an entirely (or mostly) male community. The focus on masculine communities and general exclusion of women help to mitigate the effects of Mowgli and Kim being at times simultaneously androgynous and hypermasculine, attractive to both men and women because of their superior cunning, beauty, and/or strength. In the case of the Scouting movement, such a masculine focus and community helped remove or mitigate the supposedly "feminine" aspects of a focus on domestic duties. As if he feared he wasn't clear enough, Baden-Powell even dedicated *The Wolf Cub's Handbook* to Kipling and masculinity: "To Rudyard Kipling, who has done so much to put the right spirit into our rising manhood" ([1916] 1918: 7).

Another means by which Baden-Powell makes his domestic socialization of boys successful is by emphasizing, as Ewing's story hints, that, like Mowgli and Kim, Cub and Boy Scouts should be self-sufficient. Every Cub should know and accomplish domestic, social and other obligations otherwise viewed as typically feminine. A Cub must learn to cook, should fold his clothes daily/nightly as a means of "being prepared," and "a Cub is not much good who does not know how to use a needle" ([1916] 1918: 113–14). Baden-Powell dedicated a badge to "House Orderly," wherein Cubs are encouraged to help their mothers and where "minding baby" and "looking after your little brothers and sisters" is honored, as "it shows great confidence on the part of the Old Wolf to trust its precious Baby Wolf in the care of the Wolf Cub—so live up to it!" (192, 194). To successfully attain a "Homecraft" badge, the Wolf Cubs' club room must be "a marvel of cleanliness and neatness. It should be the envy and despair of Scoutmasters—who will begin to wish the Scouts had a Homecraft Badge, to teach them this, and give them a real keenness about orderly work" (195). Other ways of procuring the badge include "if 'mother' ... says there is nothing in the world like the Cub movement for making little boys helpful and useful and polite" and "the examiner really *enjoys* the cup of tea [made by the Cub]: it will put him in a good temper to pass your boots and your windows and even your greens!" (195; emphasis in the original). In his socializing Scouting movement (the subtitle of his original *Scouting for Boys* [1908] is *A Handbook for Instruction in Good Citizenship*), Baden-Powell used fairy tales to help emphasize values such as helpfulness, politeness, and usefulness—the same values also promoted to girls through fairy tales.

FAIRY TALES, FURTHER CLASS SOCIALIZATION, AND CHILD AUTHORITY

As Troy Boone has shown, the Scouting movement was primarily a middle-class project promoting middle-class values, even when it occasionally directed its attention to members of the lower and working classes; fairy tales of the period follow a similar trend. Frequently, they address middle-class audiences and promote middle-class values, yet not infrequently they also call such values into question, either by pointing out the problematic nature of class or by calling into question notions of adult and child authority.[15] In the late seventeenth century, Perrault's version of "Cinderella" offered a subtle critique of class when, after Cinderella flees the palace after midnight, "the guards at the palace gate were asked if they had not seen a princess go out, and they replied they had seen nobody go out but a young girl, very meanly dressed, and who had more the air of a poor country girl than of a young lady" ([1697] 2000: 20). Perrault shows that class is merely equated with dress and therefore easily changeable, a theme he further offers in his moral to "The Master Cat; or, Puss in Boots": the miller's youngest son's marriage to a princess is described as "It's due to good manners, looks, and dress / That inspired her deepest tenderness / And always help to win the day" ([1697] 2001a: 401). Robert Louis Stevenson also critiques the conflation of poverty in dress, goods, or treats and poor behavior or manners. In "System" from *A Child's Garden of Verses* (1885), Stevenson's naïve speaker points to the social and societal "System" in which a child does not get an orange for a treat either because he has not behaved or because his father cannot afford one. The poor child, because of this lack, is assumed by the speaker to be naughty (Stevenson [1885] 1994: 21).

Such a conflation of class and behavior is also found in McLoughlin Brothers' card game version of Cinderella, or Hunt the Slipper (1887). Like many fairy-tale-based games of the era, the game begins with a simplified adaptation of the fairy tale "used by the Reader in the Game," in this case Perrault's "Story of Cinderella" (Cinderella, or Hunt the Slipper 1887).[16] While McLoughlin Brothers' "Little Red" game highlights good conduct, its "Cinderella" focuses on bad behaviors, even remarking "how [Cinderella] had a bad habit of sitting in the ashes and cinders, from which she got the name of Cinderella" (Cinderella, or Hunt the Slipper 1887). In this version, it is Cinderella's own poor manners that result in her insulting nickname (and, by extension, her impoverished appearance, if not condition). The game continues its theme by highlighting Cinderella's impoverished situation, featuring cards with "ragged," "broken," or "old-fashioned" items, with the goal of the game to discover what "historians" do not tell us. When Cinderella returns home with only one slipper, the fairy godmother is likely to be displeased with the loss and the neglectful behavior it represents, so she must look everywhere, even if she doesn't find exactly what she's searching for (Cinderella, or Hunt the Slipper 1887: instruction booklet and game cards). Items on the cards include a "ragged" cushion and hat and a broken pan, gridiron, dipper, and horn-comb. To implicate the child player in Cinderella's own supposed poor decision-making and behavior, the game offers an extensive nota bene: "During the game, whenever matches are played with boots, shoes, slippers, socks, or moccasins on them ... the Reader may fine or punish the person who is so stupid as to think that *that* could possibly be Cinderella's beautiful Slipper." The "fines" can be as cruel, silly, or embarrassing as the "Reader" pleases. Readers may require players to "humbly ask pardon; to spell Cinderella or some other word backward; to pay a forfeit; to tell a riddle for the amusement of the company; to make a speech, with slipper, boot, and shoe in it; to say something very silly; to describe the lady (or gentleman) he loves best, &c" (Cinderella, or Hunt the Slipper 1887: instruction booklet; emphasis in the original). Even for its child audience, in other words, the game focuses on poor behavior and, as Tatar observes for fairy tales, embarrassment or punishment as the remedy to help the child player "return" to good behavior and thereby maintain appropriate class status.

Unlike McLoughlin's "Cinderella" game and like Nesbit's "Fortunatus Rex & Co.," fortunately, many fairy-tale writers and adapters of the period critiqued rather than conflated class and (bad) behavior. In Andersen's version of "The Princess and the Pea" (1835), for example, as with Perrault's earlier "Cinderella," class cannot be determined by dress or appearance, as the waterlogged maiden who appears at the castle door truly is a princess and as the king himself, we are told, goes to answer the door on the stormy night (Andersen [1835] 2000: 118). Charles Dickens describes a king's household as a version of the lower-middle-class family into which he was born, satirizing both the English monarchy and the ideas, such as those put forth by Ruskin, of every man as a king in his own home and every wife as queen. Dickens's fairy tale "The Magic Fish-Bone" (1868), attributed to "Miss Alice Rainbird, Aged Seven," surrounds a supposed "king" and "queen" and their large royal family (somehow nineteen children between the ages of seven months and seven years). The "king" is described as "in his private profession, Under Government"—satirizing, in other words, all subjects as under the authority of the government, working for the government as family man, being under the purse-power of Parliament as a king, and ultimately, kings as in constant need of money—while "the Queen's father had been a medical man out of town" (Dickens [1868] 1988: 107). The "royal" family has a hard time making ends meet, a fact that becomes all the harder when the "queen" falls ill. Yet Alicia, their eldest daughter, manages to keep everything together until one day we learn the "moral" of the story: "when we have done our very best, papa, and that is not enough, then I think the right time must have come for asking help of others" (113). At this point, Alicia uses the magic fishbone acquired through her "Good Fairy Grandmarina," who makes all their problems vanish and marries off Alicia to "Prince Certainpersonio" (a rub at the irrelevance of princes' names and personalities in many fairy tales) with a "duchess" (Alicia's favorite doll) as bridesmaid (114). At this point, too, the true—or a seemingly better—moral emerges, with the Grandmarina bestowing gifts like the fairies in versions of "Sleeping Beauty": "My dears, you will have thirty-five children, and they will all be good and beautiful. Seventeen of your children will be boys, and eighteen will be girls. The hair of the whole of your children will curl naturally. They will never have the measles and will have recovered from the whooping-cough before being born" (115). The conclusion blends satire with naivete, with its emphasis on what young girls like Alicia and the purported author Alice seemingly want or should want (preferences for large families, if not girls, beauty, curly hair, and well-behaved children), but there is also admission of *actual* blessings: no measles or whooping-cough, potentially dangerous and deadly childhood illnesses. The tale also, likely to the amusement of child readers, repeatedly mocks the idea of adults as all-knowing authority figures and underscores child power (Alicia persistently saves the day after all). The Fairy Grandmarina chastises the King frequently, telling him such things as "Don't be impatient, sir ... Don't catch people short, before they have done speaking. Just the way with you grown-up persons. You are always doing it" and "*Will* you be good, sir? ... The reason for this, and the reason for that, indeed! ... I am sick of your grown-up reasons" (108; emphasis in the original). Turning the tables on the patriarchal father figure—and "king" to boot—the tale makes clear that children can know what they are doing. Like a Wordsworthian Romantic child, though more practical, Alicia is wiser than her father.

Kenneth Grahame presents a similarly wise figure in "The Reluctant Dragon" (1898), though in this child's case his parents acknowledge it, for "he was treated more or less as an equal by his parents," who leave "the book-learning" to him. We are told "what the Boy chiefly dabbled in was natural history and fairy tales, and he just took them as they came, in a sandwichy sort of way, without making any distinctions; and really his course of reading strikes one as rather sensible" (Grahame [1898] 1988: 327). And "sensible" it must be, as the boy saves his town from its proclivities toward gambling and fighting and makes friends out of both St. George and the dragon. Yet, by the end of the tale, Grahame differs from Dickens. While Dickens is content to leave Alicia with her authority intact, imitating a child's perspective to undercut adult societal values even while potentially reinforcing them with didactic morals, Grahame returns his boy to a child's (seemingly) powerless state. After the boy, who frequently worries about his mother having to sit up waiting for him, has done all the work and fixed everything, St. George and the dragon resume their supposedly rightful roles of being good adult authority figures by nicely taking the tired boy home and putting him to bed, something he suddenly cannot do for himself (344). As Grahame's example indicates, adults generally maintain authority in the tales even as child characters consistently call into question or even undercut the socializing forces supposedly controlled by adults. Nesbit's "Fortunatus Rex & Co.," for instance, generally accedes adult authority (at least with regard to Miss Fitzroy Robinson), but still at times offers the child authority and power. The most significant example arrives at the tale's end, when each prince kisses the wrong princess but is told that their parents "must put up with your choice" as "it's the common lot of parents" and "they can't change," for "when a Prince has picked a gold apple that has a Princess in it, and has kissed it till she comes out, no other Princess will ever do for him, any more than any other Prince will ever do for her" (Nesbit [1901] 1992: 204).[17]

FAIRY TALES AND PARADOXICAL NOTIONS OF SOCIALIZATION

Other fairy tales of the long nineteenth century critique children's socialization practices alongside governmental and cultural systems. In Mary De Morgan's "A Toy Princess" (1877), the danger is unnatural socialization based on repression of feeling and expression. The end result is that the king and his people prefer a "wood-and-leather" "doll" to a living princess. The princess Ursula is exchanged for a toy by her fairy godmother, who realizes how unhappy she is under a socializing regime that demands she be inhumanly genteel (De Morgan [1877] 1991: 173–4). The Toy Princess can do nothing but mutter empty polite expressions, for as the fairy godmother instructs its maker, "it need not be at all talkative ... It need only say, "'If you please,' 'No thank you,' 'Certainly,' and 'Just So'" (167). Princess Ursula grows up happily in the home of a fisherman and his wife, where she "waited on them and cleaned the house, and did the needlework, and was so useful that they could not have done without her" (171). She ends up marrying their son and living quite happily, successfully socialized into practical feminine values of cleanliness, needlework, and usefulness rather than gentility, mere politeness, and endless fancywork.

Ursula's (feminine) socialization—even as she is replaced in her biological home by a magical robot—stands in stark contrast to Carlo Collodi's *The Adventures of Pinocchio* (1883) where Pinocchio, the puppet, wants to be human but succumbs at times to bad behavior, his poor socialization threatening his hopes of becoming "real." Engaging in bad behavior even before he is fully formed, Pinocchio discovers that his ability to become a real boy is consistently thwarted, delayed by his naughty refusal to attend school to be educated and learn proper behaviors and skills. As he admits in one of his encounters with the blue-haired fairy, unlike "good boys," "I am never obedient ... And I am an idle vagrant all the year round ... And I always tell lies ... And school gives me a pain" (Collodi [1883] 1996: 148). His unwillingness to adopt good behaviors and attend school to be educated and socialized results in his transformation into the donkey about which he has been warned. This transformation is of course a punitive measure of the sort Tatar indicates was displayed in fairy tales to encourage or, really, threaten and force cultural ideals of good behavior and socialization (211). It is only after the death of his peer, Lampwick, who was also turned into a donkey, that Pinocchio finally reforms and becomes the better socialized and better behaved child the blue-haired fairy and Geppetto have been encouraging him to be, willing to sacrifice and work hard for his parental figures and earning the privilege of becoming a "real" boy (258). The late nineteenth- and early twentieth-century child study movement, and eventually Disney itself, recognized the aims of socialization embedded in the Italian text, and cast Pinocchio, Nicholas Sammond discerns, as a representative of "working-class and immigrant children (and, to some extent, adults) [who] were to be assimilated into American culture through social and educational programs that inculcated in them white, Protestant, middle-class values such as self-denial and deferred gratification" (2005: 84).

Perhaps the fairy-tale writer who is the most insistent in critiquing nineteenth-century notions of civilization and socialization is Oscar Wilde, who famously claimed he wrote his fairy tales "not for children, but for childlike people from eighteen to eighty" ([1889] 2000: 388). His fairy-tale collections, *The Happy Prince and Other Tales* (1888) and *A House of Pomegranates* (1891), regularly end tragically, reflecting his own views of socialism (like Nesbit and De Morgan, Wilde had radical ideas for his time), where society is in dire need of change, but that change cannot be accomplished by individuals alone. Both the Happy Prince and the Star-Child discover in their eponymous tales that their unselfish actions may temporarily affect the world, as when the Happy Prince donates precious jewels and metals to the populace, but eventually his beloved swallow dies and he is destroyed, leaving no real change in the town. Neither do the Star-Child's lessons in humility and sacrifice lead to permanent change, for "he ruled not long, so great had been his suffering ... and he who came after him ruled evilly" (2003: 163).

Even as Wilde's fairy tales offer at times radical critiques of civilization and socialization, however, they align with other fairy tales of the era in reflecting Western fascination with "the exotic" East and Middle East, a fascination set against and spurred by the persistent backdrop of imperialism and nationalism that pervaded late nineteenth-century British culture. Wilde's "The Birthday of the Infanta," for instance, highlights exoticism with its Spanish setting, Moorish references, and its portrayal of a dwarf, just as McLoughlin's "Little Red" game highlights the exotic luxury of a "Morocco work-box." Richard Burton engaged the British public with his extended travels and 1885 publication of his translation of Middle Eastern and South Asian folk and fairy tales, *The Book of the Thousand Nights and a Night* (*Arabian Nights*). Andrew Lang published his own versions of "Arabian Nights" tales, including in his famous *Colored Fairy Books* (1889–1913), in which he collected and published stories not only from European but other traditions, including works by Marie-Catherine d'Aulnoy as well as Japanese, Chinese, Turkish, Persian, Indian, and African fairy tales. "Arabian Nights" stories also formed the basis of later nineteenth-century games, such as J. H. Singer's Game of Ali Baba, or the Forty Thieves (*c.* 1900), the game board of which pictorially retells the tale.

Similar fascinated exoticism applied to fairy tales is notable in Milton Bradley's Game of Beauty and the Beast (1905; Figure 7.2), which, despite its cover depicting a young girl and a lion, seems to have very little to do with versions of the "Beauty and the Beast" fairy tale. Instead, according to the game's instructions, ideally with the help of "two good fairies," "the object of the game is to take a trip to Fairyland, avoiding the monsters and obstacles in the enchanted forest" (Game of Beauty and the Beast 1905: "Directions"). These "monstrous" obstacles—goblin, giant, bear, lion, elephant—consist of beings both real and imaginary, with many of the real ones surfacing from, to

FIGURE 7.2: Milton Bradley's Game of Beauty and the Beast, 1905. Reproduced with the permission of The Strong, Rochester, New York.

those in the United States and United Kingdom, generally exotic, colonized locales and surprising additions to fairyland, even in a forest setting.

Mixing the fantastic, the real, the colonial, and the "exotic" in nineteenth-century fairy tales helps to draw readers' and players' attention to notions of space and place and their own roles in the creation of places and spaces, through images invoking imperialism, nationalism, and nation-building. In Barrie's fairyland of Neverland (itself populated by wolves, bears, crocodiles, and lions), when confronted with the traitorous pirates, John Darling and his peers refuse to give up being "respectful subjects of the King," Curly exhorts "Rule Britannia," and Wendy channels what she believes the Lost Boys and her own brothers' actual mothers would want: "We hope our sons will die like English gentlemen" (Barrie [1911] 2004: 120–1). British imperial, national might, in other words, is protected and on patriotic display in Barrie's fairyland world. Even as Barrie parodies colonial enterprises through the romanticized "desert isle" motif of the island of Neverland itself, he naturalizes them through the portrayal of Neverland as the rightful playland for English gentlemen, who are also, particularly with the case of Peter, portrayed as its rightful rulers. The native fairies treat Peter differently from all other inhabitants and even the "redskins," problematically portrayed to reflect prejudicial and colonial stereotypes, recognize him as "The Great White Father" (88).[18] Albert A. Hill's US game of Right and Wrong, or The Princess Belinda (1876), whose very title touts its socializing message, is just as forthright in its mixing of fairy tales and nationalism. Seeking to create a fairy tale that "promises to become as popular as the famous story of *'Cinderella; or, the Glass Slipper,'*" Hill designed the game's narrative entirely as a fairy tale to be disrupted at key times by players (Right and Wrong, or The Princess Belinda 1876: directions card). The game's narrative tells the story of Belinda, who undertakes a world and universe tour, the culmination of which is her leaving England to cross "the Atlantic in a cockle-shell, the sails of which were the wings of THE AMERICAN EAGLE. Strange as had been the adventures of Belinda, she was glad to reach once more her HOME IN WONDERLAND" (directions card, emphases in the original). This reimagining of Wonderland as the United States would likely be unrecognizable to Carroll and his Alice but accords with US assertions of national greatness in comparison with other nations, especially the UK.

Time and again throughout the nineteenth century, fairy tales were used—in their adapted original forms, in new mocking or critiquing versions, and in transformations into such things as children's and family games—to familiarize, if not initiate, youth and others into nineteenth-century values and beliefs, particularly as they related to views of gender, class, governmental and societal or cultural systems, and even nationhood and citizenship. Encouraging civilizing behavior and socialization, as critics have frequently suggested, was often the point of fairy tales, including nineteenth-century fairy tales. Indeed, nineteenth-century fairy tales often coalesced around purposes of promoting middle-class ideas, such as those emphasized at the end of the century by Baden-Powell and Kipling through fairy-tale writers such as Ewing and others: earnestness, duty, conformity, and imperial and national fitness. Yet many fairy-tale writers of the time could not resist using and critiquing fairy tales to offer children and others alternate pathways, alternate possibilities, for civilization and socialization, and, really, alternate worlds and lives, perhaps even promises or potentials for difference and change. Adapting fairy tales for use in nineteenth-century children's and family games was yet another way to imagine, if not create, different, alternate, and even new worlds.

CHAPTER EIGHT

Power

MOLLY CLARK HILLARD

This is a chapter about the fairy tale and its relationship to mechanisms of power in Victorian England. Fairy tales and modern technocracy "grew up" together during the nineteenth century. Though common rhetorical representation now often separates the Enlightenment or positivist discourses of scientific and technological theory from the imaginative styling of fairy tales, in reality, a kinship was forged between these epistemologies in the literary landscape. Until recently, we have thought of folkloric and scientific discourse merging only in late Victorian England with the rise of the social sciences. Richard Dorson's history of British folklore told us that the grandfathers (and one grandmother) of the scientific method in folklore study—namely, Edwin Sidney Hartland, George Lawrence Gomme, Joseph Jacobs, Andrew Lang, David MacRitchie, and Marian Roalfe Cox—were all late Victorians (Dorson 1968), and this narrative has been hard to disrupt. By contrast, this chapter suggests that certain Victorian media productions not only anticipated but also actually modulated and enabled the linkages between technology, the fairy tale, and discourses of power that we usually associate with the late nineteenth century.

This chapter is grounded in the formulation in 2015 of the V21 Collective research consortium, especially its call to *strategic presentism*, which V21 moderators Anna Kornbluh and Benjamin Morgan define in this way: "our interest in the [Victorian] period is motivated by certain features of our own moment. In finance, resource mining, globalization, imperialism, liberalism, and many other vectors, we *are* Victorian, inhabiting, advancing, and resisting the world they made" (Kornbluh and Morgan 2015; emphasis in the original). Like these scholars, I am interested in what light may be shed upon how and why we read and reread nineteenth-century literatures: how they direct us to a variety of institutional spaces that we in the twenty-first century still inhabit, for better and for worse, but also what they may offer to us in the way of resistance.

But why put fairy tales and technocratic events—Victorian and contemporary—into conversation at all? What good could it do to know that fairy tales lived and live still in the rhetorical spaces of our neoliberal accumulations and catastrophes? A group of critics have begun to grapple with our colossal failures in humanity by insisting first on the urgency of immersive storytelling, and second on what Bruno Latour calls "networks." Latour tells us that we must be concerned "not with nature or knowledge, with things-in-themselves, but with the way all these things are tied to our collectives" (1993: 4). Building upon Latour and speaking specifically about literatures, Rita Felski contends that "the social just is the act and the fact of association, the coming together of phenomena to create multiple assemblages, affinities, and networks. It exists only in its instantiations, in the sometimes foreseeable, sometimes unpredictable ways in which ideas, texts, images, people, and objects couple and uncouple, attach and break apart" (2011: 578). In Rebecca Walkowitz's terms, "translation and global circulation create many books out of single texts, transforming old traditions and inaugurating new ones" (2007: 226). Wai Chee Dimock has called this way of seeing "diachronic historicism," where "the text [is] a temporal continuum, thick with receding and incipient nuances" (1997: 1061).

In fairy-tale studies, this work is aligned with the critical trend in the last decade or so toward interdisciplinarity. Jennifer Schacker's newest work investigates the exchange between the European fairy tale and the nineteenth-century English drama (Schacker 2018); Carolyn Sumpter examines the role of Victorian periodical publication in shaping the fairy-tale genre, and vice versa (Sumpter 2008); Laurence Talairach-Vielmas explores the relation between Victorian natural history and the fairy tale (Talairach-Vielmas 2014); my own *Spellbound* explores the interrelation between the fairy tale and canonical Victorian literature (Clark Hillard 2014). All of these examples demonstrate what Mikhail Bakhtin would call the dialogic imagination, the conversation between mutually interacting texts over time, texts that simultaneously inform and are informed by previous and future texts. Though, ironically, Bakhtin was speaking of literature other than fairy tales, and in fact did not grant fairy tales discursive authority, current patterns in fairy-tale studies situate the fairy-tale genre firmly in the dialogic, networked structure of the Victorian mediascape (Bakhtin 1981b: 15). For these reasons, I propose that in examining the "sociability" between power systems and fairy tales in select nineteenth-century literary events, we might further illuminate the persistent cultural power of fairy tales—a gain in itself for fairy-tale scholars.

Bear with me, then, as I begin, not in the nineteenth century, but in a very different time and place—in the United States, in 2012 to 2018. As we look into our own very recent history, at three massive failures of humanity, three instances of our unchecked capitalist technocracy and the brutalities it enables, we should note the ways that fairy tales and folk narratives inhabit these spaces too. It is not my intention to suggest that the fairy tale served solely as a mechanism for perpetuating or defending technocratic power. Feminist fairy-tale scholars, myself included, have demonstrated the ways in which the fairy tale—as a fluid, flexible, and largely feminine (or feminized, or even queer) genre—can be transgressive, resistant, and subversive, can both stand in counterpoint to conventional (patriarchal) literary cultures and soak into them, threatening to engulf them entirely. As Schacker notes: "Although Mother Bunch is not connected to potential transgression via ink, she is ... associated nevertheless with a number of other densely symbolic fluids that threaten (or promise) to obfuscate boundaries, that intoxicate, impregnate, and nourish, that defy efforts to contain them" (2008: 14–15; see also Schacker 2011). I still firmly believe this to be true about the fairy tale and its uses across times and cultures, as this chapter will eventually show. Nevertheless, what follows demonstrates that the fairy tale has been and continues to be manipulated and coopted as a technology of fear and control, especially of women, children, people of color, and the poor. If we are going to celebrate the fairy tale's fluidity, its subversive potential, we will also have to reckon with its power to damage and harm.

2012–18

Sandy Hook

In December 2012, twenty children and seven adults were murdered in the Sandy Hook Elementary School massacre. Though the Columbine High School shooting had happened in 1997, the Amish school girl murders in 2006, the Virginia Tech shooting in 2007, and the Aurora movie theater shooting earlier in 2012, the Sandy Hook murders, as a mass-shooting in an elementary school, broke upon the United States with a new kind of horror. In January 2013, the newly formed[1] Moms Demand Action released an advertisement that drew together the fairy tale "Little Red Riding Hood" (ATU 333)[2] and an assault rifle (Figure 8.1).

On the floor of a school library two unsmiling little girls sit cross-legged. The girl on the left holds a copy of *Little Red Riding Hood* (retold and illustrated by beloved artist and author Trina Schart Hyman). The girl on the right holds an AR-15 semi-automatic rifle. Only one of these items kills children, the poster insists, and it is not the banned item. At first read, then, there is a seemingly stark difference between the contents in these little girls' hands. At this level of interpretation, the fairy tale and the weapon are meant to present a grimly

FIGURE 8.1: "'Choose One'—Little Red Riding Hood or an Assault Weapon?," Moms Demand Action.

ironic inversion—the innocent book banned for the "bottle of wine in [Riding Hood's] basket," the assault weapon endorsed for its deadly technology.

And yet, arguably, the advertisement captures something else about the fairy tale, something not quite innocent. The subtext of the image reads "we keep 'Little Red Riding Hood' out of schools … Why not assault rifles?" The superintendents who banned the book in 1990 and 1991 in a few counties in California and Florida purportedly did so because the bottle of wine in the basket sent the wrong message to children about alcohol consumption (Jacobs 2013). But this is hardly the most disturbing thing about the tale. As Jack Zipes ([1983] 1993), Alan Dundes (1989), Catherine Orenstein (2002), and I (2014) have previously argued, "Little Red Riding Hood" throughout its long history has been a narrative of a male predator enacting—or threatening to enact—sexualized violence against a little girl. As the tale passed through the moralizing and patriarchal filter of Perrault and the Grimms, the tale was reshaped to blame the victim for her own demise. Because the children in the image are little girls, perhaps the advertisement has something to say about gendered mechanisms of power; about the sick young men who represent the majority of our school shooters, about paramilitary fetishism stoked by America's imperial machinations and neo-nationalist turn since 9/11, about toxic masculinity combined with unchecked technology. So, at a deeper level of interpretation, we might look at the two little girls seated in mirrored poses, book and gun in laps, and conclude that the fairy tale is also an explosive technology, a mechanism of power; at times, it has been used to wield fear and control in ways adjacent to our deadliest science.

Detention Centers

In July 2019, Karen Greenberg wrote for *Salon*:

> Lately, I've been thinking about the Grimm's fairy tale, "Hansel and Gretel." Terrified by cruel conditions at home, the brother and sister flee, winding their way, hungry and scared, through unknown woods. There, they encounter an old woman who lures them in with promises of safety. Instead, she locks one of them in a cage and turns the other into a servant, as she prepares to devour them both.
>
> Written in nineteenth-century Germany, it should resonate eerily in today's America ... girls and boys by the hundreds fleeing cruelty and hunger ... believing that they will find a better life in the United States, only to be thrown into cages by forces far more powerful and agents much crueler than that wicked old woman.
>
> (Greenberg 2019)

The United States operates the world's largest immigration detention system. Detention has steadily risen, and detention centers have expanded, since the beginning of the twenty-first century, but with the 2017 inauguration of Donald Trump, and as an explicit part of his platform, detentions have skyrocketed. Though reported numbers vary, at the time of writing between 42,000 and 49,000 people are held daily in detention facilities, including at least 11,000 children (Joung 2019), with the Trump administration planning for an increase to 50,000 in 2020 (Buchholtz 2020). While public awareness of the foul and inhumane conditions of detention centers has been on the rise since Trump's election, US detention policy came to the forefront of public discourse only in April 2018, when the Trump administration issued a "Zero-Tolerance" policy for illegal border crossings, which further escalated detentions (Cheng 2018). When the American Civil Liberties Union (ACLU) sued the Trump administration in federal court in June 2018, the court ordered the government to return all children under five years old to their parents. But between April and June 2018 alone, over 2,500 children of asylum-seekers and border-crossers were separated from their parents (ACLU n.d.). In spring 2019, various media reports and congressional visits to detention facilities confirmed that the process of family separation has continued despite its illegality (Romero et al. 2019).

What is it about detention facilities that takes Greenberg to the fairy tale? Not just the plotline of "Hansel and Gretel" (ATU 327A), which is only thinly connected to the facts of US detention centers; surely it is also the casual, normalized cruelty we find in the fairy-tale form: the psychological violence of Hansel and Gretel's mother, the nightmarish qualities of her abandonment mirroring, not immigrant families, but the "caretaking" of the US Department of Health and Human Services to whom refugee children are turned over; the brutal, consumptive energies of the fairy-tale witch, the glittering lure of her gingerbread house like the empty promise of the American Dream. More obliquely, the Grimms' part in the nationalist project of early nineteenth-century Germany makes Greenberg's selection of tales especially resonant. The Grimms' versions of the tales are often moralistic, punitive, and misogynistic. Joan Acocella argues that they are also "premier representatives of the nationalism that became Aryanism in the nineteen-twenties and thirties" (Acocella 2012). While fairy-tale scholars have pointed out that the nationalism of the Grimms is not necessarily or teleologically connected to Nazism, the incarceration of children in the nineteenth-century German tale nevertheless points a ghostly finger to Germany's concentration camps in the twentieth, and thence to our own in the twenty-first.

Michael Brown

In August 2014, in Ferguson, Missouri, white police officer Darren Wilson fatally shot unarmed eighteen-year-old Michael Brown, a recent high school graduate, as he and his friend Dorian Johnson walked home after shoplifting some cigarillos. Wilson contended that Brown attacked him in his squad car, while Johnson testified that Wilson initiated the confrontation by grabbing Brown by the neck from the car and shooting at him. Brown and Johnson fled, with Wilson chasing. Wilson stated that Brown stopped and charged him after a short pursuit. Johnson contradicted this account, stating that Brown turned around with his hands raised after Wilson shot at his back. During the entire altercation, Wilson fired a total of twelve times, and hit the unarmed Brown six times. In November, a grand jury and the US Department of Justice each investigated, and both refused to indict Wilson, concluding that he killed Brown in self-defense. Brown's murder sparked the subsequent unrest in Ferguson, during which police issued curfews and deployed riot squads to keep "order," in many instances with unwarranted and unlawful militarized violence.

In his testimony before a grand jury, the 6-foot 4-inch (193-centimeter), 210-pound (95-kilogram) Darren Wilson repeatedly described the 6-foot 4-inch (193-centimeter), 292-pound (132-kilogram) Brown in both subhuman and preternatural terms: "He looked up at me and had the most intense, aggressive face. The only way I can describe it, it looks like a demon" (Wilson 2014: 225); "I don't know how many I shot, I just know I shot it" (228); "I felt like a five-year-old holding onto Hulk Hogan" (212); "it looked like he was almost bulking up to run through the shots, like it was making him mad that I'm shooting at him" (228). Several media responses in the wake of the November 24 acquittal commented on the police officer's depiction of the teenager as larger in spite of their equal statures, and identified Wilson's fear of Brown, his frequent slide into the "it" pronoun, as a projection of widespread racial fears and myths. Jamelle Bouie rightly connected Wilson's testimony to histories of white supremacist rhetoric of black men as "brutes": menacing, powerful, and unable to feel the pain of torture and punishment (Bouie 2014). But whereas Bouie and others compare Wilson's figurative language to comic book superhumans, at least two opinion pieces noticed the folk-narrative qualities of Wilson's testimony. Dexter Thomas notes that "there might have been a human out there in the street, but Wilson didn't see him. He saw a demon" (Thomas 2014). Amy Davidson Sorkin reflects that "Brown comes across as a big, mad genie," and points out that "there is not really a cross-examination, or any interrogation of the portrait of a young man who would run, enraged and magically indifferent, toward a volley of bullets, as if this were somehow a familiar, easily recognizable character" (Davidson Sorkin 2014). While there is no overt connection to the fairy tale in this reception, Thomas and Davidson Sorkin's focus on demons, genies, and the magical underscore the enduring connections between racial and physiognomic categorization and legends of the supernatural, such as fairies, goblins, and demons.

So then: three (and only three of many) contemporary crises. Three events in which our children are abandoned, tortured, and murdered in their schools and streets. How did we get here? And how does a girl holding a copy of *Little Red Riding Hood* in place of a gun, a boy compared to a demon, or Hansel and Gretel recast as refugees come to occupy, and even stand in for, the West's other travesties—its mythologies of safety, of equality, of opportunity? How do they come to signify on deadly technological advance? We shall see that the fairy tale is imbricated in—implicated in—various social, historical, and technological shifts, and the uses and abuses of power that accompanied them. This can be seen in the intersections of technological and fairy-tale print histories; it can also be witnessed through the ways in which fairy tales (and their literary vehicles) absorbed and reflected scientific and technological discourses. Finally, in the transforming hands of certain white male authors, the fairy tale has been wielded to consolidate power in the same fashion and against the same populations as these contemporary instances.

1842

Now consider a second span of time (1842, a single year in the nineteenth century), and another set of events. As with the contemporary markers detailed above, these Victorian events are harbingers of sorts: canaries in the coal mine, reflective of the technocratic regimes that were to come. Some of these scientific, industrial, or technological events were benign or beneficial; comparative anatomist and early paleontologist Richard Owen coined the term *Dinosauria* to describe and unify the reptile fossils that had been found in England since the late seventeenth century (Mullen 2015). Charles Darwin moved in and set up his worm bins at Down House, the home from which he would write all his evolutionary treatises (Darwin 1842). Edwin Chadwick published his *Report on the Sanitation of the Labouring Population*, which demonstrated the correlation between overcrowding, the lack of sanitation, and high rates of disease and mortality (Chadwick 1842). The *Mines Report* shocked the public with accounts of child labor and abuses, and the Mines and Collieries Act was passed that same year to prohibit all females and boys under ten years old from working in coal mines (Great Britain Commission 1842).

But many of the scientific, industrial, and technological advances of that year served as mechanisms for consolidating power within emerging paradigms of capitalism, imperialism, and racism. For example, Samuel George Morton, whose theory of craniometry—the argument that cranial capacity determines intellectual ability and comparative levels of "civilization" among races—had been published as *Crania Americana* (1839), was riding his wave of popularity with a lecture tour and a further publication ("An inquiry into the distinctive characteristics of the aboriginal race of America") en route to his second volume, *Crania Aegyptiaca* in 1844. Queen Victoria became the first steam-powered monarch when she rode the rails from Slough in Berkshire to London Paddington Station ("Her Majesty's First Trip By Railway" 1842). England's first locomotive rail line was laid in 1825: by 1850 rail would connect virtually all cities, towns, and villages in Britain, a technology that would effectively complete the shift from agrarian to industrial primacy. The advent of the railroad also enabled England to consolidate power in English colonies. The East India Company introduced rail to India in 1845, when it was primarily used to transport materials; after the 1857 rebellion, passenger train use accelerated for England to effectively move troops throughout the nation (Encyclopedia Brittanica n.d.; Jedwab, Kerby, and Moradi 2017; Tharoor 2017).

War technology also advanced: the 1842 Pattern Smoothbore Musket, a percussion cap rather than flintlock rifle, entered production; and the Royal Brass Foundry revolutionized its cannon and other gun production by switching to steam power (Wikipedia 2020). These advances coincided with the end of the First Opium War (1839–42) and the First Afghan War (1839–42), and no doubt aided imperial wars over the next decade: the Sikh Wars (1845–6, 1848–9), the Second Burmese War (1852–3), and the Crimean War (1853–6).

Separated as they are by 170 years, the differences between these contemporary and Victorian temporal coordinates are obvious: but their similarities bear marking. These are not magical dates but merely snapshots—almost (but not quite) incidental case studies. Both are poised on the verge of big changes in Great Britain and the United States, respectively. The period 2012–18 captures a time after the second tech boom produced by the rise of social media, and the concomitant increase in a globalized economy supported by that technology. Paradoxically, it also shows a nation in the midst of a sharp rise in white nationalism, as well as moments just before and just after the 2016 presidential election, an event indivisible from that rise, and strongly marked by various technologies of voter fraud. Meanwhile, 1842 captures the rise and solidity of modern capitalism, the faltering of the Chartist movement, the wheels of globalism and imperialism set in motion. These sets of years, disparate as they are, similarly bear witness to the mobilizing of technocratic regimes. Grand narratives of progress circulate around these time periods: in the nineteenth century, narratives of industry, prosperity, and advance; in the twenty-first century, the dawn of social media, the righting and globalization of the economy, the first black president. But as we know, some of our most trenchant, most pressing crises in the twenty-first century were enabled by the technological "breakthroughs" of the nineteenth.

How did the fairy tale enter into this fraught network of relationality? What place did the fairy tale hold in English culture in 1842? As I have demonstrated in *Spellbound: The Fairy Tale and the Victorians*, over the span of the nineteenth century, the fairy tale became entrenched in the Victorian literary community, in print media, theatrical performance, and visual art (Clark Hillard 2014). By 1842 the fairy tale is very much present in Victorian media, but not yet ubiquitous. The fairy pantomimes of the 1840s to 1880s; the fairy paintings of the late 1840s to 1890s by artists such as Joseph Noel Paton, John Anster Fitzgerald, Richard Doyle, Richard Dadd, John Everett Millais, and Edward Burne Jones; the rise of the children's book market, and the fairy-tale contributions there by the likes of John Ruskin, Lewis Carroll, George MacDonald, and Anne Thackeray Ritchie; the fairy and fairy tale's embeddedness in literary production for adults by authors including Brontë, Dickens, Eliot, and Christina Rossetti: all of this was yet to come. Therefore, let us shift attention to two poetic interventions in fairy-tale history, elaborating upon the ways in which Alfred Tennyson's and Robert Browning's interest in fairy tales and technological "progress" in their poetic works of 1842 cascaded into the nineteenth century, affecting other artistic media in the decades that followed.

"THE FAIRY TALES OF SCIENCE"

One important catalyst for the networking of science, technology, and the fairy tale came, not from science or fairy-tale publications but from literary production. Eighteen-forty-two was also the year Alfred Tennyson published his third volume of poetry, titled *Poems*, the work that secured his fame. Published in May of that year, *Poems* contains some of Tennyson's most anthologized, most often-adapted verse. Unsurprisingly, this volume is rich with the scientific influences that surrounded it. Tennyson was a lifelong learner, especially devoted to scientific readings, and he apocryphally divided up his week into self-taught units of study: "Monday. History, German./Tuesday. Chemistry, German./Wednesday. Botany, German./Thursday. Electricity, German./Friday. Animal Physiology, German./Saturday. Mechanics./Sunday. Theology" (Gold 2010: 37). What we don't often note is that in this 1842 volume, Tennyson meditated upon the fairy tale in equal measure with scientific advances (the word "fairy" appears twelve times across the two volumes). I'm proposing here that these studies were, for Tennyson, concurrent and mutually informative.

Poems was a two-volume set; the first volume offered revisions of poems from his 1830 volume, *Poems, Chiefly Lyrical*, and his 1832 volume, *Poems*. These included such works as "Mariana," "The Kraken," "The Lady of Shalott," and "The Palace of Art." The second volume contained new poems, including "The Epic," "Ulysses," "The Day Dream," and "Locksley Hall" (Tennyson 1842: vii–x). A merger of past and present work, then, this volume exhibits Tennyson's poetic practice, which drew upon the scientific methods of repetition, revision, and synthesis—methods that he absorbed with his course of self-guided education.

Several poems in the 1842 work treat folkloric subjects. "The Kraken" loosely adapts Norse legendry, while "Ulysses" takes the Greco-Roman hero legend as its subject. In the verse diptych "The Merman" and "The Mermaid" form a watery pastoral in which the speaker imagines the merman kissing and chasing mermaids, and the mermaid combing her hair until every sea creature falls in love with her. A series of other poems—"The Lady of Shalott," "The Epic," "Sir Galahad," "Sir Launcelot and Queen Guinevere"—treat Arthurian legend. One poem explores a specific fairy tale, "The Day Dream," Tennyson's adaptation of "Sleeping Beauty." In that poem, the fairy tale absorbs Tennyson's meditation upon temporality, ranging from timescales geologic, historical, and artistic, to timescales personal, gestational, and circulatory. As I discuss at length in *Spellbound*, Briar Rose's hundred years of sleep and resurrection gave Tennyson a language by which to articulate his poetic project, and a model by which to express his emerging philosophies of time and history (Clark Hillard 2014: 92–107). For the purposes of this chapter, though, I would like to focus on a different poem in the volume: "Locksley Hall" (Tennyson 1842: lines 92–111). Far from treating any single fairy tale, "Locksley Hall" devotes but a single line to the *concept* of the fairy tale. Nevertheless, I would argue that this line is crucial to the poem, to the volume as a whole, and to Victorian receptions and iterations of the fairy tale that were to come. It serves to frame and rationalize the other fantastic poems in the work, and it offers a methodology for uniting fairy-tale and technological discourses that other literary and visual artists adopted and carried forward into the century.

In Tennyson's dramatic monologue, the speaker is a soldier whose regiment is on the march near the eponymous Locksley Hall, his uncle's house where he was raised as an orphan with his cousin Amy (after his mother died in his infancy, and his father was killed in battle somewhere in India, where the speaker was also born). He sends his comrades on ahead while he lingers to reminisce:

> Here about the beach I wander'd, nourishing a youth sublime
> With the fairy tales of science, and the long result of Time;
> When the centuries behind me like a fruitful land reposed;
> When I clung to all the present for the promise that it closed:
> When I dipt into the future far as human eye could see;
> Saw the Vision of the world and all the wonder that would be.
> (Tennyson 1842: 93)

What does Tennyson mean by "the fairy tales of science?" Because of Locksley Hall's beach setting, the "fairy tales of science" may refer to natural history pursuits, or could refer to the fossil record visible on many of England's shorelines, which drew holidaymakers and amateur fossil hunters during the early half of the nineteenth century. If it weren't for the other fairy poems in the 1842 volume, we might conclude that he simply means something like "science and technology so unfamiliar that it seems outlandish, like fairy-tale magic." But as we move through "Locksley Hall," we can see a deeper resonance for Tennyson between the fairy tale and scientific epistemologies. Both rely on succinct, procedural, or episodic stories that serve to explain phenomenology of various kinds. Both are preoccupied with timescales and the relationship between time and human endeavor. And both are fundamentally immersed in, inured to, and even dependent upon violence to consolidate power.

The lines that follow "the fairy tales of science" suggest that the phrase causes the speaker to dilate on past, present, and future, to slip along time coordinates. In fact, the phrase seeps into the rest of the poem, causing a temporal rupture that affects its very structure; for the remainder of the poem, the speaker oscillates between past and present tense—sometimes to the point of readerly confusion as to just when we are. He remembers a much more recent past, in which he and Amy fall in love, but are parted when Amy's parents marry her off to a wealthy dullard. Reeling with grief, and excoriating Amy's inconstancy, the speaker—possessing neither money nor title, indeed nothing but an "angry fancy" (Tennyson 1842: 102)—resolves to "mix with action" by joining the military. Struggling to find a worldview that transcends personal love, the speaker "dip't into the future" (though when this takes place we can't be sure) and in this second reverie, he anticipates air travel, as well as globalized commerce, warfare, and government:

> Saw the heavens fill with commerce, argosies of magic sails,
> Pilots of the purple twilight dropping down with costly bales;
> Heard the heavens fill with shouting, and there rain'd a ghastly dew
> From the nations' airy navies grappling in the central blue;

> Far along the world-wide whisper of the south-wind rushing warm,
> With the standards of the peoples plunging thro' the thunder-storm;
> Till the war-drum throbb'd no longer, and the battle-flags were furl'd
> In the Parliament of man, the Federation of the world.
>   (Tennyson 1842: 104–5)

The past tense of this section connects it at least tacitly with the visions of his youth. It is "the fairy tales of science" that shall bring about and power the "magic sails" of commercial and military airships (moving, in other words, from the naturalizing of geologic timescales to the technology of the Anthropocene). Tennyson's speaker imagines this technology—including the technology of war and death—advancing a globalized civilization. But it bears noting that this is the future conjured by the "angry fancy" of this military speaker. It is the same fancy that calls his erstwhile beloved a "shallow-hearted" (line 39), "servile" "puppet" (Tennyson 1842: 96). It is the same fancy that imagines killing her and then himself (Tennyson 1842: 97). It is the same fancy that imagines a "retreat" to the "Orient," where the speaker "will take some savage woman, [who] shall rear [his] dusky race". The speaker almost immediately rejects this vision of "mating" and "herding" with "lower foreheads" "like a beast" (Tennyson 1842: 109) in favor of "forward" progress, concluding, "better fifty years of Europe than a cycle of Cathay" (Tennyson 1842: 110). The speaker's casual misogyny, racism, and nationalism are sublimated within his narrative of European expansion; nevertheless, they are tied directly to the "fairy tales of science." Therefore, for Tennyson's speaker, fairy tales crescendo to English imperial violence across the poem.[3] What is more, the "ghastly dew" of bloodshed foretold in "Locksley Hall" is echoed by the 1842 advances in gun manufacture (the percussion cap rifle and steam-powered cannon) that would make Sandy Hook possible 170 years later.

It is therefore not difficult to perceive the connection between "Locksley Hall" and cycles of power enacted over generations—the tyranny within domestic spaces echoed and compounded in imperial violence over the course of the poem. Nor is it necessary to belabor the ways in which Victorian advances in science are consolidated into brutalities of power in this poem. Less obvious is the case for numbering "Locksley Hall" among Tennyson's fairy poems, and connecting Tennyson's fairy poems to systems of gender and imperial violence and power. "Locksley Hall" is certainly not "fairy" like "The Day Dream" or other folkloric poems in the 1842 volume, nor "fairy" like those that followed on from it (Rossetti's *Goblin Market*, for instance).[4] Nevertheless, I would argue that it *is* a fairy poem in the sense that it advances a theory of interlocking and interdependent time scales—fairy-tale time, deep (or geologic or scientific) time, and human time. As I have shown elsewhere (Clark Hillard 2014: 92–107), Tennyson's first three volumes of poetry reveal his preoccupation with human progress and limitation: his speakers struggle to adopt and adapt to a model of time that is fundamentally "scientific"—linear, progressive, enlightened, and rational: in other words teleological—in the face of the overwhelming urge to double back, cycle through, and inhabit the past. As Kirstie Blair puts it, Tennyson was "writing into a heightened anxiety about relationships between the ticking of the clock, the motions of universe, and the rhythm of poetry" (Blair 2006: 81). Victorian interest in linear temporality dovetailed with scientific and technological developments of the first half of the century: Charles Lyell's *Principles of Geology*, the second law of thermodynamics, Darwin's *Origin of Species*, the relative affordability of the pocket watch and mantle clock.[5] It is not, as earlier critics[6] suggested, that these innovations created a new sense of time, or vice versa; rather, these scientific and industrial changes provided a new set of metaphors and analogues with which to imagine time, and—significantly—to imagine the interlocking relationships between time, the fairy tale, and power structures.

Because of its very connection to capitalist and technocratic structures, linearity is associated with masculinity, while cyclicality is both feminized (through female biology) and racialized ("better fifty years of Europe than a *cycle* of Cathay"; my emphasis). According to Julia Kristeva, the trope of linear time is imagined as a "prospective unfolding," including within its terms departure, progression, and arrival (Kristeva 1981: 17). In these terms, linear time occupies even the basic level of "language considered as the enunciation of sentences" and that "mastery of language is mastery of time" (17). Departure, progression, arrival: narrative, which shares these characteristics of "unfolding," might be conceived of as the "natural" mode of articulation of a normative "masculine time." Fairy tales, whether their print histories reflect a primarily male or female authorship, are often identified as a female cultural production, reflective not of temporalized narrative but of ineffable space. Perhaps this is because they take place in an abstract, historically unverifiable time and place ("once upon a time"). This is what Kristeva calls "matrix space": that is, "extrasubjective," "cosmic time," or "monumental temporality," which "has so little to do with linear time (which passes) that the very word 'temporality' hardly fits" (Kristeva 1981: 16). We need not look far to find evidence of the tyrannies of masculine time: the railroad and its clock; the factory and its assembly line; the increasing mechanization of war; the regulation and subordination of women through wage disparity (women's labor is less valuable to industry) and educational disparity (women as irrational, cyclical creatures are unfit for rational, intellectual heavy lifting); the justification of empire (indigenous populations, like women, are "extrasubjective" and thus incapable of self-governance). All of these are instances of how temporality itself was used to reify carceral power regimes.

Scientific (masculine) and fairy tale (feminine) time should be incompatible, therefore, but in "Locksley Hall," Tennyson appears to claim the fairy tale in the name of science. As previously noted, the very processes of the scientific method are iterative and cyclic, as was Tennyson's composition process. "Locksley Hall" engages in what feel like increasingly desperate attempts by the speaker to impose harsh, macho linearity and futurity on what he suspects to be cyclic and feminine within himself. The speaker's oscillation between tenses and his tendency toward melancholic retrospection stand in contrast to his ameliorative bombast throughout. Moreover, the speaker twice refers to his contemporary moment as his "Mother Age" (Tennyson 1842: 103, 110), a phrase that reads ironically coming from this poster boy for toxic masculinity. By the end of the poem, it's clear that the speaker means by "Mother Age" the agent that gives birth to technological innovations, much as the "fairy tales of science" in his past give way to the scientific "inspiration" (Tennyson 1842: 93, 111) of the future. As if anticipating what Vladimir Propp would later propose, that "Folklore is the womb of literature ... Folklore is the prehistory of literature ... Literature, which is born of folklore, soon abandons the mother that reared it" (Propp 1984: 14), in "Locksley Hall" the fairy tale appears to be the womb of science as well as literature.

This single verse line in "Locksley Hall" evokes an entire genre and its complex networks, and therefore demonstrates the extent to which the fairy tale had already entered public imagination and discourse. It also set the stage for the resonance between fairy tales and science that endured thereafter. Later in the century, authors played with Tennyson's "Locksley Hall" quote, "the fairy tales of science." Possibly the first adaptation of this kind was John Cargill Brough's *The Fairy Tales of Science: A Book for Youth* (1859). The book uses the conventions, narrative structure, and what Brough calls the "attractive garb" of folk narrative to "clothe" science for children (iii). More specifically, Brough organizes the book around various scientific inquiries dressed in the vocabulary of the marvelous: "The Age of Monsters" on the fossil record, "The Amber Spirit" on electricity, "The Mermaid's Home" on oceanography, "The Gnomes" on speleology, "The Wonderful Lamp" on steam technology, and so forth. The work is fascinating in and of itself, but also in that it seems to have ushered in a subgenre of works in the same vein, among them Arabella Buckley's *The Fairyland Of Science* (1879), Forbes E. Winslow's *Fairy Geography,* and Charlotte Tucker's *Fairy Know-A-Bit* (1868).

Over three decades later, solicitor and president of the Folklore Society Edwin Sidney Hartland published *The Science of Fairy Tales*: *An Inquiry into the Fairy Mythology* (1891). Hartland's title both recalls and inverts Tennyson's "Locksley Hall" phrase. He reads the structure of fairy legends (not tales) through the lens of the survival theory so popular at the time. No doubt indebted to the organization of Brough's *Fairy Tales of Science*, Hartland organizes his book conceptually, with chapters on, for instance, "Fairy Births and Human Midwives," "Changelings," "Robberies from Fairyland," "The Supernatural Lapse of Time in Fairyland," and "Swan Maidens." Hartland makes clear in his preface that the book is not intended for children but, rather, "to exhibit to readers who are not specialists, the application of the principles and methods which guide investigations into popular traditions" (1891: v). Where Brough hopes to win readership by demonstrating the resonance between scientific and fantastic epistemologies, Hartland is clearly at pains to position folkloric study squarely within the scientific framework as it existed at the end of the century.

It is important to emphasize the extent to which work like Brough's and Hartland's depend upon the placement of the "Locksley Hall" speaker, standing on both a physical and temporal shore, looking into the future of human intellectual enterprise and its modes and forms of power. These authors take up Tennyson's challenge to imagine progress in several ways. First, they particularize Tennyson's "fairy tales of science" into a kind of taxonomy; in Brough's case, the branches of science are governed by fairy-tale narrative intervention, and in Hartland's, a fairy-tale taxonomy is ordered and explained through Victorian ethnographic methods. Second, through taking up Tennyson in this way, these authors insert themselves into his paradigm of "the long result of time" as practitioners after Tennyson who undo rigid distinctions between science and the fairy tale. Finally, they follow Tennyson in imagining how this unification of science and the fairy tale might be leveraged for power. This is not to suggest that all Victorian interest in the fairy tale, or science and the fairy tale, flows from Tennyson. The fairy tale's points of entry were too many and too diffuse for that to be true. However, it is also important to take full measure of Tennyson's tremendous influence upon later Victorian artistic media. The "angry fancy" of the "Locksley Hall" speaker seems to have struck an answering chord in young male artists for decades thereafter.

"SOME SUBTERRANEOUS PRISON"

If Tennyson's reception of and intervention into the fairy tale facilitated the neoliberal, nationalistic manipulation of the genre, Robert Browning's experimentation with the tale form showcases the tale as a resistant and subversive technology. In November 1842, Browning published his volume *Dramatic Lyrics*, which, as with Tennyson, included some of his most famous poetry, including "Porphyria's Lover," "My Last Duchess," and "Soliloquy of the Spanish Cloister." It also included "The Pied Piper of Hamelin," a poem he had originally written for his friend William Macready's young son Willy to illustrate while he was sick in bed (Queenan 1978). The poem was based on the medieval German legend "Der Rattenfanger von Hameln" ("The Ratcatcher of Hamelin"), specifically, the English translation by Richard Verstegan from 1605.[7] In Browning's poem, the riverside town of Hamelin is plagued by rats; the townspeople threaten to sack the "Mayor and Corporation" (1842: line 33) unless they can solve the vermin problem. Sitting in council at Town Hall, they are interrupted by a knock on the door, and in walks a man wearing a "pied" coat of red and yellow, with "sharp blue eyes ... and light loose hair, yet swarthy skin ... There was no guessing his kith and kin" (line 64). "Pied" in both dress and nationality, then, he advertises himself as an international vermin hunter, one who has magically exterminated "mole and toad and newt and viper" (line 78), as well as gnats, vampire bats, and scorpions (line 92) from "Tartary" to Asia to Afghanistan (line 89). He offers to rid the town of rats by means of a charm for a thousand guilders. The Mayor agrees, and the man plays a tune on his pipe, which brings all rats running to the River Weser, where they are drowned. The Mayor then refuses to pay the piper, offering him fifty guilders instead. The piper refuses, and pipes again, this time charming the town's children. They follow the piper to a "door in the mountainside" (line 231) where they are lost to Hamelin forever. However, the speaker tells us, a story goes that Transylvania was settled by a group of people who had "risen / Out of some subterraneous prison / Into which they were trepanned" from Hamelin (line 294–6).

"The Pied Piper" was a last-minute addition to *Dramatic Lyrics*; this may have been in part because Browning noticed the immense popularity of the folkloric material in Tennyson's *Poems*, published six months before, and was hoping to appeal to readers with similar fare. However, it also might have had something to do with the publication of the *Report of the Children's Employment Commission* in May (Wood 1842), and the passage of the Mines Act in August 1842. Most of literate Britain had read—with absorption and horror—what was familiarly called the *Mines Report*, the result of a three-year Royal Commission investigation, led by Lord Ashley, Earl of Shaftesbury, into working conditions in mines and factories in Britain. There the public read testimony from child miners, some as young as five, and learned that children were five times cheaper to employ than adults, and were expected to work the same shifts, separated from their parents, from eleven to fourteen hours per day. They learned that working conditions in the mines were perilous, sometimes fatally so, and that children were often given tasks with the highest likelihood of cave-ins, flooding, and suffocation. They learned that child miners, not exclusively but especially the girls, were exposed to sexual assault by both adult and juvenile miners. In other words, middle- and upper-class England was forced to see what it would rather not: that its industrial and technological power was carried on the backs of exploited working-class children. To ensure swift legislation, Lord Ashley and his investigators focused their rhetorical attentions on the "moral" problem of children in the mines, not of the mine owners themselves: that women and girls wore trousers in the mines blurred gender binaries, and that children went naked underground provoked "immoral" behavior. Investigators' reports both animalized and eroticized child bodies, tactically underscored by the report's accompanying engravings.[8] Put another way, the *Mines Report* made clear both the shocking, inhumane treatment of children, but also the Victorian belief in a fundamental difference in humanity between working-class and middle-class children.[9]

The subtitle of Browning's "Pied Piper" is "A Child's Story," and its prosody—full of feminine rhyme and skipping, jingling meter—at first seems to reinforce its title. However, Browning is hardly known for his children's poetry: "Pied Piper" is unique among his oeuvre. Tucked in with his *Dramatic Lyrics*, it seems an odd fit with poems like "Porphyria's Lover" and "My Last Duchess." In fact, "Pied Piper" was not remarketed for children until Kate Greenaway published her illustrated version of 1889, just after Browning's death. This would suggest that the poem first written for an eight-year-old middle-class child's amusement also holds at its core a critique—though a very subtle one—of child labor practices. Elizabeth Barrett published "Cry of the Children"—her poem explicitly about child miners—in August 1843, a year before Browning met her. Barrett and Browning shared progressive political convictions: indeed, it was one of the factors that drew them together. It is therefore not much of a stretch to think that Browning may have been using the "Pied Piper" legend to contribute his own commentary on the horrors of mine technology. Unlike Tennyson, then, Browning would have evoked folk narrative to damn, rather than celebrate, English "progress."

For one thing, the poem implicitly correlates children with rats. Whereas the charmed rats are anthropomorphized (likened to an "army" [Browning 1842: line 107], whose "muttering grew to a grumbling" [line 108], and as "families by tens and dozens / Brothers, sisters, husbands, wives" [line 117]), the charmed children are dehumanized (moving with a "rustling" [line 198], a "pattering" [line 199], and "like fowls in a farm-yard when barley is scattering" [line 201]). One is reminded of various Victorian epithets for working-class children, among them "street vermin," "street Arabs," and "dock" or "wharf rats." Even though all of Hamelin's children are abducted—presumably irrespective of caste difference—one wonders whether Browning was thinking of the dehumanization of laboring children in this elision between human and animal. For another thing, the children are lured away to a "cavern" (line 229), into which they are "trepanned," and Browning's verb choice is telling: "trepan" means both to bore or drill and to entrap or beguile. If the bodily movement of rats and children converge, so too do their respective ends: the one death by drowning, the other to exile in a "subterraneous prison." These are different fates, to be sure, but both life sentences; indeed, in mining history, the two fates frequently converged. The report on the labor condition for child

FIGURE 8.2: William (Willie) C. Macready Jr, "Pencil Illustration III," from Robert Browning's "The Pied Piper of Hamelin" (1842). Browning Collections. Armstrong Browning Library, Baylor University, Waco, TX.

miners came about after an accident in 1838 at Huskar Colliery in Yorkshire, in which twenty-six children were drowned when their ventilation system flooded ("The Huskar Pit Disaster, 1838" 2004). One might even go so far as to say that Willy Macready's illustration for the "door in the mountainside"—whether intentionally or not—looks like the entrance to a mine (Figure 8.2).

In bearing witness to children in US detention camps, Karen Greenberg was reminded of "Hansel and Gretel." But in reflecting on the networks of 1842 and 2019, I wonder whether "The Pied Piper of Hamelin" might also offer a folk narrative connection. In the Browning poem, in mining history, and in our contemporary immigration crisis, children are separated from their parents, trepanned into prison, dehumanized, endangered, and even doomed by broken promises and the greed of politicians and for-profit industries, including prisons. Latent in the piper's song is the promise "of a joyous land … / Where waters gushed, and fruit-trees grew / And flowers put forth a fairer hue, / And everything was strange and new" (Browning 1842: 240–4). What is this if not the abominable lie of the capitalist dream, which promises safety and refuge, victory and plenty, to those who work hard and sacrifice?[10]

COLORED FAIRIES
Visual Imagery

The influences of 1842 resounded throughout the rest of century, both in the expansion of the technocratic regime, and in the legacy of Tennyson and Browning. As England's poet laureate, Tennyson was by far more popular (and more mainstream) than Browning in the middle of the century. The bellicose "angry fancy" of "Locksley Hall" seems to have outweighed the resistant symbolism of Browning's "child's story" for the reading public. Tennyson's poetry was among the most popular subjects for mid- to late Victorian visual artists: illustrators, painters, and photographers alike.[11] Of course, another popular subject for painters was fairies and fairy tales in works such as John Everett Millais's "Little Red Riding Hood" (1864), Edward Burne-Jones's "Cinderella" (1863) and "Briar Rose" series (1885–90), and the fairy paintings of Joseph Noel Paton, Richard Doyle, John Anster Fitzgerald, and Richard Dadd.[12] These fairy subjects were influenced by a variety of cultural sources, such as the pantomime and circulation of fairy tales and legends in print media. Tennyson's poetry was one of the influences here, too: Burne-Jones commented that he derived his subjects "from vague impressions left by poems which I have forgotten."[13]

As previously mentioned, one of the "fairy tales of science" to emerge in and around 1842 was Morton's pseudo-scientific theory of craniometry. We can see it taking root in "Locksley Hall," when the speaker first imagines "tak[ing] a savage woman" and creating a "dusky race" of "iron-jointed, supple-sinew'd" (Tennyson 1842: line 169) people, then turns in disgust at the thought of "herd[ing] with narrow foreheads ... like a beast with lower pleasures, like a beast with lower pains" (lines 175–6). Craniometry and its ills can also be seen in later Victorian visual art, and nowhere better than its fairy paintings.

For instance, in a detail of Paton's painting *Quarrel of Oberon and Titania* (1849), a border of white-skinned, blond fairies chase, caress, and woo each other, while a group of fairies with racially caricatured faces and animalistic bodies occupies the center, kneeling before the largest of their number, a black-skinned fairy; hats in hand, and looking terrified, they appear to offer him up a slug.[14] Doyle's *Fairy Tree* (1870) also associates fairy otherness with racial difference. The fairies sit on the branches of a tree, reminding us of Darwinian phylogeny. Several of Doyle's fairies are rendered with racially stereotyped facial features and bodies, clearly drawing upon the craniometric grotesquery of racial caricature. All fairies orient to the white-skinned king seated in the middle of the tree, and march toward him to pay him tribute.[15] John Anster Fitzgerald's painting *The Fairy's Lake* (1866; Figure 8.3) features a white-skinned, winged fairy splashing happily in the water. Behind her, a red-skinned, top-knotted fairy, flying astride an owl or bat-like creature appears to be on the verge, either of impaling her with a spear or snatching her up with a clawed hand.

FIGURE 8.3: John Anster Fitzgerald, *The Fairy's Lake*, exhibited 1866. Oil paint on board. Tate. Reproduced with the permission of Tate Images.

The faces of these fairies are caricatured with all of the physiognomic poison of craniometry, which said that the brains of women and people of color were smaller and therefore inferior; which theorized that "prognathous" (or protruding) jaws were inherent to nonwhite (but especially "negro") faces, compared to the "orthognathous" (or vertical) profile of Westerners (or "Caucasians"), and this "proved" the evolutionary superiority of whites. Doyle's racialized fairies are meant to evoke laughter, like his *Punch* cartoons.[16] But Paton's and Fitzgerald's racial fairies are monstrous. They leer with flaming eyes, or gape with teeth bared. They are drawn to frighten. They are meant to evoke the goblinish, demonic side of the fairy folk.[17]

Michael Brown died because Darren Wilson looked at a young black man and thought, "the *only way I can describe it*, it looks like a demon." Wilson's tunnel vision, the delimited possibilities for his looking and describing, was created by the last two hundred years of scientific racism, grandfathered by Morton's theory of craniometry, among other pseudosciences. But those theories became instantiated, popularized, made palatable or titillating or comical in visual artistry of all kinds, among which are the fairy paintings I've described. It is significant that Wilson's racist visual transposition is not exactly animalistic, not precisely the "black beast" of Reconstruction, but demonic, supernatural.[18] Though the path is winding and the tributaries many, the racism of Victorian fairy paintings are a strand in the cultural network that murdered Michael Brown.

The Social Sciences

In the last third of the Victorian period, roughly 1870–1910, the relationship between fairy tales and science/technocracy became formalized. Edwin Sidney Hartland's aforementioned indebtedness to Tennyson in his *Science of Fairy Tales* was one example of how folklore as a whole was folded into the emerging social science disciplines of anthropology/ethnography, sociology, and psychology—first obliquely through the works of Edward Tylor, and then more specifically through what Richard Dorson has called "The Great Team" of British folklorists. This period of time, and this group of people, were characterized by shared goals as well as coterie scholarship and production. They founded the first Folklore Society (1878), launched the first folklore journal (1890), and held the first International Folklore Congress (1891). The group included theorists, collectors, publishers, and popularists. Among them, in addition to Hartland, were George Lawrence Gomme (*Ethnology in Folklore* [1892], *Folklore as Historical Science* [1908]), Joseph Jacobs (*English Fairy Tales* [1890], *Celtic Fairy Tales* [1891], *Indian Fairy Tales* [1892]), Marian Roalfe Cox (*Cinderella: Three Hundred and Forty-Five Variants* [1893]), Andrew Lang (the *Colored Fairy Books* [1889–1913], among many other publications), and David MacRitchie (*Testimony of Tradition* [1890], *Fians, Fairies, and Picts* [1893], and *Hints of Evolution in Tradition* [1902]).

While these scholars succeeded in a great deal of preservational and archival work, and dignified the study of folklore into an academic (if still leisured) discipline, they were also largely guided by the racism and imperialism of scientific enterprise. Nearly all of these scientific folklorists believed in "savage" survivals theory; that folk narrative was "the tattered remnants" of a past oral tradition that "trickled up" from primitive people to literate Europeans (Dorson 1968: 191). Through this theory, the purported "savagery" of folklore may be conflated with the bodies that produce it in all directions. For instance, theorist MacRitchie developed a euhemeristic theory of fairies, in which he argued that fairy legends originated as a "folk memory" of an aboriginal race that occupied the British Isles before Celts and other groups arrived. When white explorers discovered "pygmy" tribes in Africa and Asia, they latched on to MacRitchie's theory, likening the "seemingly magical appearance" of the people they "found" to the "brownies and goblins of our fairy stories" and "the gnomes and elves of European legend" (Silver 1999: 136).[19]

Lang's twelve books of collected folk and fairy tales were familiarly called the *Colored Fairy Books* (though little of their contents included stories of the fairies per se). Lang was listed as the sole compiler of these phenomenally popular books, but in reality his wife Leonora Blanche Alleyne and a host of mostly female translators and adaptors did the bulk of the collection and editorial work (Day 2017). In his prefaces to the volumes, Lang both racialized and feminized the process of narration and transmission. Tales, he says, are ancient, first told by "naked savage women to naked savage children" (1901: vii). He explained over and over, across the twelve books in the series, that folk and fairy tales' "irrational and 'infantile' character ... is derived from their origin, if not actually among children, at least among childlike peoples, who have not arrived at 'raison,' that is, at the scientific and modern conception of the world and of the nature of man" (Lang 1911: 370). The popular work of the Langs is the closest thing to a global fairy-tale tradition at the end of the nineteenth century. The *Colored Fairy Books* are perhaps something that Tennyson (who died in 1892) would have imagined among the artifacts of the "Parliament of man / The federation of the world." The bulk of the tales are European, but there are also selections from Africa, the Americas, Australia, China, Japan, Serbia, and the Middle East. In the prefaces, Lang frequently expresses frustration that people think he wrote what he purports to have collected. In this maneuver the power structures of the editorial and publishing processes are writ plainly: he downplays the extent to which the tales are wrung through a British translational, creative, and editorial mangle, a rhetorical move that, ironically, stills both the voices of color that came out of and the female labor that went into the tales. Like Tennyson and others before, Lang claims the fairy tale in the name of science, and capitalizes on both its feminine and racial "qualities," but simultaneously distances himself from the "infantile" oral narrative, framing himself as the learned man of letters who offers (but of course, what he was really doing was commoditizing and selling) the stories to white families.

So, when did the books come to be familiarly called the "*Colored* Fairy Books"? Lang never called them so in any of his prefaces. But at least by 1906, book reviewers seemed to be commonly referring to the books in this way (Wilkenson 1906). Given the opposition the Langs' fairy books created between the "children black and brown and yellow" from whose countries the stories originated and those of "the white-skinned race" (Anonymous 1906) for whom the books were intended, we might wonder about the history of the word "colored" as it describes racial difference. It would be natural to assume that "colored" was a product of the racially segregated American South, perhaps especially the period between the 1930s and 1960s. But not so: the word has explicitly "denoted a member of any dark-skinned group of peoples ... a person of sub-Saharan African or ... South Asian origin or descent ... in earliest use with reference to South America" since at least 1758, and was apparently in common use throughout the nineteenth century. This coinage of the word, therefore, has to do with the moment of European (specifically Anglo-European) consciousness of things that are not itself. And since fairy tales and legends are also very much about these same moments, this same consciousness of difference, Lang's work offers an especially apt confluence as a case study in late-century fairy media production and its mechanisms of power. However subtly, "colored" becomes another word, another weapon, in the technocratic, pseudoscientific arsenal; becomes another way in which the fairy tale's flexible powers were diverted to support England's industrial and imperial projects.

2019

This chapter needs a conclusion: something triumphal and upbeat, something wise and definitive. But it cannot be concluded, for (and this is if we are very lucky) we are in the midst, not at the end, of the tragedies unleashed by our technocratic regimes and their abuses of power. Since Sandy Hook, Ferguson, and the election of 2016, the United States has been subject to one onslaught after another of nationalism, misogyny, and racism. And as my contemporary case studies indicated, the fairy tale is so embedded in our scientific and technological power structures that its misuses can be very hard to disrupt. The "Sleeping Beauty" tale still haunts the narrative of conception in certain biology textbooks, in which "the spermatic hero actively pursues the egg, surviving the hostile environment of the vagina and defeating his many rivals. The large and placid egg, like Sleeping Beauty, drifts unconsciously along the fallopian tube, until awakened by a valiant sperm" (Schiebinger 1999: 145). Nanotechnologists rely on the word origin *Nano*, dwarf in Italian as well as classical Latin and Greek, in their publication and visual representation, making connections between microtechnology and the little people. Perhaps the originators of the word meant to evoke associations with the labor of dwarves and goblins on behalf of humans; but because of the Victorian connection of the dwarf/goblin with nonwhite people, "nanos" also have disturbing associations with unpaid, forced labor.

And yet, the fairy tale *can* be used to call out the West's mythologies too, to speak truth to power, as the Moms Demand Action visual and the Greenburg essay on detention centers certainly demonstrate. Perhaps, then, the best way to end this chapter is to return for a moment to the Brownings. While Tennyson may have taught a generation of young male artists to claim the fairy tale in the name of neoliberal "progress," it is worth considering that "The Pied Piper of Hamelin" wound in and through Elizabeth Barrett and Robert Browning's meeting, and in some fashion guided their subsequent personal and political action. In 1842 Robert Browning published "Pied Piper," arguably critiquing child labor. In 1843 Elizabeth Barrett published "Cry of the Children," a poem explicitly critiquing child labor. In 1845 the two began to correspond and, after a while, to meet: they were already deep admirers (and in their words, "students") of each other's poetry and politics (Barrett, January 11, 1845; Browning and Barrett 1900), and they rapidly fell deeply into both friendship and love. On September 12, 1846, they secretly married and eloped to Italy, where they lived for the next sixteen years, until Barrett's death. It has often been described as among the most egalitarian of Victorian marriages, refusing the normalized power abuses of the Victorian marriage market and domestic sphere.

I do not recall this most tender of Victorian love stories to suggest that in the face of our global dumpster fire we should retreat to the domestic, the individual, or the heterosexual contract. On the contrary, Barrett and Browning's love was to themselves very much a symbol of being affiliated with the world:

> Here is the whole wondrous Ba [Barrett's nickname] filling my whole heart and soul; and over-filling it, because she is in all the world ... Am I not with you in the world? ... In my secret heart I know what my "mission of humanity" means [a code term for their secret meetings], and what telescopic and microscopic views it procures me.
> (Browning, February 25, 1846; Browning and Barrett 1900)

Barrett and Browning left England to escape Barrett's despotic father, who refused to allow his children to marry, and who had all but confined Barrett to the house as an invalid. They remained to pursue life on their own terms; lives of political activism (specifically antislavery, anti-Semitism, and feminism) and of avant-garde poetry. The activism begun on their own, on English soil, was stronger together, in love and in Italy; so too their writing: their removal from England allowed them an expansion of perspective that led to their finest work. In 1850 Barrett was passed over for Poet Laureate in favor of Tennyson. But, arguably, it didn't matter: as laureate, she would have belonged to England, and would have been compelled to compose poetry in conformity to its national ethos, to its burgeoning capitalism and imperialistic power mongering. In Italy, she could write *Sonnets from the Portuguese* and *Aurora Leigh*, her amatory and feminist masterpieces. Without travel, without Browning, they would not have been written at all. They may have joked about a "mission of humanity," but what was their union, their writing, if not this?

Lastly, but importantly for this chapter, Barrett and Browning agreed about what made successful fairy tales: Barrett complained about another poet's attempt at an "Elf-story": "I can take delight in the fantastical, and in the grotesque ... but ... the elf is no elf and speaks no elf-tongue: it is not the right key to touch ... for supernatural music" (Barrett, January 6, 1846; Browning and Barrett 1900). Browning concurred: "fairy stories, the good ones, were written for men and women, and, being true, pleased also children; now, people set about writing for children and miss them and the others too" (Browning,

January 7, 1846; Browning and Barrett 1900). However briefly touched upon, this is a conversation about the power of fairy tales, their capacity to encode adult meaning. To speak in "elf-tongue" was to tap into the discursive potency of narrative folklore and the literary fairy tale, and so to speak truth to power, to enact change. Surely the Brownings instantiate what Latour and Felski mean by a network, the "sometimes ... unpredictable ways in which ideas, texts, images, people, and objects couple [and] attach." And if so, then perhaps they offer a model for how we might continue to read, study, critique, and adapt the Victorian fairy tale: a model for how we might network the fairy tale into our actions of resistance and resilience, hope and love, as we move into this most uncertain of futures.

NOTES

Introduction

1. See Michelle Beissel Heath, this volume.
2. See, among others, Bottigheimer (1986); Haase (1993); Tatar (2003); and Zipes (2014).
3. James MacPherson's poetry by the purported third-century bard Ossian (1760) was widely read and celebrated, and it fueled interest in folk poetry. "Herder's admiration for Ossian and for the folk poetry collected in Thomas Percy's antiquarian *Reliques of Ancient English Poetry* (1765) … compels him to issue an impassioned call to his compatriots to begin the vital task of collecting this cultural treasure before it vanishes altogether" (Lokke 2006: 140). In France, Hersart de la Villemarqué likewise presented *Barzaz-Breiz: chants populaire de la Bretagne* (1839) in the Celtic style as the work of an ancient Breton bard.
4. U. C. Knoepflmacher, indeed, reads the entire story as demonstrating Ruskin's fundamental resistance to growth and full adulthood, associating nature and the fairy tale with childlike innocence (Knoepflmacher 1998). Nicole Thesz expands on this point in her chapter in this volume.
5. Kingsley's epigraph to chapter 1 cites the first two stanzas of William Wordsworth's "Lines Written in Early Spring" (1798).
6. Charles Kingsley's *The Water-Babies*, and George MacDonald's *At the Back of the North Wind* (1871), among others, also make use of this imagery. See Wood (2004).
7. Maria Tatar's note 3 to "The Happy Prince" (2017b: 338).
8. Caroline Sumpter observes that this lively recollection invites Dickens's readers to pity his child self (2008: 25); yet his own literary career exploited such devices to grand effect—Fagin, Bill Sikes, Daniel Quilp, and other Dickensian villains arguably draw their macabre vitality from similar sources.
9. Maria Tatar points out that the Grimms did not achieve a bestseller until they copied the success of this edition. The Grimms' 1825 abridged, illustrated, and lower-priced edition finally met with "full-scale popular success" (Tatar 2003: 19).
10. A partial list includes "The Golden Key" (1867), *The Princess and the Goblin* (1872), *The Princess and Curdie* (1882), *At the Back of the North Wind* (1871).

11 See Amy Billone, this volume.
12 For more on Carroll's revolutionary effect on the fairy tale, see Jan Susina, this volume.
13 See also Marsh (2008).

Chapter 1

1   Because of the pervasive influence and strength of puritanism in Britain, with its emphasis of reason and morality, it is often arguably believed that before the Romantic period, unlike in France and in Germany, imaginative reading (particularly represented by fairy tales) was banned from British children's bookshelves. Throughout the eighteenth century, moreover, as accounts of English children's literature have often suggested, children were nurtured by didactic stories in the vein of Maria Edgeworth's narratives and sermons (a classic writer for children very much involved in educational issues), and protected from the dangers of the imagination so as to become industrious and responsible citizens. Studies by Mitzi Myers, Alan Richardson, and Donelle Ruwe have since revised these conceptions of eighteenth-century English children's literature, proposing a much more nuanced view of early Georgian educationalists, which illustrates that their moral and rational tales never truly banished fairy-tale plots and patterns but often adapted them instead, especially using their moralization potential (see Richardson 2010; Ruwe 2005: 117). As James Holt MacGavran contends, indeed, the fairy tale was "never truly banished" although it remained "outside the mainstream of acceptable children's literature" ([1991] 2009: 17). As one of the key pedagogues of the last decades of the eighteenth century, Anna Laetitia Barbauld proposed increasingly amusing narratives, adding motifs borrowed from the world of fairy tales to her stories, as in her six-volume collection *Evenings at Home* (1792–6). Though still very much instructive and didactic and highly repressing fancy, her method was, however, disapproved of by Sarah Trimmer (1741–1810), who strictly condemned fairy stories. Trimmer was known for launching the *Family Magazine* (1788–9), which contained moral tales and sermons, and wrote on education; her *Guardian of Education* (1802–6) directly addressed parents and governesses and warned them about the qualities or dangers of newly published children's literature. Mary Sherwood (1775–1851) similarly disliked fairy tales. When she re-edited Sarah Fielding's *The Governess* in 1820, she deleted the two fairy tales. See Myers (1986).
2   Many gothic novels published during the first wave of gothic novels (1764–1824) also recurrently used fairy-tale motifs and plot-patterns, especially those published by the Minerva Press.
3   Silver analyses here Blake's romantic fairies.
4   Fairy painting drew heavily upon Shakespeare's *A Midsummer Night's Dream* and *The Tempest* (Wood 2000: 13). In addition to Fuseli and Blake, Silver mentions David Scott's *Puck Fleeing From the Dawn* (1837), Richard Dadd's *Puck*, Robert Huskisson's *The Midsummer Night's Fairies*, Sir Joseph Noel Paton's *Oberon Watching a Mermaid* (1883), Edwin Landseer's *Titania and Bottom*, and John Simmons's oil paintings and watercolors of Titania as major fairy paintings derived from *A Midsummer Night's Dream*. John Stothard, Francis Danby, Henry Thomason, and Joseph Severn contributed Shakespearian fairy paintings as well; see Silver (1999: 19–20, 215). Victorian fairy painting changed after 1850, freeing itself from literary influences.

5 The fairy tale was included in an educational book, *Magasin des enfans, ou dialogues entre une sage gouvernante et plusieurs de ses élèves de la première distinction* and published in 1757. When Leprince de Beaumont reworked Villeneuve's "Beauty and the Beast," she changed the fairy tale into a moral lesson intended for a young, mainly female audience. Villeneuve's long romance, published in *La jeune amériquaine, et les contes marins*, was dramatically shortened by Leprince de Beaumont, who, in particular, cut the long descriptions of Beauty's entertainments at the palace and the dream sequences in which a prince and a fairy appeared to Beauty to encourage her not to be deceived by appearances; see Hearne (1989: 26).

6 John Harris was the successor of John Newbery, who had launched the market for children's literature in the middle of the eighteenth century, merging instruction and amusement in his publications for children. Harris was famous for his amusing stories for children, such as Sarah Catherine Martin's *The Comic Adventures of Old Mother Hubbard and Her Dog* (1805), William Roscoe's *The Butterfly's Ball* (1807), and Catherine Dorset's *Peacock "At Home"* (1807).

7 Regarding children's literature and censorship, see Knoepflmacher (1998).

8 Carroll regularly called his fantasy a "fairy tale," such as when he wrote to a professional illustrator (Tom Taylor) to ask him for advice on the title: "I should be very glad if you could help me in fixing on a name for my fairy-tale" (Charles Dodgson to Tom Taylor, June 10, 1864, quoted in Cohen [1982] 1989: 29).

9 The story is also said to come from the narrator's godmother's grandmother's grandmother, foregrounding a matrilineal line of storytellers.

10 Ritchie knew classical fairy tales; she translated and wrote an introduction to Marie-Catherine d'Aulnoy's fairy tales.

11 As I have argued elsewhere, unlike Ritchie, however, who uses the modern building to epitomize her heroine's soaring desire, Andersen's tale used the Great Exhibition to stress the taming of the Dryad's "nature." See Talairach-Vielmas (2014: 93–9).

12 See Bown's analysis of Edward Hopley's *Puck and a Moth* (1854) (Bown 2001: 41–3).

13 See, for instance, Rev. John George Wood, *Common Objects of the Microscope* (1861). This idea is further developed in my *Fairy Tales, Natural History and Victorian Culture* (2014: chs 1 and 2).

14 Though Victorian fairy painting was not a movement in itself, its golden age was between 1840 and 1870; after 1870, fairies mainly appeared in children's literature and illustrations, in particular Arthur Rackham's and Edmund Dulac's (Wood 2000: 11).

15 These are aspects developed further in Bown (2001).

16 This point is further developed in Talairach-Vielmas (2014).

17 See, for instance, Michael Aislabie Benham's pamphlet, *A Few Fragments of Fairyology, Shewing its Connection with Natural History* (1859), which tries to connect fairy slippers, stones (Encrinites and Entrochi), butter (Tremella mesenterica), pipes (smoking pipes), cups, cauldrons, elf locks, elf shots (flint), fairy children (changelings—in fact often idiots) with nature (Benham 1859).

18 The giant seabird became extinct in the middle of the nineteenth century due to humans' overhunting.

19 This essay was included in the third volume of Thomas Crofton Croker, *Fairy Legends and Traditions of the South of Ireland* (1825–8).

20 Around the same period, "Beauty and the Beast" was also illustrated by Eleanor Vere Boyle in 1875 and H. J. Ford (in Andrew Lang's *The Blue Fairy Book* [1889]).

21 Defined as the "Academician of the Nursery," Crane constantly sought to innovate and experiment in his illustrations. Crane's meeting with Edmund Evans in 1863 launched his career, as Evans first hired Crane to draw cover illustrations for his yellowbacks then as a children's book illustrator. Once his contract with Routledge ended, Crane continued to illustrate different kinds of children's books, among which were Molesworth's fairy tales (see Meyer 1983: 79–93).

22 Ritchie (1871, 1872). Both short stories were reprinted in *Bluebeard's Keys and Other Stories* (1874: 1–118, 119–97).

23 "Beauty and the Beast" was first published in *The Cornhill Magazine* (vol. 15, June 1867: 676–709).

24 Silver contends that many of these spectacular productions were Shakespeare's fairy plays, *A Midsummer Night's Dream* and *The Tempest* (Silver 1999: 4).

25 Ritchie's rewriting of "Little Red Riding Hood" illustrates this point: the heroine's encounter with the wolf takes place at the theater, where she sees a play, "a grand fairy piece—where a fustian peasant maiden was turned into a satin princess in a flash of music and electric light." The choice of a theater brings home the heroine's sexual maturation. The transformation staged in the embedded fairy play thus mirrors the heroine's, while the male character (Rémy de la Louvière) metamorphoses into a wolf "ready to eat [Patty] up" (Ritchie 1868: 151–225, 199, 200).

26 Allusions and references to fairy tales are numerous throughout the novel. The introduction of Heathcliff to the family as one of the presents brought back by the father reads like a darker version of "Beauty and the Beast"; after the visit of Catherine's ghost Heathcliff believes that "she must have been a changeling"; Nelly Dean also says that Heathcliff's cake and cheese, untouched, have been left "for the fairies" (Brontë [1847] 1985: 69, 96).

27 See, in particular, Lady Audley's description by her nephew: "'She's the prettiest little creature you ever saw in your life, George,' he cried, when the carriage had driven off and he returned to his friend. 'Such blue eyes, such ringlets, such a ravishing smile, such a fairy-like bonnet—all of a-tremble with heart's-ease and dewy spangles, shining out of a cloud of gauze'" (Braddon [1862] 1987: 56); Lady Audley's "fairy-like note" (64), "fairy-like boudoir" (29), and "fairy-like, silver-mounted embroidery scissors" (77) also partake of her characterization.

28 Sybilla Rothesay is described as "a flesh-and-blood fairy" (Craik [1850] 1996: 9).

29 For more on Victorian rewritings of "Beauty and the Beast," see Talairach-Vielmas (2010).

30 The tale was first published in the *Cornhill Magazine* (vol. 16, October 1867: 440–73).

31 "All manner of relics were produced out of the old lady's ancient stores to adorn Miss Patty's crisp locks and little round white throat and wrists; small medallions were hung round her neck, brooches and laces pinned on, ribbons tied and muslins measured" (Ritchie 1868: 196).

32 For more on Ritchie's and Childe-Pemberton's rewritings, see Talairach-Vielmas (2009).

Chapter 3

1 See Auerbach and Knoepflmacher (1992). Also consult Jarvis and Blackwell (2001). See also Day (2017).

2 In Naomi Wood's words, "In addition to capturing little girls' interest with stories, Lewis Carroll provided himself with pins when he went to the beach so as to be able

to help them tuck up their skirts; John Ruskin fell desperately in love with nine-year-old Rose La Touche; J. M. Barrie was hopelessly devoted to the family of five boys for which he created Peter Pan; and many others violated or contemplated violating the boundaries our culture has placed between children and adult sexualities" (2002: 156).

3 Oscar Wilde's scandalous trials and imprisonment from 1895 to 1897 for "gross indecency" threw many into panic. According to Ellen Bayuk Rosenman, "By the 1880s, incremental changes in women's roles crested into a full-blown crisis ... While at midcentury a range of ideas existed, it was relatively narrow compared to the torrent of arguments at play at the end of the period" (2013: 54–5).

4 See Joosen and Lathey (2014: 1). This multicultural study expands from Donald Haase's insightful collection of essays that focus on Western countries, *The Reception of Grimms' Fairy Tales: Responses, Reactions, Revisions* (1993).

5 See Seifert (2015). For an interesting study of later work, see Duggan (2013).

6 This argument is made by Kay Turner and Pauline Greenhill in their introduction to *Transgressive Tales: Queering the Grimms* (2012).

7 In their book, *Reading Children's Literature: A Critical Introduction* (2013), Carrie Hintz and Eric L. Tribunella mention only two fairy-tale (short-story) writers from the "traditional canon" as being especially open to queer readings: the Grimm brothers and Oscar Wilde.

8 According to Zipes in *The Original Folk and Fairy Tales of the Brothers Grimm* (2014), "The second version of 'The Frog King,' which was called 'The Frog Prince,' was deleted in all the following editions" (xxxvii).

9 In the words of Michelle Ann Abate, "The Grimm Brothers' version of 'Snow White' is not only the most popular but also the most homicidal" (2012: 179).

10 Of course, giving Rapunzel power was not new to the Grimms. In Giambattista Basile's "Petrosinella" (1634), Rapunzel both successfully drugs the ogress every night with a "narcotic" so that she can sleep with the prince and through a wild trial of adventures involving a "Corsican hound," a "ferocious lion," and a wolf, manages to kill the ogress at the end of the story. See Zipes (2001: 478).

11 According to Zipes, Tieck "was the first to introduce a hunter who saves Red Cap's life" (2001: 744).

12 Fairy tales also made their way not only into drama but also into canonical Victorian poetry and fiction. In *Spellbound: The Victorians and the Fairy Tale* (2014), Molly Clark Hillard makes this argument "specifically to address and counter the persistent idea that the fairy tale is and was a subject only for children" (18).

13 For information about the invention and distribution of fairy-tale postcards during the long nineteenth century, consult Zipes, *Tales of Wonder: Retelling Fairy Tales Through Picture Postcards* (2017).

14 Jennifer Schacker provides a helpful overview of how nineteenth-century pantomime influenced fairy-tale interpretation in *Staging Fairyland: Folklore, Children's Entertainment, and Nineteenth-Century Pantomime* (2018).

15 Burnett is best known for her novels *Little Lord Fauntleroy* (1885–6), *A Little Princess* (1905), and *The Secret Garden* (1911).

16 Burnett's *Little Lord Fauntleroy* was serialized in *St. Nicholas's Magazine* between 1885 and 1886, before being published as a novel in 1886.

17 Jeannine Blackwell poses the question nicely in the introduction to *The Queen's Mirror: Fairy Tales by German Women, 1780–1900*: "When and why did women in

18 In Maria Tatar's words, "Andersen scholars frequently point out that the tale ["The Little Mermaid"] was begun the day after Jonas Collin's son Edvard married, and that 'The Little Mermaid' could be an expression of the writer's anguish that his friend had an attachment to a woman with whom he could never compete" (2007).
19 Leland G. Spencer argues that queer criticism needs to be employed to understand how "The Little Mermaid" reads as "a story about a performance of transgender identity" (2014: 112). Spencer argues that parallels exist between transgender identity development and mermaid narratives.
20 In "The Ugly Duckling's Legacy: Adulteration, Contemporary Fantasy, and the Dark" (2006), Wood describes the bittersweet tone of "The Little Mermaid" and of Andersen's other stories as well.
21 In "Gay-Related Themes in the Fairy Tales of Oscar Wilde," John-Charles Duffy explains that the Dwarf's grotesqueness may mark him as a signifier for the homosexual, given the Victorian press's custom of referring to homosexuals as monstrous (2001: 348).
22 "The Star-Child," which closes Wilde's fairy-tale collection *A House of Pomegranates*, has been read as showing a "queer interval" that interferes with the Victorian model of maturation. See Simonsen (2014).
23 In "Creating the Sensual Child," Wood argues that Wilde drew from the mid- and late Victorian period "pederasty," which was "tacitly promoted by J. A. Symonds and Walter Pater as the truest expression of the classical heritage" (2002: 158).
24 In *Child-Loving: The Erotic Child and Victorian Fiction*, James Kincaid maintains that "no children have ever been more desirable" than Lewis Carroll's Alice and J. M. Barrie's Peter Pan (1992: 275).
25 All quotations from Carroll's *Alice's Adventures in Wonderland* (1865) and from *Through the Looking-Glass* (1871) are taken from Martin Gardner's *The Annotated Alice: The Definitive Edition* ([1960] 2000). Karoline Leach argues that Lewis Carroll "never confused Alice [Liddell] with 'Alice' as we do. She was never his 'dream-child,' and he never pretended that she was" ([1999] 2009: 174). Leach's field-changing work notwithstanding, Carroll gives figurative information through his texts and through his photographs that continue to puzzle readers and scholars about the conflation of Alice Liddell with the fictional Alice.
26 For Gillian Beer, "Alice has a double nature: she is hybrid across fiction and the living" (2016: 9).
27 See the argument made about the juxtaposition between Barrie's Peter Pan and Carroll's Alice in Billone (2004a, 2016).
28 In spite of the way that Carroll radically altered the fairy-tale tradition, he also drew from his vast knowledge of the tradition when composing his Alice books. According to Jan Susina, "For far too long, Wonderland has been seen as the originator of a genre, while, in fact, it represents an important synthesis of the tradition of literary fairy tales for children" (2010: 73).
29 Wood explains that Victorian literary works "divide themselves based on conflicting constructions of the child" (2012: 116).
30 See Laura Tosi's and Peter Hunt's analysis in *The Fabulous Journeys of Alice and Pinocchio: Exploring their Parallel Worlds*: "But unlike characters in a postmodern fairy tale, they do not know that they are fictional, and so dramatic illusion is not broken" (2018: 32).

31 For an interesting comparison between Collodi's Pinocchio and Hoffmann's Olympia, see Lucas (2012: 49–61).
32 MacDonald has also been read as queering the fairy tale. See McGillis (2003).
33 According to U. C. Knoepflmacher, "If Carroll's publication in 1865 of *Alice's Adventures in Wonderland* owed much to the entire MacDonald family's sympathetic encouragement of his original manuscript, George MacDonald greatly profited from the success of his friend's masterpiece" (1999: xviii).
34 For an analysis of how levity and innocence are linked in "The Light Princess," see Billone (2004b).
35 In Alison Lurie's words, "Oz is also, as several critics have noted, both a kind of socialist utopia and a deeply matriarchal and occasionally transsexual one" (2000).
36 On the subject of translation, Maria Nikolajeva explains that "one of the most popular books among Russian children, which has sold many millions of copies, is closely based on *The Wizard of Oz*" (1995: 106). The book is not a translation but the "cultural isolation of the Soviet Union guaranteed that no charges of plagiarism" would be made in the case of famous works such as *The Wizard of Oz* or *Pinocchio* (106).
37 "However, it is generally acknowledged that fairy tales came of age in America with L. Frank Baum's 1900 Wizard of Oz" (Blackford 2015: 231–2).
38 According to Kenneth Kidd, "Long before Bruno Bettelheim, analysists wrote about the psychosexual uses of enchantment, and queer-leaning psychoanalytic work on children's classics like *Alice's Adventures in Wonderland* and *The Wonderful Wizard of Oz* dates back to the 1930s" (2011: 183–4).
39 Jacqueline Rose uses the example of J. M. Barrie's *Peter and Wendy* to conclude that authors of children's fiction in general try to trick and seduce child audiences: in children's literature, for Rose, "the adult always comes first (author, maker, giver) and the child comes after (reader, product, receiver)" ([1984] 1993: 1–2).
40 Tatar clarifies, "The play, which existed only in performance for many years, underwent multiple revisions. Barrie attended rehearsals and was constantly cutting, revising, and adding new material, collaborating with the actors and the actresses to improve dialogue and staging" (2011: xvii). According to Gubar, "Barrie incorporated the names of all five Llewelyn Davies boys into the dramatis personae and gave the costume designer a basketful of their clothes so that he could base his designs for the Darling children and the Lost Boys on them" (2011: 481).
41 The sudden and accidental death of Barrie's older brother when Barrie was only six years old may have provided the initial inspiration for Peter Pan: "Most famously, this ghost appears in the shape of Peter Pan—a boy who materializes from the world of children's dreams" (Billone 2005: xvi).

Chapter 4

1 "Naturpoesie" was not necessarily related to nature, but did presuppose a lack of artifice seen in artistic poetry, or "Kunstpoesie." On the Grimms' preference for the former, see Zipes (1988: 33). Oral literature such as folksong and folktale were examples of "Naturpoesie," and German authors of literary fairy tales such as Tieck, Goethe, or Hoffmann were clearly inspired by this genre even as they pursued more complex scenarios of human encounters with various non-human entities. In the context of German Romanticism, Deborah Janson (2018) discusses proto-ecological elements in Bettina von Arnim's literary tale "The Queen's Son."

2   In a letter by Jacob Grimm to Achim von Arnim, May 20, 1811 (quoted in Steig and Grimm 1904: 119; my translation).
3   The Aarne-Thompson-Uther (ATU) system categorizes international folk and fairy tales according to plot lines.
4   It should be noted that folktales such as "Der Räuberbräutigam" ("The Robber Bridegroom," KHM 40) and "Fitchers Vogel" ("Fitcher's Bird," KHM 46) allow for a more positive reading of female curiosity, since the brides' strategic inquisitiveness saves their lives.
5   See, for example, Robin McKinley's *Beauty* ([1978] 1993) and Alex Flinn's *Beastly* ([2007] 2012).
6   In Brie Spangler's *Beast* (2016) an ungainly, unusually tall outcast falls in love but has to prove his loyalty to his partner after he initially recoils upon finding out she is transgender. The novel is as much about the Beast's need to become comfortable being a "beastly" human on the exterior as about accepting that "Beauty" is less narrowly defined than he believed.
7   In contrast, in Catherine Bernard's lesser-known version of "Riquet à la houppe" ("Riquet with the Tuft," [1696] 2001), the heroine rebels against the marriage to the deformed gnome Riquet, and the story resolves without a happy end.
8   The hare that is jilted at the altar, so to speak, in "Häsichenbraut" ("The Hare's Bride," KHM 66), is "trurig" (sad) but does not die (Grimm and Grimm 1997: 358; Zipes 2003: 244); unlike the temporary non-humans, the hare is not seeking transformation, though he does try to pressure the maiden to marry him (Zipes 2003: 243). As such, KHM 66 connects animal groom stories with tales about murderers who ensnare brides: whereas the hare's bride escapes by leaving behind a straw doll, the heroine in "Fitcher's Bird," which resembles Perrault's "Bluebeard," disguises herself as a birdlike figure.
9   "Puddocky" resembles Afanasev's "The Frog Princess," but Büsching's tale emphasizes the youngest son's choice of the unbeaten track in venturing out to fulfill the father's three demands, which are satisfied by the frog (a girl transformed by a witch to prevent her beauty from wreaking havoc); the frog bride has been banished to remote swamps, matching German folktales' proto-ecological emphasis on nature as solitude and as a healing entity (Tatar 2017a: 182–7).
10 As Jeana Jorgensen determines by means of a digital humanities analysis, "transformation" tends in the Grimms' tales to be associated with males (2014: 130), although there are exceptions, such as "Jorinda and Joringel," in which the bride is turned into a bird.
11 See Zipes's use of this term to describe the impact of the Grimms' lives on the editing of the *Kinder- und Hausmärchen* in "Dreams of a Better Bourgeois Life: The Psycho-Social Origins of the Tales" (Zipes 1988: 28–42).
12 Max Lüthi points out that the "theme of separating, judging, and arranging is present in the motif of the sorting out of the lentils" (1970: 62), although he does not elaborate on the difference between the utilitarian sorting of lentils (a process whose calculated use is emphasized by the fact that the stepmother assigns this task to exclude Cinderella) and the moral judgment on the part of the birds. Yet his idea that this harsh justice is simply a continuation of human activity—the stepsisters' self-mutilation (62)—suggests that the role of nature (in the birds and hazel tree) is less pronounced than one might at first glance assume.

13 As a singular, male entity, as opposed to the birds, the fish (a masculine noun, "der Fisch," in German) speaks sternly throughout KHM 19 and therefore relates more explicitly to monotheistic and patriarchal symbolism.
14 Additionally, Bottigheimer's argument concerning the "injunction to silence" (1986: 123) applies particularly well to "The Fisherman and His Wife" since the tale's logic is directed at criticizing the wife's attempts to exert verbal and then political power.
15 A similar series of tasks appears in "Die Bienenkönigin" ("The Queen Bee," KHM 62; Zipes 2003: 232–3) involving ants, ducks, and a bee; the two unsuccessful brothers are temporarily turned into stone, which means that "The Queen Bee" connects elements of "The White Snake" (similar animal helpers) with "Faithful Johannes" (petrification). Rather than allude to the ants' proverbial industriousness, as in "The Queen Bee" or "The White Snake," the tale "Löwe, Storch und Ameise" ("Lion, Stork, and Ant"), collected by Ignaz Vinzenz Zingerle and Joseph Zingerle, draws on the ant's small size, which allows the protagonist to slip into a narrow space in his quest to save the princess (1854: 3–4).
16 The mysterious fairy-tale forest reappears in contemporary culture in numerous works, albeit often adopting the frightening atmosphere of "Hansel and Gretel" or "Little Red Cap" as opposed to the benign nature mysticism of "Cinderella." Trees are not imbued with any helpful magic in the Harry Potter series (1997–2007), though different woods carry various magical properties, but forests are a backdrop for spooky exploration, while one individual tree stands out as the irritable "Whomping Willow." Trees become increasingly hostile and even murderous in Lois Lowry's *The Messenger* (2004).
17 See Iovino and Oppermann's "Introduction" to *Material Ecocriticism* (2014: 1–17).
18 The verb "*sprang*" ("jumped") is already found in the first edition, see Grimm and Grimm (1812). In the 1810 manuscript, the verb is "*fiel*" (infinitive: "fallen," i.e., "to fall"), though followed by "*warf ihn todt*" ("struck him dead"), which does suggest agency (Rölleke 1975: 336). Although the choice of verbs seems to have been the Grimms' personal one, the reading of purposeful action is further supported by the other animals' and objects' careful positioning prior to Herr Korbes's return.
19 After the French Revolution, the color red became associated in Europe with workers' movement and the political Left.
20 The implication that "Herr" refers to social standing is found in the 1810 manuscript, which reads: "wie sie in dem Herrn Korbes sein Haus kamen, war der Herr nicht da" ("when they came to Herr Korbes's house, the gentleman wasn't there"; Rölleke 1975: 334; my translation). This reference to status is lost in the published tale: the 1812 version uses the full name, "der Herr Korbes." I am indebted to James M. McGlathery's lecture on the Grimms' fairy tales at the University of Illinois at Urbana-Champaign for the argument concerning "revolution."
21 In a letter to Edgar Taylor, the English translator of the tales, the Grimms noted that "*Korbes*" meant "bogeyman" (Zipes 2003: 734).
22 These early humans are effigies that play a role in the process of becoming human in the *Popol Vuh*: "They were merely an experiment, an attempt at people" (Christenson [2003] 2007: 70). I would like to thank Jeb Card for this reference.
23 See "The Revolt of the Objects" and reference to the Quechuan "pachacuti," which alludes to "social upheaval or cataclysm" (Dumbarton Oaks n.d.).
24 I would like to thank Naomi Wood for commenting on the influence of Catholic and Protestant contexts on the perceptions of magic and ritual.

25 On Schulz as the Grimms' source, see Zipes (2003: 732).
26 In the 1812 versions of these tales, the mother figure is still the biological mother, but is edited to a stepmother in later versions. See Ashliman (2000–2, 1998–2013).
27 Notably, Tieck enhances the non-human's power by describing how Christian begins his descent into madness by accidentally pulling out a mangrove root (Tieck 1992: 27).

Chapter 5

1 Maria Tatar has elaborated on how the Grimms' *Nursery and Household Tales*, for example, represent "a class of hybrid texts," situated in the early nineteenth century between oral folk tales and printed children's literary texts (2003: 32–3).
2 Ignácz Kúnos was a Hungarian linguist whose main interest became Turkish folklore following his travels to Turkey. He was a pupil of Ármin Vámbéry, a prominent Hungarian Turkologist during the nineteenth-century Ottoman era. His anthology of *Turkish Fairy Tales* published in 1889 was translated into English by Nisbet Bain. In 1913, Kúnos translated a selection from the collection into English himself, which was published as *Forty-four Turkish Fairy Tales* in London. As Kúnos writes in his preface to the 1913 book, he collected the stories by "jot[ting] them down from time to time" as he heard them "daily in the purleieus of Stamboul [Istanbul] where the native women relate them to their children and friends" to "present them, a choice bouquet, to the English reading public" (1913: ix).
3 Jennifer Shacker has observed that nineteenth-century "folktale collections were framed not as mollifying trifles but as both entertaining and instructive. The objectives of amusement and instruction are often regarded … as a dichotomy and one that is paralleled by child versus adult" (2003: 11). Alan Richardson has noted that placing child and adult categories in opposition to one another in our assessment of nineteenth-century fairy tales may obscure the shared political motives of amusement and improvement in the anglophone tradition (1991: 34–53). And, as I have argued elsewhere, fairy-tale authors such as Oscar Wilde purposefully deployed the genre expressly for reception by parent-child dyad readers, not for one age group or the other. "It is the duty of every father," Wilde famously quipped, "to write fairy tales for his children" (Marsh 2008: 72–87; Wilde quoted in Marsh 2008: 72).
4 As Cohen notes, the "monster" is in this way the living embodiment of the phenomenon Jacques Derrida has famously labeled the "supplement" (*ce dangereux supplément*): it breaks apart bifurcating, "either/or" syllogistic logic with a kind of reasoning closer to "and/or," introducing what Barbara Johnson has called "a revolution in the very logic of meaning" (Johnson quoted in Cohen 1997: 46). Monsters enact this lexical revolution not only through Derridean bifurcation but also through the grammatical fusion of both-and.
5 In the English translation, lexical play on the word "kid" further elides the boundary between this story's human and goat categories. This pun does not exist in the original German.
6 For more on the relationship between humans and animals in Islamic tradition, see Nursi (2011).
7 Readers interested in this tale type will also find useful the B640 designation of the "Marriage to person in animal form" tale type in the Aarne-Thompson-Uther Index (Thompson 1995).

8 The Turkish word "dew" literally translates as "giant." However, in his "Meaning of Turkish Words Used in the Text" Kúnos translates "dew" as "evil spirit" or "devil."
9 See "The Horse-Devil and The Witch," "The Silent Princess," "Shah Jussuf," and "The Laughing Apple and The Weeping Apple."
10 As mentioned above, the Turkish word "dew" literally translates as "giant." However, in his "Meaning of Turkish Words Used in the Text" Kúnos translates "dew" as "evil spirit."
11 For example, Linley Sambourne's 1889 illustrations of the text emphasize the darkness of Tom's skin in the scene where he gazes on the sleeping Ellie.
12 The "Tar Baby" tale type is listed in the Aarne-Thompson-Uther Index as Types 175 and 1310A (Thompson 1995).
13 For more on slavery in the Ottoman Empire, see Çakir (2014) and Bayarslan (2017).
14 Complicating the mystery is the high number of Hungarian slaves in the Ottoman Empire; was Kúnos censoring the monstrous depiction of his ancestors?
15 A Hungarian-American, Willy Pogany, is an acclaimed illustrator who is known for his art nouveau-style contributions to myth and fable drawings. He has also illustrated hundreds of famous works and volumes, including *The Rime of the Ancient Mariner* (1910), *Faust* (1908), *Gullivers Travels* (1917), *Arabian Nights* (1915), and *Alice's Adventures in Wonderland* (1929).

Chapter 7

1 Many thanks to Naomi Wood for her helpful suggestions as I revised this chapter. I am also indebted to archival research graciously offered to me by The Strong National Museum of Play, the Lilly Library at Indiana University, the Library of Congress, the V&A Museum of Childhood, the British Library, and the Bodleian Library and made possible by the generous support of a Children's Literature Association Faculty Research Grant, an Everett Helm Visiting Fellowship from the Lilly Library, a Mary Valentine and Andrew Cosman Research Fellowship from The Strong, a Cosmos Club Foundation Grant, and multiple University of Nebraska, Kearney, Research Service Council Grants.
2 Playground activities were recorded by the Playground Association of America in its monthly journal, *The Playground*. The association wasn't formed until the first years of the twentieth century but it developed out of the playground movement at the end of the nineteenth century. Photographed playground reenactments in Dayton, Ohio, of Snow White with some dwarves and the Mad Hatter's Tea Party from Lewis Carroll's *Alice's Adventures in Wonderland* appear in the January 1914 issue of *The Playground*, while the April 1916 issue documents "about five hundred children" offering "*Mother Goose in Fairyland*" during a "Play Day" that drew "between 12,000 and 13,000 people" in Johnstown, Pennsylvania (*The Playground* 1914: 410–11; "Play Days" 1916: 8–9).
3 For other cultural and historical views of fairy tales, see, for example, the work of Marina Warner and Ruth B. Bottigheimer.
4 For the fad of using "pretty" "little bird[s]" as pets and middle-class luxury status items at the time, see Rothfels (2007).
5 For examples of Yonge's texts that at times consider women's work and usefulness, see *The Clever Woman of the Family* ([1865] 2001), *The Daisy Chain* (1856) and its sequel *The Trial* (1864), and her treatise on *Womankind* (1877).

6 The "Fitzroy" of Miss Fitzroy Robinson's name may be another mocking jab, as surnames beginning with "Fitz" have historically been associated with nobility and even the illegitimate sons of royalty and the upper class in the UK.
7 See Ruskin's "Of Queens' Gardens" ([1865] 2002) and Patmore's *The Angel in the House* (1854, 1891).
8 For other analyses of the Grimms' work, see *The Reception of Grimms' Fairy Tales: Responses, Reactions, Revisions*, edited by Donald Haase (1993).
9 This interpretation accords with Zipes's view, as he suggests "these passages again reveal how the Grimms had an entirely different socialization process in mind when they altered the folk tales. Snow White is given instructions which are more commensurate with the duties of a bourgeois girl, and the tasks which she performs are implicitly part of her moral obligation. Morals are used to justify a division of labor and the separation of the sexes. Here, too, the growing notion that the woman's role was in the home and that the home was a shelter for innocence and children belong to a conception of women, work, and child-rearing in bourgeois circles more so than to the ideas of the peasantry and aristocracy" ([1988] 1991: 53).
10 Though Andersen was Danish and Bottigheimer acknowledges that the preference was not the same in every Western European country, it is notable that she discerns that in "mid-nineteenth century Germany" "a vigorously championed German ethic … was that of the silent woman" (1986: 115).
11 For analysis of some of the erotic and consumer consumption aspects of the poem, see, for example, Lorraine Janzen Kooistra's "*Goblin Market* as a Cross-Audienced Poem: Children's Fairy Tale, Adult Erotic Fantasy" (1997) and Krista Lysack's *Come Buy, Come Buy: Shopping and the Culture of Consumption in Victorian Women's Writing* (2008).
12 Both *Alice's Adventures* and *Peter and Wendy* inspired their own games throughout the long nineteenth century.
13 For other considerations of socialization and violence in Carroll's work, see Jennifer Geer's "'All sorts of pitfalls and surprises'" (2003) and Nancy Armstrong's "The Occidental Alice" (1990).
14 See Jacqueline Rose, *The Case of Peter Pan, or The Impossibility of Children's Fiction* (1993), particularly the chapter "Peter Pan and Literature for the Child."
15 See "The Boy Scouts and the Working Classes" in Troy Boone, *Youth of Darkest England: Working-Class Children at the Heart of Victorian Empire* (2005).
16 Hunt the Slipper is also a game commonly found in games manuals of the period, an activity where players sit in a circle while trying to hide an item—a slipper, whistle, etc.—from another player who is supposed to guess who has it.
17 In another mockery of fairy-tale conventions, Nesbit's princes and princesses in the tale are generally numbered, not named: Secundus, Tertius, Quinta, etc. The youngest, Daisy and Denis, are named but are siblings, which leaves readers another mocking conundrum: since Denis kissed Daisy, what will become of them?
18 As Peter stands guard over the little house (and falls asleep) during the night Wendy and her brothers arrive in Neverland, the fairies pass by: "Any of the other boys obstructing the fairy path at night they would have mischiefed, but they just tweaked Peter's nose and passed on" (Barrie [1911] 2004: 66).

Chapter 8

1. Moms Demand Action was formed as a Facebook group the day after Sandy Hook (https://momsdemandaction.org/about/).
2. The ATU (Aarne-Thompson-Uther) Index is a classification system of folktale types.
3. One might think here too about the European collection, translation, and alteration of, for instance, the *Arabian Nights Tales* (e.g., Galland, Lane) and Indian tales (e.g., Jacobs, Lang) as its own, less violent but equally engulfing, wielding of imperial power. For further reading see, for example, Sadhana Naithani, *The Story-Time of the British Empire. Colonial and Post Colonial Folkloristics* (2010).
4. See, for example, Clark Hillard (2014: 154–69).
5. See, for example, Peter Burke, "Reflections on the Cultural History of Time" (2004); Elizabeth Campbell, *Fortune's Wheel: Dickens and the Iconography of Women's Time* (2003); Steven Dillon, "Watches, Dials and Clocks: Victorian Illustrations of Time" (2002); N. N. Feltes, "To Saunter, To Hurry: Dickens, Time, and Industrial Capitalism" (1977); Patricia Murphy, *Time is of the Essence: Temporality, Gender, and the New Woman* (2001).
6. Especially Jerome Buckley, *The Triumph of Time. A Study of the Victorian Concepts of Time, History, Progress and Decadence* (1966).
7. *A Restitution of Decayed Intelligence: in Antiquities, concerning the most noble and renowned English Nation* (1605) (Verstegan 1634). The Grimms' version, "The Children of Hameln" (Grimm and Grimm 1816: 245) in *Deutche Sagen* (1816) was not translated into English until 1981.
8. See, for instance, "Colliers Picking the Coal" in *The Condition and Treatment of the Children employed in the Mines and Colliers of the United Kingdom Carefully compiled from the appendix to the first report of the Commissioners With copious extracts from the evidence, and illustrative engravings* (1842).
9. The Mines Act prohibited women and children under the age of ten from working in the mines. Of course, it did nothing to address the loss of employment for those families that depended upon the wages of women and child miners.
10. It is no coincidence that during the Second World War, the child evacuation program was called Operation Pied Piper. Here, too, primarily working-class children were separated from their parents and sent away—in some cases for years. This was purportedly for their safety, and nominally voluntary. But it was also to affect greater governmental control of the cities, and to streamline their parents' attention on their labor for the war effort. Investigations into the lasting trauma of this separation are only just now beginning, and early findings compare evacuation to family separation of US detainees (Wang 2018).
11. John Everett Millais's "Mariana" (1851) may have been the earliest artistic interpretation of the poet's work. Henry Alexander Bowler's "The Doubt: Can These Dry Bones Live?" (1855) gives shape to the play of faith and doubt in *In Memoriam*. The Moxon edition of Tennyson's *Poems* (1857) included eighteen drawings by Millais, seven by William Holman Hunt and five by Dante Gabriel Rossetti. While the book was not commercially successful (of the 10,000 copies printed, fewer than 3,000 sold), and while Tennyson himself disliked the edition, both established and incipient artists read and admired the book, and it proved foundational to later Victorian artistry. Some of the volume's illustrators, such as Holman Hunt, used their drawings as the bases for later, finished paintings (for instance, Hunt's "The Lady of Shalott," completed in 1905). As the parts of *Idylls of*

the King advanced through publication, these, too, inspired later Victorian painters, for instance William Morris and Burne-Jones.
12 See, for instance, Clark Hillard (2014: 131–53) and Martinau (1997).
13 See Powell (1986: 15–28, 21).
14 Joseph Noel Paton, *The Quarrel of Oberon and Titania*, 1849, detail. Oil. National Galleries of Scotland.
15 Richard Doyle, *The Fairy Tree*, 1870. Watercolor. Doyle painted a similar picture, "The Enchanted Fairy Tree, or a Fantasy Based on *The Tempest*" in 1845. The painting depicts a palm tree on Prospero's island, entirely wreathed around with fairies. Created before Darwin published *Origin of Species*, it is not the clear phylogenetic tree that "Fairy Tree" is, and is less overtly imperial: other than Caliban the nonwhite fairies are not grotesquely caricatured as they are in "Fairy Tree."
16 Doyle was an illustrator for *Punch* from 1843 to 1850.
17 In Victorian understanding, goblins were the branch of the fairies considered to be "malevolent or demonic" (OED Online 2020b: s.v. "goblin"). See Silver (1999), Purkiss (2000), and Clark Hillard (2005).
18 In 1993, Rodney King was also described as supernatural and monstrous. See James Earl Jones (1993: 268), Daniel B. Wood (1993).
19 See Sidney Hinde, "The Pygmies and Ape-Like Men of the Uganda Borderland" (quoted in Silver 1999); Anonymous, "Negro Nileand and Uganda" (1901); Guy Burrows, *In the Land of the Pygmies* (1898); Albert Lloyd, *In Dwarf Land and Cannibal Country* (1899, quoted in Silver 1999).

REFERENCES

Abate, Michelle Ann (2012), "'You must kill her': The Fact and Fantasy of Filicide in 'Snow White,'" *Marvels & Tales*, 26: 178–203.

Abbott, Edwin A. ([1884] 2002), *The Annotated Flatland: A Romance of Many Dimensions*, intro. and notes Ian Stewart, Cambridge: Perseus Publishing.

Acocella, Joan (2012), "Once Upon a Time: The Lure of the Fairy Tale," *New Yorker Magazine*, June 23. Available online: https://www.newyorker.com/magazine/2012/07/23/once-upon-a-time-3 (accessed September 10, 2020).

Aesop (sixth *c*. BCE), "The Ant and the Grasshopper," Library of Congress. Available online: http://read.gov/aesop/052.html (accessed December 13, 2020).

American Civil Liberties Union (ACLU) (n.d.), "Family Separation by the Numbers." Available online: https://www.aclu.org/issues/immigrants-rights/immigrants-rights-and-detention/family-separation (accessed September 10, 2020).

Andersen, Hans Christian (1869), "The Dryad," trans. A. M. Plesner and Augusta Plesner, *Aunt Judy's Magazine*, 6 (34) February 1: 237–47; 6 (35) March 1: 286–96.

Andersen, Hans Christian ([1835] 2000), "The Princess and the Pea," in John W. Griffith and Charles H. Frey (eds.), *Classics of Children's Literature*, 5th edn., 118, Upper Saddle River, NJ: Prentice Hall.

Andersen, Hans Christian ([1837] 2000), "The Little Mermaid," in John W. Griffith and Charles H. Frey (eds.), *Classics of Children's Literature*, 5th edn., 105–18, Upper Saddle River, NJ: Prentice Hall.

Andersen, Hans Christian ([1865] 1949), "The Will-o'-the Wisps Are in Town," trans. Jean Hersholt, *The Complete Andersen*, New York: The Limited Editions Club. Available online: https://andersen.sdu.dk/vaerk/hersholt/TheWillOTheWispsAreInTown_e.html (accessed December 19, 2020).

Andersen, Hans Christian (1974), *The Complete Fairy Tales and Stories*, trans. Erik Christian Haugaard, New York: Doubleday.

Anderson, Benedict (1991), *Imagined Communities: On the Rise and Spread of Nationalism*, London: Verso.

Anonymous (1901), "Negro Nileland and Uganda," *The Quarterly Review* (387) October: 1–32.

Anonymous (1906), "Serious Reading for Boys and Girls: *The Orange Fairy Book* and Other Fairy Tales," *The New York Times*, November 3: 718.

Armstrong, Nancy (1990), "The Occidental Alice," *Differences: A Journal of Feminist Cultural Studies*, 2 (2) (Summer): 3–40.

Ashliman, D. L. (1998–2013), "Snow-White and Other Tales of Aarne-Thompson-Uther Type 709." Available online: https://www.pitt.edu/~dash/type0709.html#snowwhite (accessed December 14, 2020).

Ashliman, D. L. (2000–2), "'Hansel and Gretel': A Comparison of the Versions of 1812 and 1857." Available online: https://www.pitt.edu/~dash/grimm015a.html (accessed December 14, 2020).

Auerbach, Nina (1982), *Woman and the Demon: The Life of a Victorian Myth*, Cambridge, MA: Harvard University Press.

Auerbach, Nina and U. C. Knoepflmacher, eds. (1992), *Forbidden Journeys: Fairy Tales and Fantasies by Victorian Women Writers*, Chicago: University of Chicago Press.

Axton, W. F. (1977), "Victorian Landscape Painting: A Change in Outlook," in U. C. Knoepflmacher and G. B. Tennyson (eds.), *Nature and the Victorian Imagination*, 281–308, Berkeley: University of California Press.

Bachelard, Gaston ([1958] 1964), *The Poetics of Space*, trans. Maria Jolas, Boston: Beacon Press.

Baden-Powell, Robert ([1916] 1918), *The Wolf Cub's Handbook*, New York: The Boy Scouts of America.

Bakhtin, Mikhail (1981a), *The Dialogic Imagination*, trans. Caryl Emerson and Michael Holquist, Austin: University of Texas Press.

Bakhtin, Mikhail (1981b), "Epic and Novel: Toward a Methodology for the Study of the Novel," in Michael Holquist (ed.), *The Dialogic Imagination*, 3–40, Austin: University of Texas Press.

Baldwin, James (1972), *No Name in the Street*, New York: The Dial Press.

Barrett, Elizabeth (1843), "The Cry of the Children," *Blackwood's Magazine*, 54 (334). Available online: http://www.gutenberg.org/files/25065/25065.txt (accessed September 10, 2020).

Barrett, Elizabeth (1898), *The Letters of Elizabeth Barrett Browning*, vol. 1, ed. Frederick Kenyon, London: Smith, Elder, and Co.

Barrie, J. M. (1902), *The Little White Bird*, London: Hodder and Stoughton.

Barrie, J. M. ([1911] 1999), *Peter Pan in Kensington Gardens* and *Peter and Wendy*, ed. Peter Hollindale, Oxford: Oxford University Press.

Barrie, J. M. ([1911] 2004), *Peter and Wendy*, in Jack Zipes (ed.), *Peter Pan*, 5–153, New York: Penguin.

Baum, L. Frank ([1900] 1987), *The Wonderful Wizard of Oz*, New York: Harper Collins.

Baum, L. Frank ([1900] 2000), *The Annotated Wizard of Oz*, ed. Michael Patrick Hearn, New York: W. W. Norton.

Bayarslan, Hüseyin (2017), "Slavery and Emancipation Methods in the Ottoman Empire," *UlakBilge*, 5 (10): 439–52.

Beer, Gillian ([1983] 2000), *Darwin's Plots: Evolutionary Narrative in Darwin, George Eliot and Nineteenth-Century Fiction*, Cambridge: Cambridge University Press.

Beer, Gillian (2016), *Alice in Space: The Sideways Victorian World of Lewis Carroll*, Chicago: University of Chicago Press.

Benham, Michael Aislabie (1859), *A Few Fragments of Fairyology, Shewing its Connection with Natural History*, Dunhelm: Will, Duncan and Son.

Bernard, Catherine ([1696] 2001), "Riquet with the Tuft," in Jack Zipes (ed.), *The Great Fairy Tale Tradition: From Straparola and Basile to the Brothers Grimm*, 717–21, New York: W. W. Norton.

Bernheimer, Kate and Andrew Bernheimer (2018), "Fairy Tale Architecture," *Places*. Available online: https://placesjournal.org/series/fairy-tale-architecture/ (accessed January 10, 2020).

Bettelheim, Bruno (1976), *The Uses of Enchantment: The Meaning and Importance of Fairy Tales*, London: Thames and Hudson.

Billone, Amy (2004a), "The Boy Who Lived: From Carroll's Alice and Barrie's Peter Pan to Rowling's Harry Potter," *Children's Literature*, 32: 178–202.

Billone, Amy (2004b),"Hovering between Irony and Innocence: George MacDonald's 'The Light Princess' and the Gravity of Childhood," *Mosaic: A Journal for the Interdisciplinary Study of Literature*, 37 (1): 135–48.

Billone, Amy (2005), "Introduction, Notes, and for Further Reading," in *Peter Pan*, New York: Barnes and Noble Classics.

Billone, Amy (2016), *The Future of the Nineteenth-Century Dream-Child: Fantasy, Dystopia, Cyberculture*, New York: Routledge.

Blackford, Holly (2015), "Transformations of E. T. A. Hoffman's tales from Hawthorne to Oz," in Maria Tatar (ed.), *The Cambridge Companion to Fairy Tales*, 220–35, Cambridge: Cambridge University Press.

Blair, Kirstie (2006), *Victorian Poetry and the Culture of the Heart*, Oxford: Clarendon.

Blake, William ([1974] 2018), *Songs of Innocence and of Experience*, in *The Norton Anthology of English Literature: The Romantic Period*, vol. D, ed. Deidre Shauna Lynch, gen. ed. Stephen Greenblatt, 127–45, New York: Norton.

Boone, Troy (2005), *Youth of Darkest England: Working-Class Children at the Heart of Victorian Empire*, New York: Routledge.

Bottigheimer, Ruth B. (1986), "Silenced Women in the Grimms' Tales: The 'Fit' Between Fairy Tales and Society in Their Historical Context," in Ruth B. Bottigheimer (ed.), *Fairy Tales and Society: Illusion, Allusion, and Paradigm*, 115–31, Philadelphia: University of Pennsylvania Press.

Bottigheimer, Ruth B. (1987), *Grimms' Bad Girls and Good Boys: The Moral and Social Vision of the Tales*, New Haven, CT: Yale University Press.

Bouie, Jamelle (2014), "Michael Brown Wasn't a Superhuman Demon," *Slate*, November 26. Available online: https://slate.com/news-and-politics/2014/11/darren-wilsons-racial-portrayal-of-michael-brown-as-a-superhuman-demon-the-ferguson-police-officers-account-is-a-common-projection-of-racial-fears.html (accessed September 10, 2020).

Bown, Nicola (2001), *Fairies in Nineteenth-Century Art and Literature*, Cambridge: Cambridge University Press.

Braddon, Mary Elizabeth ([1862] 1987), *Lady Audley's Secret*, Oxford: Oxford University Press.

Briggs, K. M. ([1967] 1978), *The Fairies in Tradition and Literature*, London: Routledge & Kegan Paul.

Brontë, Emily ([1847] 1985), *Wuthering Heights*, ed. David Daiches, London: Penguin.

Brough, John Cargill (1859). *The Fairy Tales of Science: A Book for Youth*, London: Griffith and Farren.

Browning, Robert (1842), *Dramatic Lyrics*, London: Edward Moxon.

Browning, Robert and Elizabeth Barrett (1900), *The Letters of Robert Browning and Elizabeth Barrett*, London: Smith, Elder, and Co.

Buchholtz, Katharina (2020), "Number of Immigrant Detainees Rises Quickly," *Statista*. Available online: https://www.statista.com/chart/17977/number-of-detainees-in-facilities-of-dhs-immigration/ (accessed September 10, 2020).

Buckley, Jerome (1966), *The Triumph of Time: A Study of the Victorian Concepts of Time, History, Progress and Decadence*, Cambridge, MA: Harvard University Press.
Burke, Peter (2004), "Reflections on the Cultural History of Time," *Viator*, 35: 617–26.
Burrows, Guy (1898), *The Land of the Pigmies*, London: C. Arthur Pearson Limited.
Çakir, İbrahim Etem (2014), "Slaves and Female Slaves in Ottoman Society, Sofia 1550–1684," *Selçuk University Türkiyat Research Journal*, 36: 201–16.
Campbell, Elizabeth (2003), *Fortune's Wheel: Dickens and the Iconography of Women's Time*, Athens: Ohio University Press.
Carpenter, Humphrey (1985), *Secret Gardens: The Golden Age of Children's Literature*, Boston: Houghton Mifflin.
Carroll, Lewis ([1865] 2013), *Alice's Adventures in Wonderland*, in Donald J. Gray (ed.), *Alice in Wonderland*, 3rd edn., 1–97, New York: W. W. Norton.
Cecire, Maria Sachiko, Hannah Field, Kavita Mudan Finn, and Malini Roy, eds. (2015), *Space and Place in Children's Literature, 1789 to the Present*, London: Routledge.
Chadwick, Edwin (1842), *Report on the Sanitary Condition of the Labouring Population of Great Britain*, London: W. Clowes and Sons.
Cheng, Amrit (2018), "Fact-Checking Family Separation," ACLU, June 19. Available online: https://www.aclu.org/blog/immigrants-rights/immigrants-rights-and-detention/fact-checking-family-separation (accessed September 10, 2020).
Childe-Pemberton, Harriet Louisa ([1882] 1987), "All My Doing; or Red Riding Hood Over Again," in Jack Zipes (ed.), *Victorian Fairy Tales*, 209–48, London: Routledge. (Originally published in *The Fairy Tales of Everyday*, London: Christian Knowledge Society, 1882.)
Christenson, Allen J., trans. and commentary ([2003] 2007), *Popol Vuh*, Norman: University of Oklahoma Press. Available online: https://www.mesoweb.com/publications/Christenson/PopolVuh.pdf (accessed December 13, 2020).
Cinderella, or Hunt the Slipper (1887) [Board Game], New York: McLoughlin Brothers.
Clark Hillard, Molly (2005), "Dangerous Exchange: Fairy Footsteps, Goblin Economies and *The Old Curiosity Shop*," *Dickens Studies Annual*, 35: 63–86.
Clark Hillard, Molly (2014), *Spellbound: The Fairy Tale and the Victorians*, Columbus: Ohio State University Press.
Clauson, Christopher (1982), "Home and Away in Children's Fiction," *Children's Literature*, 10: 141–52.
Coats, Karen and Farran Norris Sands (2016), "Growing up Frankenstein: Adaptations for Young Readers," in Andrew Smith (ed.), *The Cambridge Companion to Frankenstein*, 241–55, London: Cambridge University Press.
Cody, Lisa Foreman (2005), *Birthing the Nation: Sex, Science, and the Conception of Eighteenth-Century Britons*, London: Oxford University Press.
Cohen, Jeffrey Jerome (1997), "Monster Culture (Seven Theses)," in *Monster Theory: Reading Culture*, 3–25, Minneapolis: University of Minnesota Press.
Cohen, Morton N., ed. ([1982] 1989), *The Selected Letters of Lewis Carroll*, Basingstoke: Macmillan.
Collodi, Carlo ([1883] 1996), *Pinocchio*, trans. E. Harden, London: Penguin Puffin.
The Condition and Treatment of the Children employed in the Mines and Colliers of the United Kingdom Carefully compiled from the appendix to the first report of the

Commissioners With copious extracts from the evidence, and illustrative engravings (1842), London: William Strange.

Cooper, Melinda (2008), "Monstrous Progeny: The Teratological Tradition in Science and Literature," in Christa Knellwolf and Jane R. Goodall (eds.), *Frankenstein's Science: Experimentation and Discovery in Romantic Culture, 1780–1830*, 87–97, Aldershot, England: Ashgate.

Cott, Jonathan, ed. (1973), *Beyond the Looking Glass: Extraordinary Works of Fairy Tale & Fantasy*, New York: Stonehill Publishing Company.

Craik, Dinah Mulock ([1850] 1996), *Olive and the Half-Caste*, Oxford: Oxford University Press.

Croker, Thomas Crofton (1825–8), *Fairy Legends and Traditions of the South of Ireland*, London: Macmillan.

Darwin, Charles (1842), "August 31," in Darwin Correspondence Project, University of Cambridge. Available online: https://www.darwinproject.ac.uk/letter/?docId=letters/DCP-LETT-640.xml;query=31%20august%201842;brand=default (accessed September 10, 2020).

Darwin, Charles (1859), *On the Origin of Species by Means of Natural Selection, or Preservation of Favoured Races in the Struggle for Life*, London: John Murray.

Davidson Sorkin, Amy (2014), "Darren Wilson's Demon," *New Yorker*, November 26. Available online: https://www.newyorker.com/news/amy-davidson/demon-ferguson-darren-wilson-fear-black-man (accessed September 10, 2020).

Day, Andrea (2017), "'Almost wholly the work of Mrs. Lang': Nora Lang, Literary Labour, and the Fairy Books," *Women's Writing*, 19: 400–20.

De Morgan, Mary ([1877] 1991), "A Toy Princess," in Jack Zipes (ed.), *Victorian Fairy Tales: The Revolt of the Fairies and Elves*, 163–74, New York: Routledge.

De Morgan, Mary ([1880] 1988), "The Necklace of Princess Fiorimonde," in Michael Patrick Hearn (ed.), *The Victorian Fairy Tale Book*, 211–27, New York: Pantheon.

Dickens, Charles ([1850] 1990), *David Copperfield*, ed. Jerome H. Buckley, New York: W. W. Norton.

Dickens, Charles ([1853] 1976), "Frauds on the Fairies," in Lance Salway (ed.), *A Peculiar Gift: Nineteenth Century Writings on Books for Children*, 111–18, Harmondsworth, UK: Kestrel Books.

Dickens, Charles ([1865] 1997), *Our Mutual Friend*, ed. Adrian Poole, New York: Penguin Books.

Dickens, Charles ([1868] 1988), "The Magic Fish-Bone," in Michael Patrick Hearn (ed.), *The Victorian Fairy Tale Book*, 107–15, New York: Pantheon Books.

Dillon, Steven (2002), "Watches, Dials and Clocks: Victorian Illustrations of Time," in Richard Maxwell (ed.), *The Victorian Illustrated Book*, 52–90, Charlottesville: University Press of Virginia.

Dimock, Wai Chee (1997), "A Theory of Resonance," *PMLA*, 112 (5): 1060–71.

Dorson, Richard (1968), *The British Folklorists: A History*, Chicago: University of Chicago Press.

Duffy, John-Charles (2001), "Gay-Related Themes in the Fairy Tales of Oscar Wilde," *Victorian Literature and Culture*, 29 (2): 327–49.

Duggan, Anne (2013), *Queer Enchantments: Gender, Sexuality, and Class in the Fairy-Tale Cinema of Jacques Demi*, Detroit, MI: Wayne State University Press.

Dumbarton Oaks (n.d.), "Narrative Themes." Available online: https://www.doaks.org/resources/moche-iconography/narrative-themes (accessed December 14, 2020).

Dundes, Alan (1989), *Little Red Riding Hood: A Casebook*, Madison: University of Wisconsin Press.

Dusinberre, Juliet (1987), *Alice to the Lighthouse: Children's Books and Radical Experiments in Art*, Basingstoke: Palgrave Macmillan.

Empson, William ([1935] 1995), "Alice in Wonderland: The Child as Swain," *Some Versions of Pastoral*, 201–33, London: Chatto and Windus.

Encyclopedia Brittanica (n.d.), s.v. "British Railways." Available online: https://www.britannica.com/topic/British-Railways (accessed September 10, 2020).

English, Mary, and Xavier Vendrell (2018), "Little Red Riding Hood," *Places Journal* (December). Available online: https://placesjournal.org/article/fairy-tale-architecture-little-red-riding-hood/ (accessed January 10, 2020).

Espinosa, Aurelio (1943), "A New Classification of the Fundamental Elements of the Tar-Baby Story on the Basis of Two Hundred and Sixty-Seven Versions," *Journal of American Folklore*, 56 (219): 31–7.

Ewing, Juliana Horatia ([1870] 1992), "Amelia and the Dwarfs," in Nina Auerbach and U. C. Knoepflmacher (eds.), *Forbidden Journeys: Fairy Tales and Fantasies by Victorian Women Writers*, 105–27, Chicago: University of Chicago Press.

Ewing, Juliana Horatia (1871), *The Brownies and Other Tales*, London: Society for the Promotion of Christian Knowledge.

Ewing, Juliana Horatia ([1888] 2015), "'Preface' to *Old-Fashioned Fairy Tales*," in Michael Newton (ed. and intro.), *Victorian Fairy Tales*, 395–6, Oxford: Oxford University Press.

Felski, Rita (2011), "Context Stinks!," *New Literary History*, 42 (4): 573–91.

Feltes, N. N. (1977), "To Saunter, To Hurry: Dickens, Time, and Industrial Capitalism," *Victorian Studies*, 20: 245–67.

Flinn, Alex ([2007] 2012), *Beastly*, New York: HarperTeen.

Freedgood, Elaine (2006), *The Ideas in Things: Fugitive Meaning in the Victorian Novel*, Chicago: University of Chicago Press.

Gaiman, Neil (2016), "Foreword," in Shaun Tan, *The Singing Bones*, 1–4, New York: Scholastic.

Game of Ali Baba, or the Forty Thieves (*c.* 1900), [Board Game] by J. H. Singer, New York.

Game of Beauty and the Beast (1905), [Board Game] Springfield, MA: Milton Bradley.

Gardner, Martin, ed. ([1960] 2000), *The Annotated Alice: The Definitive Edition*, New York: Norton.

Gates, Henry Louis, Jr. (2018), "Foreward: The Politics of 'Negro Folklore,'" in Henry Louis Gates and Maria Tatar (eds.), *The Annotated African American Folktales*, xxiii–lii, New York: Liveright Publishing Corporation.

Gates, Henry Louis and Maria Tatar (2018), *The Annotated African American Folktales/Edited with a Foreword, Introduction, and Notes by Henry Louis Gates Jr. and Maria Tatar*, New York: Liveright Publishing.

Geer, Jennifer (2003), "'All sorts of pitfalls and surprises': Competing Views of Idealized Girlhood in Lewis Carroll's Alice Books," *Children's Literature*, 31: 1–24.

Gere, Charlotte (1997), "In Fairyland," in Jane Martineau (ed.), *Victorian Fairy Painting*, 62–73, London: Royal Academy of Arts.

Gilbert, Sandra M. and Susan Gubar (1979), *The Madwoman in the Attic: The Woman Writer and the Nineteenth-Century Literary Imagination*, New Haven, CT: Yale University Press.

Gold, Barri (2010), *ThermoPoetics: Energy in Victorian Literature and Science*, Cambridge, MA: MIT Press.

Goldney, Rev. S. (1885), "Fables and Fairy Tales," in Michael Newton (ed.), *Aunt Judy's Annual Volume*, 20–32, London: Hatchards.

Grahame, Kenneth ([1898] 1988), "The Reluctant Dragon," in Michael Patrick Hearn (ed.), *The Victorian Fairy Tale Book*, 327–44, New York: Pantheon Books.

Grahame, Kenneth ([1898] 2015), "The Reluctant Dragon," in Michael Newton (ed. and intro.), *Victorian Fairy Tales*, 342–65, Oxford: Oxford University Press.

Gray, William (2010), *Fantasy, Myth and the Measure of Truth*, Basingstoke: Palgrave Macmillan.

Great Britain Commission (1842), *The Condition and Treatment of the Children employed in the Mines and Collieries of the United Kingdom*, London: William Strange.

Greenberg, Karen (2019), "No Fairy Tale: The Trump Administration's Declaration of Inhuman Rights," *Salon*, July 29. Available online: https://www.salon.com/2019/07/29/no-fairy-tale_partner/ (accessed September 10, 2020).

Grenby, M. O. (2006), "Tame Fairies Make Good Teachers: The Popularity of Early British Fairy Tales," *Lion & Unicorn*, 30 (1): 1–24.

Grimm, Jacob and Wilhelm Grimm (1812), "Die drei Raben." Wikisource. Available online: https://de.wikisource.org/wiki/Die_drei_Raben_1812_ (accessed December 13, 2020).

Grimm, Jacob and Wilhelm Grimm ([1812, 1815] 2014), *The Original Folk and Fairy Tales of the Brothers Grimm*, ed. and trans. Jack Zipes, Princeton, NJ: Princeton University Press.

Grimm, Jacob and Wilhelm Grimm ([1812, 1857] 1999), "Little Red Cap," in Maria Tatar (ed.), *The Classic Fairy Tales*, 13–16, New York: W. W. Norton & Company.

Grimm, Jacob and Wilhelm Grimm (1816), *Deutsche Sagen*, Berlin: Nicolai.

Grimm, Jacob and Wilhelm Grimm (1825–8), "On the Nature of the Elves," in Thomas Crofton Croker (ed.), *Fairy Legends and Traditions of the South of Ireland*, vol. 3, 1–153, London: Macmillan.

Grimm, Jacob and Wilhelm Grimm (1857), "Aschenputtel," in *Kinder- und Hausmärchen* [Children's and Household Tales—Grimms' Fairy Tales], 7th edn., 137–44, Göttingen: Verlag der Dieterichschen Buchhandlung.

Grimm, Jacob and Wilhelm Grimm (1988), "The Wolf and the Seven Little Kids," in *The Complete Fairy Tales of the Brothers Grimm*, ed. and trans. Jack Zipes, Toronto: Bantam.

Grimm, Jacob and Wilhelm Grimm (1997), *Kinder- und Hausmärchen: Ausgabe letzter Hand*, ed. Heinz Rölleke, Stuttgart: Reclam.

Grimm, Jacob and Wilhelm Grimm (2012), *Fairy Tales from the Brothers Grimm: A New English Version*, trans. Philip Pullman, New York: Penguin Classics.

Griswold, Jerry (2004), *The Meanings of "Beauty and the Beast": A Handbook*, Peterborough, ONT: Broadview Press.

Gubar, Marah (2009), *Artful Dodgers: Reconceiving the Golden Age of Children's Literature*, Oxford: Oxford University Press.

Gubar, Marah (2011), "Peter Pan as Children's Theater: The Issue of Audience," in Julia Mickenberg and Lynne Vallone (eds.), *The Oxford Handbook of Children's Literature*, 475–95, Oxford: Oxford University Press.

Gutman, Marta and Ning de Coninck-Smith (2008), "Introduction: Good to Think With—History, Space, and Modern Childhood," in Marta Gutman and Ning de Coninck-Smith (eds.), *Designing Modern Childhoods*, 1–19, New Brunswick, NJ: Rutgers University Press.

Haase, Donald, ed. (1993) *The Reception of Grimms' Fairy Tales*, Detroit, MI: Wayne State University Press.

Hale, Piers J. (2013), "Monkeys into Men and Men into Monkeys: Chance and Contingency in the Evolution of Man, Mind, and Morals in Charles Kingsley's 'Water Babies,'" *Journal of the History of Biology*, 46 (4): 551–97.

Hall, Stuart ([1981] 2005), "Notes on Deconstructing 'The Popular'," in Raiford A. Guins and Omayra Zaragoza Cruz (eds.), *Popular Culture: A Reader*, 64–71, London: Sage Publications.

Hartland, Edwin Sidney (1891), *The Science of Fairy Tales: An Inquiry into the Fairy Mythology*, London: Walter Scott.

Hearn, Michael Patrick, ed. and intro. (2000), "Introduction to The Annotated Wizard of Oz," in L. Frank Baum, *The Annotated Wizard of Oz*, xiii–cii, New York: W. W. Norton.

Hearne, Betsy (1989), *Beauty and the Beast: Visions and Revisions of an Old Tale*, Chicago: University of Chicago Press.

"Her Majesty's First Trip By Railway" (1842), *Bristol Mercury*, June 18. British Newspaper Archive. Available online: https://www.britishnewspaperarchive.co.uk/ (accessed September 10, 2020).

Hermansson, Casie E. (2009), *Bluebeard: A Reader's Guide*, Jackson: University Press of Mississippi.

Hinde, Sidney Langford (1897), *The Fall of the Congo Arabs*, London: Methuen.

Hintz, Carrie and Eric L. Tribunella (2013), *Reading Children's Literature: A Critical Introduction*, New York: St. Martin's Press.

Hofer, Margaret K. (2003), *The Games We Played: The Golden Age of Board and Table Games*, New York: Princeton Architectural Press.

Hoffman, E. T. A. ([1818] 2004), "The Sandman" trans. R. J. Hollingdale, in *Tales of Hoffman*, 85–126, New York: Penguin.

Huet, Marie-Hélène (1993), *Monstrous Imagination*, Cambridge, MA: Harvard University Press.

Hunt, Peter (2015), "Unstable Metaphors: Symbolic Spaces and Specific Places," in Maria Sachiko Cecire, Hannah Field, Kavita Mudan Finn, and Malini Roy (eds.), *Space and Place in Children's Literature, 1789 to the Present*, 23–37, London: Routledge.

Hutcheon, Linda (2012), *A Theory of Adaptation*, 2nd edn., New York: Routledge.

Ingelow, Jean ([1869] 1992), *Mopsa the Fairy*, in Nina Auerbach and U. C. Knoepflmacher (eds.), *Forbidden Journeys: Fairy Tales and Fantasies by Victorian Women Writers*, 215–316, Chicago: University of Chicago Press.

Ingwersen, Niels (2000), "Asbjørnsen, Peter Christen (1812–85) and Moe, Jørgen (1813–82)," in Jack Zipes (ed.), *The Oxford Companion to Fairy Tales*, 27–8, Oxford: Oxford University Press.

Iovino, Serenella and Serpil Oppermann, eds. (2014), *Material Ecocriticism*, Bloomington: Indiana University Press.

Jacobs, Lewis (2013), "Moms Demand Action Says 'Little Red Riding Hood' Has Been Banned, But Assault Weapons Haven't," *Politifact*, August 27. Available online: https://www.politifact.com/truth-o-meter/statements/2013/aug/27/moms-demand-action-gun-sense-america/moms-demand-action-says-little-red-riding-hood-has/ (accessed September 10, 2020).

Janson, Deborah (2018), "The Path Not (Yet) Taken: Bettina von Arnim's Ecological Vision in Her Romantic Fairy Tale 'The Queen's Son,'" *Feminist German Studies*, 34: 1–24.

Jarvis, Shawn C. and Jeannine Blackwell, eds. (2001), *The Queen's Mirror: Fairy Tales by German Women, 1780–1900*, Lincoln: University of Nebraska Press.

Jedwab, Rémi, Edward Kerby, and Alexander Moradi (2017), "How Colonial Railroads Defined Africa's Economic Geography," VOX CEPR Policy Portal. Available online: https://voxeu.org/article/how-colonial-railroads-defined-africa-s-economic-geography (accessed September 10, 2020).

Johns, Andreas (2004), *Baba Yaga: The Ambiguous Mother and Witch of Russian Folktale*, New York: Peter Lang.

Jones, James Earl (1993), *Voices and Silences*, New York: Scribner.

Joosen, Vanessa and Gillian Lathey, eds. (2014), *Grimms' Tales Around the Globe: The Dynamics of their International Reception*, Detroit, MI: Wayne State University Press.

Jorgensen, Jeana (2014), "Quantifying the Grimm Corpus: Transgressive and Transformative Bodies in the Grimms' Fairy Tales," *Marvels & Tales*, 28 (1): 127–41.

Joung, Madeline (2019), "What is Happening in Migrant Detention Centers? Here's What to Know," *Time*, July 12. Available online: https://time.com/5623148/migrant-detention-centers-conditions/ (accessed September 10, 2020).

Keene, Melanie (2015), *Science in Wonderland: The Scientific Fairy Tales of Victorian Britain*, Oxford: Oxford University Press.

Kidd, Kenneth (2011), "Queer Theory's Child and Children's Literature Studies," *PMLA*, 126 (1): 182–8.

Killick, Tim (2008), *British Short Fiction in the Early Nineteenth Century: The Rise of the Tale*, Abingdon: Taylor and Francis.

Kincaid, James (1992), *Child-Loving: The Erotic Child and Victorian Fiction*, New York: Routledge.

Kingsley, Charles ([1863] 1910), *The Water-Babies*, illustrated by Linley Sambourne, London: Macmillan.

Kingsley, Charles ([1863] 1995), *The Water-Babies: A Fairy Tale for a Land-Baby*, London: Penguin.

Kingsley, Charles ([1863] 2008), *The Water-Babies*, ed. Richard Kelly, Peterborough, ONT: Broadview Press.

Kingsley, Charles ([1870] 1888), *Madam How and Lady Why; or, First Lessons in Earth Lore for Children*, New York: Macmillan & Co.

Knoepflmacher, U. C. (1998), *Ventures into Childland: Victorians, Fairy Tales, and Femininity*, Chicago: University of Chicago Press.

Knoepflmacher, U. C., ed. (1999), *George MacDonald: The Complete Fairy Tales*, New York: Penguin.

Knoepflmacher, U. C. and G. B. Tennyson, eds. (1977), *Nature and the Victorian Imagination*, Berkeley: University of California Press.

Kooistra, Lorraine Janzen (1997), "*Goblin Market* as a Cross-Audienced Poem: Children's Fairy Tale, Adult Erotic Fantasy," *Children's Literature*, 25: 181–203.

Kornbluh, Anna and Benjamin Morgan (2015), "Manifesto of the V21 Collective," *V21: Victorian Studies for the 21st Century*. Available online: http:v21collective.org/manifesto-of-the-v21-collective-ten-theses/ (accessed September 10, 2020).

Kristeva, Julia (1981), "Women's Time," *Signs*, 7 (1): 13–35.
Kúnos, Ignácz (1913), *Forty-Four Turkish Fairy Tales*, London: George G. Harrap & Co.
La Belle et la Bête [Beauty and the Beast] (1946), [Film] Dir. Jean Cocteau, France: Les Films André Paulvé.
La Fontaine, Jean de (1668), "The Grasshopper and the Ant," Wikisource. Available online: https://en.wikisource.org/wiki/Fables_La_Fontaine,_tr._Wright_/The_Grasshopper_and_the_Ant (accessed December 13, 2020).
Lambourne, Lionel (1997), "Fairies and the Stage," in Jane Martineau (ed.), *Victorian Fairy Painting*, 46–53, London: Royal Academy of Arts.
Lang, Andrew ([1892] 1976), "Modern Fairy Tales," in Lance Salway (ed.), *A Peculiar Gift: Nineteenth Century Writings on Books for Children*, 133–6, Harmondsworth: Kestrel Books.
Lang, Andrew (1901), *The Violet Fairy Book*, London: Longmans, Green and Co.
Lang, Andrew (1911), "Tales," in *Encyclopaedia Britannica*, 11th edn., 369–71, New York: Encyclopaedia Britannica.
Latour, Bruno (1993), *We Have Never Been Modern*, Cambridge, MA: Harvard University.
Leach, Karoline ([1999] 2009), *In the Shadow of the Dreamchild: A New Understanding of Lewis Carroll*, London: Peter Owen.
Levine, George ([1988] 1991), *Darwin and the Novelists: Patterns of Science in Victorian Fiction*, Chicago: University of Chicago Press.
Levine, George (2006), *Darwin Loves You: Natural Selection and the Re-Enchantment of the World*, Princeton, NJ: Princeton University Press.
Lewis. C. S., ed. (1986) "Preface," in *George MacDonald: 365 Readings*, xxi–xxxiv, New York: Macmillan.
Lhéritier [sic], Marie-Jeanne ([1696] 2001), "The Enchantments of Eloquence; or, The Effects of Sweetness," in Jack Zipes (ed.), *The Great Fairy Tale Tradition*, 550–64, New York: W. W. Norton.
Little Red Riding Hood (1887), [Board Game] New York: McLoughlin Brothers.
Lloyd, A. B. (1899) *In Dwarf Land and Cannibal Country: A Record of Travel and Discovery in Central Africa*, New York: Charles Scribner's Sons.
Lokke, Kari (2006), "The Romantic Fairy Tale," in Michael Ferber (ed.), *A Companion to European Romanticism*, 138–55, Hoboken, NJ: John Wiley & Sons.
Lovell-Smith, Rose (2007), "Eggs and Serpents: Natural History Reference in Lewis Carroll's Scene of Alice and the Pigeon," *Children's Literature*, 35: 27–53.
Lowry, Lois (2004), *The Messenger*, Boston: Houghton Mifflin.
Lucas, Ann Lawson (2012), "Puppets on a String: The Unnatural History of Human Reproduction," in Katia Pizzi (ed.), *Pinocchio, Puppets, and Modernity: The Mechanical Body*, 49–61, New York: Routledge.
Lurie, Alison (2000), "The Oddness of Oz," *The New York Review of Books*, December 21. Available online: https://www.nybooks.com/articles/2000/12/21/the-oddness-of-oz/ (accessed March 8, 2020).
Lüthi, Max ([1962] 1976), *Once Upon a Time: On the Nature of Fairy Tales*, trans. Lee Chadeayne and Paul Gottwald, Bloomington: Indiana University Press.
Lüthi, Max (1970), *Once Upon a Time: On the Nature of Fairy Tales*, trans. Lee Chadeayne and Paul Gottwald, New York: Frederick Ungar.
Lüthi, Max ([1975] 1985), *The Fairytale As Art Form and Portrait of Man*, trans. Jon Erikson, Bloomington: Indiana University Press.

Lysack, Krista (2008), *Come Buy, Come Buy: Shopping and the Culture of Consumption in Victorian Women's Writing*, Athens: Ohio University Press.
MacCulloch, J. A. (1905), *The Childhood of Fiction: A Study of Folk Tales and Primitive Thought*, New York: E. P. Dutton.
MacDonald, George (1858), *Phantastes: A Faerie Romance for Men and Women*, London: Smith, Elder and Co.
MacDonald, George ([1858] 1983), *Phantastes: A Faerie Romance for Men and Women*, London: Everyman.
MacDonald, George ([1864] 1999), "The Light Princess," in U. C. Knoepflmacher (ed.), *George MacDonald: The Complete Fairy Tales*, 15–31, New York: Penguin.
MacDonald, George ([1871] 2011), *At the Back of the North Wind*, ed. Roderick McGillis and John Pennington, Peterborough, ONT: Broadview.
MacDonald, George ([1871, 1881] 1990), *The Princess and the Goblin and The Princess and Curdie*, ed. Roderick McGillis, New York: Oxford University Press.
MacDonald, George ([1874] 1999), "Cross Purposes," in U. C. Knoepflmacher (ed.), *The Complete Fairy Tales*, 103–19, New York: Penguin.
MacDonald, George (1895), "The Fantastic Imagination," in *A Dish of Orts: Chiefly Papers on the Imagination and on Shakspeare*, 313–22, London: S. Low, Marston.
MacDonald, George ([1895] 1976), "The Fantastic Imagination," in Lance Salway (ed.), *A Peculiar Gift: Nineteenth Century Writings on Books for Children*, 162–7, Harmondsworth, UK: Kestrel Books.
MacDonald, George ([1895] 2001), *Lilith: First and Final*, Whitehorn, CA: Johannesen.
MacGavran, James Holt, ed. ([1991] 2009), *Romanticism and Children's Literature in Nineteenth-Century England*, Athens: University of Georgia Press.
Macready, William (Willie) C., Jr. (1842), "Pencil Illustration III," in Robert Browning, "The Pied Piper of Hamelin," H0088, Browning Collections, Armstrong Browning Library, Baylor University, Waco, Texas.
Marsh, Sarah (2008), "Twice Upon a Time: The Importance of Rereading 'The Devoted Friend,'" *Children's Literature*, 36: 72–87.
Martineau, Jane, ed. (1997), *Victorian Fairy Painting*, London: Royal Academy of Arts.
Marzolph, Ulrich (2011), "Arabian Nights," in Charlie T. McCormick and Kim Kennedy White (eds.), *Folklore: An Encyclopedia of Beliefs, Customs, Tales, Music, and Art*, 2nd edn., 124–9, Santa Barbara, CA: ABC-CLIO.
McGillis, Roderick (2003), "'A Fairytale Is Just a Fairytale': George MacDonald and the Queering of Fairy," *Marvels & Tales*, 17 (1): 86–99.
McGlathery, James M. (1991), *Fairy Tale Romance: The Grimms, Basile, and Perrault*, Urbana: University of Illinois Press.
McKinley, Robin ([1978] 1993), *Beauty: A Retelling of the Story of Beauty and the Beast*, New York: Harper Trophy.
Mellor, Anne K. (1980), *English Romantic Irony*, Cambridge, MA: Harvard University Press.
Merrill, Lynn (1989), *The Romance of Victorian Natural History*, Oxford: Oxford University Press.
Meyer, Susan E. (1983), *A Treasury of the Great Children's Book Illustrators*, New York: Harry N. Abrams.
Michaels, Walter Benn (1992), "Race into Culture: A Critical Genealogy of Cultural Identity," *Critical Inquiry*, 18 (4): 655–85.

Molesworth, Maria Louisa ([1893] 1976), "Hans Christian Andersen," in Lance Salway (ed.), *A Peculiar Gift: Nineteenth Century Writings on Books for Children*, 137–46, Harmondsworth: Kestrel Books.

Morton, Samuel George (1839), *Crania Americana*, London: Simpkin, Marshall, and Co.

Moss, Anita (1988), "Mothers, Monsters, and Morals in Victorian Fairy Tales," *The Lion and the Unicorn*, 12 (2): 47–60.

Mullen, Tom (2015), "Richard Owen, The Man Who Invented the Dinosaur," *BBC News*, February 26.

Murphy, Patricia (2001), *Time is of the Essence: Temporality, Gender, and the New Woman*, Albany: State University of New York Press.

Myers Mitzi (1986), "Impeccable Governesses, Rational Dames, and Moral Mothers: Mary Wollstonecraft and the Female Tradition in Georgian Children's Books," *Children's Literature*, 14: 31–59.

Naithani, Sadhana (2010), *The Story-Time of the British Empire. Colonial and Postcolonial Folkloristics*, Jackson: University Press of Mississippi.

Nesbit, E[dith] ([1900] 1987), "The Last of the Dragons," in Jack Zipes (ed.), *Victorian Fairy Tales: The Revolt of the Fairies and Elves*, 353–8, New York: Methuen.

Nesbit, E[dith] ([1901] 1992), "Fortunatus Rex & Co.," in Nina Auerbach and U. C. Knoepflmacher (eds.), *Forbidden Journeys: Fairy Tales and Fantasies by Victorian Women Writers*, 192–205, Chicago: University of Chicago Press.

Nesbit, E[dith] ([1904] 2012), *The Phoenix and the Carpet*, London: Puffin Books.

Neumann, Siegfried (1993), "The Brothers Grimm as Collectors and Editors of German Folktales," in Donald Haase (ed.), *The Reception of Grimms' Fairy Tales: Responses, Reactions, Revisions*, 24–40, Detroit, MI: Wayne State University Press.

Newton, Michael, ed. (2015), *Victorian Fairy Tales*, Oxford World's Classics, Oxford: Oxford University Press.

Nikolajeva, Maria (1995), "Russian Children's Literature Before and After Perestroika," *Children's Literature Association Quarterly*, 20 (3): 105–11.

Novalis [Friedrich von Hardenberg] ([1802] 2007), *Heinrich von Ofterdingen*, commentary by Andrea Neuhaus, Frankfurt: Suhrkamp.

Novalis [Friedrich von Hardenberg] (2017), "Epigraph," in George MacDonald, *Phantastes: Annotated Edition*, ed. John Pennington and Roderick McGillis, Hamden, CT: Winged Lion Press.

Nursi, Bediuzzaman Said (2011), "The Third Matter of 'The First Chapter,'" in *The Staff of Moses: Reflections on Islamic Faith, and Divine Existence and Unity*, New York: The Light.

OED Online (2020a), s.v. "coverture, n.," Oxford: Oxford University Press, December. Available online: https://www.oed.com/view/Entry/43385 (accessed December 20, 2020).

OED Online (2020b), s.v. "goblin, n1," Oxford: Oxford University Press, December. Available online: www.oed.com/view/Entry/79613 (accessed December 21, 2020).

Orenstein, Catherine (2002), *Little Red Riding Hood Uncloaked: Sex, Morality, and the Evolution of a Fairy Tale*, New York: Basic Books.

Pask, Kevin (2013), *The Fairy Way of Writing: Shakespeare to Tolkien*, Baltimore: Johns Hopkins University Press.

Patmore, Coventry (1854), *The Angel in the House*, London: John W. Parker & Son.

Patmore, Coventry (1891), *The Angel in the House*, London: Cassell & Company. Project Gutenberg. Available online: http://www.gutenberg.org/files/4099/4099-h/4099-h.htm (accessed December 13, 2020).

Perrault, Charles ([1697] 2000), "Cinderella, or the Little Glass Slipper," in John W. Griffith and Charles H. Frey (eds.), *Classics of Children's Literature*, 5th edn., 17–21, Upper Saddle River, NJ: Prentice Hall.

Perrault, Charles ([1697] 2001a), "The Master Cat; or, Puss in Boots," in Jack Zipes (ed.), *The Great Fairy Tale Tradition*, 397–401, New York: W. W. Norton.

Perrault, Charles ([1697] 2001b), "Riquet with the Tuft," in Jack Zipes (ed.), *The Great Fairy Tale Tradition: From Straparola and Basile to the Brothers Grimm*, 722–7, New York: W. W. Norton.

"Play Days" (1916), *The Playground*, 10 (1) (April): 8–9.

The Playground (1914), 7 (10) (January): 410–11.

Powell, Kirstin (1986), "Edward Burne-Jones and the Legend of Briar Rose," *Journal of Pre-Raphaelite Studies*, 15 (4): 15–28.

Prickett, Stephen (2005), *Victorian Fantasy*, 2nd edn., Waco, TX: Baylor University Press.

Propp, Vladimir J. (1984), *Theory and History of Folklore*, Minneapolis: University of Minnesota Press.

Pugh, Tison (2008), "'There Lived in the Land of Oz Two Queerly Made Men': Queer Utopianism and Antisocial Eroticism in L. Frank Baum's Oz Series," *Marvels & Tales*, 22 (2): 217–39.

Purkiss, Diane (2000), *Troublesome Things: A History of Fairies and Fairy Stories*, London: Allen Lane, The Penguin Press.

Queenan, Bernard (1978), "The Evolution of the Pied Piper," *Children's Literature*, 7: 104–14.

Ramazani, Jahan, ed. (2018), *The Norton Anthology of English Literature: The Twentieth and Twenty-First Centuries*, vol. F, gen. ed. Stephen Greenblatt, 10th edn., New York: W. W. Norton.

Reynolds, Kimberley (2006), "Nonsense," in Jack Zipes (ed.), *The Oxford Encyclopedia of Children's Literature*, vol. 3, 165–8, New York: Oxford University Press.

Richardson, Alan (1991), "Wordsworth, Fairy Tales, and the Politics of Children's Reading," in James Holt McGavran (ed.), *Romanticism and Children's Literature in Nineteenth-Century England*, 34–55, Athens: University of Georgia Press.

Richardson, Alan (2010), *Literature, Education and Romanticism: Reading as Social Practice, 1780–1832*, Cambridge: Cambridge University Press.

Right and Wrong, or the Princess Belinda (1876) [Board Game] published by Albert A. Hill.

Ritchie, Anne Thackeray (1867a), "Beauty and the Beast," in *Beauty and the Beast*, 1–24, Boston: Loring.

Ritchie, Anne Thackeray (1867b), "Little Red Riding Hood," *The Cornhill Magazine*, (16) October: 440–73.

Ritchie, Anne Thackeray (1868), *Five Old Friends and a Young Prince*, London: Smith, Elder, & Co.

Ritchie, Anne Thackeray ([1868] 1987), "Cinderella," in Jack Zipes (ed.), *Victorian Fairy Tales: The Revolt of the Fairies and Elves*, 101–26, New York: Methuen.

Ritchie, Anne Thackeray (1871), "Bluebeard's Keys, Part I," *Cornhill Magazine* (23) February: 192–220; "Bluebeard's Keys, Part II," (23) June: 688–709.

Ritchie, Anne Thackeray (1872), "Riquet à la Houppe, Part I," *Cornhill Magazine*, (25) January: 45–59; "Riquet à la Houppe, Part II," (25) February: 177–95.

Ritchie, Anne Thackeray (1874), *Bluebeard's Keys and Other Stories*, London: Smith, Elder and Co.

Robson, Catherine, ed. (2018), *The Norton Anthology of English Literature: The Victorian Age*, vol. E, gen. ed. Stephen Greenblatt, 10th edn., New York: W. W. Norton.

Rölleke, Heinz, ed. (1975), *Die älteste Märchensammlung der Brüder Grimm: Synopse der handschriftlichen Urfassung von 1810 und der Erstdrucke von 1812*, Cologny: Fondation Martin Bodmer.

Romero, Simon, Zolan Kanno-Youngs, Manny Fernandez, Daniel Borunda, Aaron Montes, and Caitlin Dickerson (2019), "Hungry, Scared and Sick: Inside the Migrant Detention Center in Clint, Tex.," *The New York Times*, July 19. Available online: https://www.nytimes.com/interactive/2019/07/06/us/migrants-border-patrol-clint.html?mtrref=time.com&assetType=REGIWALL (accessed September 10, 2020).

Rose, Jacqueline (1984), *The Case of Peter Pan: Or, the Impossibility of Children's Fiction*, London: Macmillan.

Rose, Jacqueline (1993), *The Case of Peter Pan; or, The Impossibility of Children's Fiction*, Philadelphia: University of Pennsylvania Press.

Rosenman, Ellen Bayuk (2013), "Bodies and Sexuality," in Teresa Mangum (ed.), *A Cultural History of Women: In the Age of Empire*, 54–5, New York: Bloomsbury.

Rossetti, Christina ([1862] 1973), *Goblin Market*, in Jonathan Cott (ed.), *Beyond the Looking Glass: Extraordinary Works of Fairy Tale & Fantasy*, 469–519, New York: Stonehill Publishing Company.

Rossetti, Christina ([1862] 1988), *Goblin Market*, in Michael Patrick Hearn (ed.), *The Victorian Fairy Tale Book*, 193–208, New York: Pantheon Books.

Rothfels, Nigel (2007), "How the Caged Bird Sings: Animals and Entertainment," in Kathleen Kete (ed.), *A Cultural History of Animals in the Age of Empire*, 95–112, Oxford: Berg.

Ruskin, John ([1868] 1905), "Fairy Stories," in E. T. Cook and Alexander Wedderburn (eds.), *The Complete Works of John Ruskin*, vol. 19, 233–9, London: George Allen.

Ruskin, John ([1851] 1973), "The King of the Golden River, or The Black Brothers," in Jonathan Cott (ed.), *Beyond the Looking Glass: Extraordinary Works of Fairy Tale & Fantasy*, 5–37, New York: Stonehill Publishing Company.

Ruskin, John ([1851] 1987), "King of the Golden River," in Jack Zipes (ed.), *Victorian Fairy Tales: The Revolt of the Fairies and Elves*, 15–36, New York: Methuen.

Ruskin, John ([1865] 2002), "Of Queens' Gardens," in Deborah Epstein Nord (ed.), *Sesame and Lilies*, 68–93, New Haven, CT: Yale University Press.

Ruskin, John ([1869] 2015), "'Introduction' to the Grimm Brothers, *German Popular Stories*," in Michael Newton (ed. and intro.), *Victorian Fairy Tales*, 391–5, Oxford: Oxford University Press.

Ruwe, Donelle, ed. (2005), *Culturing the Child, 1690–1914: Essays in Memory of Mitzi Myers*, Lanham, MD: Scarecrow Press.

Said, Edward W. (1978), *Orientalism*, London: Routledge & Kegan Paul.

Sammond, Nicholas (2005), *Babes in Tomorrowland*, Durham, NC: Duke University Press.

Schacker, Jennifer (2003), *National Dreams: The Remaking of Fairy Tales in Nineteenth-Century England*, Philadelphia: University of Pennsylvania Press.

Schacker, Jennifer (2008), "Generic Transformation and the Body of Mother Bunch," unpublished conference paper.
Schacker, Jennifer (2011), "Fluid Identities: Madame d'Aulnoy, Mother Bunch, and Fairy Tale History," in Ray Cashman, Tom Mould, and Pravina Shukla (eds.), *The Individual and Tradition: Folkloristic Perspectives*, 249–64, Bloomington: Indiana University Press.
Schacker, Jennifer (2018), *Staging Fairyland: Folklore, Children's Entertainment, and Nineteenth-Century Pantomime*, Detroit, MI: Wayne State University Press.
Schiebinger, Londa (1999), *Has Feminism Changed Science?*, Cambridge, MA: Harvard University Press.
Seifert, Lewis C. (2011), "Animal-Human Hybridity in d'Aulnoy's 'Babiole' and 'Prince Wild Boar,'" *Marvels & Tales*, 25 (2): 244–60.
Seifert, Lewis C. (2015), "Introduction," in "Queer(ing) Fairy Tales," special Issue of *Marvels & Tales*, 29 (1): 15–20.
Shaw, W. C. (1981), "Folklore Surrounding Facial Deformity and the Origins of Facial Prejudice," *British Journal of Plastic Surgery*, 34 (3): 237–46.
Shelley, Mary (1999), *Frankenstein; Or, The Modern Prometheus*, Toronto: Broadview Literary Texts.
Showalter, Elaine (2018), *A Vindication of the Rights of Monsters*, Washington, DC: American University.
Shuttleworth, Sally (2010), *The Mind of the Child: Child Development in Literature, Science, and Medicine, 1840–1900*, Oxford: Oxford University Press.
Silver, Carole G. (1999), *Strange and Secret Peoples: Fairies and Victorian Consciousness*, New York: Oxford University Press.
Silver, Carole G. (2000), "Wilde, Oscar [1854–1900])," in Jack Zipes (ed.), *The Oxford Companion to Fairy Tales*, 549–51, Oxford: Oxford University Press.
Silver, Carole G. (2016), "Animal Bride, Animal Groom," in Anne E. Duggan and Donald Haase (eds.), *Folktales and Fairy Tales: Traditions and Texts from around the World*, 2nd edn., vol. 1, 40–2, Santa Barbara, CA: ABC-CLIO.
Simmons, Clare A. (2011), *Popular Medievalism in Romantic-Era Britain*, New York: Palgrave Macmillan.
Simonsen, Rasmus R. (2014), "Dark Avunculate: Shame, Animality, and Queer Development in Oscar Wilde's 'The Star-Child,'" *Children's Literature*, 42: 20–41.
Spangler, Brie (2016), *Beast*, New York: Alfred A. Knopf.
Spariousu, Mihai (1997), *The Wreath of Wild Olive: Play, Liminality, and the Study of Literature*, New York: State University of New York.
Spencer, Leland G. (2014), "Performing Transgender Identity in *The Little Mermaid*: From Andersen to Disney," *Communication Studies*, 65 (1): 112–27.
Steig, Reinhold and Herman Grimm, eds. (1904), *Achim von Arnim und die ihm nahe standen*, vol. 3, *Achim von Arnim und Jacob und Wilhelm Grimm*, ed. Reinhold Steig, Stuttgart: J. B. Cotta.
Stevenson, Robert Louis ([1885] 1994), "System," in *A Child's Garden of Verses*, 21, London: Puffin Penguin.
Stewart, Susan (1993), *On Longing: Narratives of the Miniature, the Gigantic, the Souvenir, the Collection*, Durham, NC: Duke University Press.
Stone, Harry (1979), *Dickens and the Invisible World: Fairy Tales, Fantasy, and Novel-Making*, Bloomington: Indiana University Press.
Sumpter, Caroline (2008), *The Victorian Press and the Fairy Tale*, Basingstoke: Palgrave Macmillan.

Susina, Jan (2003), "'Like the fragments of coloured glass in a kaleidoscope': Andrew Lang Mixes Up Richard Doyle's *in Fairyland*," *Marvels & Tales*, 17 (1): 100–19.

Susina, Jan (2010), *The Place of Lewis Carroll in Children's Literature*, Abingdon: Routledge.

Sylva, Carmen (Elisabeth of Rumania) (2001), "Furnica, or The Queen of the Ants," in Shawn C. Jarvis and Jeannine Blackwell (eds.), *The Queen's Mirror: Fairy Tales by German Women, 1780–1900*, 325–33, Lincoln: University of Nebraska Press.

Talairach-Vielmas, Laurence (2009), "Rewriting *Little Red Riding-Hood*: Victorian Fairy Tales and Mass Visual Culture," *The Lion and the Unicorn*, 33: 259–81.

Talairach-Vielmas, Laurence (2010), "Beautiful Maidens, Hideous Suitors: Victorian Fairy Tales and the Process of Civilization," *Marvels and Tales*, 24 (2): 272–96.

Talairach-Vielmas, Laurence (2014), *Fairy Tales, Natural History and Victorian Culture*, Basingstoke: Palgrave Macmillan.

Tan, Shaun (2016), "Little Red Cap," in *The Singing Bones: Inspired by Grimms' Fairy Tales*, foreword by Neil Gaiman, intro. by Jack Zipes, 20–1, New York: Scholastic.

Tatar, Maria (1992), *Off with Their Heads! Fairy Tales and the Culture of Childhood*, Princeton, NJ: Princeton University Press.

Tatar, Maria, ed. (2002), *The Annotated Classic Fairy Tales*, New York: W. W. Norton.

Tatar, Maria (2003), *The Hard Facts of the Grimms' Fairy Tales*, 2nd edn., Princeton, NJ: Princeton University Press.

Tatar, Maria, ed. (2007), *The Annotated Hans Christian Andersen*, New York: Norton.

Tatar, Maria, ed. (2011), *The Annotated Peter Pan: The Centennial Edition*, New York: Norton.

Tatar, Maria, ed. (2017a), *Beauty and the Beast: Classic Tales About Animal Brides and Grooms from Around the World*, New York: Penguin.

Tatar, Maria, ed. (2017b), *The Classic Fairy Tales*, 2nd edn., New York: W. W. Norton.

Tennyson, Alfred (1842), *Poems*, London: Edward Moxon.

Tennyson, Alfred Lord ([1850] 1973), *In Memoriam*, ed. Robert H. Ross, New York: W. W. Norton & Co.

Thackeray, William Makepeace ([1854] 2015), "The Rose and the Ring; or, The History of Prince Giglio and Prince Bulbo: A Fire-Side Pantomime for Great and Small Children," in Michael Newton (ed.), *Victorian Fairy Tales*, 38–114, Oxford World's Classics, Oxford: Oxford University Press.

Tharoor, Shashi (2017), "'But What About the Railways?' The Myths of Britain's Gifts to India," *The Guardian*, March 8. Available online: https://www.theguardian.com/world/2017/mar/08/india-britain-empire-railways-myths-gifts (accessed September 10, 2020).

"The Huskar Pit Disaster, 1838: Why 28 Children Died" (2004), BBC Radio 4. Available online: http://www.bbc.co.uk/radio4/history/making_history/makhist10_prog8a.shtml (accessed December 13, 2020).

Thesz, Nicole (2019), "Eco-Critical Perspectives: Nature and the Supernatural in the Cinderella Cycle," in Andrew Teverson (ed.), *The Fairy Tale World*, 426–37, London: Routledge.

Thomas, Dexter (2014), "Michael Brown Was Not a Boy, He Was a Demon," *Al Jazeera*, November 26. Available online: https://www.aljazeera.com/indepth/opinion/2014/11/michael-brown-demon-ferguson-2014112672358760344.html (accessed September 10, 2020).

Thomas, Keith (1983), *Man and the Natural World: Changing Attitudes in England, 1500–1800*, London: Oxford University Press.
Thompson, Stith (1995), *Motif-Index of Folk-literature: A Classification of Narrative Elements in Folktales, Ballads, Myths, Fables, Mediaeval Romances, Exempla, Fabliaux, Jest-books, and Local Legends*, Bloomington: Indiana University Press.
Thurston, Robert W. (2007), *The Witch Hunts: A History of the Witch Persecutions in Europe and North America*, New York: Pearson Longman.
Tieck, Ludwig (1992), "Der Runenberg," in *Der blonde Eckbert. Der Runenberg. Die Elfen*, Stuttgart: Reclam.
Tilley, Roger (1973), *A History of Playing Cards*, London: Studio Vista.
Todd, Dennis (1995), *Imagining Monsters: Miscreations of the Self in Eighteenth-Century England*, Chicago: University of Chicago Press.
Todorov, Tzvetan (1975), *The Fantastic: A Structural Approach to a Literary Genre*, trans. Richard Howard, Ithaca, NY: Cornell University Press.
Tosi, Laura and Peter Hunt, eds. (2018), *The Fabulous Journeys of Alice and Pinocchio: Exploring their Parallel Worlds*, Jefferson, NC: McFarland & Company.
Tucker, Holly (2003), *Pregnant Fictions: Childbirth and the Fairy Tale in Early Modern France*, Detroit, MI: Wayne State University Press.
Turner, Kay and Pauline Greenhill, eds. (2012), *Transgressive Tales: Queering the Grimms*, Detroit, MI: Wayne State University Press.
Turner, Victor (1982), *From Ritual to Theatre: The Human Seriousness of Play*, New York: Performing Arts Journal Press.
Verstegan, Richard (1634), *A Restitution of Decayed Intelligence: In Antiquities: Concerning the Most Noble and Renowned English Nation*, London: John Norton.
Walker, Barbara, K. (1993), *The Art of the Turkish Tale*, Texas: Tech University Press.
Walkowitz, Rebecca (2007), "Unimaginable Largeness: Kazuo Ishiguro, Translation, and the New World Literature," *NOVEL: A Forum on Fiction*, 40 (3): 216–39.
Wang, Amy B. (2018), "What World War II's 'Operation Pied Piper' Taught us About the Trauma of Family Separations," *Washington Post*, June 19. Available online: https://www.washingtonpost.com/news/retropolis/wp/2018/06/19/what-world-war-iis-operation-pied-piper-taught-us-about-the-trauma-of-family-separations/ (accessed September 10, 2020).
Warner, Marina (1995), *From The Beast to The Blonde: On Fairy Tales and Their Tellers*, New York: Farrar, Straus and Giroux.
Warner, Marina (2014), *Once Upon a Time: A Short History of Fairy Tale*, Oxford: Oxford University Press.
Warner, Marina (2018), *Fairy Tale: A Very Short Introduction*, Oxford: Oxford University Press.
Wells, H. G. ([1895] 2005), *The Time Machine*, ed. Patrick Parrinder, New York: Penguin Books.
Wikipedia (2020), "1842 in Great Britain." Available online: https://en.wikipedia.org/wiki/1842_in_the_United_Kingdom (accessed September 10, 2020).
Wilde, Oscar ([1888] 2017), "The Happy Prince," in Maria Tatar (ed.), *The Classic Fairy Tales*, 2nd edn., 334–41, New York: W. W. Norton.
Wilde, Oscar ([1889] 2000), "15 January: Oscar Wilde to Amelie Rives Chanler," in Merlin Holland and Rupert Hart-Davis (eds.), *The Complete Letters of Oscar Wilde*, 388, New York: Henry Holt & Company.
Wilde, Oscar (1919), *The Happy Prince and Other Fairy Tales*, New York: G.P. Putnam's Sons.

Wilde, Oscar (2003), *Complete Short Fiction*, London: Penguin.
Wilkenson, Florence (1906), "The Literary Activity of Andrew Lang: Two New Books from His Rapid Pen, a Life of Sir Walter Scottand a Volume of Collected Poems," *The New York Times*, April 7: 224.
Wills, W. H. and George A. Sala (1853), "Fairyland in 'fifty-four'," *Household Words*, 193 (3): 313–17.
Wilson, Darren (2014), "Read Darren Wilson's Full Grand Jury Testimony," *Washington Post*, November 25. Available online: http://apps.washingtonpost.com/g/page/national/read-darren-wilsons-full-grand-jury-testimony/1472/ (accessed September 10, 2020).
Wilson, Phillip K. (2002), "Eighteenth-Century 'Monsters' and Nineteenth Century 'Freaks': Reading the Maternally Marked Child," *Literature and Medicine*, 21 (1): 2–3.
Winchester, Simon (2011), *The Alice Behind Wonderland*, Oxford: Oxford University Press.
Wood, Christopher (2000), *Fairies in Victorian Art*, Woodbridge: Antique Collectors' Club.
Wood, Daniel B. (1993), "Rodney King Takes Stand in L.A. Police Officer Trial," *Christian Science Monitor*, March 11. Available online: https://www.csmonitor.com/1993/0311/11082.html (accessed December 23, 2020).
Wood, Naomi (2002), "Creating the Sensual Child: Paterian Aesthetics, Pederasty, and Oscar Wilde's Fairy Tales," *Marvels & Tales*, 16 (2): 156–70.
Wood, Naomi (2004), "(Em)Bracing Icy Mothers: Ideology, Identity, and the Environment in Children's Fantasy," in Sid Dobrin and Kenneth Kidd (eds.), *Wild Things: Children's Literature and Ecocriticism*, 198–214, Detroit, MI: Wayne State University Press.
Wood, Naomi (2006), "The Ugly Duckling's Legacy: Adulteration, Contemporary Fantasy, and the Dark," *Marvels & Tales*, 20 (2): 193–207.
Wood, Naomi (2012), "Angelic, Atavistic, Human: The Child of the Victorian Period," in Adrienne E. Gavin (ed.), *The Child in British Literature: Literary Constructions of Childhood, Medieval to Contemporary*, 116–30, New York: Palgrave.
Wood, William Rayner (1842), *Report of the Children's Employment Commission*, London: William Clowes.
Yonge, Charlotte (1856), *The Daisy Chain, or, Aspirations: A Family Chronicle*, London: John W. Parker & Son.
Yonge, Charlotte (1864), *The Trial: More Links of the Daisy Chain*, London: Macmillan.
Yonge, Charlotte ([1865] 2001), *The Clever Woman of the Family*, ed. Clare A Simmons, Peterborough, ONT: Broadview Literary Texts.
Yonge, Charlotte (1877), *Womankind*, London: Mozley and Smith.
Zanger, Jules (1977), "Goblins, Morlocks, and Weasels: Classic Fantasy and the Industrial Revolution," *Children's Literature in Education: An International Quarterly*, 8 (4): 154–62.
Zingerle, Ignaz Vinzenz and Joseph Zingerle (1854), "Löwe, Storch und Ameise," in *Kinder- und Hausmärchen aus Süddeutschland*, 1–5, Regensburg: Pustet.
Zipes, Jack (1983a), *Fairy Tales and the Art of Subversion: The Classical Genre for Children and the Process of Civilization*, New York: Routledge.
Zipes, Jack (1983b), *The Trials and Tribulations of Little Red Riding Hood: Versions of the Tale in Sociocultural Context*, South Hadley, MA: Bergin & Garvey Publishers.

Zipes, Jack, ed. and intro. (1987), *Victorian Fairy Tales: The Revolt of the Fairies and Elves* London: Routledge.
Zipes, Jack, ed. ([1983] 1993), *The Trials and Tribulations of Little Red Riding Hood*, New York: Routledge.
Zipes, Jack (1988), *The Brothers Grimm: From Enchanted Forests to the Modern World*, New York: Routledge.
Zipes, Jack ([1988] 1991), *Fairy Tales and the Art of Subversion: The Classical Genre for Children and the Process of Civilization*, New York: Routledge.
Zipes, Jack (1999), *When Dreams Came True: Classical Fairy Tales and Their Tradition*, New York: Routledge.
Zipes, Jack (2000a), "Kalevala," in Jack Zipes (ed.), *The Oxford Companion to Fairy Tales*, 274–5, Oxford: Oxford University Press.
Zipes, Jack, ed. (2000b), *The Oxford Companion to Fairy Tales*, Oxford: Oxford University Press.
Zipes, Jack (2001), *The Great Fairy Tale Tradition: From Straparola and Basile to the Brothers Grimm*, New York: W. W. Norton.
Zipes, Jack, trans. and ed. (2003), *The Complete Fairy Tales of the Brothers Grimm*, New York: Bantam.
Zipes, Jack (2006), *Why Fairy Tales Stick: The Evolution and Relevance of a Genre*, New York: Routledge.
Zipes, Jack (2012), *The Irresistible Fairy Tale: The Cultural and Social History of a Genre*, Princeton, NJ: Princeton University Press.
Zipes, Jack, trans. (2014), "Introduction: Rediscovering the Original Tales of the Brothers Grimm," in Jack Zipes (ed. and trans.), *The Complete First Edition of The Original Folk and Fairy Tales of the Brothers Grimm*, xix–xliii, Princeton, NJ: Princeton University Press.
Zipes, Jack (2017), *Tales of Wonder: Retelling Fairy Tales Through Picture Postcards*, Minneapolis: University of Minnesota Press.

CONTRIBUTORS

Michelle Beissel Heath is Professor of English at the University of Nebraska, Kearney, where she specializes in children's literature and in nineteenth-century British literature. Her book, *Nineteenth-Century Fictions of Childhood and the Politics of Play*, was published in 2018.

Amy Billone is Professor of English at the University of Tennessee, Knoxville. She is the author of *The Future of the Nineteenth-Century Dream-Child: Fantasy, Dystopia, Cyberculture* (2016) and *Little Songs: Women, Silence, and Nineteenth-Century Sonnet* (2007). She also wrote the Introduction and Notes to the Barnes and Noble Classics edition of J. M. Barrie's *Peter Pan* (2005).

Zeynep Cakmak is a graduate student at Montclair State University's Clinical Mental Health Counseling program. She has an MA in Literature from American University in Washington, DC, where she taught as an instructor in the Writing Studies Program. Her most recent work, "The Muslim Heroines of the American Screen: Re-Writing or Recycling the Narrative?" examines the quality "inclusive" political dramas and their use of stereotypical Muslim characters.

Molly Clark Hillard is Associate Professor of English at Seattle University, where she specializes in Victorian literature. She is the author of *Spellbound: The Fairy Tale and the Victorians* (2014), and has contributed essays to journals and volumes such as *SEL, Narrative, VLC, b2O, Journal of Narrative Theory*, and the *Oxford Handbook on Dickens*. She is currently at work on a book-length project titled *Literary Subject* on readerly bodies and the persistence of Victorian narratives in contemporary novels.

Sarah Marsh is appointed jointly in the Department of Literature and the Department of Critical Race and Gender Studies at American University, where she teaches at the intersection of literature, medical humanities, and the legal history of the body. Her book project, *Constituting Britons: Law, Medicine, and the Roots of White Supremacy in Anglo-American Culture*, shows that an English ideal of embodied liberty—the "ancient constitution"—is a major source of white supremacy in Britain's western Atlantic colonies and the early United States.

John Pennington is Professor of English at St. Norbert College in Wisconsin. His latest publications include a critical edition, with Roderick McGillis, of George MacDonald's *Phantastes* (2017) and an edited collection of essays *Crossing a Great Frontier: Essays on George MacDonald's* Phantastes (2018).

Jan Susina is Professor of English at Illinois State University, where he teaches courses in Children's Literature, Victorian Studies, and Visual Culture. He coedited, with Andrea Immel, *Considering the Kunstmärchen: The History & Development of the Literary Fairy Tale*, a special issue of *Marvels & Tales* (2003) and he is the author of *The Place of Lewis Carroll in Children's Literature* (2010).

Laurence Talairach is Professor of English Literature at the University of Toulouse Jean Jaurès and associate researcher at the Alexandre Koyré Center for the History of Science and Technology. She is the author of *Gothic Remains: Corpses, Terror and Anatomical Culture, 1764–1897* (2019), *Fairy Tales, Natural History and Victorian Culture* (2014), *Wilkie Collins, Medicine and the Gothic* (2009), and *Moulding the Female Body in Victorian Fairy Tales and Sensation Fiction* (2007).

Nicole Thesz is Professor of German at Miami University, Ohio. She has published articles on the German fairy tale, ecocriticism, post–Second World War literature, the GDR, German film, protest movements, and science and the humanities. Her monograph, *The Communicative Event in the Works of Günter Grass: Stages of Speech, 1959–2015*, appeared in 2018.

Naomi J. Wood is Professor of English at Kansas State University, where she teaches graduate and undergraduate courses in children's and young adult literature, fantasy, and Victorian studies. Since 2009, she has coedited *The Lion and the Unicorn*, with David Russell and Karin Westman. She writes about Charles Kingsley, George MacDonald, Hans Christian Andersen, Oscar Wilde, and their twentieth-century heirs.

INDEX

Notes: Page locators in *italic* refer to illustrations.
n = endnote.

Abbott, Edwin A. 124, 125
adaptations 43–62
   children's literature and fairy tales 51–61
   crossover texts 43–8
   Dickens's argument against 13, 52, 131, 142
   nursery rhymes and nonsense rhymes 48–51
   racist stereotypes 61–2
Adela Cathcart 40, 54, 134
adults, fairy tales for 1, 3–7, 46–7, 120–2, 146
advertising 39
Aesop's fables 55
Afanasyev, Aleksandr 8
African American
   folk tradition 55, 116–18
   writers 62
Alcott, Louisa May 44
"Alice on Stage" 56
Alice's Adventures in Wonderland
   in canon of Victorian literature 145
   as a fairy tale 53, 198*n*28
   feminine socialization 155–6
   figures from nursery rhymes 51, *51*
   gender and sexuality 73–8
   illustrations *50*, 54–5, 55–6, 142–3
   imitations 56–8
   influence of *On the Origin of Species* 33–4
   liminal space 137, 138
   non-book items 58–9
   nonsense literature 21, 22, 28, 50–1
   People's Edition of Alice 61
   process of creating 54
   shift from education to entertainment 52–3
   similarities with Pinocchio 77
   theater adaptations 47, 56
   translations 56
Alice's Adventures Under Ground 54, 56, 73, 78
Andersen, Hans Christian 23, 27–8, 51, 130, 133–4
   "The Dryad" 31
   gender and sexuality 71, 72, 73
   "The Little Mermaid" 71, 72, 72, 73, 87, 155, 198*n*18
   "The Nightingale" 12–13, 23
   "The Princess and the Pea" 160
   "The Snow Queen" 5–6, 13, 134
   "Thumbelina" 18–19
animals
   human domination over 108
   -human hybrids 107–8
   judges 89–93, 102
   spouses 87, 88–9, 108–10, 111
   stories of humanized 55

INDEX

ants 92–3
Arab slaves 118–19
The Arabian Nights 11–12, 13, 134, 164
architecture, fairy tale 125–6
art fairy tales 3–7, 10
Asbjørsen, P. C. 8, 69
Auden, W. H. 145–6

Baba Yaga 101, 157
Bachelard, Gaston 127–8, 135
At the Back of the North Wind 135, 136, 140, *143*, 144
Baden-Powell, Robert 157–9
Bakhtin, Mikhail 128, 168
Ballantyne, M. 45
ballets 39, 47
Barrett, Elizabeth 183, 189–91
Barrie, J. M. 70, 79–80, 165, 199n41
    Llewelyn Davies brothers and 79–80, 81
    Peter Pan in Kensington Gardens 19, 138–9
    Peter Pan, or The Boy Who Wouldn't Grow Up 42, 59, 66, 67, 80
    (*see also Peter and Wendy*)
Basile, Giambattista 93–4, 131, 197n10
Baum, L. Frank 22, 49, 58, 79, 142, 146, 157
"beast marriages" 87, 88–9, 108–10, 111
"Beauty and the Beast" 27, 37–9, 109–10, 116, 129, 131–2, 195n5
    Crane's illustrations 37–8
    games 164–5
    struggle for humanity 85–9, 102
Bernheimer, Kate and Andrew 125, 126
bestiality 36, 41, 111
Bettelheim, Bruno 145
"The Birthday of the Infanta" 163–4
births, monstrous 107, 112, 121
Blake, William 26, 27, 147
The Blue Fairy Book 16, 43, 46, 48, 109
"Bluebeard" 12, 20, 85, 110–11, 129
Bottigheimer, Ruth 15, 87, 93, 94, 154
Bowdler, Thomas 45
Bown, Nicola 30, 34
The Boy Castaways of Black Lake Island 19, 59, 80
Braddon, Mary Elizabeth 40
"Briar Rose" 65, 94–5, 176
Brontë, Charlotte 15, 39, 40

Brontë, Emily 39, 196n26
"The Brother and Sister" 107, 108, 118–19
Brough, John Cargill 180, 181
Brown, Michael 172–3, 186–7
Browne, Frances 52
Browne, Maggie 56, 58
"The Brownies" 16, 62, 157–8
Browning, Robert 181–4, 185, 189–91
Buckley, Arabella 35, 180
Bunyan, John 43, 44
burlesque 20–1, 69
Burne Jones, Edward *141*, 185
Burnett, Frances Hodgson 52, 59, 70
Burton, Richard 12, 164
Büsching, Johann Gustav 87, 88, 89

Caldecott, Randolph 48
canon of Victorian literature, fairy tales in 145–6
capitalism, monstrosity of 120
Carpenter, Humphrey 129
Carroll, Lewis 21, 22, 28, 33–4, 47, 50–1, *50*, *51*, 70, 145, 195n8, 198n28
    and Alice Liddell 74–6, *74*, *76*, 198n25
    "'Alice' on Stage" 56
    Alice's Adventures Under Ground 54, 56, 73, 78
    feminine socialization 155–6
    finding an illustrator 54–5
    liminal space 137, 138
    The Nursery "Alice" 55–6
    shift from education to entertainment 52–3
    (*see also Alice's Adventures in Wonderland; Through the Looking-Glass and What Alice Found There*)
castles 129
"The Cat Cinderella" 93–4
censorship 28, 32
chapbooks 3, 44, 46
Chase, Pauline 66, 67–8, 75
child miners 182–4
Childe-Pemberton, Harriet Louisa 41
children, sexualization of 69–70, 73–5
Children's and Household Tales (Kinder- und Hausmärchen) 4, 27, 64, 83, 84, 86, 87, 89, 90, 91, 92, 93, 94, 95, 96, 97, 99, 100, 101, 102, 116, 130, 132

children's literature
   and concerns over fairy tales 15, 44, 46, 152, 194n1
   creating a space for childhood 138
   crossover texts 43–8
   fantasies and fairy tales 13–20, 26–30, 44, 46–8, 51–61
   golden age 61
   racist stereotypes 61–2, 115–20
   shift from education to entertainment 52–3, 61
"Christabel" 5
Christian socialism 140, 141
Christian symbolism 91
Christian teachings 16, 27–8, 52, 99–100, 120, 142
   reconciling science and 34–5
chronotope 128
"Cinderella" 59, 80, 91, 93–4, 159
   games 159–60, 164
   Grimms' version 65, 90, 93–4, 95, 114
   Perrault's 159, 160
class socialization 159–62
Clifford, Lucy Lane 113
Cohen, Jeffrey Jerome 105, 106, 107, 108, 110, 112, 121
Coleridge, Samuel Taylor 4–5, 136
Coles, Henry 51
Collodi (Carlo Lorenzini) 76–7, 162–3
Colored Fairy Books 2, 38, 43, 46, 48, 59, 109, 164, 187–9
consumerism 39, 152, 154
The Coral Island 19, 45
Cottingley fairies 2, 42
coverture 110
Craik, Dinah Mulock 29, 39–40
Crane, Walter 37–8, 39, 48, 55, 196n21
craniometry 174, 185–7
Croker, Thomas Crofton 8, 36
cross-dressing 69
"Cross Purposes" 40, 124
crossover texts 43–8
Cruikshank, George 13, *14*, 15, 27, 47, 52, 132, 139, 142
"Cry of the Children" 183, 189
Crystal Palace 30–1
Cubs 157–9

Dadd, Richard 31, 144
Darwin, Charles 26, 33, 34, 35, 36, 38, 111, 174, 179

d'Aulnoy, Marie-Catherine 44, 47, 85, 87, 88, 91
De Morgan, Mary 29, 123–4, 162
Defoe, Daniel 43, 44
Denslow, W. W. 49, 146
detention centers 171–2, 184
deus ex machina 105
development, theories of 2
"The Devoted Friend" 23, 120
Dickens, Charles 13, 15, 17, 29, 45–6, 130–1, 160–1
   "Frauds on the Fairies" 13, 52, 131, 142
didactic fairy tales 12, 15–16, 27–8, 142, 194n1
Doré, Gustave 47, 144–5
Doyle, Richard 17, *18*, 47, 60, 142, 185, 186, 206n15
"The Dryad" 31
Du Bois, W. E. B. 62

ecology, fairy tale 9–10
eighteen forty-two (1842) 172–5
Eliot, T. S. 145, 146
English folklore 47–8
English, Mary *125*, 126
environmental issues 35–6, 84
evolutionary theory 34, 35, 36, 38, 111
Ewing, Juliana Horatia 15–16, 28–9, 40, 53, 157–8
the "exotic" 10, 13, 134, 146, 163–5

The Fairy Feller's Master Stroke 31, 144
In Fairy Land 17, *18*
The Fairy Tales of Science: A Book for Youth 180
Fairy Tree 185, 206n15
The Fairy's Lake 185, *186*
"Faithful Johannes" 92
Farrow, G. E. 58
female sexuality 17, 36, 39, 40, 41
feminine socialization 154–7, 204n9
fish 90–1
"The Fisherman and his Soul" 23, 71–3, 120
"The Fisherman and his Wife" 90, 91
"The Fitcher's Bird" 110
Fitzgerald, John Anster 27, 32, 185, *186*, 186
Five Children and It 35, 61, 147

Flatland: A Romance of Many Dimensions 124, 126
flora 93–5, 102–3
Folklore Society 180, 187
forbidden love, tales of 71–3
forests 129, 201*n*16
"Fortunatus Rex & Co." 152–4, 162
Fouqué, Friedrich de la Motte 4, 47, 133
Frankenstein 121
"Frauds on the Fairies" 13, 52, 131, 142
freak shows 113
French fairy tales 27, 44, 131
Freud, Sigmund 2, 133
"The Frog King, or Iron Heinrich" 64, 86, 87, 88
"The Frog Prince" 65
"Furnica" 92–3

Galland, Antoine 11–12, 134
games 150–2, 159–60, 164–5
Gates, Henry Louis 117–18
gender and sexuality 63–81
    Alice books 73–8
    Andersen 71, 72, 73
    Goblin Market 17, 155, 204*n*11
    Grimm brothers 64–6, 107, 110, 114, 129
    from illustrations to postcards 66–8
    monsters and 39, 41, 107–115
    performing fairy tales 69–71
    Peter Pan 66, 79–81
    swan maidens 36
    Wilde 71–3
    The Wonderful Wizard of Oz 79
German fairy tales
    nationalist project of collecting 4, 7, 46–7, 132, 172
    (see also Grimm, Jacob and Wilhelm)
German Popular Stories 15, 46, 47, 52, 132
German Romanticism 3–7, 47, 84, 132–3, 135
Goblin Market 17, 145, 146, 155
"Godfather Death" 94
Goethe, Johann Wolfgang von 84, 93
"The Golden Children" 90, 94
"The Golden Key" 136, 139, 146
Goldney, Reverend S. 25
"The Goose Girl" 91
Grahame, Kenneth 22, 55, 147, 161–2

Great Exhibition
    1851 30
    1867 31
Greek mythology 16, 46, 85, 114
Greenaway, Kate 48–9, 183
Greenberg, Kate 171
Grimm, Jacob and Wilhelm 4, 46–7, 83–103
    alterations to fairy tales 70, 151, 154–5
    animals as testers and helpers, tales of 90, 91–2
    "Beauty and Beast" type tales 86, 87–9
    dangerous objects 96–9
    gender and sexuality 64–6, 107, 110, 114, 129
    isolation of women 93, 94
    nationalist project of collecting and transcribing fairy tales 4, 7, 46–7, 132, 172
    physical and liminal spaces 123, 132–3
    plant world 93–5
    supernatural women 99, 100–101, 102
    translations 15, 27, 46–7, 64
    (see also Kinder- und Hausmärchen (Children's and Household Tales))
Gulliver's Travels 20, 43

Haeckel, Ernst 2
Hampton Normal School 116
"Hans My Hedgehog" 87
"Hansel and Gretel" 99, 100, 129, 171–2
"happily ever after" 124, 128, 134
"The Happy Prince" 12, 13, 31, 73, 163
The Happy Prince and Other Tales 51, 71, 120, 140, 141–2
Harris, Joel Chandler, 55, 117
Hartland, Edwin Sidney 180–1, 187
Hawthorne, Nathaniel 16, 46, 113
"Herr Korbes" 96–7
Hill, Albert A. 165
Hoffmann, E. T. A. 3, 47, 77, 78, 84, 133
Hoffmann, Heinrich 49, 51, 53, 61
Holiday House 51, 134
Holmes, Oliver Wendell 113
"The Horse Dew and the Witch" 109, 114–15
A House of Pomegranates 51, 71, 120, 140–1, 163
Houseman, Laurence 146

Hughes, Arthur 49, 54, 78, 143–4, *143*
human-animal hybrids 107–108

illustrations 17, 142–5, 146
    Aesop's fables 55
    Alice's Adventures in Wonderland 50, 54–5, 55–6, 142–3
    "Beauty and the Beast" 37–8
    Caldecott Medal 48
    "Little Red Riding Hood" 127, *144*, 145
    nursery rhymes and nonsense rhymes 48–50, *50*
    "The Pied Piper of Hamelin" 184, *184*
    postcards 66
    Tennyson's work 185, 205–206*n*11
    Turkish fairy tales 108–09, 118, *119*
    The Wonderful Wizard of Oz 146
    The Wood Beyond the World 141
    (*see also* paintings, fairy)
Ingelow, Jean 28, 57, 136–7
interdisciplinarity 168
Ireland 7, 8, 29
Italian fairy tales 8, 76–7, 131

Jacobs, Joseph 26, 48
"Jorinda and Joringel" 94, 123
The Jungle Books 55, 148, 158
"The Juniper Tree" 93, 95, 96

Keats, John 5
Killick, Tim 7, 8–9
Kinder- und Hausmärchen (Children's and Household Tales) 4, 27, 64, 83, 84, 86, 87, 89, 90, 91, 92, 93, 94, 95, 96, 97, 99, 100, 101, 102, 116, 130, 132
"The King of the Golden River" 9–10, 31, 47, 78, 139, 140, 142
Kingsley, Charles 10, *11*, 35, 36, 46, 52, 115, 118, 135–6
Kipling, Rudyard 35–6, 55, 148, 158
Knatchbull-Hugessen, Edward 57
Kúnos, Ignácz 106, 107, 109, 114, 118, 119, *119*, 120, 202*n*2

"La Belle Dame Sans Merci" 5
Lamb, Charles and Mary 45

Lang, Andrew 16, 17, 19, 26, 31, 46, 59–60
    Colored Fairy Books 2, 38, 43, 46, 48, 59, 109, 164, 187–9
"The Last of the Dragons" 146–7
Latour, Bruno 168
Lear Edward 49–50, 53
Leprince de Beaumont, Jeanne-Marie 27, 38, 85, 86, 87, 88, 109, 110, 195*n*5
"The Lettuce Donkey" 94, 101
Lewis, C. S. 131, 132, 145, 148
Liddell, Alice 74–6, *74*, 76, 198*n*25
life and death, discussions of 136
"The Light Princess" 54, 77–8, 130, 139–40
Lilith 123, 124, 135
limericks 50
liminal space 133, 134–9
Linnaeus, Karl 107–108
"Little Brother and Little Sister" 99
Little Lord Fauntleroy 70
"The Little Match Girl" 134
"The Little Mermaid" 71, 72, *72*, 73, 87, 155, 198*n*18
A Little Princess 52, 59
"Little Red Riding Hood" 128
    architecture 124–6
    card game 150–2
    Grimms' version 65, 129, 151
    illustrations 127, *144*, 145
    Moms Demand Action advertisement 169–71
    in pantomime 69
    Perrault's version 40, 65, 69, 126, 129, 145
    Ritchie's version 40–1, 196*n*25
Llewelyn Davies brothers 79–80, 81
"Locksley Hall" 176–8, 180, 181
Lönrott, Elias 8

MacDonald, George 4, 16, 29, 47, 54, 123
    Adela Cathcart 40, 54, 134
    At the Back of the North Wind 135, 136, 140, *143*, 144
    "Cross Purposes" 40, 124
    "The Fantastic Imagination" 4, 47
    "The Golden Key" 136, 139, 146
    "The Light Princess" 54, 77–8, 130, 139–40

INDEX 233

Lilith 123, 124, 135
Phantastes 78, 123, 133, 135, 144, 145
The Princess and Curdie 47, 140
Macready, Willy, Jr. 181, 184, *184*
MacRitchie, David 187
magazines 7–8, 37, 62, 118
"The Magic Fish-Bone" 160–1
"Maid Maleen" 95
"The Maiden Without Hands" 94, 95, 99
maternal
   body as a source of childhood trauma 113
   imprinting 112–13, 115
   monsters 113, 114–15
McLoughlin Brothers 150–2, 159–60
Merrill, Lynn 31
Mines Report 174, 182–4
miniature, aesthetic of 17–19
modern and aesthetic space, fairy tales in 145–8
Moe, Jørgen 8, 69
Molesworth, Maria Louisa 6, 29, 40
Moms Demand Action 169–71
monogenesis 116
the monstrous 105–122
   for adults and children 120–2
   function in nineteenth-century tales 106
   gender, sexuality and 39, 41, 107–115
   inventions of race and 115–19
Mopsa the Fairy 28, 57, 136–7
moralistic tales 15–16, 29, 49, 52, 53, 54, 61
Morris, William 140, *141*
Morton, Samuel George 174, 185
Mother Goose 44, 48, 49
"Mother Holle" 101
mothers (*see* maternal)
Müller, F. Max 2
mythology 16, 46, 85, 114

nano 189
nationalism and fairy tales 7–9, 106, 112, 116, 165, 172
natural poetry 7, 84
natural world 32–6
   flora 93–5, 102–103
   Grimms' commentary on 84
"The Necklace of Princess Fiorimonde" 123–4

Nesbit. E. 22–3, 35, 46, 61, 146–7, 152–4, 162
"The New Mother" 113
Newbery, Francis 44
newspapers 7, 37, 77
"The Nightingale" 12–13, 23
non-humans in fairy tales 83–103
   animal judges 89–93, 102
   "Beauty and Beast" 85–9, 102
   dangerous objects 95–9, 103
   plant world 93–5, 102–3
   supernatural women 99–102
nonsense, literary 21–2, 28, 48, 49–51
Novalis (Friedrich von Hardenberg) 3, 93, 133, 135
novels, fairy-tale influence on 131
The Nursery "Alice" 55–6, 73
nursery rhymes 48–9, *50*, 51
"Nutcracker and the Mouse-King" 47, 84, 133

objects, dangerous 95–9, 103
"once upon a time" 123–4, 128
oral tradition 134, 187
   African American 55, 116–17
   preservation of 3, 4, 7–9, 106
Orientalism 10–13, 111
On the Origin of Species 26, 33, 34, 35, 38, 111, 179

Paget, F. E. 51–2
paintings, fairy 31–3
   microscopic realism 31, 32
   popular subjects 185
   racialized 185–6
   Shakespearian fairies 26–7, 45, 144, 194n4
   (*see also* illustrations)
pantomimes 20, 44, 47, 52, 53, 59, 69, 111, 149, 185
parody 20, 21, 51, 57, 165
Paton, Joseph Noel 145, 185, 186
patriarchy 28, 39, 110, 170
performing fairy tales 69–71
   (*see also* theater productions)
Perrault, Charles 20, 37, 44, 47, 48, 65, 86, 95, 130, 131
   "Bluebeard" 85, 110
   "Cinderella" 159, 160
   "Little Red Riding Hood" 40, 65, 69, 126, 129, 145

Peter and Wendy 19–20, 42, 45, 59, 80, 147, 155, 156–7, 199n40
   gender and sexuality 66, 79–81
   liminal space 138–9
Peter Pan in Kensington Gardens 19, 138–9
Peter Pan, or The Boy Who Wouldn't Grow Up 42, 59, 80
   postcards 66, 67
Phantastes 78, 123, 133, 135, 144, 145
The Phoenix and the Carpet 22–3, 61
"The Pied Piper of Hamelin" 181–4, 189
Pilgrim's Progress 43, 44
"The Pink Flower" 94, 99
Pinocchio 76–7, 162–3
Pitrè, Giuseppe 8
plant world 93–5, 102–103
poetry
   Barrett 183, 189
   Browning 181–4, 189
   children's 49–51
   Coleridge 5, 136–7
   Naturepoesie 7, 84
   Rossetti 17, 145, 146, 155
   Tennyson 175–9, 180, 181, 185
Pogany, Willy 118, 119, 203n15
polygenesis 116
Pope, Alexander 20
postcards 66, 67–8, 71, 72
Potter, Beatrix 55
power 167–91
   1842 172–5
   2012–2018 169–73
   2019 189–91
   Barrett and Browning's personal and political action 189–91
   detention centers 171–2, 184
   "fairy tales of science" 175–81
   Michael Brown 172–3, 186–7
   "The Pied Piper of Hamelin" 181–4, 189
   racialized visual imagery 185–7
   Sandy Hook 169–71
   social sciences and 187–9
Prickett, Stephen 5
primitive stories of humankind 2, 33, 36, 111, 112, 187, 188
The Princess and Curdie 47, 140
"The Princess and the Pea" 160
"The Princess Nobody" 17, 60, 60, 62

'Principal Boy' 69, 70
Propp, Vladimir 8, 180
Puck of Pook's Hill 35–6, 148
"Puddocky" 87, 200n9
Puritans 46, 194n1
purity of fairy tales, cultural 106, 112, 116

Quarrel of Oberon and Titania 185
queer fairy-tales 64, 70, 71, 73, 79

racism
   craniometry and 174, 185–7
   in "fairy tales of science" 178
   monstrosity and scientific 115–19
   perception of Michael Brown 172–3, 186–7
   social sciences and 187–9
   stereotypes of nonwhite children 61–2
railways 174
"The Ram" 85, 86, 88
"Rapunzel" 65, 94, 95, 99, 100, 129, 197n10
"The Reluctant Dragon" 22, 147, 161–2
research, folklore 7–9, 26, 36, 112, 167, 187
"Riffraff" 97
Right and Wrong, or The Princess Belinda 165
The Rime of the Ancient Mariner 5, 136
Ritchie, Anne Thackeray 29, 30–1, 38–9, 40–1, 86, 88, 196n25
Robinson Crusoe 43, 44, 45
Romantic movement 2, 3–7, 26–7, 47, 84, 132–3, 135
   irony 21–3
The Rose and the Ring 21–2, 52
"The Rose Beauty" 109
Rossetti, Christina 17, 28, 49, 53, 138, 145, 146, 155
roundness 128
"The Runenberg" 102
Ruskin, John 4, 9–10, 13, 16, 20, 31, 47, 70, 78, 131, 132, 139, 140, 142
Russian fairy tales 8, 130

Sala, George A. 30
"The Sandman" 77, 84, 133
Sandy Hook 169–71
"savage" survivals theory 187

Scandinavian fairy tales 8
Schacker, Jennifer 8, 12–13, 69, 112, 168–9, 197n14
Schlegel, Friedrich 21
science
　fairy tales and popular 10, 30–6, 180–1
　fairy tales of 175–81
The Science of Fairy Tales: An Inquiry into the Fairy Mythology 180–1, 187
Scotland 7, 8–9
Scott, Sir Walter 8, 26
scouting movement 157–9
"The Selfish Giant" 73, 141
"The Seven Ravens" 97–9
Sewell, Anna 55
sexuality
　female 17, 36, 39, 40, 41
　(*see also* gender and sexuality)
sexualization of children 69–70, 73–5
"Shah Jussuf" 109
Shakespeare, William 45, 46, 144
Shakespearian fairies 26–7, 45, 144, 194n4
Shelley, Mary 121
Sherwood, Mary Martha 44, 54
Silver, Carole 9, 23, 26, 36, 42, 88, 187
Sinclair, Catherine 51, 53, 134
"The Singing Bone" 96
The Singing Bones 126, 127
"The Singing, Springing Lark" 87, 88–9
"Sleeping Beauty" 20, 129, 130, 136, 176, 189
"The Snow Queen" 5–6, 13, 134
"Snow White" 65, 100, 129, 154–5
social discourse, fairy tales a means of purveying 28
social sciences 187–9
socialism 120, 141, 163
socialization, fairy tales for purpose of 149–66
　alternative pathways of expectations for girls 152–4
　boys' domestication 157–9
　class socialization and child authority 159–62
　feminine socialization 154–7, 204n9
　games 150–2, 159–60, 164–5
　paradoxical notions of socialization 162–6
The Soul of Man Under Socialism 141

space 123–48
　of Andersen 133–4
　Brothers Grimm and German Romantics 132–3
　of childhood 138
　exotic 134
　foundational 129–31
　home and away 128, 129
　illustrative 142–5
　influential maps 131–9
　liminal and crossing 133, 134–9
　modern and aesthetic 145–8
　poetics of 125–31
　time and 123–4, 128–9, 133, 137, 179
　utopian 139–42
Speaking Likenesses 28, 138
"The Star Child" 73, 163
Stevenson, Robert Louis 45, 159
Stone, Harry 29, 130
"The Storm Fiend" 114
strategic presentism 167
Struwwelpeter 49, 61
successful fairy tales, Brownings' reflect on 190–1
supernatural
　racial categorization and connection to legends of 172–3
　women 99–102
Swift, Jonathan 20, 43
Swiss Family Robinson 44–5
Sylva, Carmen 92–3

Tan, Shaun 126, *127*
"Tar Baby" 117–18
Tatar, Maria 64, 85–8, 106, 110, 116–18, 150, 154, 160, 163
Taylor, Edgar 15, 17, 27, 46, 47, 52, 132, 142
The Tempest 45, 144–5
Tenniel, John 50, 54–5, 55–6, 58, 142–3
Tennyson, Alfred 6, 175–8, 180, 181, 185, 188, 190
　illustrations 185, 205–6n11
Thackeray, William Makepeace 21–2, 52
theater productions 47, 149
　cross-dressing 69
　gender and sexuality 69–71
　pantomimes 20, 44, 47, 52, 53, 59, 69, 111, 149, 185

'Principal Boy' 69, 70
sexualization of child actors 69–70
souvenir postcards 66, 67
"The Three Orange Peris" 119
"The Three Ravens" 98
"The Three Snake Leaves" 91–2
Through the Looking-Glass and What Alice Found There 22, 33, *50*, 51, 55, 73, 77, 137, 142, 145
"Thumbelina" 18–19
Tieck, Ludwig 3, 65, 84, 102, 133
time
    linear 178–9
    masculine and feminine 179, 180
    and space 123–4, 128–9, 133, 137, 179
The Time Machine 124, 147
Todorov, Tzvetan 133
Toft, Mary 112
Tolkien, J. R. R. 131, 145, 148
toy books 37–8
"A Toy Princess" 162
Treasure Island 45
Turkish fairy tales 106, 107, 108, 109, 114–15, 120
    Arab slaves 118–19
    illustrations 118, *119*

"The Ugly Duckling" 40
Undine 4, 39, 47, 133
utopian space 139–42

V21 Collective research consortium 167
Vendrell, Xavier *125*, 126
Verne, Jules 45
Victoria, Queen 30, 174
Villeneuve, Gabrielle-Suzanne de 27, 85, 109, 131, 195*n*5
"The Virgin Mary's Child" 87, 93, 95, 99

Walker, Barbara 114–15, 120, 121
war technology 174, 178
Warner, Marina 130

The Water-Babies 10, *11*, 35, 52, 115, 118, 135–6
Wells, H. G. 124, 147
"The White Snake" 91, 92
Wilde, Oscar 23, 29, 70, 71–3, 145, 146
    "The Birthday of the Infanta" 163–4
    critique of capitalism 120
    "The Devoted Friend" 23, 120
    fascination with "the exotic" 163–4
    "The Fisherman and his Soul" 23, 71–3, 120
    "The Happy Prince" 12, 13, 31, 73, 163
    The Happy Prince and Other Tales 51, 71, 120, 140, 141–2
    A House of Pomegranates 51, 71, 120, 140–1, 163
    "The Nightingale and the Rose" 23
Wills, W. H. 30
Wilson, Darren 172–3, 186–7
The Wind in the Willows 55, 147
"The Wolf and the Seven Little Kids" 107
women
    androgynous/genderqueer roles in theatre for 69, 70
    "angel in the house" 111, 113
    "curiosity" of 110–11
    feminine socialization 154–7, 204*n*9
    ideal of "silent woman" 87–8
    violence towards 65, 110–11
    work and usefulness 152–4
The Wonderful Wizard of Oz 22, 49, 58, 79, 142, 146, 157
The Wood Beyond the World 140, *141*
Wyss, Johann David 44–5

"Yeh-Hsien" 91
Yonge, Charlotte 152

Zipes, Jack 3, 7, 8, 13, 15, 27, 28, 29, 64, 66, 86, 87, 90, 91, 93, 94, 95, 96, 97, 100, 101, 111, 149, 154, 170